Revelation, the Crown-Jewel of Biblical Prophecy

The Book of Revelation

By

W. C. STEVENS

Christian Publications, Inc.
Harrisburg, Pa.

Printed U.S.A.

Contents

THE BOOK OF REVELATION

3

Introduction

THE last book of the Bible is a revelation, not an obscuration. We may believe on *a priori* grounds that it would be understood by those to whom it was addressed. The first of its seven beatitudes invokes a special blessing upon all who read, learn, mark and inwardly digest its contents. It possesses a peculiar sanction in proceeding, as does the Great Commission, from the glorified state. As it closes the sacred Canon, it is the final gleam of light upon the Jew, the Gentile and the Church of God until the second coming of Christ.

Any reverent attempt to explain its symbols, indicate its divisions and unfold its meaning is praiseworthy and gratifying. No Bible teacher of today is better qualified to discuss prophetic themes than the author of these volumes. No more satisfactory treatment can be discovered than that which he has adopted.

In this illuminating interpretation of the Apocalypse will be found the antidote to an adulterated Gospel on the one hand and to an emasculated Gospel on the other hand. From the viewpoint of literary excellence, exact scholarship and high spirituality, it leaves little to be desired.

F. W. FARR.

Preliminary Survey

THE reader is invited to make in advance a cursory reading of this last book of the Bible, with sufficient attention to detect its fivefold division. Such attention will also discover that each division focusses upon the Church of Jesus Christ in some distinctive aspect. Hence the entire book consists of a very comprehensive disclosure of our Lord concerning His Church.

But the first sentence describes "the revelation" as consisting of "things which must shortly come to pass." The "revelation," then, is the prophetic unveiling of future events to "come shortly to pass," "shortly" meaning swiftly in occurrence. The "revelation," then, constitutes the unveiling of a great chapter in Church history which will rapidly transpire in its time. And that "time is at hand," that is, next impending, v. 3.

Such a revelation we do not meet with until Chapter 4, and then it extends nearly through the rest of the book.

But in Chapter 1 we have a different kind of revelation, one pertaining to the Church of Jesus Christ. In Chapters 2 and 3 we have another different kind of revelation, also pertaining to the Church. Then, in Chapter 20 we have another revelation, which, while prophetical in character, yet relates to the Church, not in a short period, but in the long period of the thousand years. Finally, in Chapters 21 and 22 we have another prophecy relating to the Church, but in the unmeasured ages beyond the millennium.

It becomes evident, therefore, that "the revelation," in the distinctive sense, is to be found in Chapters 4-19 (more precisely 19:10), and that we are to note a distinction between "the revelation" itself and the "book" of the revelation, the former embracing the great central

9

body of the book, the latter embracing besides two brief preceding revelations concerning the Church and two succeeding ones. Recognition of these distinctions will afford us a very easy entrance into the unfolding of the entire book.

The Church Mystical

CHAPTER I.

EXPLANATORY PROLOGUE, 1 : 1-3

"1 The Revelation of Jesus Christ, which God gave unto him, to shew unto his servants things which must shortly come to pass; and he sent and signified it by his angel unto his servant John: 2 Who bare record of the word of God, and of the testimony of Jesus Christ, and of all things that he saw. 3 Blessed is he that readeth, and they that hear the words of this prophecy, and keep those things which are written therein: for the time is at hand."

THE TITLE

THE simple title of this book is "The Revelation." The word "Revelation," as it comes from the Latin, means an unveiling, drawing aside the curtain of concealment. The alternative word "Apocalypse," as it comes from the Greek, means an uncovering, bringing out from hiding.

This title intimates the nature of the book,—it is a clear disclosure of what would otherwise remain wholly hidden and unknown. If a curtain be drawn back the scene beyond is plainly exposed; if a covering be removed that which is hidden becomes manifest. The title assures us that what was hidden is now disclosed, the matter is no longer concealed. It assures us that this book is of itself the light, the full light, the manifest light upon its subject.

To treat the Book of Revelation as still a mystery is to deny what it professes to be; to treat the book as cryptic is surely to miss its revelation. To go "behind the scenes" is to go without the pale of reality into that of fancy and falsity; to introduce "theories" or "keys of interpretation" is to mystify what must be self-evident, or it is not revelation.

The nature of the book, and the principle of understanding it, which is implied by its title, is all-important, and it should be heeded from the outset. The book offers itself to everybody as his own independently, even as a mountain scene which spreads itself before all beholders alike. One may perceive much that another does not; but it is not because anything is concealed, or that one has a prerogative of understanding not enjoyed by all others. The only "authority on the Book of Revelation," which should be accorded to anyone, is that of being able to make self-evident to another from the book itself what the other had not before perceived. It is the prerogative, and it is the responsibility, of every one, while receiving what is offered "with all readiness of mind," yet to search the Scriptures daily whether those things be so. It is evident that if this book be read by all on the principles just explained,—without importing interpretation into it—it will not suffer from any great diversity of understanding.

Of course translation has much to do with ready and correct understanding. The author has felt the special value of variant translations of the Book of Revelation, and he will make occasional references thereto with careful discrimination. This will place no reader at any disadvantage as to independent understanding, for only readily accessible translations will be cited. And the author wishes the reader to understand that he is not by these references to be taken as expressing preference or endorsement on points of question connected with these versions in general. A. V. stands for the Accepted (King James) Version, R. V. for the Revised Version, 1911 for the American Revised and Corrected, G. for Godbey's Translation and C. V. for the Concordant Version.

MARVELLOUS ORIGIN OF THE REVELATION

The expression, "The Revelation of Jesus Christ," does not make Jesus Christ the subject of the revelation. "Of" here is the preposition of source, meaning from or by. This is made certain by the words following: "The Revelation of Jesus Christ, which *God gave unto him.*" That Jesus Christ is not the subject of the Revelation is confirmed by the further words, "to shew unto his servants *things which must shortly come to pass.*" These last seven words show what is revealed in this book; it is not a person, but "things,"—coming events. What is shown in regard to the origin of the Revelation is that it came from the Father by the Son.

The words, "which God gave unto him," if taken by themselves, would seem to imply that the Father first made the revelation outright to Jesus Christ. The words just following, "to shew unto his servants," may be taken to throw the weight of thought not upon the giving of the revelation to Jesus Christ, but upon the giving to Him to show the revelation to His servants. It would then mean not so much a matter of original disclosure to the Son, as a matter of authorizing Him to make this disclosure to His servants. This turn of thought is supported by the Revised Version, which reads, "The Revelation of Jesus Christ, which God gave him to show unto his servants, *even* the things which must shortly come to pass."

While this understanding of the original text frees it from undue emphasis upon the dependence of Jesus Christ upon the Father for His own first knowledge of the Revelation itself, yet it does harmonize with that sort of secondary place in relation to the Father which Jesus Christ Himself uniformly delighted to acknowledge while upon the earth. "He that sent me is true; and I speak to the world those things which I have heard of [from] him" (John 8:26). "The words that I speak

unto you I speak not of [from] myself: but the Father
that dwelleth in me, he doeth the works'' (John 14:10).
''I have given unto them the words which thou gavest
me; and they have received them, and have known surely
that I came out from thee, and they have believed that
thou didst send me'' (John 17:8). ''When ye have lifted
up the Son of man, then shall ye know that I am be,
and that I do nothing of myself; but as my Father hath
taught me, I speak these things. And he that sent me
is with me: the Father hath not left me alone; for I
do always those things that please him'' (John 8:28, 29).
While in His state of humiliation the Son of man seems
to have been limited and dependent both in knowledge
and in foreknowledge, although it is a great mystery
to us; yet it is not to be supposed that in His bodily
restoration to former glory His omniscience longer suf-
fers limitation.

A further stage in the origin of the Revelation is
marked by the statement, ''and he sent and signified it
by his angel unto his servant John.'' Besides the twofold divine source of the Revelation, there is a further
celestial source, an angel who served as its medium to
John.

What notable reflections this excites! It cannot imply
independent foreknowledge, yet it plainly does imply
angelic foreknowledge of this Revelation. It is charming to think of the interest taken by the holy angels in
the purposes and plans of God, especially of His redemptive doings. It is suggested that the angels have
even more than intelligent interest,—that they are
actually taken into coöperation with God in carrying
forward His plans. This we have already repeatedly
found in previous Scriptures to be true; and we will
find the truth of it further illustrated in this book. But
more captivating to the imagination is the picture that
can be justly drawn of the interviews held between
Jesus Christ and this particular angel, for the purpose

of instructing and preparing the latter for his notable mission. This mission was much more elaborate than that of the angel that enlightened Zechariah, or even Gabriel's mission to Daniel. By the way, it is not an illegitimate surmise that the particular angel here designated as "His [Christ's] angel" was Gabriel.

The fourth link in the chain of the origin of this revelation was the Apostle John, Jesus Christ's "servant John." What more suitable human source for this closing book of prophecy could have been chosen? Yet he carefully subordinates himself duly as but a servant and witness.

THE OBJECT OF THE REVELATION

The object of the Revelation is plainly stated: "to shew unto his [Christ's] servants things which must shortly come to pass." As has already been noted, the subject of the Revelation was declared to be coming events. The object of God was to have Jesus Christ show these coming events to His servants in the earth. This makes it plain for whom the Revelation was designed; namely, for the servants of Jesus Christ. No discrimination of classes or times is indicated, but the Revelation is for all Christ's servants as such and in all the generations from first to last. The expression "shew" implies perfectly clear disclosure, as clear at one time as another. And this word "shew" is peculiar, indicating a panoramic method of unveiling the coming events. It is further specified of these events, "which *must shortly* come to pass." Does this mean that the events will soon arrive, or that they will take place very swiftly in their time? The word "must," instead of will, indicates the latter idea. We understand, then, that the Revelation was intended to unfold to the view of servants of Jesus Christ ever since that day the drama of unique events which, in the nature of the case, must transpire very quickly in their day.

THE AUTHENTICITY OF THE REVELATION

It is important to notice the threefold authenticity of this book for which John vouches: "Who bare record (1) of the word of God, (2) and of the testimony of Jesus Christ, (3) and of all things that he [John] saw." As a revelation given by Jesus Christ from God, it bears the original imprimatur of "the word of God." As a revelation delivered by express angelic messenger from Jesus Christ, it came as "the testimony of Jesus Christ," who always speaks exactly and only, as He said, "as my Father hath taught me." As a record from the hand of John of the angel's panoramic communication of the Revelation, the book is authenticated by John as a faithful "record . . . of all things that he saw." We must be impressed that it is intended that this book should be received with perfect assurance of its reliability and with reverent obedience to its authority.

BEATITUDE FOR FULL USE OF THE BOOK

"Blessed is he that readeth." Strictly speaking, this refers not to private reading, as the book could not when given be multiplied for private use. The blessing was promised for the public reading by the minister of the congregation. While the want of public reading and teaching of this book does not now close its contents to believers generally, yet it is not at all strained to find in these words a benediction for the public ministers of this book of Scripture today. And it is true that the lack of such ministry results in comparatively little use of the book in private. "And they that hear the words of this prophecy." The transition from "he" to "they" confirms the reference of the first expression to the minister. The blessing also awaits all believers in their attentive attitude toward this book, both under public ministry and in private reading and study. The lack of this attitude costs God's children the loss of an explicit benediction.

It is to be noted here that the Revelation is described as "the words of this prophecy." This word "prophecy" excludes from the Revelation itself everything of other than prophetical nature and proves that nothing in the Revelation is to be related to times prior to John's reception of the Revelation. This leads to a clear distinction between the Revelation itself and the "Book of Revelation." The book contains the Revelation, but the Revelation does not embrace the entire book. The Revelation is limited to the "things which must shortly come to pass," while the "Book of Revelation" embraces also whatsoever is not thus included. For instance, this Preface is not part of the Revelation. We expect the line of division to be perfectly plain as we progress within the book.

"And keep those things which are written therein." This applies to the hearers directly, and it shows that the nature of this book is not immediately and practically unimportant, but just the reverse. The word "keep" implies that the contents of Revelation put the Christian under spiritual mandate as much as the words of John's Gospel or of his Epistles. Revelation is, then, not a book of speculative, conjectural or theoretical use, but something to be intelligently received and practically observed.

There is another important point made apparent from the present tense of the words, "readeth," "hear" and "keep." This point is made the more striking by Godbey's very literal translation: "Blessed is the one reading, and those hearing the word of this prophecy, and keeping the things which have been written in it." The present participles emphasize the continuousness of these acts and indicate the repeated practice of so doing as a settled habit. Here again the practical, everyday usefulness of this portion of Scripture is implied.

"THE TIME IS AT HAND"

The reason given for inciting such faithful, practical attention to the public ministry and to the personal appropriation of Revelation is thus stated, "for the time is at hand." This shows that the coming events belong to a "time," or epoch, of their own. This is important; the Revelation unfolds the events of a distinctive period of history. It is further shown that in relation to times current this "time" is proximate,—next immediately subsequent. This too is a very important characteristic, —the "time" of the Revelation is relatively imminent and yet distinct from the present accustomed course of events.

OUR BEARINGS

This brief preamble to the Book of Revelation gives us most important bearings before we are inducted into the book as such. We are shown: 1. That something plain, not mysterious and puzzling, lies before us. 2. That it is designed to be self-evident to the servants of the Lord without distinction of class or generation. 3. That the Revelation embraces only coming events. 4. That these events constitute a brief time of swift occurrence. 5. That relative to the existing course of things, this time is entirely distinct and abruptly to succeed. 6. That the nature of these coming events is such as to call for an habitual attention and practical use of the prophetic drama from the time it was given until it shall be brought to pass.

CHAPTER II.

APOSTOLICAL GREETING TO THE SEVEN CHURCHES

I. The Salutation, v. 4a

"John to the seven churches which are in Asia."

THE purely personal greeting, "John," without any official addition, is striking. While it makes the least of himself possible, yet it is likewise a testimony to the unique position of this particular John among the churches of Asia (the Roman Province of Asia only), that no further designation was necessary. It is also noteworthy that John addressed certain definite churches of this certain section of country just as definitely as did Paul when he addressed a letter to "the churches of Galatia,"—another Roman Province of Asia Minor adjacent to the Province of Asia on the east. Two things are implied. First, a very personal relationship between John and those churches is implied; this may have been the field of John's special apostolical labors. The second thing implied is that this writing from John's hand applied immediately, distinctly and wholly to those seven churches, without any immediate view to any other bodies any more than was true in the case of Paul's letter to the Romans. This fact should check us from expounding the book in whole or in part from any primary standpoint other than that of those literal churches.

II. The Invocation, vs. 4b-6

"4 Grace be unto you, and peace, from him which is, and which was, and which is to come; and from the seven Spirits which are before his throne; 5 And from Jesus Christ, who is

the faithful witness, and the first begotten of the dead, and the
prince of the kings of the earth.   Unto him that loved us, and
washed us from our sins in his own blood,   6 And hath made us
kings and priests unto God and his Father; to him be glory and
dominion for ever and ever.   Amen.''

It is the rule with the opening greetings of apostolical
writings to associate with the common invocation of
"grace," "mercy" and "peace," descriptive expressions relating to the divine source of those gifts, which
descriptions forecast and are pertinent to the subject
matter of the writings themselves.   The descriptive expressions employed by John in this greeting are quite
unusual in their fulness and in their character, and they
are to be taken as an impressive forecast of what is to
follow in the book.   The first notable feature is the vivid
presentation they offer of trinitarian distinctions in the
Godhead.   The second notable feature consists of the
significant material employed in distinguishing between
the three divine persons.   The third and last notable
feature is the striking place and fulness of characteriza-
tion given to the second person of the trinity.   These
features will all appear as the passage is expounded
consecutively.

1. ''From him which is, and which was, and which is to come.''

This is the simple, although very impressive, charac-
terization of God the Father as the Eternal One, the
existing One, and existing in the beginningless past and
in the endless future.   (''Which is to come'' manifestly
does not refer to an act or event of coming, but only to
coming endless existence.)   With reference to the Father,
then, this book, greeting the churches from the Eternal
One, may be expected to be characterized by this aspect
of the first person of the trinity.

2. ''And from the seven Spirits which are before his throne.''

The connection leaves us with no doubt that this is
the designation of the Holy Spirit, an unique designa-

tion that is peculiarly characteristic of and appropriate
to this book. We are not to be hindered from taking
the expression "seven Spirits" as referring to the Holy
Spirit, by the apparent plurality of persons indicated.
This peculiar expression seems to indicate rather the
plurality of aspects and attributes belonging to the one
infinite Holy Spirit. The Scriptures speak, for instance, of the Spirit of love, and of the Spirit of power;
but these two Spirits are one and the same Holy Ghost.
We may not know just how to make out the list of "the
seven Spirits," in this sense of one sevenfold Spirit,
from the description given in the Word; but the following is offered as at least approximately correct:

(1) "The Spirit of God," or "the eternal Spirit."

(2) "The Spirit of His Son," "of the Lord," "of
Christ," "of Jesus Christ," or "of power," or "of
life."

(3) "The Spirit of holiness," or "The Holy Spirit."

(4) "The Spirit of wisdom," or "the Spirit of truth."

(5) "The Spirit of love."

(6) "The Spirit of grace."

(7) "The Spirit of glory."

These titles or insignia of the third person of the
Godhead call for at least brief notice in particular.

(1) He is Himself eternal and personal deity.

(2) He is the other self of the second person of the
trinity; the Scriptures love to expatiate upon the inef-
fable relationship between the two. Whether our
Saviour be designated in His sonship residing eternally
in the bosom of the Father, the third person is the Spirit
of the Son's eternal generation from and communion
with and image of the Father; or whether it be the
Son as Lord, entrusted with full regency by the Father,
the Holy Ghost is the Spirit of Him as Lord; so also
of Him as the eternally Anointed, the Christ, the one
walking in all majesty and grace through all the pages
of Old Testament history, poetry and prophecy; so also

of Him as Jesus Christ, the Son of man, the manifestation of the second person in New Testament story, doctrine and prophecy, as well as in the present priesthood before the face of God in "heaven itself." As the Spirit of the Son of God, of the Lord, of Christ, of Jesus Christ,—He is the Spirit of power; He is the power, or empowerer, of all the capacities of the second person of the deity, and He is the Spirit of life; namely, of the life in Christ Jesus.

(3) He is possessed of and the executive of all the holiness which has the "Holy Father" as its infinite, inexhaustible source.

(4) Infinite and eternal wisdom is found in Him essentially and potentially; and all truth, as it is in God the Father or in His Son Jesus Christ—He is the Spirit of it all.

(5) So also of love,—the very essence of God, that which sums up God ("God is love") as naught else does, that which always governs God,—of that love He is the Spirit.

(6) So also of grace,—"God's grace," that favor which is life, the withholding of which is death,—of "all grace" He is the Spirit.

(7) Finally also of Glory,—"the glory of God," "of the Father," the glory which the Son had with the Father before the world was and to which He was restored bodilywise, and the glory which Jesus prayed that His followers might hereafter behold, share with Him and manifest,—of that glory also He is the Spirit. Yes, He is Himself the "seven Spirits," the manifold, infinite and divine perfection of Spirit-being and potency. But may God forgive the poverty of our highest human conceptions of this mystery!

"The seven Spirits which are before his throne." The position of the seven Spirits is significant and appropriate. Before the throne is the place of immediate procession from and access to the King Eternal upon the throne. So Jesus speaks in John 15:26 of the Comforter as the "Spirit of truth which *proceedeth from the Father*." All manifestation, all outgoing from the Father, must be by the Spirit. So too, "we . . . have access by one Spirit unto the Father" (Eph. 2:16). Even praying to the Father must be "in the Holy Ghost" (Jude 20), as well as in the name of Jesus Christ. Hence the "grace" and the "peace" of the Eternal Father can issue unto the seven churches only "from the seven Spirits," and can be entered into by those churches only by the Holy Ghost. Now it is to be remembered that it is as "the seven Spirits" that we are to expect the third person of the trinity to appear characteristically in the Book of Revelation.

3. "And from Jesus Christ." No more can "grace" and "peace" be sent forth from the King Eternal and Almighty, or be entered into, but "from Jesus Christ" and through Him. How absolutely equal in deity is the "Son of man" shown to be! It is noticeable, however, that although the Son of God is the second person of the trinity, as Jesus Christ He here stands third and last in order. That is, of course, perfectly right, whether we apprehend the reason for it or not. It is customary to find apostolical invocations of grace, mercy and peace offered from God the Father and the Lord Jesus Christ only, and in that order, of course. This is the only instance of a trinitarian invocation. There is a trinitarian benediction found once in the New Testament, in 2 Cor. 13:14, where the blessing of "the communion of the Holy Ghost" comes last in order.

This much is in striking evidence,—that there is a strong climax to this invocation resting upon "Jesus Christ."

(1) Jesus Christ is first presented here in His three offices of Prophet, Priest and King. These offices are eternal in Him as Christ the Son of God. In Him, however, as Jesus Christ, the Son of God incarnate as

Son of man, these offices are entered into at appropriate points of time. And reference is here made to Him in His exercise of these offices in human manifestation.

a. He is first described as "the faithful witness." This has respect especially to His prophetic ministry on earth as man. With great dignity and emphasis Jesus insisted upon the authority and integrity of all His teaching and preaching, as well as of His wondrous works. At the close He could say right to the Father who sent Him, "I have glorified thee on the earth; I have finished the work which thou gavest me to do. . . . I have manifested thy name unto the men which thou gavest me out of the world; . . . I have given unto them the words which thou gavest me" (John 17:4, 6, 8). While all this refers only to the prophetic ministry of Jesus Christ on earth in visible body, yet as has already been intimated, He was thus only manifesting His eternal character and office as the Almighty Father's prophet. In His preëxistence He was the manifest medium of the Father's communications to all creatures even when He employed intermediate channels. This was because He Himself was and evermore is the "Word" of God. All that the Father has to communicate, whether of Himself or from Himself, is embodied and personified in the Son, and it can be communicated only through and from Him. "All the counsel of God," which "at divers times and in divers manners" has been written into the Holy Bible, both reveals Christ and was revealed by Him.

b. Jesus Christ is next described as "the first begotten from the dead." By His resurrection from the dead He entered bodily into His office as High Priest. Several things of deep importance are to be noted under this representation.

(a) In the first place, the phrase "the dead" shows that the death of Jesus Christ belongs to His priestly office. A priest must have a sacrifice to offer. In all previous priestly transactions the priest and the sacrifice were distinct; no priest had ever before come to the altar excepting "with blood of others." But in the case of Jesus Christ the Lamb offered and the one offering the same are both embraced in one,—Jesus was both the Lamb and the Priest offering the same. Jesus as Priest offered Himself as the sacrifice, and as the resurrected Lamb He "entered . . . into heaven itself, now to appear in the presence of God for us," where "He ever liveth to make intercession for us" (Heb. 9:24 and 7:25).

As has been intimated, this office was not new to the Son of God. In all times past penitent mortals had crept up successfully to the throne of the Almighty and come back with shining faces of conscious acceptance. Yea, forgiven mortals had walked for years in unbroken communion with most awful deity, like Enoch and Noah of even antediluvian times. And David, Isaiah and all the prophets knew full well that the Lord God could not be pleased with thousands of rams and rivers of oil; that, in fact, God needed from man no lamb or bullock, but only a contrite, broken and trusting heart. So there was access to God before Calvary the same as afterwards. The meaning of the beasts of sacrifice did not consist primarily in their typical import,—pointing down to Calvary's mute victim; but primarily those substitutes for guilty man bore witness that in the unseen there was One who was already taking away the sins of the world. Indeed, the love of God for the world, which moved Him to give up His only begotten Son to save sinners, eternally and essentially carried redemption in its exercise, so that that gift was no new prompting of love, no new gift of love, but the bursting forth of eternal redemptive love with its eternal redemptive gift into the awful chasm of human need, like the waters already prepared in reservoir to inundate the horrid "Death Valley."

(b) The words, "the first begotten from the dead," embrace another thing of importance. It is not said that He was the first to be raised from the dead. Others had already been brought out of their graves, and some had passed into glory without seeing death. Paul calls Jesus Christ "the firstfruits of them that slept." This means the choicest sample. The "first begotten" means especially the inheritor of all. Paul calls Jesus the "firstborn of every creature." This designates Jesus Christ not as a mere creature, but as the head and heir of all creation. "For by him were all things created, that are in heaven, and that are in earth, visible and invisible, whether they be thrones, or dominions, or principalities, or powers; all things were created by him, and for him: and he is before all things, and by him all things consist" (Col. 1:15-17). Jesus Christ arose from the dead as the inheritor of the kingdom of death. He arose not merely as others, raised from death; He arose as "the resurrection and the life." Death and the grave have become a rich spoil to Him. And through Him "all things are yours; . . . whether . . . life, or death, . . . all are yours." "Death is swallowed up in victory."

There is significance in the resurrection of Jesus Christ which the Church today seems not to be comprehending and emphasizing as did the apostolic Church. The resurrection of Jesus was the crowning, overwhelming demonstration of His deity and Messiahship. His dying for our sins, His burial under death as the supreme power of the devil and of the curse, and His resurrection in evidence that "it was not possible that he should be *holden* of it," constitute the essential testimony of the Scriptures and of the Gospel. Of this last event the second Psalm speaks: "The Lord said unto me, Thou art my Son; this day have I begotten thee." In seeking for an apostle to succeed Judas the requisite stated was that of all candidates "must one be ordained to be a witness with us of his resurrection" (Acts 1:22). And it is recorded that "with great power gave the Apostles witness of the resurrection of the Lord Jesus" (Acts 4:33).

(c) Jesus Christ is next and finally described as "the Prince of the kings of the earth." This clearly describes our Lord in His kingship as Son of man, as He shall assume earthly sovereignty at His approaching second coming.

The subject of the earthly kingship of Jesus Christ is very important. The Son of God created this earth and its heavens in the Father's name. His is by original right the sovereignty of the same; He has ever been, is now, and ever shall be the divine ruler thereof for His father. "All things were created by him and for him: and he is before all things, and by him all things consist" (Col. 1:16, 17).

All the divine rule and authority in evidence throughout the Old Testament Scriptures was that of Christ the Son of God. The recognition of this fact at once opens up the Old Testament clearly to one's understanding. The Old Testament predictions of One to come who shall rule over all the earth and heavens, indicated no change of rule and authority from the hands of one to those of another—as from the hands of the Father to those of the Son—but only a change of rule and authority from One invisible and purely divine to that same One in visible and human form and manifestation. The consequence is that, in order to know that ruler and His ways in His divine character, the Old Testament is to be searched; while, to know that same ruler and His ways in human manifestation, the Jesus of the New Testament is to be observed. The Almighty Sovereign—"the Prince of the kings of the earth"—is even now Jesus Christ, the incarnate Son of God. "Thou crownedst him with glory and honor, and didst set him over all the works of thine hands; thou hast put all things in subjection under his feet. . . . But now we *see* not yet all things put under him'' (Heb. 2: 7, 8). It is just this visible demonstration of the subjection of all things in skies and earth under Him, which in the Book of Revelation we are given to foresee by apocalypse while awaiting the actual historical manifestation of it.

The emphasis of the expression under consideration rests upon the princeship of Jesus Christ over all earthly kings. This is now true mystically; His impending visible return will demonstrate it openly. The ruling powers of the earth should even now put their necks under His feet; very soon they will literally be ''the footstool of his feet.'' To this the faithful servants of Jesus Christ are under commission to bear fearless testimony, and according to this truth they should adjust their present citizenship. No Scripture is so pertinent to these ends as the Book of Revelation. Like so much of Biblical prophecy it is highly political in character. In this respect this book is applicable at all times and should never be discarded, neglected or treated as unintelligible.

(2) Besides dwelling so extensively upon Jesus Christ in the three offices just considered, the invocation of John upon the seven Churches further characterizes in a threefold way what Jesus has done for ''us,'' His servants.

a. ''Unto him that loved us.'' How well the Apostle John knew to designate the first and chief thing that the Lord Jesus has done for us! John's sense and appreciation of Christ's love had not diminished with the intervening decades since he leaned upon that sacred, tender breast. It is significant that the ''Apostle of love''—of the fourth Gospel and of those three Epistles which are so fragrant with love—should be chosen as the recipient of this revelation. It intimates that not less than those does this book throb with the Saviour's love. This needs to be observed all the way through in searching this book. The princeship of Jesus Christ is held in love, and even His fearful judgments are dictated by love. The unending, unswerving, the inevitable love of Jesus Christ is aptly indicated by the usual later translations of the phrase under consideration,—"Unto him that loveth us," or "To the one loving us," instead of "who loved us." "He loved them unto the end" not only long ago; but He is loving them—us—on to the further end.

b. "And washed us from our sins in his own blood." This is a noteworthy expression as well as a glorious truth. In the first place it leaves no uncertainty in regard to the vicarious character of the atonement,— "In *his own* blood." It implies that blood only could wash away sins, and it asserts that He did this with His own blood in place of ours. But it declares that Jesus Christ "*washed us*," and it is a past and accomplished work. He washed us "*from* our sins." And when it is added that He did this "in His own blood," the picture is completed of our Saviour's taking us, as a filthy garment is taken, and thoroughly washing us from the accumulation of sins and even from the most penetrating stain, as a diligent washerwoman leaves no trace of uncleanness or spot behind. It is into such an experience and life of moral cleanness and spotlessness that we are privileged and called now to enter to His glory and as the true meetness for His coming.

c. "And hath made us kings and priests unto God and his father." Other translations generally make an important distinction here, reading this sentence thus: "And made us a kingdom, priests unto God and his Father." The whole expression is in accord with other important Scriptures. Two points are worthy of careful consideration.

(a) "Made us a kingdom." The term kingdom is variously applied in Scripture, but it always has the same fundamental idea; it means that which is obedient to the divine will and rule through Christ.

The expression, ''the kingdom of God'' represents the ''kingdom'' as to its ultimate headship. The expression, ''the kingdom of heaven,'' represents that same ''kingdom'' as to its sphere, the sphere where the will and rule of God have always obtained. Originally the creature heaven and earth were embraced in the kingdom of God and of heaven, because the will of God was done there as in ''heaven itself.'' The rebellion of the delegated prince of this ''heaven and earth,''—Satan —while not overthrowing the divine sovereignty over our earth and skies, yet did bring heaven and earth directly under the sway of darkness and evil. The restoration of ''the heaven and the earth'' of Gen. 1: 1 from the ruinous condition brought upon it by Satan through God's judgment as pictured in Gen. 1: 2, constitutes the drama unfolded in all the Bible beginning with the last sentence of Gen. 1: 2, ''And the Spirit of God moved upon the face of the waters.'' After the restoration of the earth to an habitable condition, the first Adam was given dominion over all by Christ, only under His direction and for His glory. So long as Adam served ''the Lord God,'' in the loving obedience and intelligent capability of his first creation, the kingdom, or rule, or will, of God was prevailing through him on earth as in heaven.

But Satan, ''the prince of the power of [resident in] the air'' (skies), intruded and secured the defection of Adam; and so again the earth, as well as ''the heaven,'' was in revolt, and it still is. The promise, however, then and there shone forth that a second Adam—''seed'' of the woman—should crush the serpent's headship and restore this revolted province of God's universe to its appointed place in ''the kingdom of God'' and ''of heaven.'' This glorious consummation will be found depicted at large in the closing chapters of Revelation.

(b) "Priests unto God and his Father." When the Son of God called Israel at Mount Sinai as a great people to Himself—"a peculiar treasure . . . above all people" —it was to be "a kingdom of priests." This meant, in the first place, that Israel was called as a nation to be subject to God, to have Jehovah as their King instead of having a visible ruler, as did the other nations; Israel was called a theocratic kingdom and to represent on earth "the kingdom of God" and "of heaven." In the next place, they were called as such a kingdom to the priestly character and office; the entire nation, as a kingdom among the kingdoms of the earth, was to be "a kingdom of *priests*." That is, they as a kingdom-body were to be presenting all other nations before the throne of God's grace in intercession, and they were to be God's ministers of that grace unto all nations. All the Mosaic legislation was to the end of maintaining this high and holy calling. Dismally as Israel failed to fulfil this great calling, yet it has never been revoked; and it is to be gloriously fulfilled by the restored millennial kingdom of Israel. This is distinctly proved by the words of Isa 61:6: "But ye [restored Israel] shall be named the Priests of the Lord: men shall call you the Ministers of our God."

Now it is after the analogy of Israel's national calling that the Church of the present age is called in relation to mankind. Peter, in writing to Hebrew believers "scattered throughout Pontus, Galatia, Cappadocia, Asia, and Bythnia,"—writing to them not primarily as Hebrews, but as Christian believers—after speaking of them in familiar figures as "a spiritual house, an holy priesthood, to offer up spiritual sacrifices, acceptable to God by Jesus Christ," still further reminds them in equally familiar figures that they were "a chosen generation, a royal *priesthood*, an holy nation, a peculiar people" (1 Peter 2:5, 9). This is a literal application to Hebrew Christians as Christians and as representa-

tives of the whole living Church of this age, of all the
terms applied in Ex. 19:5, 6 to Israel at Mount Sinai.
And it must be confessed that the Church of this age,
as an outward body, is proving to be about as unfaithful
to this high calling of representing "the kingdom of
God" and "of heaven" on the earth as the Church
which came out of the wilderness did.

We now return to John's application of all this to the
seven churches of Asia, when he speaks of Jesus Christ's
having made them "a kingdom [of] priests unto God
and his Father."

Not by themselves separately, yet in themselves in
their own particular place and also in their representative capacity, representing the whole Church of this
age, they, as subjects of the heavenly King and as
priests under His headship as the great High Priest,
represented the present dispensational form of "the
kingdom of God" and "of heaven" on the earth. Believers are not yet actually "kings" on earth, for Jesus
their Head is not such as yet. But believers are "a
kingdom" on earth as subjects of the will and rule of
God through Christ by His Spirit. "The kingdom of
God is . . . righteousness, and peace, and joy in the Holy
Ghost" (Rom. 14:17). Not a separate and entire nation,
as Israel of old, but the Church, embracing the called-
out of all nations, is now the representation of "the
kingdom of God" and "of heaven" on earth. In the
next age, the millennial, the prince of darkness will be
in exile from both heaven (skies) and earth, and glorfied
saints will then be kings with Christ, co-rulers with Him
in the skies and over the earth, and Israel will be the
national, earthly and worthy representation of "the
kingdom of God" and "of heaven" in the earth. In
the postmillennial and everlasting reconstruction of the
earth and skies that will be perfectly realized which we
daily pray for, "Thy kingdom come. Thy will be done
in earth, as it is in heaven."

"To him be glory and dominion for ever and ever. Amen." As the intelligent and appreciative reader reaches this high climax of John's greeting, it is with throbbing heart and exultant response that these concluding words are read. It is a well deserved ascription to the Son of Man. It is with deep sense of Jesus' love, of His sacrificial work, and of the high dignity to which we are appointed in and with Him, that all our glory is given unto Him, that we invoke upon Him all glory, and that we acclaim the Father's will that everlasting dominion be in His hands. This is the pose into which we are placed at the very outset, and it is in this sentiment and attitude that we are to follow the Book of Revelation to the end. It reminds us of the acme of acknowledgment of faith to which Jesus brought the Disciples as voiced by Thomas in John 20:28: "My Lord, and my God!"

It has already been stated that Jesus Christ is forevermore to sway the scepter of dominion over the earth and the heaven. This is corroborated by the invocation, "unto him be . . . dominion for ever and ever." The reader's mind may, however, revert at once to a passage which is often taken to teach otherwise. The passage referred to is found in 1 Cor. 15:28: "And when all things shall be subdued unto him [Jesus Christ], then shall the Son also himself be subject unto him that put all things under him, that God may be all in all." This does not teach, however, that, when redemption shall have completed its object in restoring all things under divine sovereignty, the Son will vacate His lordship in favor of the Father; but it teaches that, when the great end shall be attained by the Son,—"when he shall have delivered up the kingdom [restored] to God, even the Father; when he shall have put down all rule and all authority and power"—He will still continue in the self-subjection to the Father which He has ever exercised, instead of then leading off earth and skies in a

revolt against the Father's sovereignty as did Satan
long ago. As the Book of Revelation itself elsewhere
shows, the throne of earth and skies in future everlasting ages will be "the throne of God and of the
Lamb" (Rev. 22:3).

III. THE ANNUNCIATION OF THE OBJECTIVE OF THE BOOK, vs. 7, 8

"7 Behold, he cometh with clouds; and every eye shall see
him, and they also which pierced him: and all kindreds of the
earth shall wail because of him. Even so, Amen. 8 I am Alpha
and Omega, the beginning and the ending, saith the Lord, which
is, and which was, and which is to come, the Almighty."

Abruptly verse 7 throws upon the screen the objective
of the book, "Behold, he cometh with clouds: and every
eye shall see him, and they also which pierced him:
and all kindreds of the earth shall wail because of him."
The visibility to this earth of the returning Jesus—
while it is not here flashed upon the reader's first attention as the theme of Revelation—is yet presented
as the great focal event of all the contents of the book.
It gives the reader his proper position and attitude in
confronting the whole book.

From whom this awesome, arresting and pregnant
message comes seems to be to us indeterminate. It may
be "his angel" who thus begins his distinguished service
in the drama of Revelation. It may be John's own comprehensive forecast of the great denouement of the
book. From whatsoever source it came, it challenges
attention and commands reverent awe from believer,
terrified apprehension from unbeliever. This is the
event which, next after Calvary, focalizes all rays of
Scriptural prediction from Gen. 3:15 onward.

It is not, here, our Lord's coming to our skies where
we expect to meet Him, but it is His appearing in
visible descent from the skies "with clouds" of angels
and glorified saints. It is a spectacle worldwide and

especially significant to them "which pierced him"—
the Jews. The effect upon earth's unprepared hearts
is faintly illustrated by that produced upon Joseph's
guilty brethren when he made himself known to them,
or like that produced upon the mob in the Garden when
Jesus calmly confronted them with the words, "I am
he." A universal wail will arise from earth's beholders
"because of him."

How plain it is that the world in general will not be
expecting Jesus' return, will not be prepared for Him
or favorable to His coming! To the world in general
Christ's abrupt appearing will spell C-A-L-A-M-I-T-Y.
And the Church had better be found busy in the day
of His coming fulfiling the Master's one commission
than be found absorbed in some "New Era" or Modern-
ist scheme for "bringing in the kingdom." The annunciation of this august event will evoke from the
sanctified heart a fervent "Even so. Amen."

But, as verse 8 shows, the solemnity of this momentous
event will spring from the majesty of the Coming One
Himself.

"I am Alpha and Omega, the beginning and the
ending, saith the Lord, which is, and which was, and
which is to come, the Almighty." This is His own
testimony of Himself—He is the ever-existent One, the
Almighty Himself, who compasses in His existence all
history and holds it all in His control, who is Himself
the beginner and the consummator of history (His
story).

CHAPTER III.

THE CIRCUMSTANTIAL ORIGIN OF REVELATION, vs. 9-11

"9 I John, who also am your brother, and companion in tribulation, and in the kingdom and patience of Jesus Christ, was in the isle that is called Patmos, for the Word of God, and for the testimony of Jesus Christ. 10 I was in the Spirit on the Lord's day, and heard behind me a great voice, as of a trumpet, 11 Saying, I am Alpha and Omega, the first and the last: and, What thou seest, write in a book, and send it unto the seven Churches which are in Asia; unto Ephesus, and unto Smyrna, and unto Pergamos, and unto Thyatira, and unto Sardis, and unto Philadelphia, and unto Laodicea.''

1.

EVIDENTLY Revelation was born out of tribulation. John was in the island of Patmos. This is an isle of the Ægean Sea, located some twenty-four miles off the western shore of Asia Minor, and consisting of barren masses of volcanic hills. It was a suitable place for the confinement of criminals. The Roman Emperor Domitian is the authority generally held to have banished the Apostle John to this lonely and forbidding spot. There is a monastery upon the summit of the most central height which was dedicated to "Saint John" about eight centuries ago. Nearby is a cave where tradition holds that John received his vision, and he is said to have labored in mines of the island. He is said to have been about one hundred years old when released by the Roman Emperor Nerva.

John's exile is plainly attributable to persecution for his faith. It was on account of fidelity to "the Word of God" and to "the testimony of Jesus Christ." This represents a twofold steadfastness in the face of official opposition,—steadfastness in obedient hearing and in courageous speaking.

From Eden down the children of God have been tested by the word spoken unto them, whether the word be the commandment of the Lord, on the one hand, or the insinuation of the devil, on the other hand. The inner spiritual life depends upon whose word is given entrance to mind and heart. "Man shall not live by bread alone, but by every word that proceedeth out of the mouth of God" (Matt. 4:4). "The entrance of thy word giveth light" (Psa. 119:130). "The seed is the Word of God" (Luke 8:11). "Faith cometh by hearing, and hearing by the Word of God" (Rom. 10:17). Keeping the Word of the Lord is the test of love, for the expressed will of the Lord is the food of love.

Contrariwise, Satan prevails, not by tormenting, oppressing, destroying a soul, but altogether by getting his word into mind and heart. Thus he procured the fall of the first human pair. Thus he now "worketh in the children of disobedience" (Eph. 2:2). His destructive copulation with the spirit is accomplished through gaining lustful consent to receive seed out of his hellish mouth. Satan uses not only a serpent, but all manner of media as the channels of this deadly coition. So it comes, that his word through the channel of human authorities brings the Lord's servant to the alternative of adhering to the Word of God and to the commandment of Jesus Christ, or of yielding to the word of Satan through the mandate of contrary human authority. The invariable rule for Christian action is expressed in the words of the Apostles: "We ought to obey God rather than men" (Acts 5:29).

But obedient hearing governs speech and action. If the tempter cannot get the ear of the heart, he will still seek to defeat God's child by the plea, "If you do keep the faith, keep it to yourself." But Jesus says: "Ye shall be witnesses to me" (Acts 1:8). It is by "testimony'' that He is made known to the salvation of others. Testimony is the banner which the valiant soldier of the cross holds aloft right in the enemy-country, in the hottest conflict, not counting life dear unto himself. We may not succeed in silencing our Lord's traducers, but we have the victory over them if we faithfully confess Him. We have this strikingly taught in 1 John 4: 1-6. After saying that ''many false prophets are gone out into the world,'' John lays down the criterion for testing the Spirit of God in a confessor: ''Every spirit that confesseth that Jesus is Christ come in the flesh is of God.'' The contrary confession is declared to be ''that spirit of Anti-Christ.'' But John adds, ''Ye are of God, little children, and *have overcome them* because,'' as the confession proves, ''greater is he that is in you, than he that is in the world''; namely, this spirit of Anti-Christ.

This twofold aspect of loyalty to Jesus Christ is illustrated by the example of the early Apostles and pithily expressed by them in the bold utterance before the authorities: ''Whether it be right in the sight of God to hearken unto you more than unto God, judge ye. For we cannot but speak the things which we have seen and heard'' (Acts 4: 19, 20).

There is a probable hint of the crucial point of John's testing implied in the expression, ''the testimony of Jesus Christ.'' No combination of the name of Christ was so offensive, to the disbelieving Jew especially, but also to the Gentile authorities, as *''Jesus* Christ.'' To the Jew it identified Christ with Jesus whom he hated and crucified. And even the Gentiles, while they tolerated adherence to different invisible divinities, yet they detected, like Herod of old, an official rival in a God-man, a man who was represented to be God manifest in the flesh to rule the world. The appellation ''Jesus Christ'' bears little of this significance in common Christian thought now, and it does not often expose one to bitter persecution. What has been said applies equally under the reading of the Revised Version which omits the word "Christ."

Further evidence that Revelation is the child of early persecution is found in John's humble, tender and sympathetic expression of comradeship with those whom he addresses, "in tribulation, and in the kingdom and patience of Jesus Christ," or "of Jesus," as reads the R. V. This expression is impressive in that it identifies Jesus with this testing. It is His own testing really, not theirs; especially are the kingdom and patience of Him. "Kingdom" here is doubtless to be taken in the sense of Rom. 14:17: "The kingdom of God is—righteousness, and peace, and joy in the Holy Ghost." "Patience" has the sense of steadfast endurance. The combined thought is, then, that of fellowship in victorious endurance of tribulation through the kingdom power of the Holy Spirit of Jesus Himself. Jesus repeats His own victorious endurance of "the contradiction of sinners against himself" by the power of the Holy Spirit in His persecuted followers.

Such fidelity to the Word of God and to the testimony of Jesus is a frequent note of this book. "And when he opened the fifth seal, I saw under the altar the souls of them that were slain for the Word of God, and for the testimony which they held" (6:9). "And the dragon was wroth with the woman, and went to make war with the remnant of her seed, which keep the commandments of God, and have the testimony of Jesus" (R. V.), (12:17). "Here is the patience of the saints: here are they that keep the commandments of God, and the faith of Jesus" (14:12). Tribulation is not only a time for displaying victorious Christian fortitude and fidelity, but it also seems to be almost necessary for arousing and sustaining the same. And it is a notable fact that this book has always been a favorite Scripture with faithful believers in times of acute persecution throughout the age.

Such, then, were the outward circumstances under which this vision was received by the Apostle John. The circumstances might seem to have been unpropitious; but in God's economy they were peculiarly suited to the occasion. Human misery attracts divine pity; human guilt attracts vicarious expiation; the rule is, that the opposite poles of the human and the divine meet in power. Hence, the cruel conditions of John upon Patmos attracted the glories of heaven, and the narrow and forbidding confines of his environment invited and favored the unbounded, transporting, magnificent revelation of the visions given him.

2.

Quite in contrast with the aforementioned physical circumstances attending the origin of Revelation were the spiritual circumstances related in verse 10: "I was in the Spirit on the Lord's day."

It is probably difficult for us to realize the significance of the Lord's day as did John. He had been brought up under "the Sabbath of the commandment." As such, it was intended to be a day of "rest and gladness." Quite likely, however, John, as one of the "sons of thunder," was brought up under rabbinical interpretation of Sabbath, by which he knew little of its "joy and light." But the Master, by teaching and illustration, had shown John the significance of Sabbath as a day of freedom from bondage to toil in order to full opportunity for worship and works of mercy, so that he had come to "call the Sabbath a delight, the holy of the Lord, honorable" (Isa. 58:13).

But, just as the old dispensation,—although it was, when rightly understood and applied, full of spiritual life and fruit—yet was in all respects expectant of "some better thing," so the Sabbath of the law was expectant of another and better Sabbath, a "Sabbath on the eighth day," the "morrow after the Sabbath" of the seventh day.

Such a Sabbath was appointed by the law for the day following the regular Sabbath of the Passover week. It was not only a further Sabbath, but it was a different and an unique one. It occurred at the beginning of barley harvest, the earliest grain to ripen. The law read: "Ye shall bring a sheaf of the firstfruits of your harvest unto the priest: and he shall wave the sheaf before the Lord, to be accepted for you [as representative of the whole harvest]: on the *morrow after the Sabbath* the priest shall wave it. . . . And ye shall eat [from the new harvest] neither bread, nor parched corn, nor green ears, until the self-same day that ye have brought an offering unto the Lord" (Lev. 23:10, 14).

The law prescribed another eighth day Sabbath: "And ye 'shall count unto you from the morrow after the [Passover] Sabbath, from the day that ye brought the *sheaf* of the wave offering; seven Sabbaths shall ye complete: even unto the *morrow after the seventh Sabbath* shall ye number fifty days; and ye shall offer *a new meat offering* unto the Lord. Ye shall bring out of your habitations *two wave loaves* of two tenth deals: They shall be of *fine flour;* they shall be taken *with leaven;* they are the firstfruits unto the Lord. And ye shall proclaim on the selfsame day, that it may be *an holy convocation* unto you: ye shall do no servile work therein" (Lev. 23:15-17, 21). This "feast of weeks," or of "the fiftieth day" from the Sabbath of Passover, we commonly call Pentecost.

The distinction between these two offerings of "firstfruits" was that the sheaf signalized and sanctified the beginning of reaping the fields of the standing grain, while the two loaves (in the dough) signalized and sanctified the beginning of the use of the newly threshed and ground grain just stored in their habitations for daily bread through the ensuing year.

Now to an early Hebrew follower of Jesus like John —and to John especially, the bosom intimate friend of

Jesus—the fulfillments in Jesus of these typical Sabbaths made Sabbath, especially "the Lord's day," "the morrow after the Sabbath" "of the [fourth] commandment," a day suited to the highest spiritual occasion. By His resurrection "on the morrow after the Sabbath" of the Passion and of His crucifixion, Jesus was revealed to John—as he "went in" to that vacated sepulcher, "and he saw, and believed"—as "the firstfruits of them that slept." And when, on that "morrow after the seventh sabbath,"—"the day of Pentecost"—the promised outpouring of the Holy Ghost came upon John, with the rest, Jesus was revealed to him, out of "the fulness of the godhead . . . in him bodily," as the twofold bread of life—for soul and body—of the world. These glories of "the Lord's day" seem almost obsolete, almost forgotten at least, in the Church today, so that the significance of John's noting that it was on this day that "the revelation of Jesus Christ" was opened to him is easily overlooked.

The spiritual state of John on this "Lord's Day" was likewise highly significant and appropriate: "I was in the Spirit." Since resurrection and Pentecost, the first day of the week is for the wholly devoted Christian peculiarly the Spirit's day. Well were it for believers to memorialize and utilize each Lord's Day as the perpetuation of the Holy Spirit in quickening with "newness of life" and in flooding consciousness afresh from the fulness of the glorified Jesus. Most probably the aged John had ceaselessly thus embraced the privilege and opportunity of each succeeding Lord's Day from the time of Christ's resurrection and of the coming of the Spirit of the glorified Jesus.

But the expression here used by John doubtless means something extraordinary. "In the Spirit" seems clearly to imply a transported state of consciousness, transported out of consciousness of Patmos not only, but of flesh and blood itself. It may be related to Paul's experience when "caught up to the third heaven . . . into Paradise," when he heard "unspeakable words"; or John's state may be likened to the coming change when "mortality [shall] be swallowed up of life." Or John's state may be likened to that of Ezekiel, when, as he says, "the Spirit lifted me up between the earth and the heaven, and brought me in the visions of God to Jerusalem" (Ezek. 8:3). In fact, Ezekiel's introduction to his book might well serve for John's Book of Revelation, "the heavens were opened, and I saw visions of God." It is more than having the Spirit indwelling, more than being filled with the Spirit; it may be described as being transported out of ordinary state, even most spiritual, into the Spirit Himself, ensphered in Him, raptured in Him. And thus John could in experience be readily placed anywhere desired in the supernal realms, and be enabled to perceive and comprehend whatsoever the angel unveiled to him from Jesus Christ.

Suddenly from behind, John heard in trumpet tone the mighty voice of Christ, who declared Himself as the all-comprehending one, and gave John direction to write what he saw in a book. This book John was directed to send unto the seven churches in Asia severally, which have already been named,—"unto Ephesus, and unto Smyrna, and unto Pergamos, and unto Thyatira, and unto Sardis, and unto Philadelphia, and unto Laodicea."

These churches are mentioned in the order of geographical circuit, which, with the repetition of the preposition "unto" seems to picture to our minds the delivery of the book across the water from Patmos to the nearest point, Ephesus, first, from which it was to be borne from place to place in regular circuit. This impression is important. It makes real to us that, had the Book of Revelation never been circulated further, its full immediate purpose would still have been accomplished. Primarily it was meant exclusively for each one and for all of just these seven literal churches. What the book contains at all and for any of the Lord's servants it was meant to convey in finished revelation and finished purpose to these seven literal churches.

CHAPTER IV.

CHRIST AMIDST THE CANDLESTICKS, vs. 12-20

"12 And I turned to see the voice that spake with me. And being turned, I saw seven golden candlesticks; 13 And in the midst of the seven candlesticks one like unto the Son of man, clothed with a garment down to the foot, and girt about the paps with a golden girdle. 14 His head and his hairs were white like wool, as white as snow; 15 And his eyes were as a flame of fire; And his feet like unto fine brass, as if they burned in a furnace; and his voice as the sound of many waters. 16 And he had in his right hand seven stars: and out of his mouth went a sharp twoedged sword: and his countenance was as the sun shineth in his strength. 17 And when I saw him, I fell at his feet as dead. And he laid his right hand upon me, saying unto me, Fear not; I am the first and the last: 18 I am he that liveth, and was dead; and, behold, I am alive for evermore, Amen; and have the keys of hell and of death. 19 Write the things which thou hast seen, and the things which are, and the things which shall be hereafter; 20 The mystery of the seven stars which thou sawest in my right hand, and the seven golden candlesticks. The seven stars are the angels of the seven churches: and the seven candlesticks which thou sawest are the seven churches."

THIS vision constitutes the portal, so to speak, of the Book of Revelation. A right entrance is afforded by it, superseding everything speculative and fanciful in the way of perspective.

THE CANDLESTICKS AND THE STARS

It is to be noticed that these two symbols are placed in first prominence both in the vision and in the closing interpretation. What is meant by the symbols is literally explained. The seven candlesticks represent "the seven churches," the stars their angels, or message-bearers. In other words, the candlesticks represent these same seven literal churches of Asia Minor already specified

by name, and the stars symbolize Christ's message-
bearers, or ministers, set over them to feed and lead
them by His word.

The source of the symbol of the candlestick is beyond
question. Each church of Asia was represented to John
after the figure of the golden candlestick of the Tabernacle of Israel. A complete description of the divine
design of this beautiful article of furniture is found
in Ex. 25 : 31-40, and one of the exact finished replica
is found in Ex. 37 : 17-24. The lampstand was made
of pure gold in one beaten piece, which embraced the
glistening shaft, terminating in a central lamp, and
three branches on either side in opposite pairs, terminating in like manner in lamps, making seven lamps in
all: The whole standard was elaborately ornamented
by skillfully embossed figures and flowers. Though
hollow within, the whole standard weighed one hundred
pounds, some say nearly two hundred, and it stood
nearly five feet in height and nearly three and one-half
in width. The Lord specially directed that a talent of
gold should be used in the structure, representing a
value, some estimate, of nearly $25,000.

According to Ex. 27 : 20, 21, the lamps were to be
supplied with ''pure oil olive beaten,'' and the candelabra was to stand in the Holy Place on the south side,
facing the veil of the Holiest of All and over against
the table of shewbread, with the golden altar of incense
between the two.

The purpose of the candelabra was to give the light
in the Holy Place by night. The Lord greatly emphasized the charge to have the lights kept always burning
night after night. Aaron was to light the lamps at
sundown, when he also burnt the holy incense on the
golden altar, and in the morning before offering the
incense he was to ''dress'' the lamps. The articles required for snuffing, trimming, etc., were to be of pure
gold. The lamps were to be left through the day perfectly

clean from soot and replenished with oil ready to be lighted again at night.

While the "Tabernacle of the Wilderness" was provided with only one candelabra, the temple of Solomon had five on each side of the Holy Place, or ten candelabra in all, 1 Kings 7:49. Here, then, is precedent for a plurality of candlesticks in John's vision.

Jesus in the Midst of the Candlesticks

It is now very obvious in what character and functions John saw "the Son of man" "in the midst of the seven candlesticks." It is in the character and functions of "the great High Priest, that is passed into the heavens, Jesus the Son of God." He is seen as it were making His morning visit in the Holy Place for the purpose of dressing the lamps and of burning the morning incense.

We now have the right basis for an intelligent spiritual study of the applications of the vision.

The Mystery of the Churches and Their Ministers

Mystery, we repeat, means not unreality, but hidden reality. And the hidden reality stands first. The seven resplendent candlesticks symbolize the hidden realities of those seven literal churches of Asia. Their first reality, the hidden, was not necessarily known or even confirmed by their apparent reality, any more than their hidden realities were produced by their apparent realities. While in practice these churches differed so much from the symbol, as chapters 2 and 3 show, yet in hidden reality the symbol truly represented them, and this stood first for all that should be or could be before the world depended upon, what they first were mystically in the sight of God in Christ. This explains also why, while they differed so much from one another in walk and

conversation, as chapters 2 and 3 again show, yet mystically, essentially, they were all alike,—seven identical
golden candlesticks. Likewise the pastors of these
churches, Christ's message-bearers to them, were mystically angels of God, stars of heaven, one and all alike.

This twofold character of literal churches and ministers, of the Church as a whole, of the ministry as a
whole,—of the individual Christian too,—is most worthy
of constant recognition; there is the inward and the
outward, the spiritual and the natural, the mystical
reality and the obvious actuality. The discrepancy between is likely at times to be very great; but it is
always to be remembered that the hidden is first, and
that the degree of excellence in the apparent is but the
measure in which the hidden is being shown forth.
And it is to be remembered that the hidden is the same
in all, and that the hidden is the constant, the apparent
is the variable; it is the state of the believers as seated
"in the heavenlies in Christ Jesus" (Eph. 2:6).

So then, these seven Asian churches in mystical reality
were severally and alike pure as finest gold, beautiful
with heavenly figures and flower, perfect in unity as
the Father and the Son, complete and blessed with all
spiritual blessings in heavenly places, entirely qualified
to give celestial radiance in the midst of terrestrial darkness. The same in principle is to be said of the pastors.

Fortunately the solution of this mystery is not left
to ourselves, but it has been given us by inspiration in
a striking illustration. With perhaps no other church
did Paul have to deal in correction of gross evils as
with the church at Corinth. Before grappling with
those great evils, however, Paul approached the church
in greeting, benediction, and gratulation from the
standpoint of their mystical character. Note how he
characterizes the church members, what favors he invokes upon them, what praise he gives on their behalf,
what wealth of endowment he credits to them, what

assurance he expresses concerning their hereafter. "Paul, called to be an apostle of Jesus Christ through the will of God, and Sosthenes our brother, unto the church of God which is at Corinth, to them that are sanctified in Christ Jesus, called to be saints, with all that in every place call upon the name of Jesus Christ our Lord, both their's and our's: Grace be unto you, and peace, from God our Father, and from the Lord Jesus Christ. I thank my God always on your behalf, for the grace of God which is given you by Jesus Christ; that in everything ye are enriched by him, in all utterance, and in all knowledge; even as the testimony of Christ was confirmed in you; so that ye come behind in no gift; waiting for the coming of our Lord Jesus Christ: Who shall also confirm you unto the end, that ye may be blameless in the day of our Lord Jesus Christ. God is faithful, by whom ye were called unto the fellowship of his Son Jesus Christ, our Lord" (1 Cor. 1-9).

One would say that this was a model, a perfect church. And so it was—in the primary, hidden, heavenly sense, as a "church of God," "sanctified in Christ Jesus." And so is every church, and so is every believer. And this is no pretense, no make-believe, no "imputed" or "positional" sense; it is real, it is vital. Were it not so—although in the hidden, and mystical—it never could be so in the apparent, the evidential. The whole Scriptural doctrine of practical holiness by the grace of Christ Jesus is based upon the fact of existing mystical holiness by creation in Christ Jesus. The act of absolute renunciation of sin and consecration unto God—when entering upon a life of entire sanctification—is consequent upon fully believing for a *fact* "yourselves to be— *dead indeed unto sin, and alive—unto—God—through— Jesus Christ our Lord,*" (that is, through spiritual existence in Him). It was because those Corinthian Christians already were "sanctified in Christ Jesus" that Paul besought them to *live out by Christ's grace* the life that He was mystically to them.

THE HIGH PRIEST

In perfect accord with what has just been expressed, the Son of God was seen in high priestly aspect and functions in the midst of the candlesticks. It was the function of the high priest of old constantly to keep the lamps perfectly dressed and burning—albeit in the hidden chamber of the Holy Place for the eyes of God alone. So the glorified Son of man—in whom those seven churches of Asia were severally created perfect as the freshly created Adam—was seen by John first of all under His faithful high priestly ministry of ceaselessly maintaining those churches perfect in purity, in unity and in heavenly radiance; i. e., mystically so, in the secret holy place where no eye but the priest's ever beheld. And as to the messengers of His word to the churches, created and subsisting in His right hand, they "shine......as the stars" (Dan. 12:3).

It is not only the function engaging the Lord Jesus in the vision,—the function of attending upon the candlesticks—that identifies Him as High Priest to those churches, but it is also the attire in which He is described. The full regalia of the priests is described in Exodus 28 and 39, and it constitutes one of the most wonderful of the creations that Moses was directed by the Lord to have made for the Levitical order. The priestly attire was called "holy garments......for glory and for beauty." The description of Christ's attire in this vision is unmistakably that of heavenly High Priest. The robe of Aaron was to reach to his bare feet and to be girded with a golden girdle. Jesus is seen clothed throughout His stature with the glory and beauty of perfect righteousness, all girt with truth as gold tried in the fire. His feet glow like molten "white bronze," as of one who has stood for us in the place of absolute divine judgment. As to the pure white priestly turban adorned with the golden miter, "Holi-

ness to the Lord," His hairs—"white like wool, as white
as snow"— are his turban, betokening His devotion
to the will and glory of God the Father. But even more
impressive are the active expressions of His person:
His eyes emit shafts of spiritual intelligence, love and
omniscience; His countenance radiates beams of spiritual power like the midday sun; His voice is resonant
with the majesty of many distant Niagaras, and out
of His mouth proceedeth utterance penetrating and
dividing like a two-edged sword.

This is a revelation of our "great High Priest,"
who "is entered......into heaven itself, now to appear [in the fulness of the Godhead bodily] in the
presence of God for us." It is that High Priest as
He stands invisibly among His people snuffing, trimming,
replenishing them, and constantly preserving them
mystically in perfect readiness to show forth His praises
in this world of darkness and evil. How little we realize
this! How little these Asian churches realized it! How
little even the beloved Apostle John had realized it!
If a radiant and mighty angel's apparition prostrated
the godly Daniel, how much more was this mighty revelation of the glorified Son of man in priestly person
and presence enough to prostrate John at His feet as
dead, although it was the very One on whose bosom he
had once leaned confidingly and unafraid! John was
restored by the glorified Jesus to his old-time ease and
rapture in His presence by the uplifting touch of His
right hand and the gracious assuring words, "Fear not."

Yet Jesus maintained His unparalleled being and
dignity by re-declaring, "I am the first and the last,
and the living one," as aptly reads the Revised Version.
Here is that "I am," (the Jehovah name of the Old
Testament), plainly identifying Jehovah in divine being
spanning the existence of eternal deity,—the living One,
the self-existing One, none other than God Himself—
with the great High Priest of the churches, Jesus Christ.

The other side of the identification is in like impressive words, "and I became dead [having to this end become flesh, John 1:14], and behold [amazing!], I am living [more literally and strikingly rendered, living I am; i. e., a resurrected, living-again "I am"] for evermore" ("unto the ages of the ages"). This is the plainest assertion by Jesus that, as the one resurrected from His death, He is humanly and bodily invested with all the fulness of His preëxistent deity. All divine glory be to the glorified Jesus! Appropriately to this latter mode of existence He adds, "I have the keys of death and of Hades." The lockers of the last enemy, death, and of the unseen realm are in His exclusive and permanent possession. What volumes of comfort and of triumph are bound up in these few words!

A word may here be fittingly injected as to the evidence afforded by this scene of the spiritual unity in Christ of Old and New Testament dispensations and of their saints. The symbol of New Testament churches is taken from the Old Testament Temple. The character and functions in which our Lord is presented are those of the Levitical order; only, here the priest is the lamb also, the slain Lamb alive for evermore. But this Lamb-Priest is the Old Testament Jehovah, who came in the flesh as "the Lamb of God that *taketh away the sin of the world*," or, as "the Lamb slain from the foundation of the world," the "I am" Lamb, whose sacrifice of Himself was *"once and for all,"* who needed not that "He should offer Himself often" in order to avail for all times and all believers.

In the Revised and other versions v. 19 opens with a "therefore." "Write therefore." "Write therefore the things which thou hast seen." Those for whom the record of this vision of John was intended were the seven Asian churches. Imagine the impression of inestimable value that the first and the repeated reading of this record was adapted to make upon their minds!

While not themselves seeing the vision, they had all its
intended and important meaning. The power of the
vision resides in the record for those who "read......
hear....keep the words." Consequently the same in-
valuable impressions are for saints of the present day,
who "read......and hear.... and keep." Of prime
need to every Christian during all the days of Christ's
concealment in heaven is a vivid and effectual impression of who is invisibly in our midst, what He is to us
as High Priest among the candlesticks, what we are as
His mystical candlesticks, and what the ministry is as
the mystical stars in His right hand. It was from this
standpoint that those Asian churches were exhorted in
chapters 2 and 3 to "show forth the praises of him who
had called them *out of darkness into his marvelous
light.*"

John's commission was to write,—besides the things
he had seen in this wonderful unfolding of mystical
realities,—"the things which are, and the things which
shall be hereafter." This verse is so important as a
synopsis of the whole book of the Revelation, that we
do well to examine a few variant translations.

The Revised Version reads: "Write therefore the
things which thou sawest, and the things which are,
and the things which shall come to pass hereafter."
Here "sawest" refers unquestionably to the things mystical which had been revealed to John, while "the things
which are" means things apparent. Accordingly the
next verse continues. "The *mystery*......which thou
sawest,"—that of the seven candlesticks and of the seven
stars, which mystery is straightway interpreted,—while
chapters 2 and 3 straightway take up "the things which
are" (not mystical or needing interpretation) in the
seven Asian churches. And the third matter for John
to write was "the things which shall come to pass hereafter." This is clearly to be identified with "the revelation" itself described in v. 1 as "things which must

shortly come to pass." Other versions put the last number of the triplet in the words "the things which are about to take place after these" (G), implying a group of events to ensue upon the order of "the things which are"; "The things which shall take place after these" (1911); "what is about to *occur after this*" (C. V.).

Paraphrased this would read: "Write, then, what, by the vision and its interpretation, you perceived the seven churches and stars to be in their hidden existence and character in their Head, and what they are in their visible practices, and what is waiting immediately to occur after this [present earthly and visible order of the churches], as verse one predicted." This now affords us a clear prospectus of the Book of Revelation. It embraces an exhibit first of the seven Asian churches in the contrast between their hidden state in Christ, their priestly Head and Presence, and their comparative manifestations of Him in their actual earthly conduct. This, however, is not "The Revelation" proper, which was to be "of things which must shortly [swiftly] come to pass," that is, of otherwise unforeseen, unforeknown, inconceivable, *events* which constitute the material of "this prophecy" (v. 3). It is perfectly plain that the prediction, or revelation of these *coming events* begins with Chapter 4. Hence we are to distinguish between "The Revelation" and "The Book of Revelation." The Book of Revelation contains more than "the revelation" itself. But the important thing to note in this peculiar construction of the book is, that the events to occur were of most direct concern and intimate relation to the seven Asian churches, so glorious and perfect in existence in their invisible priestly Head and yet so greatly needing His dealings with their actual works on earth. These dealings form the subject of Chapters II and III. All this part of the book belongs to the present order of the Church in and under Jesus Christ in glorified body as

High Priest. The Revelation proper is to take up the stirring events attending His entrance in glorified humanity into the order of the Church under and with Him as King.

The Church Militant

CHAPTER I

CHRIST AND THE SEVEN CHURCHES

I. Guiding Considerations

THE high priest had a twofold function. His first function was to represent the people before God, to negotiate their interests in the holy and mysterious courts of the Almighty, "to make reconciliation for the people." The vision just studied reveals the status in which the great High Priest, Jesus Christ, presents and preserves His people before the face of the Father. But the high priest was also to represent God before the people, to negotiate His interests in the practical walk of His people in the public, earthly sphere. In other words, while the high priest was the intercessor for his people before God in secret, he was also God's messenger, teacher and guide to the people in their walk in the sight of mankind. It is in this latter function that the great High Priest, Jesus Christ, is represented in the two chapters now to be studied. Jesus Christ functions here as the minister of God to the people regarding their practical life and service. Here, as in the previous chapter, the seven literal Asian churches are the subjects of His ministry.

This last observation is important. The more simple, literal and matter-of-fact our conception here, as elsewhere in this book, to the effect that seven existing, local, literal churches were the original readers for which this book of Scripture was designed and given,—just as in the case of Romans, Corinthians, Galatians, Ephesians, etc.,—the closer we come to a true reading of the book ourselves, and the saner, the more legitimate and pertinent application will we make of it for ourselves.

Consequently, the only warrantable view of the book in whole or in part, is the view that belongs to it as an *open book to the seven Asian churches,* and not as a matter which could not be immediately open to them and which was dependent upon some subsequent condition of understanding fulfilled for some later readers. These messages are to be taken as a practical dealing with literal, existing churches concerning actual existing conditions and with immediate practical ends in view. That the same conditions should arise with individual believers or bodies of believers at other places and times during the high priestly regime of the glorified Jesus is to be expected, and the messages here given are to be taken in appropriate application thereto. But these letters constitute no part of "the prophecy of this book," in predictive sense; they are purely hortatory, addressed to certain specified churches, and otherwise practically applicable according as conditions at other times and places during the high priestly session of Jesus Christ call for them. These considerations will preserve us from fanciful, far-fetched, strained and overly-learned, doubtful and conflicting schemes of interpretation.

II. The Messages of Jesus Christ as Glorified High Priest, to the Seven Churches.

While these seven letters are entirely distinct from one another in import, yet they are all constructed on a like pattern, and they have certain important features in common, of all which the message to Ephesus will serve as our model. The following features of this one belong in common to all seven epistles.

1. The message is addressed to the "angel" of the church (1). This, we have considered means the ministerial head, although denominated in mystical character as a "star," or a celestial luminary.

2. The Lord as High Priest issues His message in a

special attribute drawn from the mystical description of Him given in Chapter I and appropriate to His dealing with the particular church (1).

3. The standpoint of the message is expressed in the words, "I know thy works;" it is the standpoint of closest scrutiny of and acquaintance with what is going on in the church, as if to say, "I know just what you are doing" (2).

4. Then comes the bill of specifications of their works (2, 3).

5. This is followed by appropriate exhortation (4-6).

6. The conclusion (7) is based on a formula. "He that hath an ear, let him hear what the Spirit saith unto the churches; To him that overcometh," is exactly the formula—followed by a distinctive conclusion of each message—excepting that in the last four messages the two members of the form are given in reversed order.

These messages, then, are suitable dealings of the high priestly Head of the seven Asian churches,—first, from the standpoint of His solicitous, penetrating scrutiny of their practical works; secondly, from the standpoint of His gift of the Holy Spirit to teach, lead and enable them to do His works; and thirdly, from the standpoint of His high priestly captaincy over the churches in their warfare in this militant situation in the world during this present age. It is clear that Christ's objective in dealing with the churches was to cause them by the Holy Spirit "alway......to triumph in Christ" and to "make manifest the savour of his knowledge" by them in every place (2 Cor. 2:14). And this is the objective of Christ's high priestly relationship in dealing with all His churches and with all His followers in all this dispensation. These letters hang before our eyes not only literal photos of those seven churches, but types also of churches and of believers throughout the present militant career of God's children, as they march through the path of tribulation, besetment and peril till the end of the high priestly dispensation of the glorified Jesus, and as they fight in prospect of being rewarded appropriately in the way of participation with Him in the dispensation of His visible earthly reign in glorified form as King of kings and Lord of lords.

Certain pertinent Scriptures come to mind readily in this connection.

1. As to doing the works of the glorified Jesus. "Verily, verily I say unto you, he that believeth on me, the works that I do shall he do also; and greater works than these shall he do; because I go unto my Father. And whatsoever ye shall ask in my name, that will I do, that the Father may be glorified in the Son. If ye shall ask anything in my name, I will do it" (John 14:12-14). Christ's assurance here does not mean primarily that His followers shall through faith in Him repeat the works that He had done while on earth. The sense is, "the works that I am doing,"—or shall be doing from the right hand of the Father—these shall my believing servants be doing for Me instrumentally. And His works from the Father's right hand were to exceed those of His activity while in the earth. Jesus is from thence to glorify the Father as He did when here; but He has greater power now to glorify the Father since being seated glorified at His right hand. But, while He is to do these greater works by the same Spirit by whom He wrought of old, yet it is to be by the instrumentality of believers even as He humanly was the Spirit's instrument. And, just as He obtained knowledge of the Father's will and working by prayer, and offered Himself instrumentally for the execution of the same by the power of the Holy Spirit, so believers were by prayer to enter into the vision of Christ's hidden working and become able to offer themselves instrumentally for the execution of the same by the power of the Holy Spirit.

This praying is "in His name." This does not mean merely a verbal, even a perfectly sincere, use of His name. "My name" means His presence and person. This praying is, then, in such vital union with Him, and out of such personal identification with Him, that the prayer unto the Father by the believer is as truly in the person of Jesus Christ as the latter's own supplication. That this is no strained interpretation is proved by John's own experience and by that of the apostles. In John 5:19, 20, Jesus says: "Verily, verily I say unto you, the Son can do nothing of himself, but what he seeth the Father do[ing]: for what things soever he [the Father] doeth [may be doing], these also doeth the Son likewise. For the Father loveth the Son, and sheweth him all things that himself doeth [may be doing]: and he will shew him greater works than these, that ye may marvel." We get here the secret of how Jesus knew what to do and when to do it. By His identification through prayer with the Father He was given to see what the Father was doing in the unseen and to bring it instrumentally to light, the Father working with Him as His instrument. "My Father worketh hitherto, and I work," the one originally and in the unseen, the other instrumentally and in the seen. Prayer in—not His own name; i. e., in and of Himself, but in the Father's name, in and of and for Him,—was the avenue of this identity of co-working.

Now we read of the apostles, Mark 16:20: "they went forth and preached every where, the Lord working with them [that is, making them His instruments], and confirming the word [concerning His presence and working] with signs [visible manifestations] following." In like manner the Apostle Paul discloses the secret of his marvelous ministry by saying, "For I will not dare to speak of any of those things which Christ hath not *wrought by me*......through mighty signs and wonders, by the power of the Spirit of God" (Rom. 15:18, 19). We can now appreciate what the great High Priest meant each of the seven churches of Asia to realize, when

He reminded it of the facts involved by saying, "I know thy works." It was the same as to say that He was noting just in how far that church was His instrument and in how far it was not, in what respects He could not acknowledge their works as done by Himself.

2. When Jesus commissioned the apostles, He declared that they should be His witnesses, or representatives, from Jerusalem to the uttermost part of the earth. But this was not to be undertaken until the Holy Spirit had come upon them as the enabling power.

Why were they thus restrained? Was it because they had not had the Spirit before? Surely not. Jesus had sent them abroad in the land before as His representatives, and they had preached and wrought wonderfully by the same Spirit by whom He had preached and wrought. But they were now to be witnesses or representatives of Jesus, not as they had known Him or wrought under Him in the past, but as they were to know Him and to work under Him in His glorified state. What a difference this made to them! When Jesus spoke of the issues from the inmost depths of believers which were to result from the gift of the Holy Spirit which He promised, it was said, "the Holy Ghost was not yet given; because that Jesus was not yet glorified" (John 7:39).

This means that there was in store a new gift of the Holy Spirit for pouring into and through human vessels the things of Jesus Christ when glorified at the Father's right hand. Certainly the Father gave His Son to speak and work among men after coming in the flesh, even in the state of humiliation, as He had never been given to do before. But this was limited again in comparison with the "greater works" He was to do "because," said He, "I go to my Father." And a greater dispensation still awaits His return to earth in visible glory. But the Holy Spirit has been, is, and will be the agent of all Christ's words and works in these advancing dispensations. And that Spirit has been given, is given, and will be given to Christ's ministers in degrees and manifestations correspondingly. While the prophets of old made Jesus Christ known by the Holy Spirit's endowment according to the times of His pre-incarnate presence, the ministers of Christ in the days of His advent on earth had a further endowment in His name. The endowment in the present time of Christ's glorified, though invisible presence and power, is far in advance yet; and the endowment which will belong to Christ's ministers in the coming dispensation of His visible presence in glorified form will still far exceed anything now possible.

The endowment of the Spirit in all dispensations has been, so far as ministry is concerned, for the purpose of entire direction and efficiency. The law of service is expressed in the words now before us: "He that hath an ear, let him hear what the Spirit saith unto the churches." "Church work!" What a common expression! How often does it mean Holy Spirit's work? But Jesus is saying "I know your church work. My entire concern is whether it is my work by the Spirit I give you for direction and divine power. All my work through you is committed into His hands, who is given to those who will obey Him"; all "church work" that is not His work is "wood, hay, stubble." "Every man's work shall be made manifest: for the day [of Christ's judgment seat, 2 Cor. 5:10] shall declare it, because it shall be revealed by fire: and the fire [of "the Spirit of judgment, and . . . the Spirit of burning," Isa. 4:4] shall try every man's work of *what sort* it is. If any man's work, which he hath built thereupon abide [the fire test], he shall receive a reward. If any man's work shall be burned, he shall suffer loss [of reward]: but he himself shall be saved: yet so as by fire" (1 Cor. 3:13-15).

3. And how could it be otherwise than that the glorified Jesus, by "the Spirit of glory and of God," is the

sole and only sufficient author and power of the churches
to work! This is involved in the regularly recurring
phrase, "To him that overcometh." This implies conflict. And what saith the Scripture respecting Christian conflict in this age? "We wrestle not against flesh
and blood, but against principalities, against powers,
against the rulers of the [moral and spiritual] darkness
of this world, against spiritual wickedness [that is,
wicked spirits] in high [that is, celestial] places" (Eph.
6:12). This is enough to make anyone shrink from being involved in the contest with such foes. What spiritual
conflict attended the pathway of Old Testament warriors of faith is shown in Hebrews 11. Was Satanic
opposition intimidated and weakened in the days of our
Lord in the flesh? Just the contrary! Did the Satanic
enemies of Christ pale and flee when evidences of His
resurrection and glorification burst forth? Just the
contrary! Is this age to be one of gradual but sure
routing of these celestial hosts, organizations and forces?
Just the contrary, as the Book of Revelation will abundantly prove. Nowhere does the New Testament hint
that Jesus will return to receive His crown from a
pacified, reconciled, Christianized world. But the testimony is that "evil men and seducers shall wax worse
and worse, deceiving and being deceived." Never during this age more than in its last days will the charge
be more pertinent: "Be strong in the Lord, and in the
power of his might. Put on the whole armour of God,
that ye may be able to stand against the wiles of the
devil. . . . Take unto you the whole armour of God, that
ye may be able to withstand in the evil day, and having
done all [that is, having overcome all] to stand" (Eph.
6:10, 11, 13).

Hence we have given the distinguishing title to this
Part as "the Church Militant." The whole tenor
of these two chapters of Revelation is that of the warfare of faith, meeting the brunt of subtle, heavy,

dangerous opposition in various forms. Here is the Lord, in the old-time captaincy of the high priest, calling His Church to be more than conqueror over the enemies of the world, the flesh and the devil. It is the same region of battle-smoke, clash of spiritual forces, groans of suffering and shouts of victory, that are so familiar to us in the apostolical epistles.

CHAPTER II.

MESSAGES TO EPHESUS, SMYRNA AND PERGAMOS

I. *Message to the Church of Ephesus, 2:1-7.*

"1 Unto the angel of the church of Ephesus write; These things saith he that holdeth the seven stars in his right hand, who walketh in the midst of the seven golden candlesticks; 2 I know thy works, and thy labour, and thy patience, and how thou canst not bear them which are evil: and thou hast tried them which say they are apostles, and are not, and hast found them liars: 3 And hast borne, and hast patience, and for my name's sake hast laboured, and hast not fainted. 4 Nevertheless I have somewhat against thee, because thou hast left thy first love. 5 Remember therefore from whence thou are fallen, and repent, and do the first works; or else I will come unto thee quickly, and will remove thy candlestick out of his place, except thou repent. 6 But this thou hast, that thou hatest the deeds of the Nicolaitanes, which I also hate. 7 He that hath an ear to hear, let him hear what the Spirit saith unto the churches; To him that overcometh will I give to eat of the tree of life, which is in the midst of the paradise of God."

THIS church was addressed by Christ Jesus in the most prominent and comprehensive aspect of His high priestly care; namely, as "He that holdeth the seven stars in his right hand, who walketh in the midst of the seven golden candlesticks." This is a most solemn reminder of the majesty of Him with whom the church of Ephesus had to do. Strong commendation is given by Jesus to this church. It is commended for its long unflagging pull of toil and endurance; for its unyielding attitude toward evil and evil doers; for its faithful scrutiny of professing apostles and its keen detection and fearless exposure of lying claimants. It is here shown that, as Paul teaches in 1 Cor. 12:28, the order of apostles in the church was not intended

70

to be confined to the Twelve, but to be permanent, embracing others to be called by Jesus Christ from generation to generation. There were other apostles already while members of the original apostolate were still living and active, such as Paul, Barnabas (Acts 14:4), Silas, etc. What distinguished the Twelve was that they were witnesses to Jesus' ministry and resurrection (Acts 1: 21, 22). But this was not an exclusive sign of an apostle (2 Cor. 12:12). It followed, then, that the church of Ephesus, as other churches, needed to "try the spirits" claiming to be apostles and even appearing to be. Doing this so faithfully, the church had been kept uncorrupted in doctrine and ministry. But it is evident that Ephesus had had repeated, protracted, unending tests upon patience and endurance. She had, however, borne all unwearyingly because of Jesus' name, His person, His presence, His will and honor and truth.

It could be said with strong color of truth, "How few churches of the age or of the present day have proved so true to Jesus!" And yet Ephesus had not proved true to *Jesus*. What is it to be true to Jesus? Is it to be true to His form of doctrine and of ministry, or to be true to His person and Spirit? While the former is very important and commendable, yet without the latter, it is to Jesus disappointing and intolerable. Said one minister to another, "I cannot be true to Jesus and be peaceable." The other replied, "I cannot be true to Jesus and not be peaceable." In the one case it meant the impossibility of maintaining Jesus' doctrine without hostile contention; in the other it meant the impossibility of contending for the faith without fulfiling the injunction, "If it be possible, as much as lieth in you, live peaceably with all men" (Rom. 12:18); or, more apropos, "The servant of the Lord must not strive, but be gentle unto all men, apt to teach, patient [forbearing], in meekness instructing those that oppose themselves; if God peradventure will give them repentance to the acknowledging of the truth; and that they may recover themselves out of the snare of the devil, who are taken captive by him at his will'' (2 Tim. 2:24-26).

While Ephesus had stuck to the straight path of Christian rectitude, orthodoxy, zeal, faithful exposure of the evil and false, yet she had ''fallen''; she had deserted her Lord in the pathway of His love. Once she had walked with Him in the love that ''beareth all things, believeth all things, hopeth all things, endureth all things'' (1 Cor. 13:7). It was not that Ephesus had done anything wrong in form that Jesus chided her; but it was that somewhere on the way she had deserted Him in respect to the motive, the spirit, and the end of her deeds of patience, zeal and purity.

And the great High Priest treats this falling-out with Him most seriously; He regards it as fatal, so far as service in the works is concerned. He regards the light of Ephesus in the world as a false light, which He must remove from its appointed place—except there be repentance and return—as has long ago occurred. Take the story of Paul's farewell talk to the Ephesian elders in Acts 20:28-30. ''Take heed therefore unto yourselves, and to all the flock, over the which the Holy Ghost hath made you overseers, to feed the church of God, which he hath purchased with his own blood. For I know this, that after my departing shall grievous wolves enter in among you, not sparing the flock. Also of your own selves shall men arise, speaking perverse things, to draw away disciples after them.'' Did the elders come at some time to fulfil this injunction in unyielding form, but out of communion of the Holy Spirit; and, as a result, had wolfish spirits been bred out of their own midst? What became of the Ephesian candlestick?

And yet there is a hate which is true to love, the reverse side of love. This is exemplified in the Lord's afterthought in regard to the attitude of Ephesians toward "the Nicolaitanes." It is to be noticed that Jesus says, "Thou hatest the *deeds* of the Nicolaitanes, which I also hate." Ah! This discloses the secret probably. In hating evil deeds Ephesus had doubtless fallen into hate of the doers thereof. Here lies the test in contending for the truth and the right. It is human to have a malice toward offenders. Many a Christian and many a church has "fallen" right here. It is fellowship with and true service of Christ to strive against sin "with malice toward none." The necessity for "laying aside all malice" is pressed by Peter (1 Peter 2: 1) lest, like bile in the stomach, one's own necessary food of God's word be turned into further corruption in the system.

It is not so important for us to know just what was meant by "the Nicolaitanes" as to learn the lessons of the case. Yet the following seems the best we can gather from traditional sources regarding the Nicolaitanes. The following is extracted from the International Standard Bible Encyclopedia: "A sect or party of evil influence in early Christianity, especially in the seven churches of Asia. Their doctrine was similar to that of Balaam, who taught Balak to cast a stumbling-block before the children of Israel, to eat things sacrificed to idols, and to commit fornication. . . . The problem underlying the Nicolaitan controversy......was in reality most important, and concerned the whole relation of Christianity to paganism and its usages. The Nicolaitanes disobeyed the command issued to the Gentile Churches, by the apostolic council held at Jerusalem in 49-50 A. D., that they should refrain from the eating of 'things sacrificed to idols' . . . to prevent a return to a pagan laxity of morals. To this danger the Nicolaitanes were themselves a glaring witness, and therefore St. John was justified in condemning them."

"To him that overcometh." Of course this means, to him that overcometh under the particular circumstances of testing. And it means that trying conditions are the setting of a spiritual warfare. Worldly enticement, fleshly repugnance and satanic pressure convert the given situation into an assault upon spiritual position in Christ. The peculiar nature of the conflict springs from the peculiar setting of trial, and the particular reward held out to the overcomer doubtless stands related to the special nature of the conflict. To the Ephesian overcomer is promised the unspeakable privilege of partaking of "the tree of life, which is in the midst [center] of the paradise [or garden] of God."

This peculiar expression refers us back to Adam's first condition in Eden's garden. The things spiritually real to him were kept before his eyes by symbols. As we saw when studying that interesting period, Adam having been created in Christ as his Head—living in Him, moving in Him, having his being in Him—had this symbolically represented to him in "the tree of life . . . in the midst of the garden" (Gen. 2:9), of which he was privileged freely to eat along with all the other non-symbolical trees. Only of "the tree of knowledge of good and evil" he was not to eat, for in so doing he would be spiritually partaking of the false head, the devil. Christ, Himself, was the real tree of life.

What an appropriate promise! The testing of Ephesus had caused her to fall out of the love of Christ; victory under the testing meant continuing in the love of Christ; and this brings the reward of partaking of Christ's very being which is love. "Continue ye in my love" is Christ's first commandment, and the first condition of abiding in Him and of bearing His fruit.

II. *Message to the Church of Smyrna, 2: 8-11.*

"8 And unto the angel of the church in Smyrna write; These things saith the first and the last, which was dead and is alive; 9 I know thy works, and tribulation, and poverty, (but thou art

rich) and I know the blasphemy of them which say they are
Jews, and are not, but are the synagogue of Satan. 10 Fear
none of those things which thou shalt suffer: behold, the devil
shall cast some of you into prison, that ye may be tried; and
ye shall have tribulation ten days: be thou faithful unto death,
and I will give thee a crown of life. 11 He that hath an ear
to hear, let him hear what the Spirit saith unto the churches;
He that overcometh shall not be hurt of the second death.''

Smyrna was addressed by her great High Priest in
the character of the ''first and the last, which was dead
and is alive''; that is, of the timeless Christ in His deity
and of the resurrected One in His humanity. And not
merely timeless. ''The first'' means more than first in
point of time; it means the very archetype; and ''the
last'' means the consummation of all. He is man's, He
is creation's, A and Z, beginning and ending, fountain-
head and perfect realization. The first word to be
spoken of humanity is Christ and Him crucified and
risen again.

How appropriate is Jesus' introduction of Himself
to Smyrna! It shows in what character Jesus wants
His servants to conquer through Him when tried after
Smyrna's fashion.

Smyrna evidently was suffering distress, loss and
calumny from persecutors, called Jews as they were by
race, but, for their evil spirit and deeds, more properly
called Satan's synagogue. This fiery trial was being
so borne as to be greatly enriching Smyrna spiritually.
As an old missionary in Chosen remarked regarding the
spiritual effect of the Japanese persecution of the Corean
Church: ''Japan could not have planned better for
the Corean Christians if she had tried.'' ''Take away
the dross from the silver, and there shall come forth a
vessel for the finer.'' This is Jesus' method of preparing for Himself vessels for personal use. ''In the
world ye shall have tribulation; but be of good cheer,
I have overcome the world.'' Hence ''in all these things
we are more than conquerors through Him that loved

us." The forge, the anvil, the crucible, the mortar and pestle, the potter's wheel, the burning fiery furnace heated seven times more than it was wont to be heated, are the friendly and appropriate instruments of grace, rather than the obnoxious instruments of torture.

Hence the blessed High Priest says to Smyrna, "I am not going to take you right away out of trial, but rather prove you further yet. But let no one be fearing what you are about to be suffering. Lo, the Accuser is about to cast some of you into prison, that ye may be further tried; and you shall have tribulation ten days —an exact measure of necessary proving. Be faithful as long as you live, be faithful when it means violent death. I pledge you, it only means not merely life, but life crowned with reward and honor in the sight of three worlds—heavenly, earthly, infernal."

In entire keeping with all else is the concluding promise to the Smyrnan overcomer: "He that overcometh [under these peculiar trials] shall not be hurt by the second death." Future and everlasting security of life is being sealed by insecurity and forfeiture of present life for Jesus' sake. The Smyrnan type is found today in the bleeding Church of Christ in Russia and in the dying martyr Church of Christ in Armenia.

III. Message to the Church of Pergamos, 2:12-17.

"12 And to the angel of the church in Pergamos write; These things saith he which hath the sharp sword with two edges; 13 I know thy works, and where thou dwellest, even where Satan's seat is: and thou holdest fast my name, and hast not denied my faith, even in those days wherein Antipas was my faithful martyr, who was slain among you, where Satan dwelleth. 14 But I have a few things against thee, because thou hast there them that hold the doctrine of Balaam, who taught Balac to cast a stumbling-block before the children of Israel, to eat things sacrificed unto idols, and to commit fornication. 15 So hast thou also them that hold the doctrine of the Nicolaitanes, which thing I hate. 16 Repent; or else I will come unto thee quickly, and will fight against them with the sword of my mouth. 17 He that hath an ear, let him hear what the Spirit saith unto the churches; To him that overcometh will I give to eat of the hidden manna, and will give him a white stone, and in the stone a new name written, which no man knoweth saving he that receiveth it.''

Jesus addresses Pergamos as ''He which hath the sharp sword with two edges.'' According to the vision in the previous chapter this sword proceedeth out of His mouth. It, therefore, signifies His immediate, living, personal word. Paul calls it ''the sword of the Spirit'' (Eph. 6:17), and he introduces it as the only offensive weapon of ''the whole armour of God.'' This weapon is described in Heb. 4:12 as most effective: ''The word of God is quick, and powerful, and sharper than any two edged sword, piercing even to the dividing asunder of soul and spirit, and of the joints and marrow, and is a discerner of the thoughts and intents of the heart.'' A volume would fail to exhaust the Bible's testimony to the wonders of God's Word. It has the power to cut with absolute precision between truth and error, between right and wrong, between what saith the Lord and what saith the world, flesh or devil.

Jesus introduced Himself thus to Pergamos most aptly. There is noble commendation to be given Pergamos. Satan's presence and rule peculiarly confronted the witnesses of Jesus Christ at that center. The presence and faith of Jesus were there opposed even at the peril of death to any faithful witness. But, as at Smyrna, saints at Pergamos had not flinched even at sight of martyr blood, when even Antipas had sealed his testimony with his life right in their midst.

But, unlike Smyrna, Pergamos had much for Jesus to cut out and cut off unsparingly. Balaamites and Nicolaitanes—teaching that godliness is for gain and liberty for license, that Christian service is a cloak of mercenary greed and grace condones lasciviousness— were boldly active and unabashed in their midst.

Quick repentance is demanded under the threat of
swift and unsparing judgment according to incorruptible, uncompromising truth.   The sword of the Lord
would be drawn upon "them," the offenders; but it is
implied that it is a terrible thing for any church when
the Lord undertakes judgment against offences like
those in their midst.   An illustration of this terrible
liability is afforded by Paul's dealing with the Corinthian church in regard to a case of incest in their midst
(1 Cor. 5).   Venality in Christian ministry, and licentiousness right about the Christian altars, are not wanting among the foreign mission churches or among home
churches.   Is there no such thing as bribing ministerial
service?   Is there no such thing as making merchandise
of holy offices?   Is there no such thing as sensual laxity,
—disorder and effrontery right at home?   There is one
who says, "I know thy works," "I know what is going
on; I know about everything, whether it be secret or
public."   And church repentance and cleansing is His
demand.   Otherwise, His sword of truth and of the
Spirit brings fearful judgments.   Obedience to Him is
the path of victory.   And He has appropriate and allur-
ing promise for the overcomers.   Yet the interpretation
of this twofold promise is left considerably to conjecture.

(1) "To eat of the hidden manna."   In the first
place this stands in appropriate contrast to the strong
seduction working in the Pergamos church to "eat
things offered to idols."   To the victor over the subtle,
powerful appeal, not to go to such extreme of worldly
separation as to refuse such gratification, is promised
this sweet and high spiritual gratification.   But why is
the manna here called "the hidden manna"?   Certainly
it signifies a spiritual and not a physical food, even
though it were the manna of the wilderness.   But it
is to be remembered that a pot of the manna of the
wilderness was hidden away in the ark of the testimony,
the ark which enshrined the law of God within on the

tables of stone. This portion of manna, unlike the
common daily stock, was incorruptible, imperishable.
It is of the "incorruptible word of God" "which liveth
and abideth forever," that the soul is born again and
attains its spiritual growth (1 Pet. 1:23; 2:2). It is
on this hidden manna of God's incorruptible will that
Jesus subsisted. "I have meat to eat that ye know not
of. . . . My meat is to do the will of him that sent me,
and to finish his work" (John 4:32-34).

Under a little different construction "the hidden
manna" signified "the true bread from heaven" as
Jesus called Himself (John 6:32). The Psalmist had
sung, "He gave them bread from heaven" (Psa. 78:24).
The carnal Jews of Jesus' day interpreted this to mean
that Moses gave Israel bread from heaven in the daily
manna. But Jesus said, "Moses gave you not that bread
from heaven. For the bread of God is *he* which cometh
down from heaven, and giveth life unto the world. . . .
I am that bread of life" (John 6:32, 33, 48). Now, "ye
cannot be partakers of the Lord's table, and of the
table of devils. Do we provoke the Lord to jealousy?"
(1 Cor. 10:21, 22).

There is a striking explanation of the "hidden manna"
as a rare and choice morsel of the Son of God Himself.
The Jews use three special cakes in the Passover Supper
which successively represent Father, Son and Holy
Spirit. When, in the course of the Supper, the middle
cake, representing the Son, is reached, it is broken in
two and one-half is hidden under a pillow of the couch.
Later on this is brought to light by the head of the
family and a portion of it distributed to each person as
a surprise and as a most precious morsel in figure of
the broken Son of God.

(2) "And will give him a white stone, and in the
stone a new name written, which no man knoweth saving he that receiveth it." The white stone may probably
best be taken as the perfect, colorless diamond—which

probably constituted that mysterious Urim which was
concealed in the pocket behind the breastplate of the
high priest, and which seems to have contained the
incommunicable name of Jehovah, which it was lawful
for the high priest alone to look at and consult for
divine decisions of importance.

Now, the assaults of Satan upon Pergamos concerned
her secret spiritual sustenance and guidance from Jesus
Christ as her bread of life and her Urim of judgment.
And with many a church and many a believer ever since
—never more than today—like assaults are made, and
victory over Satan's snares must be maintained in
obedience to the Spirit, or their priceless benefits will
be lost.

CHAPTER III.

MESSAGES TO THYATIRA, SARDIS, PHILADEL-
PHIA AND LAODICEA

IV. *Message to the Church of Thyatira, 2: 18-29.*

"18 And unto the angel of the church in Thyatira write;
These things saith the Son of God, who hath his eyes like unto
a flame of fire, and his feet are like fine brass; 19 I know thy
works, and charity, and service, and faith, and thy patience, and
thy works; and the last to be more than the first. 20 Notwithstanding I have a few things against thee, because thou sufferest
that woman Jezebel, which calleth herself a prophetess, to teach
and to seduce my servants to commit fornication, and to eat
things sacrificed unto idols. 21 And I gave her space to repent
of her fornication; and she repented not. 22 Behold, I will
cast her into a bed, and them that commit adultery with her
into great tribulation, except they repent of their deeds. 23 And
I will kill her children with death; and all the churches shall
know that I am he which searcheth the reins and hearts: and
I will give unto every one of you according to your works.
24 But unto you I say, and unto the rest in Thyatira, as many
as have not this doctrine, and which have not known the depths
of Satan, as they speak; I will put upon you none other burden.
25 But that which ye have already hold fast till I come. 26 And
he that overcometh, and keepeth my words unto the end, to him
will I give power over the nations: 27 And he shall rule them
with a rod of iron; as the vessels of a potter shall they be
broken to shivers: even as I received of my Father. 28 And
I will give him the morning star. 29 He that· hath an ear, let
him hear what the Spirit saith unto the churches.''

JESUS CHRIST, the High Priest of the churches,
addresses Thyatira as Son of God, in the attributes,
taken from the previous vision, of all-searching
scrutiny and of absolute and perfect judgment. This
is appropriate as His exposure of and judgment upon
conditions in the church were intended to show: ''And
all the churches shall know that I am he which searcheth

81

the reins and hearts: and I will give unto every one of you according to your works'' (v. 23).

Much credit is allowed to Thyatira for courses of Christian love and ministry, for faith, patience and increasing activities that were commendable. But very serious protest is entered against the place of prominent, intimate, powerful and defiling influence occupied in the church by a Jezebel. At once we are reminded of the irresistible and damning power of the original Jezebel over King Ahab, over his court and over Israel of the north in general. This influence placed idolatry in power with all its corrupting accompaniments and consequences. In Elijah the Son of God stepped forth in searching exposure and swift, effective judgment. There was striking analogy between the Old Testament story and conditions in Thyatira. Wedded intimately, dominantly, to the very doctrinal administration of the Church, was teaching that sprang from ''the depths of Satan,'' and that was seducing to idolatry and fornication,—whether literal or spiritual, or both—many whom Jesus calls ''my servants.'' While not precipitate in judgment, He cannot brook refusal to repent.

Could Jesus look on this scene unmoved? No! Just as bodily pollution and commerce with devils brings swift and awful effects in disease and torment, so this unrepentant Jezebel must be visited with the due consequences of her teaching, and her followers must suffer great tribulation except they repent of her teachings and deeds. Those proving to be her very children must suffer the judgment of death itself with her, to the end that all churches and Christians may deeply learn that Jesus Christ knows exactly and judges perfectly the doings of those who profess His name.

Assurance is given to those of the church who were not spiritually involved in those evil teachings and practices, that no other judgment should be brought upon them than that of unhappy association and painful witnessing. They are charged to hold fast the true teaching which they already have till the coming again of Jesus.

There must be a vital relationship between the idolatrous and polluting movement so strongly prevailing in Thyatira, and the truth and practical expectation of the Lord's second coming. While, in the case of literal Thyatira, there was probably a more literal connivance with surrounding idolatry and licentiousness than seems to us conceivable in a Christian church, yet the supreme seriousness of the evil doctrine supporting those practices stood related to the truth and practical expectation of Christ's literal return. This is confirmed by the peculiar and striking character of the promise to the overcomer just following.

The "end" (v. 26) means the consummation of this militant age in our Lord's return. Christian victory in keeping ourselves from idols (literal or mystical,—see 1 Cor. 10 and 1 John 5:20, 21) vitally involves steadfastness in the doctrines and in the "works" of Christ in His bodily absence until He bodily reappears. Doctrinal and practical defection therefrom means idolatrous commerce with this world that tends downward to the very depths of Satan. This pernicious, anti-Christian teaching denies that the present world (age) is an evil world—evil only, irrecoverably evil—just ripening in idolatry and fornication for the judgment of the Lamb returning in wrath, after which judgment further probation will be extended only under the "rod of iron." The promise of participation with Jesus at His return in "power over the nations" springs pertinently out of the nature of the Jezebel doctrine and practice, and it is offered to those who overcome all that, by keeping true to the absentee Son of man until He returns in power and great glory to reign.

"And I will give him the morning star." In Rev. 22:16, Jesus says: "I am the root and the offspring

of David, and the bright and morning star.'' As root
of David He is the preëxistent Christ, who was the
spiritual root of life to David. As the latter's offspring
He is Jesus of Bethlehem. As the bright and morning
star He is the coming King of the millennial day. There
can, then, be no doubt that Jesus means that He will
give Himself in millennial coming to the overcomers of
Thyatira. See also 2 Peter 1:19, "whereunto ['the
more sure word of prophecy'] ye do well that ye take
heed, as unto a light that shineth in a dark place, until
the day dawn, and the day star arise in your hearts.''
Some of the Thyatirans were doing just this in that
day of Jezebel dominance—taking heed in their hearts
to the word of prophecy, which was ''more sure'' even
than the transfiguration scene. They were finding
prophecy to be a light shining in that ''dark place.''
And this is the surest light until the fore-gleams of
millennial consummation dawn and until the Sun of
righteousness Himself arise upon earthly vision as clear
as the morning sun. The hope of Christ's second coming is, then, the special weapon of victory to Thyatiran
believers, and His actual coming will have its peculiar
reward for them.

V. *Message to the Church of Sardis, 3:1-6.*

"1 And unto the angel of the church in Sardis write; These
things saith he that hath the seven Spirits of God, and the
seven stars; I know thy works, that thou hast a name that thou
livest, and art dead. 2 Be watchful, and strengthen the things
which remain, that are ready to die: for I have not found thy
works perfect before God. 3 Remember therefore how thou hast
received and heard, and hold fast, and repent. If therefore
thou shalt not watch, I will come on thee as a thief, and thou
shalt not know what hour I will come upon thee. 4 Thou hast
a few names even in Sardis which have not defiled their garments; and they shall walk with me in white: for they are
worthy. 5 He that overcometh, the same shall be clothed in
white raiment; and I will not blot out his name out of the book
of life, but I will confess his name before my Father, and before
his angels. 6 He that hath an ear, let him hear what the Spirit
saith unto the churches.''

Jesus as High Priest here speaks as the one who has the sevenfold fulness of God at His command, and who has in his hands for the ministry in Sardis the sufficiency of the mystical ideal of the ministry.

But He has no word of commendation. As a church they live only in name, in public credit. Only prompt watchfulness and pains to establish them can save what is not quite dead as yet. The Revised just here is striking, and pertinent to a merely nominal church: "For I have found no works of thine *fulfilled before my God*." That is it. The all-spiritual Christ finds no spiritual works in Sardis as a church, as a ministry, or as a body of members. All are dead, or almost expired spiritually; just a lifeless form without spiritual power.

Most appropriate is the injunction to recall how they had once received spiritually and heard, and to hold fast the remembrance and repent. Otherwise the threat is that of the Lord's coming unexpectedly upon them to snatch from them even their name to live.

How possible it is for a Christian, a local church, even for the Church general, to relapse into fulfilling accustomed and regular works only in unspiritual form and not before the Father of our Head, Jesus Christ. Nothing wrong in form of doctrine or service, and yet all of it nothing more than an empty chrysalis!

Yet even in Sardis was fulfiled in some the beautiful precept: "Let thy garments be always white, and let thy head lack no ointment" (Eccles. 9:8). Like Enoch and Noah, who in their times of spiritual darkness, coldness, hardness, "walked with God," and were "perfect"—in full accord with the Son of God—so in Sardis the Lord found some worthy to walk with Him in white, in "white-heated love" and in singular purity. What a triumph of grace, and what victory of faith!

The promise of Jesus Christ to those coming off conquerors under the conditions of Sardis is most appropriate: "the same shall be clothed in white raiment."

Taking this as a future reward, we may see here the promise of assured bodily glorification with Jesus, the radiant glory-vesture of the outer man harmonizing with the refined and lustrous holiness of the inner man. "And I will not blot out his name out of the book of life, but I will confess his name before my Father, and before his angels." Whatever danger there may be that spiritually dead Sardians will incur such calamity as is here implied, assurance is made doubly sure to the few undefiled ones, that their names shall be most heartily acknowledged on high in the great day of momentous, decisive reading of the honor roll.

VI.   *Message to the Church of Philadelphia, 3:7-13.*

"7 And to the angel of the church in Philadelphia write; These things saith he that is holy, he that is true, he that hath the key of David, he that openeth, and no man shutteth; and shutteth, and no man openeth; 8 I know thy works: behold, I have set before thee an open door, and no man can shut it: for thou hast a little strength, and hast kept my word, and hast not denied my name. 9 Behold, I will make them of the synagogue of Satan, which say they are Jews, and are not, but do lie; behold, I will make them to come and worship before thy feet, and to know that I have loved thee. 10 Because thou hast kept the word of my patience, I also will keep thee from the hour of temptation, which shall come upon all the world, to try them that dwell upon the earth. 11 Behold, I come quickly: hold that fast which thou hast, that no man take thy crown. 12 Him that overcometh will I make a pillar in the temple of my God, and he shall go no more out: and I will write upon him the name of my God, and the name of the city of my God, which is new Jerusalem, which cometh down out of heaven from my God: and I will write upon him my new name. 13 He that hath an ear, let him hear what the Spirit saith unto the churches."

The aspects in which Jesus, the High Priest, addresses this church are more elaborate than usual; and a striking peculiarity is that none of these features are taken directly from the portraiture of Him given in the vision of Chapter 1. Yet all the lineaments are true to the picture. These marks belong more to the hidden charac-

ter than to the active functions and manifestations
which could be featured in the vision. Of course these
characteristics are distinctively appropriate to the case
of Philadelphia. Not a lisp of censure or exception is
expressed toward her works in her High Priest's sight.
He that is holy and He that is true is satisfied in her;
for, though of little strength, she has been faithful to
His word and to His person. Hence He who holds the
key of royal authority in earth and in the skies had
opened to her the very door of service He chose, and
none could shut that door of service to her. Here lies
the secret of an open and an unclosable door of service
to the Philadelphian believer, minister, church; the
opening of the door and the keeping open lies with Him
who holds the key of David, while to Philadelphia it
belongs to be true to the word and the person of Him
who is holy, who is true.

The particular spiritual conflict involving Philadelphia is intimated by v. 9. In apostolical times the
false Jewish religionists were the worst foes to vital
Christianity. They were Satan's counterfeit and the
instruments of his persecuting malignity. Evidently
Philadelphia had pitted against her little earthly
strength a tremendous religious force from that quarter.
And yet Jesus promised that this proud, malicious
enemy would, willingly or unwillingly, be compelled
to acknowledge His favor toward Philadelphia. A fine
illustration of the case is furnished by the acknowledgment the full Sanhedrin was compelled to make when
they attempted to close the "open door" to Peter and
John in Jerusalem: "Now when they saw the boldness
of Peter and John, and perceived that they were un-
learned and ignorant men, they *marvelled;* and they took
knowledge of them, that they *had been with Jesus.* And
beholding the man which was healed standing with them,
they could say *nothing against it"* (Acts 4: 13, 14). "So
when they had further threatened them, they let them

go, finding nothing how they might punish them, because
of the people, for *all men glorified God for that which
was done"* (v. 21).

A very striking light is thrown upon the secret of
Christian victory over this form of conflict by the expression, "because thou hast kept the word of my patience."
Victory lies in patience, and this patience is Christ's
patience; He has left ample instruction to His followers
to maintain His patience under ecclesiastical assaults.
Herein lay the exemplariness of the prophets of old:
"Take, my brethren, the prophets, who have spoken in
the name of the Lord, for an example of suffering afflic-
tion, and of patience" (Jas. 5:10). Jesus said to the
Apostles: "Ye shall be betrayed . . . and ye shall be
hated . . . In your patience possess ye your souls" (Luke
21:16, 17, 19). "If, when ye do well, and suffer for it,
ye take it patiently, this is acceptable [thank, Marg.]
with God;" as if God said to one, "Thank you." It is
not the suffering for righteousness' sake that gives a
share with Jesus and His reward, but it is the patience
of Jesus in thus suffering. "In all things," says Paul,
(2 Cor. 6:4), "approving ourselves as the ministers of
God, in much *patience,* in afflictions, in necessities, in
distresses, in stripes," etc. That is, it is the Christlike
patience in enduring all such undue things, that is the
sign manual of being approvable "ministers of God."
This order of truth is so wide-spread in the Bible that it
is seen plainly to be fundamental.

Victory in this respect has the promise, touching the
present life, of escaping the hour of supreme testing
which is impending throughout the age. This is the way
of escaping by rapture the great tribulation whenever it
shall break upon the world. "Behold, I come quickly
[swiftly, expeditiously in due time]: hold that fast
which thou hast, that no man take thy crown." In every
generation, beginning with, but also succeeding, Philadelphia, keeping of trust patiently against pitiless oppo-

sition from religious quarters is the way of approving oneself as a translation saint, whether he lives till that time or not.

Overwhelmingly rich is the future reward promised to Philadelphian overcomers: "Him......will I make a pillar in the temple of my God, and he shall go no more out." The temple here is probably to be taken as the "habitation of God through the Spirit," "built upon the foundation of the apostles and prophets, Jesus Christ himself being the chief corner stone" (Eph. 2:22, 20); that is the finally glorified church. The Philadelphian overcomer, whose characteristic is that of *spiritual fixity* in the hottest conflict, will be made, as were "James, Cephas, and John, who seemed to be *pillars*" in the church at Jerusalem; that is, the Philadelphian overcomer will be in the Church of the New Jerusalem a kind of Jachin ("He shall stablish"), or Boaz ("In it is strength"), 1 Kings 7:21. Furthermore, "I will write upon him the name of my God, and the name of the city of my God, which is New Jerusalem, which cometh down out of heaven from my God: and I will write upon him my new name." Note the recurrence of the pronoun "my." The promise of this peculiar oneness with Jesus in future divine things is to those to whom He had said, "thou hast kept the word of *my patience*"—in the fierce conflict. "Write" means transcription by the Spirit, see 2 Cor. 3:3. The Philadelphian overcomers are to be "living epistles" of the Father of the Lord Jesus Christ, of the New Jerusalem as the final, supreme, residence of God through the Spirit.

VII. Message to the Church of Laodicea, 3:14-22.

"14 And unto the angel of the church of the Laodiceans write; These things saith the Amen, the faithful and true witness, the beginning of the creation of God; 15 I know thy works, that thou art neither cold nor hot: I would thou wert cold or hot. 16 So then because thou art lukewarm, and neither cold nor hot, I will spue thee out of my mouth. 17 Because thou sayest, I am rich, and increased with goods, and have need of nothing; and knowest not that thou art wretched, and miserable, and poor, and blind, and naked: 18 I counsel thee to buy of me gold tried in the fire, that thou mayest be rich; and white raiment, that thou mayest be clothed, and that the shame of thy nakedness do not appear; and anoint thine eyes with eyesalve, that thou mayest see. 19 As many as I love I rebuke and chasten: be zealous therefore, and repent. 20 Behold, I stand at the door, and knock: if any man hear my voice, and open the door, I will come in unto him, and will' sup with him, and he with me. 21 To him that overcometh will I grant to sit with me on my throne, even as I also overcame, and am set down with my Father in his throne. 22 He that hath an ear, let him hear what the Spirit saith unto the churches.''

The characteristics in which Jesus as High Priest addresses Laodicea, while not clearly borrowed from the vision of the Lord given in the first chapter, yet, like those in the address to Philadelphia, are in perfect harmony therewith. They are more closely identical with features appearing earlier in the chapter, and they are peculiarly solemn and significant.

He is the Amen, God's eternal, personal Verily, the So-Be-It. Whatever He is, so be it. Whatever He says as "the faithful and true winess," so let it be. "I am ......the truth." How blessed this is to those to whom, like as to the Philadelphians, He can say, "thou hast kept my word, and hast not denied my name!" "Ye in me and I in you." "He that is joined unto the Lord is one spirit." "Peter" (stone) is partaker of the Rock. But how awful is Jesus as "the Amen," "the faithful and true witness," to those in whom is yea and nay, who, like the Laodiceans, have no positive fixed character!

Jesus is also described as "the beginning of the creation of God." This does not mean that He was the first creation in the history of God's creative works. Rather does it mean that He Himself originated God's creation; or even better, as the Concordant Version so aptly puts it, "God's creative Original." Not only was all creation originally from His hand, but it also bore

His stamp, He was its archetype. How sadly was this stamp effaced by the fall! But the stamp is restored in sample in His created incarnate form. As such He is "the firstborn of every creature." "We shall be like him."

Laodicea is known to her High Priest practically for luke-warmness. Not dead cold like Sardis. She has spiritual warmth, but just enough to nauseate her glorified Head. He cannot keep her on His stomach. Dead cold would be preferable, more tolerable to Him. He cannot digest or assimilate Laodicea. The reason is because His love is so hot, so fervid, that half-hearted response is disgusting to Him. If Jesus is to be loved at all He must be loved altogether, with love "white heated." To set a low valuation upon Him practically, to offer Him an indifferent, neutral devotion, is insulting. Be out and out, one thing or the other, either frigid or fervid!

Laodicea is known to Jesus for self-complacency and worldly satisfaction. She is above need, she thinks, for anything further from Him. Her earthly and fleshly conditions are so much to her mind and are so ample, that her only regret is that her present lot must still count on death and cannot, as one regretfully admitted, "go on forever." There is a religious contentment that is blissfully, but disgustingly, ignorant of being "wretched and miserable, and poor, and blind, and naked." There are natural, social, ecclesiastical, even religious, satisfactions and plethora, which still leave true spiritual satisfaction stifled, asphyxiated.

What are these essential, incomparable, spiritual values of which the fervid Christian never has enough and of which Jesus has limitless measures to bestow. "I counsel thee to buy of me gold tried in the fire, that thou mayest be rich." This is faith, faith tested, refined, all-victorious, bought willingly at the cost of tribulation, loss, suffering, ("as though some strange thing hap-

pened,'') even at the cost of "Christ's sufferings." And,
"I counsel thee to buy of me," "white raiment, that
thou mayest be clothed, and that the shame of thy nakedness do not appear." This is holy likeness to the High
Priest Himself, in His garment of righteousness,—His
holy mind, His holy walk, His holy obedience to the
Father, His holy example, in this life, before the brethren, before the world. This, too, is worth the price that
He Himself paid in doing the will of His Father rather
than His own or that of any other. And, "I counsel thee
to" "anoint thine eyes with eyesalve, that thou mayest
see." This is spiritual vision, discernment, wisdom,
knowledge and discrimination. The anointed eye is the
"single" eye; and "if thine eye be single, thy whole
body shall be full of light."

A victoriously believing, an unsulliedly holy, a fully
enlightened and radiant life! Is this necessarily a rar-
ity? Nay, rather, is it not what Jesus as High Priest
is caring for, providing for, looking for in all His professed followers? Must not the Christian, must not the
church, that sates itself on taudry substitutes for these
"riches of grace in Christ Jesus,"—that borrows from
the world the artificial rouge painting a pallid, consump-
tive cheek, in place of that inimitable bloom of spiritual
health which Jesus only can produce,—must not such
Christianity disgust and nauseate Christ Himself?

Yet He loves, at least "as many as" He can; and
because He loves, He rebukes and chastens, He arouses
and calls to repentance. Nay, He pleads and allures.
What inimitable persuasiveness He uses! "Behold, I
stand at the door." What grace, what patience, what
lingering longing! But what a shame! He has been and
is being left by Laodicea *outside the door*. No doubt
the name of Christ is artistically inscribed on Laodicea's
doorplate; no doubt this piece of art is kept highly bur-
nished. But He Himself is kept outside the door. His
in-dwelling is displaced by selfish, worldly, temporal,

material plethora. The notice is hung outside—where He stands—"Full to capacity, from Chancel to the Doors."

Yet, even in Laodicea, as in other faithless churches, individual relationship with Jesus is a matter of free choice: "If any man." There is not only "the doors of the church;" there is the heart-door of "any man." Christ will linger, and knock, and plead for communion with a single individual in a great church which as such has not room or accommodation for Him. "I will come in to him." Within the heart chamber is Christ's only satisfying place of relationship with any soul or company of souls. "And I will sup with him." I will first gratefully receive what he has to give me. "Give me to drink," said He to the woman by the well. "And he with me." "I will spread him a table in return." The soul that gives its all to Jesus receives His all in return. It is a case of "all things in common."

It is no trifling conflict to overcome under Laodicean conditions. And it is no mean reward that is held out to the overcomer. Present communion with Jesus would seem inducement enough. But this victor will be signally honored hereafter. Jesus promises a share with Him in throne-honors and powers. It was a Laodicean church that Jesus found in His day of earthly trial. The world, the flesh and the devil offered Him everything but His Father's will, and they heaped upon Him all opprobrium for delighting only in God's will and approval. But He could always say, "I am in the Father, and the Father in me;" "the Father......dwelleth in me;" "I know that thou hearest me always." But He was also to go unto His Father; there was a "joy that was set before him." The promise to the Laodicean overcomer is modeled after His own reward: "even as I also overcame, and am set down with my Father in his throne." How far the incentive offered to the Christian reaches beyond mere eventual certain salvation, beyond even present "fulness of the blessing of the gospel of Christ!" In-

deed, how far beyond all this is the incentive offered the
Christian for the present life! The incentive offered at
the very threshhold of the true Christian life is that of
sharing with Jesus now in His Gospel ministries and sufferings, "to fill up that which is behind." "As my
Father hath sent me, even so send I you." "And, lo,
I am with you always." "The Lord working with them."
But, how much higher calling it is to share throne-powers
and activities with Him when He returns to rule over
this world which He has redeemed! How vague and hazy
this prospect is without the light of foregoing Scripture
upon the truth of Christ's return! But how powerful
the promise becomes when read in the light of Biblical
prophecy, even before the climax thereto now to be
opened in the Book of Revelation is taken in! And with
what eagerness one is now prepared to have this promise
more explicitly and magnificently unfolded!

Before leaving the messages to the seven churches behind, a few observations may be appropriate.

It corrects some fancies concerning the early Church
to find from these messages—as well as from the apostolical epistles—how imperfect and even reprehensible
churches and Christians were in those early days of privilege. How few were permanently faithful and commendable in all respects! How many were inconstant
and inconsistent! How many were even bordering on
spiritual extinction, if not already dead! What a variety
of types, whether of virtue or of blemish! What a variety of testing conditions! How noteworthy it is that
testing conditions had correspondence to peculiar existing blessings of grace and the future rewards in glory!
It is the more impressive that this great variety and
contrariety should be found in a limited circuit of about
two hundred and fifty miles, at one period of time, and
under the oversight probably of one and the same Apostle, and that such an one as John.

We are guarded not only from imputing higher general

standards to the early Church than is warranted, but also from looking at current Christianity at any epoch in too general and sweeping a light. Jesus' discernment is keen, individual, discriminating. Most likely a human historian would have written a very different story of the seven churches of Asia from that reflected in these pointed, discriminating messages.   Yet these seven churches illustrate types of churches and of Christians to be found upon close scrutiny within small radius almost any time and any where. They furnish a very essential and really the initial part of this book which it is so important to be reading, hearing and keeping. It is really more important for any church and any Christian at any day and anywhere to search in the Spirit, by means of these letters, just how they stand with the Lord, than to be well versed in acquaintance with and understanding of the panorama of final events immediately to be unfolded. To have a full, up-to-date spiritual standing with Christ Jesus is more important than to have a full and accurate chart of coming dates and events.

CHAPTER IV

EPITOME OF THE BOOK OF REVELATION

BEFORE going further we will enlarge somewhat upon the "Preliminary Survey."

It will serve to simplify and to facilitate the detailed study of the Book of Revelation, to sketch it out first in an epitome, in which the objective and the construction of the book will be made obvious. Some things will be stated in positive form, the proofs for which must wait for the detailed exposition later. The reader is advised and requested to verify this epitome carefully by reference to the book itself.

THE PERSPECTIVE

In 1:1 the special revelation of this book is described as "things which must shortly come to pass." This means, events to transpire swiftly, or in a very brief period when the time for them arrives. In 1:3 it is said that "the time is at hand." This means a time impending, next to follow the existing course of things. In 1:7 the immediate consummation of these "things," or events, is stated to be the promised visible return of Jesus Christ—especially to the Jews whose forbears crucified Him—and to the dismay of all Gentile kindreds. In 1:19, Jesus directs John to write in a book three things. These are "the things which thou hast seen," evidently referring to the vision of the golden candlesticks; "and the things which are," evidently meaning the "works," or things doing among the seven churches as dealt with by Jesus in Chapters 2 and 3; "and the things which shall be hereafter," that is, after the existing order of things, or in that "time......at hand," the time of the Lord's reappearing. That "time" is introduced with Chapter IV, and it culminates in the descent of Jesus Christ to the earth for His millennial reign as described in 19:11-20:6. And as the vision of the candlesticks and the messages to the seven churches constitute a processional to this great central panorama of the Lord's return to reign, so likewise a recessional to the same follows in the final postmillennial judgment and expulsion of all enemies from the earth (20:7-15) preparatory to the wondrous final panorama of the new heaven (earthly) and the new earth over which our Lord shall forever reign with His saints (Chapters 21, 22).

CONSTRUCTION

The Book of Revelation obviously consists of more than "the revelation" proper. The latter consists of 4:1-19:10, the interior construction of which will be left for later attention. Preceding this large division two minor divisions follow the Introduction,—which consists of the Prologue (1:1-3), the Apostolic Salutation (vs. 4-6), and the Annunciation of the central event of the Lord's coming (v. 7). These two divisions, as already intimated, consist of 1:8-21, the Vision of the Son of man in the midst of the golden candlesticks, and of Chapters 2 and 3—the Messages to the seven Asian Churches as representative of the entire Church of the whole Christian dispensation. Then following the great central division is a brief millennial section (19:11-20:15). The final main division, consisting of 21:1-22:5, portrays the arrangements of the restored and everlasting heaven (earthly) and earth, while 22:6-21 constitutes a most impressive Epilogue. This construction of the Book of Revelation may be put more graphically before the eyes in the form of an outline as follows:

OUTLINE OF THE BOOK OF REVELATION

Introduction: Prologue, 1:1-3; Salutation and Invocation, vs. 4-6; Objective, v. 7.

I. Vision of Christ among the Candlesticks, 1:8-20, "The things......seen."

II. Messages to the Seven Asian Churches, Chapters 2 and 3, "The things which are."

III. Panorama of Swift Judgments, 4:1-19:10, "The things which shall be hereafter."

IV. The Millennial Kingdom, 19:11-20:15.

V. New and Everlasting Heaven and Earth, 21:1-22:5. Epilogue, 22:6-21.

JESUS CHRIST AND HIS CHURCH IN REVELATION

This heading indicates a subject which, while not the specified subject, is yet dominant throughout the book. While the specific subject of the Lord's return to earth for millennial rule belongs directly to only the great interior of the book (4:1-20:6), this dominant, ever-present theme compasses the entire book and creates a very definite sectioning of the same, a sectioning entirely agreeing with the outline just given. This new heading indicates a very intimate relation between Jesus Christ and His Church as running through the book. This is illustrated in the very first verse of the book, where it is stated that the revelation was given by God to His Son to show to "His servants." This proves that the whole thing is projected from the standpoint of joint-interest and of reciprocal relationship between Jesus Christ and His servants of the Church. It is further strikingly illustrated by v. 5, where ascription of glory and dominion is offered to Jesus Christ, not only for His love and for the absolution of sins through His blood, but also in that "He hath made us Kings and priests [in the prospect of this book] unto God and His Father." It is thus illustrated that at every point in the book the view presented of Jesus Himself is from the standpoint of the presence and interest of His Church. It follows, as we shall see, that nowhere is such a comprehensive revelation of the Church of Jesus Christ to be found as in the Book of Revelation. In almost a paramount sense the book may be taken as Christ's own final full revelation of His precious and glorious Church.

I.   Christ's Revelation concerning His Church Mystical.

In 1: 8-21 it is the seven golden candlesticks that stand at the front with the Son of man in the midst. The symbol represents the seven Asian churches—and they as representative of the Church universal—in ideal, mystical state in Christ Jesus Himself, and in His care and keeping. Mystically the seven Asian Churches were seven perfect golden candelabra, or light-bearers.

II.   Christ's Revelation concerning His Church Militant.

In Chapters 2, 3, Christ throws upon the screen photographs of His churches as He sees them in actual earthly doings under conditions of testing and conflict, such that the supreme matter of interest is what crown He has to promise His servants who come off conquerors. This represents the churches and believers in the "present evil world," or age, of witness-bearing and of testing from the world, the flesh and the devil.

III.   Christ's Revelation concerning His Church Avenged.

In the great section of the book (4: 1-19: 10) a vast panorama is unfolded of events swiftly transpiring under an entirely new and unique order,—that of Christ's presence in the earthly skies conducting lines of action culminating in three very definite results: first, the safe gathering to Himself in the skies of all His prepared wife, the Church complete; secondly, the consummate avenging of His saints against their implacable persecutor of all the ages; and, thirdly, the millennial enthronement of the saints with Jesus Christ. The following

passages, coming at the concluding and culminating
stages of these unique events, make these results clear to
us as the objects of the drama opening with Chapter 4.
"And upon her forehead was a name written, Mystery,
BABYLON THE GREAT, THE MOTHER OF HAR-
LOTS AND ABOMINATIONS OF THE EARTH. And
I saw the woman *drunken with the blood of the saints,*
and with the *blood of the martyrs of Jesus"* (17:5, 6).
"Rejoice over her, thou heaven, and ye holy apostles and
prophets; for God hath *avenged you on her,*......And
in her was found the *blood of prophets,* and *of saints,*
and of *all that were slain upon the earth"* (18:20, 24).
"And after these things I heard a great voice of much
people in heaven [the earthly skies], saying, Alleluia;
Salvation, and glory, and honor, and power, unto the
Lord our God: for true and righteous are His judgments: for he hath judged the great whore, which did
corrupt the earth with her fornication, and hath *avenged
the blood of his servants at her hand.*......Let us be glad
and rejoice, and give honor to him: for the *marriage
of the Lamb is come,* and his wife hath made herself
ready" (19:1, 2, 7).

IV. *Christ's Revelation concerning His Church Millennial.*

Further, in 19:11-20:6, while the Lord Jesus is presented so strikingly in His descent from the skies to crush
all opposition to His long promised visible reign over
the earth for the thousand years, yet the revelation
focuses upon the part in this reign to be given to His
victorious servants. This appears from the concluding
part of the passage (20:4, 5): "And I saw thrones,
and they sat upon them, and judgment [rule] was given
unto them: and I saw the souls of them that were beheaded for the witness of Jesus, and for the word of God,
and which had not worshipped the beast, neither his
image, neither had received his mark upon their fore-

heads, or in their hands; and they *lived and reigned with Christ* a thousand years. But the rest of the dead lived not again until the thousand years were finished. This is the first resurrection''; namely, of them ''that are Christ's at his coming'' (1 Cor. 15:23).

''Blessed and holy is he that hath part in the first resurrection: on such the second death hath no power, but they shall be priests of God and of Christ, and shall *reign with him a thousand years.*''

V. *Christ's Revelation of His Church Glorified.*

After revealing the postmillennial period of satanic insurrection on earth, and of final extinction of all further satanic representation in the earth, and of the final judgment of awards before the great white throne, the never-ending age of renewed heaven (earthly skies) and earth is presented in 21:1-22:5. But most prominent here is ''the holy city, New Jerusalem, coming down from God out of heaven'' as ''the tabernacle of God.....with men''; that is, a celestial city, descending into intimate association with earthly peoples, as the very tabernacle of God with them. This same marvelous phenomenon is called in vs. 10, 11, ''that great city, the holy Jerusalem, descending out of heaven from God, having the glory of God.'' Then 21:11-22:5 greatly enlarges upon this city in both symbolical and plain language. But this city, this new and holy Jerusalem, is in 21:9 plainly declared to be ''the bride, the Lamb's wife''; that is, the Church, thus portrayed in her finally organized, glorified super-earthly condition, position and relation.

The foregoing line of progress through the Book of Revelation is so obvious, natural and simple; this constructive theme is so superior to that of a mere sequence of events; and this revelation of the marvelous fellowships between Christ and His Church is so lofty, so

worthy of constituting the climax of all Biblical prophecy, that the author feels impelled to make it the
frame-work of his exposition of this holy book. Therefore, he has thus far followed this construction and will
continue the same.

The Church Avenged

Introduction

A FEW words of general introduction to this main body of Revelation will be helpful.

In the two preceding chapters, by means of His messages to the seven Asiatic churches, Christ has shown forth the situation of conflict in which His servants stand in the present time. Promise is not extended of present forcible intervention against their foes, but only of reward, principally future, for maintaining victory in the conflict. The victory is of a purely spiritual character achieved through lending obedient ear to "what the Spirit saith unto the churches." Christ the Captain's present instructions are to this effect: "Dearly beloved, avenge not yourselves, but rather give place unto wrath: for it is written, Vengeance is mine; I will repay, saith the Lord" (Rom. 12:19); "Be patient therefore, brethren, unto the coming of the Lord" (James 5:7). It is victory by the Cross, not by the sword of judgment.

> "We must fight our battles, like the Crucified:
>   Overcome by suffering, conquer thro' defeat;
>   Tried and tested daily in the furnace heat;
>   ....Gaining as we give;
>   Crucified with Jesus, yet, in Him, we live.

> "Cross of Christ! lead onward, thro' the Holy War;
>   In this sign we conquer, now and evermore."

But the promise is, "I will repay," and the time of vengeance is at His coming. As has already been noted, it is with the swiftly-moving, astounding drama of these events that the revelation proper has to do. It is in 4:1-20:6 that "the things which must quickly come to pass" are unfolded; they were "signified" through John to Christ's servants, because these things concerned them so intimately, being the things "at hand,"—next impending—which give support and inspiration to Christian faith and courage in the midst of present conflict with the world, the flesh and the devil. As has been stated, this is "the time" of the Church's bodily translation to her Lord in the skies, the time of consummate vengeance upon her foes and the time of her entrance with Jesus into the millennial reign.

CHAPTER I

CELESTIAL PREPARATIONS, CHAPTERS 4, 5.

The Background, Chapter 4.

"After this I looked, and, behold, a door was opened in heaven: and the first voice which I heard was as it were of a trumpet talking with me; which said, Come up hither, and I will show thee things which must be hereafter," 4: 1.

THE expression, "after this I looked," implies that, whereas John's vision and attention had been protractedly held, while "in the Spirit," to the revelation of the golden candlesticks, with the glorified Jesus amidst them in high priestly attire and service, holding also the seven stars in His right hand, and to the instruction of Christ regarding the book to be written, and, more extendedly still, to the messages to be conveyed to the seven Asian Churches; yet, now, that line of vision, pertaining to the present order of a mystical and a spiritually militant Church, having been completed, a new line of vision is opened up.

And this new line of disclosure was to be given John from a new position of outlook. John saw a door "opened in heaven" and the trumpet-like voice called to him, "Come up hither." It is most important to recognize distinctly here and elsewhere in Revelation that "heaven" means the earthly heaven, our skies. The Bible will be a book of confusion to us if we fail to recognize that Gen. 1: 1 introduces a vast revelation relating to a particular part of the to us unknown, trackless and boundless material universe; namely, the dual sphere of our earth and skies. Comparatively seldom does the word "heaven" or "heavens" in the Bible mean anything but our familiar, visible, earthly skies, including atmospheric, solar and sidereal spheres. And the Book of Revelation begins at once to be a revelation to us when we understand that "heaven," from 4:1 to 21:1, without perhaps an exception, means the earth's heaven, or skies, in distinction from other creature heavens unfamiliar to us, and from "heaven itself" where our Saviour now is before the face of the Father. The new standpoint of vision for John was, then, up in the skies.

And John is told what was to be the subject of revelation now to be made to him. It was to be those aforesaid "things which must be hereafter"; that is, immediately subsequent to the order of things now, and ever "since the fathers fell asleep," prevailing. This order has been reflected in Chapters 2, 3, the order of the believer's fight of faith under a Captain invisible, far away at the right hand of the Father, and with a foe which as a "mystery of iniquity worketh hitherto." At this point, the swiftly occurring events referred to in 1:1 as belonging to "the time......at hand" (1:3), or "what is about to occur after this" (1:19), are taken up. In point of time, then, this juncture of the vision has not even yet been reached, and we are to understand the revelation from here on as disclosing events which are abruptly to intercept and radically to alter the present course of earthly affairs, whether for the world, the devil or the Church.

"And immediately I was in the Spirit" (v. 2a). This means not only a transport from ordinary bodily consciousness and possibly location, but also an extraordinary transport in the Holy Spirit as in 1:10. It was no mere natural catalepsy, with its abnormal visions, real or unreal, but it was a spiritual transport serving a prophetic purpose,—that of beholding by God's Spirit scenes and occurrences long in advance, the record of which serves for the Lord's servants the full purpose of a "prophecy" (1:3).

THE COURT SETTING

"And behold, a throne was set in heaven, and one sat on the throne" (v. 2b). "Behold, a throne set in heaven, and one sitting on the throne" (1911). "And, lo! a throne, located in heaven, and on the throne One sitting" (C. V.).

Remembering that "heaven" here means our skies, and that the throne implies direct practical sovereignty, and that that sovereignty of our skies is now (in vision) in the hands of the "One sitting," we see that in vision some wonderful exchange of sovereignty in our skies has taken place ,which is by the record of the vision predicted to us literally to take place "quickly," "hereafter," in "the time......at hand," even now directly impending. All are familiar with Scriptures which teach us who now occupies in our skies the throne of sovereignty over the earth. Even Jesus did not dispute Satan's claim to have "all the kingdoms of the world, and the glory of them" to give to any one he pleased on condition of falling before him in worship. Jesus called the devil both the prince and the god of this world. And Jesus, in vision, "beheld Satan as lightning fall from heaven"—the skies—(Luke 10:18). And Paul describes the devil as "the prince of the power of the air"; that is, the ruler whose seat of power is still, as it has been since before the temptation in the garden of Eden, in the heaven which "in the beginning God created" as celestial companion and over-sphere to the earth. John was given to see a displacing "throne......set in heaven." "And One sat on the throne." How august! A new throne is seen placed in our skies and One is seen taking His seat upon the throne! We are here reading a stupendous prophecy of a stupendous downfall of one hoary dynasty before the rise of a conquering, displacing dominion. (Psa. 94:20).

"And he that sat was to look upon like a jasper and a sardine stone: and there was a rainbow round about the throne, in sight like unto an emerald" (v. 3). The jasper and the sardine stone belong to the same group of exquisite reddish stones or gems with the ruby and the sapphire. These ruddy hues are used as similes of tints of health and beauty in body. ''Her Nazarites were purer than snow, they were whiter than milk, they were more ruddy in body than rubies, their polishing was of sapphire'' (Lam. 4:7). The combination of fleckless whiteness of skin with the ruddy glow of healthy blood means perfect health and beauty. Thus the lad David ''was ruddy, and withal of a beautiful countenance, and goodly to look to'' (1 Sam. 16:12). And again, of one of higher estate, it is written: ''My beloved is white and ruddy, the chiefest among ten thousand'' (S. S. 5:10). What a contrast, then, the personal appearance of the ''One sitting'' on the new throne in the sky will present to that of the present ruler of sky and earth, the prince of darkness, whose very countenance must betray him as the ''murderer from the beginning,'' ''the liar, and the father of it'' (John 8:44)! And what contrast to the throne of iniquity and destruction is afforded by the encircling emerald of everlasting grace and promise!

''And round about the throne were four and twenty seats [thrones]: and upon the seats [thrones] I saw four and twenty elders sitting, clothed in white raiment; and they had on their heads crowns of gold'' (v. 4).

We are still to bear in mind that we are being given description of the ''celestial preparations'' to be made in our skies in place of present long-established satanic order obtaining there. Now the order there under Satan is that of kindred ''principalities,......powers,...... rulers of the darkness of this world,...... spiritual wickedness [wicked spirits] in high [celestial] places'' (Eph. 6:12). These elders may be taken to be of glorified human order, the double-twelve representing the worthy and holy human headship of saints of both the old and the new dispensations. Further progress in this study will throw further light upon this understanding of the elders. (Psa. 96:6.)

"And out of the throne proceeded lightnings and thunderings, and voices: And there were seven lamps of fire burning before the throne, which are the seven Spirits of God. And before the throne there was a sea of glass like unto crystal" (vs. 5, 6a), or "as a glassy sea, like crystal" (C. V.).

Here are further similitudes intimating notable features and resources of divine sovereignty. The lightnings and thunderings and voices remind us that God's mighty presence is essentially unapproachable. Solomon said, "The Lord said that he would dwell in thick darkness"; "He made darkness his secret place" (the Holy of Holies). The hidden resources of "righteousness and judgment" gave even a Moses the warning, "Draw not nigh hither,......And Moses hid his face; for he was afraid to look upon God" (Ex. 3:5, 6). Also, "a fire goeth before him, and burneth up his enemies round about" (Psa. 97:3). What duty these "seven lamps of fire before the throne, which are the seven [spirits, not] Spirits of God" had already (in vision) performed in routing from the skies the Lord's enemies, we are not here informed, but are left awhile to imagine. And they stand ready to execute any further commission of sovereign authority and power. Finally, the pavement of this royal court of glory and judgment is a fitting symbol of the absolute clarity and righteousness of the Almighty as King and Judge.

"And in the midst of [i. e., centering in] the throne, and round about the throne, were four beasts [living ones] full of eyes before and hehind. And the first beast was like a lion, and the second beast like a calf, and the third beast had a face as a man, and the fourth beast was like a flying eagle. And the four beasts had each of them six wings about him; and they were full of eyes within: and they rest not day and night, saying, Holy, holy, holy, Lord God Almighty, which was, and is, and is to come" (vs. 6b-8).

These symbolic forms are already familiar to the Bible student; but they are here placed in somewhat new position. They represent those seraphic beings of the immediate heavenly and divine court, which stand in worship before their almighty Sovereign and in readiness for detective and executive service at His will. Their arrangement of worship is here emphasized, while their detective and executive engagements are especially revealed and emphasized in Ezekiel 1, and in other places in the Old Testament. Their relationship to earthly affairs seems evident, in distinction from the more specific relationship to celestial affairs on the part of the seven flaming spirits standing as counsellors and executives before the throne of God Almighty. These four beings represent in their coöperation the combination of unconquerable courage, indomitable patience, human understanding and appreciation, and lofty vision. Especially pronounced is their inescapable detective scrutiny. Their special correlation with human saints is confirmed by the fact that their figures were emblazoned upon the four standards of the four quarters of the camp of Israel.

"And when those beasts give glory and honor and thanks to him that sat on the throne, who liveth for ever and ever, the four and twenty elders fall down before him that sat on the throne, and worship him that liveth for ever and ever, and cast their crowns ("their victor's wreaths"—C. V.) before the throne, saying: "Thou art worthy, O Lord, to receive glory and honor and power; for thou hast created all things, and for thy pleasure they are [exist] and were created" (vs. 9-11).

The special, close relationship of the four "beasts" to earthly and human persons is here observable, where the former serve as leaders to the latter in worship of the Almighty, the Ever-living, the Creator of all, the One for whose pleasure all creation exists and had its origin. This concert of worship and praise on the part of beasts and elders is most impressive as a condition which waits to prevail in our skies; and the theme of praise is most pertinent in relation to the prospective subjugation of all remaining rebellion existing within the created universe of God.

Before closing this chapter, two things need to be remarked for the sake of clear understanding.

In the first place, the vision of the enthroning of the Almighty ''in heaven'' implies a heaven where the Almighty had not been holding dominion. We know of no heaven where that has been or is the case but our own earthly heaven, or skies. The Bible abundantly teaches the fact that the devil, in rebellion against God, has long had throne and seat of dominion in the skies over this earth. Therefore, ''heaven'' in this chapter and in this book is to be identified with certainty with our skies.

In the second place, the Bible is equally emphatic in stating that this rebellious dominion is to be overthrown to give place to the kingdom of God. It is not this heaven, but it is this event, which is referred to in our familiar petition, ''Thy kingdom come, Thy will be done, in earth as it is in heaven.'' It is with the fulfillment of this prayer that the apocalypse of this book is mainly taken up. Chapter 4 introduces in vision the setting up of the court of God as Sovereign in our skies. It is depicted in such a personal, apparently literalistic way as to excite the question whether we are to understand that God removes His court and capital seat from its present center to that of our skies. This question arises all the more insistently under the evidence, already quite clear, but made perfectly clear with the opening of the next chapter, that it is the Almighty Father, and not the Son, who is represented as the ''One sitting.'' In answer to the question, it is to be said unhesitatingly that no thought can be entertained of such a change of capital center of universal divine dominion. What is intended to be shown in the vision is that the antecedent of the fulfillment of ''things which must shortly come to pass'' is God Almighty's taking complete, effective ruling presence, power and manifestation in our skies just the same, we may safely assume, as prevails in all other parts of His universal realm.

THE FOREGROUND, CHAPTER 5.

The celestial throne, with its occupant, splendors and worshipping associates, now gives place as background to new disclosures still more directly and prominently related to "the things which must shortly come to pass."

"And I saw in the right hand of him that sat on the throne a book written within and on the backside, sealed with seven seals" (v. 1).

This "book" is to be understood as a scroll in sight, which, after ancient manner, would be written upon in columns beginning at the extreme right end, would be rolled up from right to left as the writing advanced, but which, when fully written, would be rolled back from left to right, so that it would be opened from right to left when read. It was seen written upon both the inside and the backside, after the manner of the "roll of a book" which the Lord in vision spread before Ezekiel (2:9, 10). In the case before us the book was seen sealed with seven seals.

A seal attached to a scroll had one or more uses. It might serve to fasten it up close, so that the seal would need to be broken or "loosed" before its contents could be read. Again, the seal commonly authenticated or validated the document as genuine and original. Furthermore, the seal might be an identification of the only rightful proprietor of or authority over the document. In the last case only the person identified by the seal had power to break it, or someone authorized by him.

"And I saw a strong angel proclaiming with a loud voice, Who is worthy to open the book, and to loose the seals thereof" (v. 2).

The language of this verse proves that this book was closed up by the seals, so that one could not read from it without loosing the seals. This feature is greatly emphasized in the next three verses, in each of which occurs the expression "to open the book," while the expression "to loose the seals thereof" also occurs again.

A very important question arising naturally right here is, How were these seven seals of the scroll arranged? By glancing forward over the succeeding chapters it is discovered that the term "opened" is used in connection with the seals, and that the seals are opened one by one with intervening chapters of stupendous—increasingly stupendous—occurrences. This shows that the book, or scroll, was unfolded by portions,—seven in all—each portion being separately sealed with one of the seven seals. This attaches the full significance of the seal to each of the seven parts of the contents of the book, and this also proves that the subject and the nature of the entire contents are of one kind, only unfolding by progressive stages from start to finish.

The solemn inquiry of the mighty angel, "Who is worthy," or as the C. V. more precisely and impressively reads, *"Is any one worthy to open the scroll, and to loose the seals?"* implies that in this case the book is fast closed to the disclosure and execution of its contents against all but one authorized and rightful candidate.

"And no man in heaven, nor in earth, neither under the earth was able to open the book, neither to look thereon" (v. 3).

This verse should read "no one" (R. V.) rather than "no man." "Heaven," of course, means the skies. Exhaustive search through angelic ranks in the skies, through human classes wherever found, living or departed, failed to discover a being with qualifications of authority or ability to undertake the opening of the book, or even to look considerately at it.

"And I wept much, because no man was found worthy [no worthy one was found, C. V.] to open and to read the book, neither to look thereupon" (v. 4).

This keen and inconsolable disappointment of John speaks eloquently for the extreme importance of the contents of this book and of having its contents revealed and executed.

"And one of the elders saith unto me, Weep not: behold the Lion of the tribe of Judah, the Root of David, hath prevailed to open the book, and to loose the seven seals thereof" (v. 5).

That it should be one of the elders thus to comfort John signifies full human sympathy and fellow-interest in the matter.

Who is this "Lion of the tribe of Judah," this "Root of David?" Of course it is Jesus Christ. But in what character do these figures represent Him, and why are these descriptions employed?

In Jacob's dying prophecy over his twelve sons (Gen. 49), Judah is given the preëminent tribal position, although Judah was not the first-born. "Judah, thou art he whom thy brethren shall praise: thy hand shall be in the neck of thine enemies; thy father's children shall bow down before thee" (v. 8). This accords the royal headship of the house of all Israel to the tribe of Judah. While it was not God's will that Israel should become a kingdom, in the sense of having an ordinary visible king like other nations, yet it was out of the tribe of Judah that the incarnate divine King of Israel was intended to come. Thus in Him Judah was to have this prophecy fulfilled unto her. But the next verse reads: "Judah is a lion's whelp: from the prey, my son, thou art gone up: he stooped down, he crouched as a lion, and as an old lion; who shall rouse him up?"

Judah had, then, her royalty first by descent,—she was a lion by virtue of being a lion's whelp. Her royalty is derived, not original. As the ruling tribe of the Hebrew monarchy, Judah derived her character and her prerogative from her own invisible royal Head, the Son of God. He was "the Lion of the tribe of Judah," the parent-lion, so to speak. It was this headship in Him which ever made Judah commanding over the other tribes and invincible over all her enemies,—that is, so long, and only so long, as she was herself obedient to Him and strong in Him alone. On such condition it was true, as the next verse reads: "The sceptre shall not depart from Judah, nor a lawgiver from between his feet, until Shiloh come; and unto him shall the gathering of the people be." Shiloh describes the Messiah with respect to true and perfect rest for His people, and the last sentence predicts the final regathering of Israel at His coming to earth to reign as King of the Jews. It is clear, then, that in this prophecy of Jacob concerning Judah we have explained, not only why the one before us in Revelation is called the Lion of the tribe of Judah, but also why he should here be introduced in that light. He was in preëxistent deity the dynastic progenitor of the house of Judah; and His being introduced just here as such implies that this "book" must relate to the fulfillment of Jacob's prophecy concerning Judah, and that it is in the capacity of the divine founder of the throne of Judah that He was found worthy and able to take the book, to loose the seven seals thereof, and to read its contents into execution.

What has just been remarked about Judah renders the description of Jesus Christ here also as "the Root of David" very readily intelligible and significant. While in human lineage Jesus Christ was "the offspring of David," yet in divine being He was the root of David, because David derived his spiritual being and his royal prerogatives from Him. And that the Lord is introduced under this designation in connection with this book implies that the book must relate to the fulfillment of the Davidic covenant; in other words, it must relate to the succession of the Messiah to David's throne in the capacity of a human-born and resurrected one from among the posterity of David.

"And I beheld, and, lo, in the midst of the throne and of the four beasts, and in the midst of the elders, stood a Lamb as it had been slain, having seven horns and seven eyes, which are the seven Spirits of God sent forth into all the earth. And he came and took the book out of the right hand of him that sat on the throne" (vs. 6, 7).

At this point the very central objective of the celestial scene so marvellously unfolded springs dramatically into view. It is the Lamb of God, Jesus Christ, even "the Lion of ......Judah, the Root of David," apparent as a slain and resurrected One. Although bearing all the marks, not only of humanity, but also of sacrificial death, yet He also appears in "all the fulness of the Godhead......bodily." The seven horns betoken the almightiness of the slain One, the seven eyes His omniscience. It is striking that His omniscience is applied here especially to the sphere of "all the earth." It implies that the contents of the book relate to things earthly, and that the Lamb's all-power is to be executed with all-scrutiny in "all the earth."

While the "seven eyes" are symbolical of Christ's omniscience, yet the qualifying expression, "Which are the seven Spirits [spirits] of God sent forth into all the earth," implies an angelic detective system rather than the mere attribute of divine omniscience. The scrutiny of the Lord's eye in all places through angelic detectives is prominently revealed in Scripture. "The *eyes of the Lord* are in every place, beholding the evil and the good" (Prov. 15:3). Just as in times especially of secret plottings of enemies, the scrutiny of our government is found to have been everywhere needed through trusty, skillful detectives, so the angels of God are ever alert to detect every movement and secret design of His enemies in earth or skies. "The eyes of the Lord run to and fro throughout the whole earth, to show himself strong in the behalf of them whose heart is perfect toward him" (2 Chron. 16:9). Especially is this form of angelic activity and service in earthly affairs made clear in Zechariah, where the angelic delegates are presented in militant symbolism as horses, chariots and riders. "These are they whom the Lord hath sent to walk to and fro through the earth" (1:10). The effect of their activities is thus described: "We have walked to and fro through the earth, and, behold, all the earth sitteth still, and is at rest'' (1:11) ; ''Behold, these that go toward the north country have quieted my spirit in the north country'' (6:8). How wonderfully angelic hosts stand mobilized for instant, effective service anywhere that God wills, is illustrated by the words of Jesus when He demurred to Peter's drawing the sword in the garden: ''Thinkest thou that I cannot now pray to my Father, and he shall presently [instantly] give me more than twelve legions of angels?'' (Matt. 26:53.)

The approach of the Lamb to the throne, and His reception of the seven-sealed book in His right hand (of power) from the Lord God Almighty sitting upon the throne, forms the dramatic climax of all these ''Celestial Preparations'' for the swift occurrence of ''the things which shall be hereafter.'' It is the signal for unparalleled celebrations of praise and honor to the Almighty and especially to the Lamb. These celebrations are seen participated in by all ranks of creatures and by numberless throngs throughout all the realms of heaven and earth.

''8 And when he had taken the book, the four beasts and four and twenty elders fell down before the Lamb, having every one of them harps, and golden vials full of odours, which are the prayers of saints. 9 And they sung a new song, saying, Thou are worthy to take the book, and to open the seals thereof: for thou wast slain, and hast redeemed us to God by thy blood out of every kindred, and tongue, and people, and nation; 10 And hast made us unto our God kings and priests: and we shall reign on the earth. 11 And I beheld, and I heard the voice of many angels round about the throne and the beasts and the elders: and the number of them was ten thousand times ten thousand, and thousands of thousands; 12 Saying with a loud voice, Worthy is the Lamb that was slain to receive power, and riches, and wisdom, and strength, and honour, and glory, and blessing. 13 And every creature which is in heaven, and on the earth, and under the earth, and such as are in the sea, and all that are in them, heard I saying, Blessing, and honour, and glory, and power, be unto him that sitteth upon the throne, and

unto the Lamb for ever and ever.   14 And the four beasts
said, Amen.   And the four and twenty elders fell down and
worshiped him that liveth for ever and ever'' (5: 8-14).

This passage embraces three oratorios of gladness and
praise.

1.   The Oratorio of the Redeemed about the Throne, vs. 8-10.

Although the four beasts have not been classed as
themselves human, but angelic beings, yet their very
special association with and leadership to the four and
twenty elders as heads of the human throng is here
again noticeable. Their figures were emblazoned upon the
standards of the four quarters of the orderly arranged
encampment of Israel of old, thus bearing witness to
this association with and leadership to the Lord's people
on the part of these angelic beings even during the earthly pilgrimage of the saints.

The beasts and the elders constitute the directors in
this oratorio. They fall in worship before the Lamb,
giving Him all divine acknowledgement. They have
harps in their hands for sweet praise, and golden vials,
or bowls, brimful of odors, or incense, which is explained
to represent the prayers of the saints.

The reading of verses 9, 10, according to the common
version, leaves no doubt that this song is to be participated in by a numberless throng of translated saints. But
all our other versions displace the pronouns of the first
person plural with pronouns of the third person, excepting in the expression ''unto our God kings and priests.''
This raises a very serious question whether translated
believers are to be considered as embraced in this scene.

But from several considerations we will assume that
a multitude of translated saints will be there to join in
this song. First, the presence of the elders proves rapture so far as they are concerned, and it implies the
presence of the congregation of whom they are the heads.

Then, the offering with thanksgiving of the prayers of
the saints implies the celebration of the answer of their
prayers. Again, the distinction of tense between the
expressions *"hast* made us unto our God kings and
priests'' and ''we shall reign on the earth,'' clearly implies that naught remains to be accomplished for these
redeemed ones, but to be inducted from the place of
meeting the Lord in the skies into their reign with Him
on the earth, and that that is just what is forthwith to
be undertaken. Finally, the reason for not using the
first person of the pronoun is simply this; that the four
beasts and the twenty-four elders lead off in the oratorio,
singing to the Lamb the praise for what He has done and
is about to do for a vast company other than themselves.
The third person would be exchanged for the first as soon
as the redeemed throng took up this part of the song.
Corroboration of this view will be encountered later in
Revelation.

This view, then, being correct, a very important factor
is supplied to us thereby relative to these ''Celestial
Preparations.'' It is this, that throughout the proceedings to be conducted from the skies by the Lamb, as represented in the succeeding vision of the opening of the
seven seals, the translated saints will be standing securely
above in glorified bodies as most deeply interested observers. In other words, the ''Celestial Preparations''
for the execution of ''the things which must shortly
[swiftly] come to pass'' (1:1), or ''the things which
shall be hereafter'' (1:19), or ''the things which must
be hereafter'' (4:1), include the gathering of resurrected
saints to Jesus in the skies.

And it is patent, that the presence of the blood-bought
saints surrounding and acclaiming the Lamb of the ages
supplies a feature of this unique occasion which could
not be spared. Redeeming blood is Christ's supreme
credential as He stands the central figure of the celestial
convention. The whole staging of the concourse on the

divine side had been to the end of delivering that book
into the only worthy and competent hands to be found.
It is the pierced hands that are extended by Him, and it
is only pierced hands, even of the eternal Son, which are
counted worthy and able. It is to the song of redeeming
love and blood that the harps of the beasts and elders
are tuned. The orchestra of musicians expressly intimates by brimming incense-bowls, that the theme to be
presented is one of answered prayers of blood-washed
saints.

Through this vision, faithfully left on record by John
the Seer, let imagination catch inspiring glimpse of that
nearing hour, so vibrant with significance to the Holy
Father, to His eternal Son, to the seven Spirits, to faithful angel ministrants innumerable, to raptured saints of
all times and tongues, and to sympathetic classes in all
spheres affected directly by redeeming blood! Then listen again to the sweet and winsome sentiment of that
enraptured orchestra as they, the nearest worshippers
before the Lamb, strike upon their lyres and release the
motif that is to radiate broadcast in ever-widening reverberations wherever redemption's work has reached.

"Thou'rt worthy to take the scroll and to open its seals,
    For Thou wast slain and dost buy for our God by
    Thy blood
    Out of every tribe and language and people and nation,
    And makest of them a kingdom and a priesthood for our God,
    And they will be reigning on the earth."

                                                    (C. V.)

Why is this called a "new song?" Not because another song will then first have been added to the hymnody
of the ages of mercy and of grace. It is rather that a
consummation has arrived, when that "song of long
ago" becomes so fresh, so real, so impressive, so far beyond all past comprehension that it seems altogether new,
We anticipate it feebly even now.

"That will be an hour of joy, Praise will then our tongues employ,
    More and more, more and more;
We shall stand before the King, And the song of triumph sing
    Evermore, evermore.
On we'll march to victory, Jesus will our Leader be,
    Jesus will our Leader be;
On we'll march to victory, To a final and a glorious victory."

The hour will have come for the saints to be brought by the "King of Saints," as "kings and priests," into the earthly, millennial reign with Him.

"Kings and priests." For the second time in this book this high calling of glorified saints in Christ Jesus is brought forward. We are to be *priest*-kings, a royal *priesthood*. While Jesus is to return as King, yet He will not discontinue His priestly functions, any more than He is now suspending prophetic functions while serving as High Priest above. The regal aspect of the millennial dispensation may be so exclusively emphasized as to overlook the sacerdotal. But it will be remembered that Israel was originally called to be "a kingdom of priests" (Ex. 19:6); that is, they were called as Christ's earthly kingdom to be engaged in negotiating the mercies of God in behalf of all other kingdoms of the earth. And Isa. 61:6 foretells the fulfillment in the millennial age of this original calling to which Israel in the past proved so recreant: "Ye shall be named the Priests of the Lord: men shall call you the Ministers of our God." So likewise the saints of this age are now mystically "a royal priesthood,"—all too remiss in duty —and they will prove to be such in truth in that coming day of the Lord.

As has already been intimated, the climax of the song is found in the closing statement, "and we shall reign on the earth." It is not so much the certainty of this event as its immediacy that is thus declared. The question arises, why the act of the Lamb in taking this book betokens immediate steps for the inaugurating of the reign of the saints with Him on the earth? This question finds its answer in a clearer view of the symbolical meaning of the scroll.

The seven-sealed book can be more readily comprehended under the light of ancient Hebrew law pertaining to the redemption of land-estates. Hebrew land-owners were forbidden to alienate a family possession. Occupancy was often forfeited for some cause. In such case, occupancy and the enjoyment of the inheritance could be regained only by waiting for the year of jubilee or by the intervention of a qualified redeemer. This redeemer must be next of kin, unless he forfeited his claim to one standing next to him in order. He must be able also to meet the obligations of the displaced owner and to dispossess the alien occupant. Moreover, the title to the property was preserved in two documents, one open, the other sealed. See Jer. 32:14. The owner alone, or his qualified redeemer in case of his own inability, had right to break the seal.

The book before us may be viewed as the close-sealed title of the saints to their original possession and dominion of the earth. Occupancy and control have been forfeited by sin to hostile, obstinate aliens; namely, the wicked of mankind, which in turn are ruled from the skies by the prince of darkness who seduced the first man from loyalty to Christ. The original title came from the Son of God, in whom man was created and for whom he was appointed to possess and rule the earth. He became Himself the Son of man by incarnation, loosed fallen man from sin and Satan by His own blood, arose from the dead, and ascended to His former glory and power to serve as fallen man's intercessor at heaven's court, and to bring every believer back with Himself into possession of the kingdom of this world. The only one to be found qualified as Kinsman and competent Redeemer, to unlock and fulfill historically the plainly prophesied, but thus far fast-closed, purposes of God for fallen man

to recover earthly dominion, is this Lamb of Calvary.
By human generation He is next of kin to fallen men;
by His blood He has paid for man the full price of
forfeited life, liberty and kingdom; in Him the
covenants of Abraham and of David were confirmed and
He, as Lion of Judah and Root of David, is almighty to
fulfill the pledges of those covenants.

2. *Oratorio of Angelic Hosts surrounding the Throne,* vs. 11, 12.

The identification of this matchless scene becomes
still more conclusive when these verses are read in the
light of Daniel 7: 9-14. Verse 9 clearly links itself with
the enthroning in our skies of the Almighty Father as
presented in Rev. 4, and it shows that hostile thrones
have to be displaced thereby. In v. 10 the same myriads
of angelic attendants are presented which are enumerated
in Rev. 5: 11. The last words of v. 10—"The judgment
was set and the books were opened"—coincide in significance with Rev. 5: 1, where the Almighty is represented
as sitting on the throne in our skies in judicial capacity
with the seven-sealed book in His right hand. Verses 11,
12 show that the sevenfold book relates in contents to
the overthrow of antichristian powers defying on earth
the right of the saints to reign. Verse 13 coincides
with Rev. 5: 2-6 in respect to the appearing of the Son
of man, the Lion-Lamb, as the only competent candidate
for the business in hand. Verse 14 explains so clearly
just what committing the seven-sealed book into the hands
of the Lamb (5: 7) meant. It is evident that the matter
pertains to the speedy acquisition of the dominion of all
the earth (as well as the skies) from satanic and antichristian hands for the saints of Christ. As Dan. 4: 18
reads: "But the saints of the most High shall take the
kingdom, and possess the kingdom for ever, even for
ever and ever."

After the raptured saints, led off by the beasts and

the elders, have sung their anthem through, those hosts
of angels, surrounding in vast circles the throne of God,
lift up their ascription of worth to the Lamb in sevenfold refrain of "power, and riches, and wisdom, and
strength, and honor, and glory, and blessing" (v. 12).
These noble beings have ever been most diligent students
and enthusiastic abetters of the eternal divine purpose
concerning the Church of Jesus Christ. "To the intent
that now unto the principalities and powers in heavenly
places might be known by the church the manifold wisdom of God, according to the eternal purpose which he
purposed in Christ Jesus our Lord" (Eph. 3:10, 11).
"That in the ages to come he might shew the exceeding
riches of his grace in his kindness toward us through
Christ Jesus" (Eph. 2:7). "Which things the angels desire to look into" (1 Pet. 1:12).

3. Oratorio of Remotest Creation, v. 13.

Finally, all the creation affected by the fall and embraced in the provisions of redemptive restoration re-
verberates with loyal praises to God and His Lamb, offering up unto them in thankful voice from all those
spheres all "Blessing, and honor, and glory, and power."
We can well understand the thrill of rapturous anticipation that will at this time animate all the waiting creation when we read a passage like Rom. 8:18-21. "For
I reckon that the sufferings of this present time are not
worthy to be compared with the glory which shall be
revealed in us"; that is, manifested to the eyes of creation in the glorified forms of the returning saints. "For
the earnest expectation of the creature [creation]
waiteth for the manifestation [from above] of the sons
of God. For the creature [creation] was made subject
to vanity [perishability], not willingly [as though
natural to it], but by reason of him [Adam] who hath
subjected the same *in hope*, because the creature [crea-

tion] itself shall be delivered from the bondage of corruption into the glorious liberty of the children of God.''

The curtain falls upon this matchless scene of ''Celestial Preparations'' with a fitting finale: ''The four beasts said, Amen. And the four and twenty elders fell down and worshipped him that liveth for ever and ever'' (v. 14).

CHAPTER II.

THE FIRST SIX SEALS OPENED, CHAPTER 6.

CERTAIN premises are strictly to be borne in mind
in entering intelligently upon the pathway of
revelation now opening concerning things to come.

1. The whole program is conducted by Jesus Christ as
the one crucified but now undertaking His long promised
seizure of earthly rule as the Lion of Judah, the Root
of David. It is the time when He shall arise to "make
his enemies his footstool."

2. The skies are viewed as already evacuated by the
forces of darkness and occupied by the undisputed and
glorious sovereignty of the Almighty.

3. The time for Satan's hostilities and resistance to
be conducted publicly through his human plenipotentiary, the Anti-Christ, is viewed as already inaugurated.

4. The order of procedure, then, is to be viewed as
issuing from the redeemed skies and as obeying the will
of the Lamb-Lion. This order is with the view of preparing the way in the earth for the kingdom of the
Lord and of His saints, which is speedily to be introduced victoriously over all effective opposition.

5. It is to the prospect of the swift accomplishment
of this end that multitudes of redeemed and raptured
saints are to be viewed as singing their joyous acclaim,
along with the other deeply interested observers, both
celestial and terrestrial.

6. It is, therefore, as dealings from the skies with the
antichristian world beneath that the panorama of inflictions now commencing is to be viewed.

"And I saw when the Lamb opened one of the seals, and I
heard, as it were the noise of thunder, one of the four beasts
saying, Come and see. And I saw, and behold a white horse:

and he that sat on him had a bow; and a crown was given
unto him: and he went forth conquering, and to conquer'' (vs.
1, 2).

From what has already been plainly found, the time
here is that of the earliest stage of Anti-Christ's times.
It has been learned from 2 Thess. 2:7, 8, that his open
revelation succeeds the removal from the earth of the
restraining agency of the overcoming saints. And from
Dan. 7:8, 20; 8:9; and 11:40-43, it is made plain that
Anti-Christ first conducts in the earth a period of sweeping, victorious warfare. The field of conflict will be the
territories of the restored northern (Syrian), southern
(Egyptian) and eastern (Mesopotamian) kingdoms of
the old Grecian Empire. The figure of a white horse,
and of his rider seated erect with drawn bow and with
victor's wreath upon his brow, is the favorite oriental
symbol of the military conqueror.

While, therefore, we are to see here visioned the early,
militant period of Anti-Christ, yet it is to be viewed as
the effect of punitive influences released from above by
the will and authority of the Lamb, when opening the
drama fulfilling the contents of the seven-sealed book.
Nowhere in the Bible is Satan or any agent of his represented by that noble animal, the horse, while uniformly
angelic persons are thus symbolized in the Bible when
they are presented in militant character and activity.
Reference may be made afresh to Zech. 1:8-11 and 6:
1-8. Here was a time when militant activities of angelic
forces, represented by horses of various colors appropriate to their special functions and bearing riders or
hauling chariot, were effecting military and political
results in the Persian Empire as determined by the Son
of God in behalf of His people, the Jews at Jerusalem,
recently returned from Babylonian captivity and lying
exposed to utmost peril from surrounding enemies. The
white horse and his rider connected with the first seal
is, therefore, to be taken as the symbolical figure of

high angelic power fulfilling the will of God and of the Lamb, in having the era of Anti-Christ's conquest projected in the appointed territories of the old imperial world.

"And when he had opened the second seal, I heard the second beast say, Come and see. And there went out another horse that was red: and power was given to him that sat thereon to take peace from the earth, and that they should kill one another: and there was given unto him a great sword" (vs. 3, 4).

This pictures the usual consequences of an outbreak of an international military struggle. War-madness seizes classes and peoples, and slaughter with the sword runs riot. What precursors and illustrations of this coming era have been recently presented among European nations, and how likely is the world to witness their recurrence in increasing horrors! The punitive angelic power superintending this stage is fitly symbolized by the red horse. The expression in v. 4, "to take peace from the *earth*," should not in this connection be taken in a general, unlimited application, but should be taken only illustratively and partially, and probably especially with respect to the Biblical "earth."

"And when he had opened the third seal, I heard the third beast say, Come and see. And I beheld, and lo a black horse; and he that sat on him had a pair of balances in his hand. And I heard a voice in the midst of the four beasts say, A measure of wheat for a penny, and three measures of barley for a penny; and see thou hurt not the oil and the wine" (vs. 5, 6).

The third quickly succeeding stage of divine infliction upon the territories of Anti-Christ's early operations is here described as a time of great straitness in food supplies. The distinction between cereal supplies and those of oil and wine indicates that famine-effects are not yet of utmost extreme, and that the military campaign involving the destruction of nature's products is during the earlier rather than the latter harvest months. The symbol of the black horse is exactly appropriate.

"And when he had opened the fourth seal, I heard the voice of the fourth beast say, Come and see. And I looked, and behold a pale horse: and his name that sat on him was Death, and Hell followed with him. And power was given unto them over the fourth part of the earth to kill with the sword, and with hunger, and with the beasts of the earth" (vs. 7, 8).

Here is represented the ultimate consequences of a time when the hounds of wide-spread, mad, ruthless warfare are unleashed. The "sallow-greenish horse" (C. V.) is the perfect symbol of days when the angels of Death and Hades stalk abroad almost as visible specters gathering up their victims. Death is not only by the more ordinary agencies of sword and of hunger, but also by pestilence and by ravenous beasts. One need not be shocked at the thought of the Lamb through angelic agents thus dealing with rebellious men. All through the Bible, Old and New Testaments, appalling physical inflictions through divine and angelic agency are faithfully and unblushingly reported. The expression, "the fourth part of the earth," is again to be taken in literal sense, yet limited and partial in scale. It does not mean one-quarter of the population of the whole earth, but it means that the death powers are given operation over one-fourth of the territory of "the earth" in the prophetic usage of the term; that is, one-fourth of the territory of the old imperial earth, more particularly of the whole old Roman Empire.

"And when he had opened the fifth seal, I saw under the altar the souls of them that were slain for the word of God, and for the testimony which they held: And they cried with a loud voice, saying, How long, O Lord, holy and true, dost thou not judge and avenge our blood on them that dwell on the earth? And white robes were given unto every one of them; and it was said unto them, that they should rest yet for a little season, until their fellow servants also and their brethren, that should be killed as they were, should be fulfilled" (vs. 9-11).

This passage throws great light for us upon the situation and the course of things during the era now under

consideration among a different and special class of
people. The company here presented is one of deceased
persons. It is plainly shown that they come to their
decease by martyrdom. The reason for their martyrdom
is their adherence to the word of God and their unflinching Christian testimony. They are seen crying to the
Lord—"holy and true"—for judgment and vengeance
upon earthly inhabitants who had been guilty of their
blood. Their position in thus imprecating vengeance
was "under the altar." This means, of course, the
golden altar where incense is offered. There they are
as "souls," evidently meaning in disembodied condition.
In response to their importunity white robes are distributed to them severally, and they are bidden to rest
yet a little season until their spiritual companions left
on the earth should in like manner and for like reason
be killed.

Several important particulars need to be elucidated
and may be enlarged upon somewhat.

1. Although the time of the Anti-Christ, as has been
seen, is subsequent to the departure of the formerly
restraining body of saints, yet Christian faith and valiant Christian testimony will still remain in the earth.
In the time when Christ shall be permitting "the man
of Sin," "the son of perdition," "that wicked, . . .
whose coming is after the working of Satan with all
power and signs and lying wonders," to be gaining
military and imperial ascendency in the earth, there
will still, thank God! be those who shall be strengthened
to love the word of God "incorruptible" more than life
and who shall seal their uncompromising testimony of
Jesus Christ with their blood. And, at the same time,
so far from the earlier martyrdoms intimidating other
believers, it will again prove that "the blood of the
martyrs is the seed of the Church." It is easy to see
that the time when divine judgments begin in the earth
the hatred against the saints will be greatly intensified.

2. Light is thrown upon the state of disembodied saints. It is seen that these saints remain in full exercise of conscious faculties of mind and spirit. They also continue in appropriate touch with earthly affairs through their relationship to Jesus. Note the expressions, "appropriate touch" and "through their relationship to Jesus." These particular martyred saints are seen engaged in imprecatory intercession unto a "holy and true" Lord with reference to the bloodthirsty persecutors and murderers of saints in the earth. And they are not repelled by the Lord for such action. On the contrary, they are evidently treated with sympathy and consideration, although they are quieted from pressing their plea for immediate vengeance. It is the time of vengeance; but it is seen to be a time of gradual progress toward final execution of vengeance.

3. The place where these "souls" are seen to be needs elucidation. It is "under the altar." This is, of course, not the altar of sacrifice, but the altar of incense, the golden altar before the inner veil. It is seen that the place of imprecatory prayer is the same as that of supplicatory and of intercessory prayer. Imprecation has its time, when supplication and intercession would be untimely and out of place, when imprecatory prayer is all that God will hear and answer. For illustrations, see Jer. 7:16; 11:14; 14:10-12; Ezek. 8:18; Prov. 1:24-28.

Now this altar is, of course, not the golden altar of the earthly temple. Right at this point in the study of Revelation, which book abounds in references like this one, it is well to note that the old-time temple furniture and functions were "patterns of things in the heavens." The "pattern showed to" Moses "in the mount" consisted of perfectly appropriate divinely designed symbols of "heavenly things." All the proceedings through the medium of the "patterns" were to have their reality and efficacy by virtue of their symbolical correspondence to the ministries "of the sanctuary, and of the true tabernacle, which the Lord pitched, and not man" (Heb. 8:2). This symbolical representation of "things in the heavens" was to be superseded by the better expression of them to be made by the great High Priest Himself over the house of God, when He should be manifested in bodily revelation. In this Book of Revelation these "things in the heavens" are called by the familiar names of their earthly "patterns." These martyred saints are, therefore, described as being engaged in the function of imprecatory prayer after manner, place and provision answering in true realities to what would be in the earth conducted through the symbolical medium of the material golden altar.

4. Answer to the question, "how long" the murderous persecutions of the saints in the earth should be allowed to continue unavenged, is found in v. 11, which verse is worthy of careful consideration. The answer is highly benignant in tone and is not disappointing. As to "how long," the answer is "for a little season, until their fellowservants and their brethren, that should be killed as they were, should be fulfilled." This translation does not make clear sense. The R. V. supplies a much clearer marginal reading,—"have fulfilled"; that is, their course. The C. V. reads, "should be completing them." The thought seems clearly to be that there is to be under Anti-Christ an era of the martyrdom of outstanding Christians, and that these martyred saints both represent an era and constitute a company gradually filling up to completion. Vengeance upon the persecutors of that era awaits the completion of the company of victims.

But meanwhile, unto these martyrs of the era of the first four seals "white robes" are to be given, even "unto every one of them." This must represent some important and blessed change in their state and also compensation for having to wait for their avenging. What is to be understood by the white robes?

It hardly seems pertinent to consider them as a change spiritually—a clothing of the spirits of these saints. There seems rather to be a connection between the white robes and the vision of these saints at the first as "souls," disembodied in condition. It leaves room for the very probable sense of the white robes as being glorified bodies given thus soon to those slain saints. This would not only be to them a great and satisfying boon, but also their qualification to be brought from the place and the engagement of imprecatory prayer, "under the altar," to the place and engagements "before the throne" of God Almighty and of the Lamb, along with the previously resurrected and glorified saints of the ages.

This introduces the idea of extended, successional, rather than single, complete, rapture of the saints. The Book of Revelation will be found to throw much and conclusive light in this direction. It may be said to be scarcely possible otherwise to read Revelation except in a cramped and far-fetched, predetermined way. In fact, without the conclusive light of Revelation, Bible readers seem to be unable to escape unhappy and heated controversy over whether all the Church will escape the tribulation by prior simultaneous rapture or all incur the tribulation before their rapture. There is also otherwise the awkward question left on hand—how it comes, if all believers are removed before the rapture, that there should be any in the earth during the tribulation to be "slain for the word of God, and for the testimony which they held."

The idea of a series of partial raptures is in entire harmony with the representation of the rapture in different places in the Epistles as a whole, without intimation of the inclusion in the whole of a series. Such mode of representation is too frequent in Scripture in various

lines; e. g., that of the Lord's coming, whether in the
two advents, or in the two stages of the second advent,
and that of the resurrection of the dead, occurring in
two parts separated by at least a thousand years—to
leave one bound up to an individual rapture. Furthermore, the idea of successional raptures comports
beautifully with urgent admonitions to be ready
for the impending call and with expressed or implied
warnings of the results of unpreparedness. In the case
of all the dead in Christ it is different. There could
be no gain in having the bodies of some lie longer in the
grave, because the intermediate state is not one of
further probation. But to be counted worthy and ready
to be caught up without dying is Scripturally a laudable
ambition and a goal of probation.

"12 And I beheld when he had opened the sixth seal, and, lo,
there was a great earthquake; and the sun became black as
sackcloth of hair, and the moon became as blood; 13 And the
stars of heaven fell unto the earth, even as a fig tree casteth
her untimely figs, when she is shaken of a mighty wind. 14 And
the heaven departed as a scroll when it is rolled together; and
every mountain and island were moved out of their places.
15 And the kings of the earth, and the great men, and the rich
men, and the chief captains, and the mighty men, and every
bondman, and every free man, hid themselves in the dens and
in the rocks of the mountains; 16 And said to the mountains
and rocks, Fall on us, and hide us from the face of him that
sitteth on the throne, and from the wrath of the Lamb: 17 For
the great day of his wrath is come; and who shall be able to
stand?" (Vs. 12-17.)

"Who is able to stand?" No wonder this question
arises. These convulsions themselves, even more especially what they portend, suffice to cause the stoutest-hearted
to reel in paralysing dismay.

This is an unprecedented concurrence of cataclysms.
Earthquakes alone have already occurred, which were as
if the foundations of the earth were utterly giving way.
What a sense of physical insecurity and helplessness is

realized! But never before such an earthquake as this! Volumes of smoke, ashes, flame, fumes and debris from gaping fissures of the earth's crust, besides the lurid glare and the columns of smoke from conflagrations of cities, hamlets, fields and forests, overspread the skies, causing the sun by day to turn black, the full moon by night blood red. Terrifying and destructive meteoric showers—sudden and thick like the falling of shrivelled figs from trees caught in a tornado—fill the atmosphere as with swift-flying fiery torches from above and pelt the earth with frightful detonations. As in rare auroral displays, the appalling celestial phenomena culminate in the appearance of a great scroll reaching from zenith to horizon all about rolling itself up. At the climax, suddenly all lights above are out, thick and awful darkness ensues. All mountains of the affected territory, and islands of the Aegean and of the Mediterranean, quiver and slip from their original settings.

But not greater is the dissolution of physical nature than that of all social classes. Ashen-faced fugitives, shaking like aspen leaves at every joint,—from thrones, from halls of State, from military Great Headquarters, from palatial mansions, from lordly castles, from slave pens and from smiling homes—huddle promiscuously in caverns and rocky recesses of the mountains. Yet there they heave no sigh of relief, for the terrors of the hour are to them but omens of more terrifying overhanging doom, from which they would have the mountains and rocks of their immediate refuge collapsing overhead emtomb them. The long-threatened, but long-flouted *Day of Doom,* is by them known now to be unmistakably announced by these terrifying portents as being right at hand. "Befriend us," "Fall on us," shriek the quaking, conscience-stricken refugees, to the mountains and rocks which had opened to them hiding places from all eyes but His. "Fall on us, and hide us from the face of him that sitteth on the throne, and from the wrath of the Lamb: for the great day of his wrath is come; and *who shall be able to stand?"*

The sign of the Son of man in the sky above had throughout the era of the preceding five seals been scorned and defied. It was but a myth, a mere natural phenomenon easily accounted for by modern science. In fact, the most up-to-date Bibles even retained no prophecies of such a thing. "Where is the promise of his coming," had "last day scoffers, walking after their own lusts," boasted. "For since the fathers fell asleep, all things continue as they were from the beginning of the creation." But now the sign of the Son of man present in the skies just above is answered to by attestations of the elements of earth and sky, and the haughtiest of men confess in view of impending divine indignation, *"Who is able to stand?"*

CHAPTER III.

FIRST CONTEMPORANEOUS INTERCALATION, CHAPTER 7.

WHILE this chapter may perhaps be warrantably confined in range of time to the period of the sixth seal, yet its extensive contents are centered so fully outside the line of the judgments upon the antichristian world, and centered so fully upon the line of matters pertaining to the Lord's faithful ones, that it may be taken as an inserted passage, not carrying the regular line of progress further, but bringing forward important information concerning the followers of the Christian faith. The vision of the fifth seal contributed information of like character; but this chapter stands out in such large proportions between chapters 6 and 8, and it stands so distinct in character from the preceding portion (6:12-17) belonging to the sixth seal, that it can be studied best as an intercalated, added or inserted, passage.

The chapter consists of two main parts or distinct divisions.

I. *Prospective, the 144,000 Sealed Israelites, vs. 1-8.*

"1 And after these things I saw four angels standing on the four corners of the earth, holding the four winds of the earth, that the wind should not blow on the earth, nor on the sea, nor on any tree. 2 And I saw another angel ascending from the east, having the seal of the living God: and he cried with a loud voice to the four angels, to whom it was given to hurt the earth and the sea, 3 Saying, Hurt not the earth, neither the sea, nor the trees, till we have sealed the servants of our God in their foreheads. 4 And I heard the number of them which were sealed: and there were sealed a hundred and forty and four thousand of all the tribes of the children of Israel. 5 Of the tribe of Juda were sealed twelve thousand. Of the tribe of

Reuben were sealed twelve thousand. Of the tribe of Gad were sealed twelve thousand. 6 Of the tribe of Aser were sealed twelve thousand. Of the tribe of Nephthalim were sealed twelve thousand. Of the tribe of Manasses were sealed twelve thousand. 7 Of the tribe of Simeon were sealed twelve thousand. Of the tribe of Levi were sealed twelve thousand. Of the tribe of Issachar were sealed twelve thousand. 8 Of the tribe of Zabulon were sealed twelve thousand. Of the tribe of Joseph were sealed twelve thousand. Of the tribe of Benjamin were sealed twelve thousand.''

All our variant versions read, ''And after this,'' instead of ''And after these things.'' This is then a new vision presented to John subsequently to that of 6:12-17, rather than a further stage of the latter vision. This vision throbs with anticipation of impending events,—it is prospective rather than being descriptive of further occurrences springing directly from the opening of the sixth seal.

Verses 1-3 imply an impending, but temporarily restrained, destruction to be inflicted upon the antichristian territory,—land, sea and vegetation. This destructive judgment is to be inflicted by angelic powers through the agency of ''the four winds of the earth.'' In Dan. 7:2 occurs the expression, ''the four winds of heaven.'' A careful examination will satisfy one that the two descriptions agree with one another, the latter indicating the celestial regions from which these forces come, the former the territorial theater of their operations. And it is evident that ''the winds'' in both cases constitute more than material atmospheric forces. We are to understand supernatural, angelic forces to be indicated. And while the directing agency is angelic, we are to understand that satanic agencies are intensely engaged in the resulting convulsions. These tremendous convulsions, while involving nature in due part—often in appalling demonstrations—yet also profoundly affect political, social and religious spheres, both on the earth and in the skies. It is for this reason, that in the present

instance the commanding angel causes the four angels in
charge of impending judgments to hold the forces in
check until the sealing of God's servants should be done.
We are, therefore, to be looking for these terrestrial
catastrophes later, while for the present there shall be
"sealed the servants of our God in their foreheads."

As to these servants of God, whether more are included
in the vision or not, twelve thousand from each of the
twelve tribes of Israel—making one hundred and forty-
four thousand in all—were specially enumerated. While
conjecture finds a fertile field for exercise right here, and
while we are left considerably to conjecture, yet this is
all deeply interesting, important and, to considerable degree, directly instructive.

The first peculiarity arresting our attention is the
exact and equal number from each tribe of Israel. This
is a selection of representatives, and it shows that in the
selection the twelve tribes were given equal consideration.
The second striking peculiarity is the make-up of the
list of twelve tribes. When the two sons of Joseph were
listed as equal tribal heirs, it made thirteen tribes including Levi. Levi, therefore, not having a landed inheritance, was usually omitted from the list of twelve
tribes. But Levi is here included and also Manasseh, one
of Joseph's two sons. In place, however, of Ephraim, the
other son, Joseph himself, is included. And yet there
are but twelve in all, as Dan is omitted altogether. The
list is described, nevertheless, as "all the tribes of the
children of Israel," and twelve there are in this list, just
equal to the original number of the sons of Jacob. We
must, therefore, take this apparently incomplete and ac-
commodated list as answering to the description, sym-
metry in the list—perhaps other conditions also—
superseding apparent exactness. The same may be true
of the identical number of sealed ones out of each of the
twelve tribes. Two things, nevertheless, are literally
evident. First, all Israel is to be on the scene con-

spicuously and nobly in the last days; second, all Israel is to contribute in those days to "the servants of our God" numerously, amply, as the number twelve, with its multiples, implies.

What are we to understand by the sealing of this multitude of Israelites at this vital stage of the preparations for our Lord's return to earth?

The first suggestion to one's mind would be that of the sealing of or with the Holy Spirit. But these persons are described as being already "servants" (slaves) of our God. And there are two other more cogent objections to the foregoing view. These Israelites were to be sealed "in their foreheads," and to be so sealed by angelic hands. Now it is manifestly true that the seat of the Spirit's sealing is not the head, but the heart, and that the Holy Spirit is never conferred upon believers by angelic hands.

The forehead is notably the seat of intelligence. The forehead of man betokens his constitution as rational and intellectual—yea, after the divine image—in distinction from the brute creation. And, besides having true hearts, the servants of God will need to be intelligent, well-informed, prepared to meet all comers with clearness of reason and knowledge, as well as with steadfastness of faith and fervency of love. At all times, especially at critical times, servants of God are needed who may be described, as was Issachar of old, as "men that had understanding of the times, to know what Israel ought to do."

But what do angels have to do with the preparation of "men of understanding of the times?" Are not wisdom and knowledge included among the gifts of the Spirit? That is true. But is it not also true that angels have at times been used of God very prominently in qualifying or in designating servants of God for great responsibility in God's service in their particular times? The career of Daniel strikingly illustrates the ministry of angels in this respect as well as in others. How largely this angelic ministry served in qualifying Zechariah with "understanding of the times, to know what Israel ought to do"! Or, take the case of John and of this very Book of Revelation. The first verse of the book informs us that Jesus Christ "sent and signified it [the revelation] by his angel unto his servant John." How richly the ministry of angels surrounded the first advent of our Lord,—instructing Zacharias, Mary, Joseph, the wise men and the shepherds! The Book of Revelation impressively discloses how, not only attending our Lord's descent from the skies, but also in the last days preceding that event, the activities of angels will be very extensive and marvellous.

Furthermore, we have light from the Old Testament to the effect that the last days will call for "men...... understanding the times," especially "to know what Israel ought to do," and that poor harassed and distracted Israel will have just such men "sealed" to be lights and guides amidst the darkness and confusion. It will be remembered that in the times of Antiochus Epiphanes—a very worthy type of the Anti-Christ—the secret of the heroism and victory of the Maccabean followers was the place filled by the "Maschilim," those who were wise for their times, able and faithful in instructing others. "They that understand among the people shall instruct many: yet they shall fall by the sword, and by the flame, by captivity, and by spoil, many days. Now when they shall fall, they shall be holpen with a little help: but many shall cleave to them with flatteries. And some of them of understanding shall fall, to try them, and to purge, and to make them white, even to the time of the end: because it is yet for a time appointed" (11 : 33-35). It will also be remembered that the expression, "to the time of the end: because it is yet for a time appointed," point to the like, and to the more critical, situation of the penitent remnant of Israel in the last days, when according to Dan. 12:2, 3, the "Maschilim," the wise ones,—"sealed......in their foreheads"—shall serve the same grand purpose. "And they that be wise [or teachers, Marg.] shall shine as the brightness of the firmament; and they that turn many to righteousness [into the right path in that desperate day] as the stars for ever and ever. But thou, O Daniel, shut up the words, and seal the book, even to the time of the end: many shall run to and fro [through its pages and visions], and knowledge [saving knowledge of the times] shall be increased." "Many shall be purified, and made white, and tried; but the wicked shall do wickedly: and none of the wicked shall understand; but the wise shall understand" (v. 10).

Is it not evident that this sealing of the 144,000 of the tribes of Israel indicates their being designated and qualified as teachers and guides, as pathfinders and inspiring examples, to perplexed, wavering, tempted fellow-Israelites in the days of far intenser tribulation immediately anticipated after the sixth seal is opened?

II. Retrospective, the White-robed Tribulation Saints, 7:9-17.

"9 After this I beheld, and, lo, a great multitude, which no man could number, of all nations, and kindreds, and people, and tongues, stood before the throne, and before the Lamb, clothed with white robes, and palms in their hands; 10 And cried with a loud voice, saying, Salvation to our God which sitteth upon the throne, and unto the Lamb. 11 And all the angels stood round about the throne, and about the elders and the four beasts, and fell before the throne on their faces, and worshipped God, 12 Saying, Amen: Blessing, and glory, and wisdom, and thanksgiving, and honour, and power, and might, be unto our God for ever and ever. Amen. 13 And one of the elders answered, saying unto me, What are these which are arrayed in white robes? and whence came they? 14 And I said unto him, Sir, thou knowest. And he said to me, These are they which came out of great tribulation, and have washed their robes, and made them white in the blood of the Lamb. 15 Therefore are they before the throne of God, and serve him day and night in his temple: and he that sitteth on the throne shall dwell among them. 16 They shall hunger no more, neither thirst any more; neither shall the sun light on them, nor any heat. 17 For the Lamb which is in the midst of the throne shall feed them, and shall lead them unto living fountains of waters: and God shall wipe away all tears from their eyes.''

Here again, the expression ''After this'' indicates merely a change of vision rather than a further chronological stage of progress. And this vision, like the one immediately preceding, does not pertain to the main line of progress,—that of the judgments on the antichristian world—but to the concerns of God's faithful and victorious witnesses of the antichristian times. The scene is shifted from a definitely numbered body, representing the twelve tribes of Israel, to a numberless throng, representing all nations, tribes, peoples and languages. Moreover, the one company is presented at a point of anticipation of an impending probation; the other at a point of recognition of a finished probation. Both companies are of God's elect, but it is almost as if the standards of the faith were viewed as being left by valiant martyred soldiers of the Church world-wide to the hands of chosen Israelites as the standard-bearers in the further antichristian times of the seventh and last seal.

THE WHITE-ROBED THRONG, VS. 9-12.

This countless multitude is seen standing ''before the throne, and before the Lamb.'' This position has been made familiar to us in Chapters 4 and 5. It is in the skies above us, where at present the prince of darkness sits exercising his malign sway over earth and skies. From the standpoint of the vision given to John the throne-presence and sway of God Almighty and of the Lamb has been there established, and it is from thence that in the vision the execution of the judgments contained

10

in the seven-sealed book is proceeding upon the antichristian world below. It is also the place whither the
raptured saints escaping the tribulation will rise "to
meet the Lord in the air" (2 Thess. 4:17). This new company is seen "clothed in white robes," which apparently
means, as in the case of the fifth-seal martyrs, resurrected and glorified bodies. Their appearance with
"palms in their hands" signifies "a final and a glorious
victory." This victory is expressed by them in a sonorous
acclamation of "Salvation to our God which sitteth upon
the throne, and unto the Lamb." This implies that their
presence there and their condition is due to signal demonstration of the saving grace and power of God Almighty
and of the Lamb. The marvel of the case is greatly
emphasized by the act of all the myriads of surrounding
angels in prostrating themselves in special worship of
God before His throne, and in their ascribing anew unto
Him "for ever and ever" "Blessing, and glory, and
wisdom, and thanksgiving, and honor, and power, and
might." So emphatic is the angelic acknowledgment,
that it is bracketed between two solemn "Amens." The
devout and the thoughtful reader must be impressed
with the profound significance of this occasion, when
not only those most intimately concerned, but also the
entire innumerable host of angels, is so deeply moved to
glorify the Almighty and the Lamb.

"WHAT ARE THESE."

The emotions and exclamations of the celestial companies implied, as has been suggested, that the white-
robed ones were well known, as was also the significance
of their victorious presence before the throne and before
the Lamb. The purpose of this vision was that the
servants of God in the earth might also know this part
of the "things which must shortly come to pass." This
is why one of the four and twenty elders opened the way
to inform John by asking him, "What are these that are

arrayed in white robes, and whence came they?" They
are evidently a throng of new-comers, having arrived
there out of special times and experiences. This is confirmed by John's disclaiming recognition of them. They
cannot, therefore, be identified with the redeemed and
glorified ones of 5:9, 10 or of 6:9-11, unless they be
taken to be foreshadowed by the closing words of 6:11,
—"until their fellow servants also and their brethren,
that should be killed as they were, should be fulfilled,"
or "completing them" (C. V.).   Most important,
therefore, is the information given by the elder to John:
"These are they which came out of great tribulation, and
have washed their robes, and made them white in the
blood of the Lamb."

All the more critical variant renderings prefix the
definite article to the phrase "great tribulation," reading "*the* great tribulation." This with certainty makes
this company distinct from and subsequent to the pre-
tribulation raptured saints, and it proves that believers
subjected to the fires of the tribulation epoch are at
intervals to be taken up into equal privilege in the skies
with those raptured and glorified before the tribulation
begins. The Book of Revelation makes plain a divisional
and successional rapture instead of a momentary complete one, one both preceding and overlapping the tribulation. All our variant renderings confirm the fact of an
extended rapture including tribulation times by a
peculiar translation of a phrase in v. 14. Instead of the
past tense, "*came* out," the present tense is given:
"These are they which *come* out of the great tribulation" (R. V.), or "*are coming* out" (C. V.). Another
careful translation adopts original manuscript authority
for a preposition which yields the rendering, "These are
those coming *up* out of the great tribulation." The
present tense implies a procession of rapture-companies
marking the tribulation times, and the expression, "coming *up*," visualizes to imagination their translation to the
skies. The whole passage (vs. 9-17) makes the white robes

of these tribulation saints the predominant feature. "Lo, a great multitude......clothed with white robes," (v. 9) ; "Who are these which are arrayed in white robes?" (v. 13) ; "These are they which came out of great tribulation, and have washed their robes, and made them white in the blood of the Lamb" (v. 14).

There must be in the figure of the white robes a special significance which is not beyond reliable interpretation. They have already been explained as signifying the resurrected and glorified bodies of the saints.

This is the reasonable and satisfactory view, considering the fact that bodily resurrection and glorification would be the paramount matter of gratulation involved in these saints' having a place before the throne and before the Lamb in the skies, just when the time has come for the saints to meet the Lord "in the air" in their resurrected and glorified bodies.

And it is entirely congruous that this occasion should call forth the praise of this white-robed multitude unto God and the Lamb for "salvation"; because it is this very consummation, which in Scripture is denominated "the redemption," yea, the "salvation," to which believers are yet looking forward, for which they long with heavy groanings, and which is to characterize the second coming of Christ: "We ourselves, which have the first fruits of the Spirit, groan within ourselves, waiting for the adoption, to wit, the redemption of our body. For we are saved by hope" (Rom. 8:23, 24). "Unto them that look for him shall he appear the second time without sin unto salvation" (Heb. 9:28).

It follows in apparently entire harmony that it is said of this new company of resurrected and glorified saints, that they had "washed their robes, and made them white in the blood of the Lamb." This implies, as has been particularly noted before in this work, that the atonement of Calvary includes our body. This sacred truth is not secondary in fact, even though it be so held in common Christian recognition, if, indeed, it be not

lost sight of altogether. The body has been purchased
with the full price of the Lamb's blood. Through that
blood the believer's body now partakes of sanctification,
of healing and of the virtue of the life of Jesus Christ,
although in respect of immortality it still remains in
humiliation—"our vile body"—and in weakness. The
very reason for this is that Christ's followers may know
"the fellowship of His sufferings," who "suffered for
us in the flesh" (1 Pet. 4:1). There is great gain prepared for the believer who embraces this fellowship; it
has direct bearing upon the standard of his resurrection.
This is plainly indicated by what is said of Old Testament heroes of faith, who "were tortured, not accepting
deliverance; that they might obtain a better resurrection" (Heb. 11:35). Paul also in similar connection
lays great weight upon difference in standards of resurrection (Phil. 3:10, 11).

Finally, our present passage, after describing the
consequent condition into which these tribulation saints
are seen to have been admitted,—"Therefore are they
before the throne of God, and serve him day and night
in his temple: and he that sitteth on the throne shall
dwell among them" (v. 15)—describes the contrast of
the condition out of which they had come entirely from
the physical side: "They shall hunger no more, neither
thirst any more; neither shall the sun light on them,
nor any heat" (v. 16). And it is from this standpoint of
explicit marvellous contrast in physical conditions that
the climax following may be read: "For the Lamb which
is in the midst of the throne shall feed them, and shall
lead them unto living fountains of waters: and God
shall wipe away all tears from their eyes" (v. 17).

Nothing is substracted from spiritual beatitude in
thus expatiating in the proper place upon the bodily
side of the wonderful salvation in store, neither is this
side of coming bliss a subject unworthy of such prominent attention and of such beautiful and glowing description.

CHAPTER IV.

THE SIX TRUMPETS, CHAPTERS 8 AND 9.

"And when he had opened the seventh seal, there was silence in heaven about the space of half an hour. And I saw the seven angels which stood before God; and to them were given seven trumpets" (8: 1, 2).

THE current of divine judicial action, arrested in the narrative at the end of Chapter 6, is now resumed. The seventh seal is opened: the concluding stage of the execution of the contents of the seven-sealed book —contents especially relating to the divine inflictions upon the antichristian world preparatory to the assumption of sovereign rule in the earth by the Lamb and His followers—is now on hand. The frantic consternation seizing the doomed victims below—so terror-stricken even under the premonitory demonstrations of the sixth seal—has been depicted in 6 : 12-17. Now, as the time for inaugurating the dreaded epoch arrives, a hush siezes the skies above and the throngs therein.

This is most impressive. The concerted arrest of all earth's sounds and activities—even for sixty seconds, for two, three, or for five minutes—as an act of reverence, of undivided recollection, of respect for some one or something notable, is indescribably impressive. How ominous and terrifying is the very stillness preceding a cyclone! How testing to an army is the hush before the crash of cannon or of arms! No such illustrations, however, are comparable with that of this "silence in heaven about the space of half an hour."

This hush is also most appropriate. The deity is not affected with the eagerness and excitability of the creatures,—human or angelic. Divine action is characterized by unhurried deliberation, by unruffled calm, by eternal peace. All creatures standing about Him as servants, or acting with Him as observers or participants, need to realize that stupendous occurrences cost divine and heavenly agencies no precipitate and noisy exertions.

That a new and important order of procedure is due, is indicated by the first feature which develops before the vision of John. A group of seven angels takes the central point of vision. These angels are called "the seven angels which stood before God," or "stand before God," R. V. In case angelic spirits are meant by those "seven lamps of fire burning before the throne, which are the seven Spirits of God" (4:5), these seven would be reasonably identified with them. To these special ministers of God is given each a trumpet. The four beasts had their time of prominent action in connection with the first four seals. Four angels "standing on the four corners of the earth, holding the four winds of the earth," a special angel "having the seal of the living God," and one of the twenty-four elders have successively come to the front in important service. But keen anticipation is excited when these seven trumpeters are introduced for service of exceeding importance, an importance corresponding to all the intimations that a period of hitherto unparalleled disclosures has arrived in the vision.

"3 And another angel came and stood at the altar, having a golden censer; and there was given unto him much incense, that he should offer it with the prayers of all saints upon the golden altar which was before the throne. 4 And the smoke of the incense, which came with the prayers of the saints, ascended up before God out of the angel's hand. 5 And the angel took the censer, and filled it with fire of the altar, and cast it into the earth: and there were voices, and thunderings, and lightnings, and an earthquake" (8: 3-5).

This highly significant transaction will bear review first. Another special angel comes upon the scene, taking his position before the (golden) altar, having a golden censer. This has a view clearly to priestly prayer—adoration and intercession—before the seat of Jehovah. An abundance of incense is given into this angel's hands, "that he may offer it with the prayers of all saints upon the golden altar before the throne." The R. V. reads, "add it unto the prayers," while the C. V. reads, "that he will be imparting to the prayers." The thought is clearly that of supplementing, reinforcing, rendering effectual. The fumes of this incense from the angel's hand offered with the prayers of saints ascend up before God with acceptance. Taking his censer, the angel fills ("crams," C. V.) it from the fire of the altar and casts it into the earth; thereupon there occur thunders and voices and lightning and an earthquake. Of course this scene is not laid in the earthly temple; it is the highly symbolical picture of "the things in the heavens," described in language taken from the earthly "patterns" thereof which were employed in the Hebrew temple of old.

From this scene we obtain much light upon the significance of the temple offices of old. For instance, the ark within the second veil represented the throne-presence and sovereignty of Christ, Israel's invisible King, the Father's Son and Mediator with man. The golden altar represented the intercessory office of Christ, through whom Israel had approach unto God and through the "much incense" of whose intercession "the prayers of all saints" were rendered effectual. These earthly and material forms did not produce the potent realities, but symbolized them to faith's vision and for faith's expression. While these forms did also foreshadow the incarnate revelation of "the heavenly things" in the Son of man, Jesus Christ, yet the heavenly things themselves did not wait for His incarnation to come into effect and to become available. The "things in the heavens" are from everlasting, they antedate man's existence as provision for his eventual need, and they have been accessible and effectual to all men throughout the history of human need, whether men possessed the Levitical ceremonial or not.

The central and predominant point in this scene is the place belonging to priestly intercession in relation especially to the new and culminating stage of judgments upon the antichristian world now reached in the vision. It is clear that the direful omens of earthly judgments described in v. 5 are directly due to the imprecatory "prayers of all saints," made effectual by the copious incense supplied by our great Intercessor, Jesus Christ, the High Priest in the house of God, whose very prayers of imprecation arise before God as grateful fumes. The fire of God—whether of almighty grace or of almighty vengeance—is thus kindled to white heat to descend into the earth to its appropriate end.

It is simple, then, to see wherein the saints' praying in the name of Jesus Christ and wherein the unstinted power of such prayer, whether for blessing or for cursing, consists. (Vengeance, however, is our God's "strange—unaccustomed—work," Isa. 28:21.) Praying in His name means so praying in the Holy Ghost as to be praying in identity with Christ Jesus Himself, and to be having copiously added to our prayers this holy incense which He alone can supply, which no one can successfully counterfeit, and which no one can safely appropriate with unholy, unlawful hand. See Korah and his company, and Uzziah. Such prayer is not only "the fervent," but also "the effectual prayer of a righteous man" which "availeth much."

There is to be found in Ezekiel a parallel to our present passage. When representing through the prophet the impending outpouring of Jehovah's wrath upon Jerusalem in her destruction by Nebuchadnezzar in 587 B. C. (Ezek. 9), the following symbolism is added, 10:1, 2, 6, 7:1,

"Then I looked, and, behold, in the firmament that was above the head of the cherubim there appeared over them as it were a sapphire stone, as the appearance of the likeness of a throne. 2 And he spake unto the man clothed with linen, and said, Go in between the wheels, even under the cherub, and fill thine hand with coals of fire from between the cherubim, and scatter them over the city. And he went in in my sight. 6 And it came to pass, that when he had commanded the man clothed with linen, saying, Take fire from between the wheels, from between the cherubim; then he went in, and stood beside the wheels. 7 And one cherub stretched forth his hand from between the cherubim unto the fire that was between the cherubim, and took thereof, and put it into the hands of him that was clothed with linen; who took it and went out."

In conclusion, we remind ourselves that already twice before the present passage under consideration the relation of the prayers of saints—imprecatory prayers—to the execution of divine judgment on the antichristian world has been intimated. When first the Lamb "had taken the book, the four beasts and four and twenty elders fell down before the Lamb, having every one of them harps, and *golden vials full of* ("brimming with," C. V.) odors, *which are the prayers of saints*" (Rev. 5: 8). A sample of such prayer is given in 6: 10: "How long, O Lord, holy and true, dost thou not judge and avenge our blood on them that dwell on the earth?" We are reminded of Christ's words as He looked forward to these very events and said, "Shall not God avenge his own elect which cry day and night unto him, though he bear long with them? I tell you he will avenge them speedily" (Luke 18: 7, 8).

"6 And the seven angels which had the seven trumpets prepared themselves to sound. 7 The first angel sounded, and there followed hail and fire mingled with blood, and they were cast upon the earth: and the third part of the trees was burnt up, and all green grass was burnt up. 8 And the second angel sounded, and as it were a great mountain burning with fire was cast into the sea: and the third part of the sea became blood; 9 And the third part of the creatures which were in the sea, and had life, died; and the third part of the ships were destroyed. 10 And the third angel sounded, and there fell a great star from heaven, burning as it were a lamp, and it fell upon the third part of the rivers, and upon the fountains of waters; 11 And the name of the star is called Wormwood: and the third part of the waters became wormwood; and many men died, because they were made bitter. 12 And the fourth angel sounded, and the third part of the sun was smitten, and the third part of the moon, and the third part of the stars; so as the third part of them was darkened, and the day shone not for a third part of it, and the night likewise'' (8: 6-12).

The striking feature of the seventh seal is that its loosing introduces a sevenfold amplification of judgment, inaugurated in seven successive stages by the successive sounding of seven trumpets by angelic trumpeters. From the peculiar descriptions which now follow the question arises, even more urgently than heretofore, whether these and similar descriptions in this book are to be taken literally or figuratively.

It must be admitted that figurative interpretation would be altogether fanciful, conjectural—''private interpretation''—because no authoritative guidance is given for it. Such interpretation proves to be wholly inconclusive because of the bewildering variety of opinions which it breeds. Whereas, in favor of the literal acceptance of these descriptions several sound considerations can be advanced.

1. There are instances in this book in which the context makes it plain that certain terms are to be understood as symbols and in which pains is taken to explain them. For example, take the seven candlesticks and the stars (1: 20); the seven lamps of fire (4: 5); the seven eyes (5: 6). Other terms are known to be symbols by previous Scriptures where they have been used and their meaning has been explained. For instance, the horses and riders, the golden altar, the censer, the incense. This habit of leaving nothing to fancy, to private interpre-

tation,—considering also that this whole book purports to
be a plain revelation to the simple reader and not a production of hidden meaning for the understanding of only
the learned and initiated—suggests that, if we even seek
for hidden and far-fetched meaning, we will surely miss
the real and immediate sense.

2. Should it be claimed that the visions of the Book
of Revelation are to be taken as symbolical, cryptic
representations of the course of Church history through
the centuries, rather than as a literal portrayal of things
which are swiftly to transpire in an extraordinary epoch,
closing the dispensation after its running for centuries
an ordinary course, the following consideration is to be
entertained. This book offers itself as an immediately
intelligible revelation, even to John himself, and to seven
specified churches of his day. Its true meaning must
then be self-evident to any and to all from the day it
was delivered: meaning that is figured out by and dependent upon the light of subsequent times is certainly
mistaken, misleading and false meaning. This book is
expressly called ''prophecy.'' Now prophecy identifies
its fulfillment, but it is not first interpreted by its fulfillment. The things which John saw according to
Chapter 1 were as intelligible to his first readers as to
us; ''the things which are,'' as given in Chapter 2 and
3, were more intelligible to them than they are to us;
if, then, from Chapter 4 on, the book is a revelation ''of
things which shall be hereafter,'' a ''prophecy'' of the
''things which must shortly come to pass,'' ''which must
occur swiftly'' and ''after this,'' we cannot with any
safety inject from our own fancy, or from the ordinary
course of Church history, any meaning which is not
self-evident from the beginning.

3. There is a remarkable similarity between the recorded ten plagues of Egypt and the predicted plagues
of Revelation, very especially those of the portion now in
hand. The object to be accomplished by God through

the two sets of plagues is exactly the same; namely, so to deal with the oppressors of His people as to compel them either to yield to God's demands, or to grow so obdurate in refusal as to bring His swift and final judgment upon their heads. If literal plagues accomplished this end in the one case, why should we doubt their efficacy in the other case and presume to "spiritualize" or symbolize the descriptions as though we could conceive of more effective agencies for God to employ? There is no reason for interpreting figuratively the plagues here presented in prediction that would not hold us to interpret figuratively the same manner of plagues there presented in history.

4. Finally, all the centuries of the Christian age must be put under requisition for the accomplishment of all that figurative interpretation demands, whereas, taking these judgments literally, the case is altogether different and very simple. God's dealings of decisive judgment are always extraordinary, sudden, and swift in execution after long toleration of obstinate wickedness under the ordinary course of things. Those plagues of Egypt occurred all within a brief space of time as compared with the dreary, weary decades and generations of oppression. The account in Exodus shows that different ones of the ten plagues lasted each but a few days, leaving us to infer that all were swift, decisive, terrible blows, of very short duration, and of quick succession. All prophecy agrees in representing just such a time in "the last days"; and the descriptions of Revelation, taken literally, depict abrupt, decisive blows of the Almighty, which are designed to carry almost instant effect.

In taking up these trumpet-judgments, we should recall that, according to 7:3, certain divine inflictions about to be visible were temporarily to be held in abeyance. "Hurt not the earth, neither the sea, nor the trees, till we have sealed the servants of our God in their

foreheads.'' In the progress of the vision this had now
been done, and the time for those inflictions has come;
and it is already indicated what manner of judgments is
to be expected, as well as what is to be the sphere of
their manifestation. The sphere is the physical realm
of the earth, and the agencies to be employed those of the
atmospheric skies directed by angelic control.

THE FIRST TRUMPET, v. 7.

''7 The first angel sounded, and there followed hail and fire
mingled with blood, and they were cast upon the earth: and
the third part of trees was burnt up, and all green grass was
burnt up.''

The first judgment in the new series consists of inflictions from above upon the vegetation beneath. The
physical agencies employed consist of hail and fire,
mingled with blood. Variant translations read, ''the
third part of the earth was burnt up, and the third part
of the trees was burnt up, and all the green grass was
burnt up,'' R. V.

Fractional devastation is characteristic of all six
trumpet-judgments of Chapters 8 and 9, one-third being
the fraction designated in all cases but that of the fifth
trumpet. This means a measured, a moderated, a probationary judgment rather than a final and conclusive
punitive one.

The effect of the first of these judgments is to ruin by
crushing hail, consuming fire and corrupting blood one-
third of the soil, one-third of the plant-life and all the
grass of the area affected. By ''the earth'' we are not
required by Scripture usage to think of the whole globe.
On the contrary, we are probably to think of no more
than the Holy Land, or of ''the earth'' lying between
the Mediterranean Sea and the Indian Ocean, between
the Red Sea and the Euphrates, or at most of the antichristian empire embracing the old imperial world. The

period of these trumpets is that of the brilliant career of the 144,000 sealed Israelites of Chapter 7. This suggests a time of special testing in their land and to their people. "The earth" is then used here probably in the sense in which it is used by Jesus when speaking of the Queen of Sheba, "of the south," coming "from the *ends of the earth*" to hear the wisdom of Solomon. It is the Promised Land in the large sense which has long before in this study been found to embrace the vast quadrangular area of the "Arabian Desert" as described just above. Not necessarily a separate one-third of this area was seen to be devastated, but rather perhaps the whole area in a fraction of one-third.

This judgment closely resembles, while exceeding in dreadfulness, the seventh plague of Egypt (Ex. 9: 22-26, 31, 32):

"22 And the Lord said unto Moses, Stretch forth thine hand toward heaven, that there may be hail in all the land of Egypt, upon man, and upon beast, and upon every herb of the field, throughout the land of Egypt. 23 And Moses stretched forth his rod toward heaven: and the Lord sent thunder and hail, and the fire ran along upon the ground; and the Lord rained hail upon the land of Egypt. 24 So there was hail, and fire mingled with the hail, very grievous, such as there was none like it in all the land of Egypt since it became a nation. 25 And the hail smote throughout all the land of Egypt all that was in the field, both man and beast; and the hail smote every herb of the field, and brake every tree of the field. 26 Only in the land of Goshen, where the children of Israel were, was there no hail...... 31 And the flax and the barley was smitten: for the barley was in the ear, and the flax was bolled. 32. But the wheat and the rye were not smitten: for they were not grown up."

The mixture of the blood with the hail and fire is entirely credible literally when likened to the first plague of Egypt, when Moses smote the Nile and all waters of the land so that "there was blood throughout all the land of Egypt" (Ex. 7: 17-21).

SECOND TRUMPET, VS. 8, 9.

"8 And the second angel sounded, and as it were a great mountain burning with fire was cast into the sea: and the third part of the sea became blood; 9 And the third part of the creatures which were in the sea, and had life, died; and the third part of the ships were destroyed.''

Here, not a literal mountain, but "as it were a mountain," all aflame, is cast into the sea. There being no warrantable reason for treating "the sea" other than as literal, we would reasonably surmise that the Mediterranean is meant. A mammoth mountain-like meteor or meteoric shower may be understood as this flaming mountain. The gases afire were of bloody hue and were seen to turn the water of the sea into blood to the extent of one-third its area and contents, by which living creatures to the extent of one-third were seen to be made to die, while even the shipping in one-third part was seen to be ruined. The plague of blood in Egypt of old referred to above is strikingly similar. "And the fish that was in the river died; and the river stank, and the Egyptians could not drink of the water of the river; and there was blood throughout all the land of Egypt" (Ex. 7:21). Doubtless that history is not more literal than this prophecy, for it is written, "According to the days of thy coming out of the land of Egypt will I shew unto him marvellous things" (Micah 7:15).

THIRD TRUMPET, VS. 10, 11.

"10 And the third angel sounded, and there fell a great star from heaven, burning as it were a lamp, and it fell upon the third part of the rivers, and upon the fountains of waters; 11 And the name of the star is called Wormwood: and the third part of the waters became wormwood; and many men died of the waters, because they were made bitter."

A great star is seen falling out of the skies, burning like a torch, smiting in one-third part the streams and springs of water; that is, the supplies of drinking water.

The effect upon the water is to turn them to absinthe, a deadly poison, from which many men were seen to die when drinking it. From Scriptural usage it would be permissible, perhaps preferable, to understand this star to be an angel of judgment in person. The effect of the infliction, so far as spoiling the drinking waters is concerned, is like to, only much more extreme than, that included in the plagues of blood with which Egypt was smitten of old.

FOURTH TRUMPET, v. 12.

"And the fourth angel sounded, and the third part of the sun was smitten, and the third part of the moon, and the third part of the stars; so as the third part of them was darkened, and the day shone not for a third part of it, and the night likewise."

This judgment consists of some physical infliction upon all the visible luminaries of the skies by which the diurnal illumination of the earth was seen to be obliterated to the extent of one-third. Suggestions of such an appalling phenomenon are not lacking in history; for example, the "Dark Day" or "Black Friday" of New England, May 19, 1780, which many in terror conceived to be the great day of judgment, or "Doomsday." The most impressive suggestion of this coming judgment is to be found in Ex. 10: 21-23, the ninth of the plagues of Egypt, that of darkness.

"21 And the Lord said unto Moses, Stretch out thine hand toward heaven, that there may be darkness over the land of Egypt, even darkness which may be felt. 22 And Moses stretched forth his hand toward heaven; and there was a thick darkness in all the land of Egypt three days: 23 They saw not one another, neither rose any from his place for three days: but all the children of Israel had light in their dwellings."

Furthermore, the prophetical Scriptures abound with descriptions of frightful and fateful atmospheric and solar phenomena as marking the Lord's judicial dealings with the earth in the last days. For example:

"The day of the Lord cometh . . .; a day of darkness and of gloominess, a day of clouds and of thick darkness, . . . the sun and the moon shall be dark, and the stars shall withdraw their shining: . . . And I will shew wonders in the heavens and in the earth, blood, and fire, and pillars of smoke. The sun shall be turned into darkness, and the moon into blood, before the great and terrible day of the Lord is come" (Joel 2: 1, 10, 30, 31).

No question is to be entertained of the physical literalness of terrestrial and celestial phenomena in those coming days, which will beggar all preceding horrors of similar kind. Neither is it necessary or possible to offer scientific explanations more than suggestively and partially, because it is to be a special, brief time when Jesus Christ "ariseth to shake terribly the earth." His personal relationship to it all, who is the creator and only upholder of physical nature, leaves us simply standing in awe before the prospect of physical phenomena of unprecedented, unexplained character,—inexplicable in character just because they are judicial instruments designed by the Almighty Himself for this unparalleled occasion. He will then have to do a new thing, to "do his work, his strange work, and bring to pass his act, his *strange* act" (Isa. 28: 21). Could we explain by anything familiar or even conceivable to us, it would not be "his strange act," His unprecedented work, foreign to any previous way of His.

"And I beheld and heard an angel flying through the midst of heaven, saying with a loud voice, Woe, woe, woe, to the inhabiters of the earth, by reason of the other voices of the trumpet of the three angels, which are yet to sound!" (8: 13).

It will be remembered that the first four seals constituted a group by themselves, the milder judgments of their series. The angel now introduced in the vision ("one eagle," as the variant readings run) announces at this point that the three remaining judgments are to be far heavier, so direful as to call for the terrifying annunciation as, like a great air ship, he swiftly flies through mid-air: ''Woe, woe, woe, to the inhabiters of the earth!''

Fifth Trumpet,—First ''Woe,'' 9:1-12.

''1 And the fifth angel sounded, and I saw a star fall from heaven unto the earth: and to him was given the key of the bottomless pit. 2 And he opened the bottomless pit: and there arose a smoke out of the pit, as the smoke of a great furnace; and the sun and the air were darkened by reason of the smoke of the pit. 3 And there came out of the smoke locusts upon the earth: and unto them was given power, as the scorpions of the earth have power. 4 And it was commanded them that they should not hurt the grass of the earth, neither any green thing, neither any tree; but only those men which have not the seal of God in their foreheads. 5 And to them it was given that they should not kill them, but that they should be tormented five months: and their torment was as the torment of a scorpion, when he striketh a man. 6 And in those days shall men seek death, and shall not find it; and shall desire to die, and death shall flee from them. 7 And the shapes of the locusts were like unto horses prepared unto battle; and on their heads were as it were crowns like gold, and their faces were as the faces of men. 8 And they had hair as the hair of women, and their teeth were as the teeth of lions. 9 And they had breastplates, as it were breastplates of iron; and the sound of their wings was as the sound of chariots of many horses running to battle. 10 And they had tails like unto scorpions, and there were stings in their tails: and their power was to hurt men five months. 11 And they had a king over them, which is the angel of the bottomless pit, whose name in the Hebrew tongue is Abaddon, but in the Greek tongue hath his name Apollyon. 12 One woe is past; and, behold, there come two woes more hereafter.''

Here is intensified severity of judgment, described at much greater length and denominated as the first ''woe.''

The ''star'' that is seen to fall from the skies, is expressly shown to be a person,—one of God's ministers of judgment. He carries authority and power to unlock ''the bottomless pit''; that is, the molten interior of our globe. We are to understand that some convulsion is to occur, by which the earth's crust will be opened where it is so appointed by our Lord.   Thus a titanic volcano is to be created, which will belch forth smoke to darken the atmosphere and obscure the sun.   The writer, who lived in the region of the awful fires which occurred in northeastern Wisconsin in 1871—where for three weeks the sun was rarely seen and then only as a globe of blood, when fire burrowed under ground, leaped in the air over great distances, lapped up bodies of water, and left the country destitute of leaf or blade of green, without the chirp of bird or any living thing—can imagine something of the frightful literalness of this description.

Out of the smoke will come locusts in countless swarms, reminding us again of the plagues of Egypt (Ex. 10: 12-15) :

"12 And the Lord said unto Moses, Stretch out thine hand over the land of Egypt for the locusts, that they may come up upon the land of Egypt, and eat every herb of the land, even all that the hail hath left.   13 And Moses stretched forth his rod over the land of Egypt and the Lord brought an east wind upon the land all that day, and all that night; and when it was morning, the east wind brought the locusts.   14 And the locusts went up over all the land of Egypt, and rested in all the coasts of Egypt: very grievous were they; before them there were no such locusts as they, neither after them shall be such.   15 For they covered the face of the whole earth, so that the land was darkened; and they did eat every herb of the land, and all the fruit of the trees which the hail had left: and there remained not any green thing in the trees or in the herbs of the field, through all the land of Egypt.''

These coming locusts are to have a scorpion-like sting, and it is to be their mission, passing by their natural field of devastation,—the vegetation—to torment unregenerate and obdurate men with their sting.   This plague is to last five months, a very protracted period for such a literal plague.   They will not kill, but they will so torture their victims as to drive them to seek death, only to be tantalized with disappointment.   Preternatural

resemblances as well as tormenting powers of these
creatures are described in vs. 7-10. They are to have as
king over them the angel of the bottomless pit, whose
name after the Hebrew is Abaddon, after the Greek
Apollyon, meaning destroyer. This angel may well be
taken as one of the primeval fallen angels mentioned in
Jude 6 as reserved in chains under darkness.   The
headship of a wicked spirit from the pit lends color to
the idea that these locusts themselves will be incarnated
imps from the pit. Of course demons can enter into and
supernaturally affect locusts as well as swine.

Before proceeding to the second "woe," we may
suitably introduce a prediction of Joel which evidently
refers to these days and to these agencies of coming
judgment upon the realm of the Anti-Christ. The description of Joel is so strikingly similar to the descriptions of the two "woes" of our present chapter, that we
cannot doubt the approximate identity in time and
character of the two. An extended quotation from Joel
will be helpful.

"1 Blow ye the trumpet in Zion, and sound an alarm in my
holy mountain: let all the inhabitants of the land tremble: for
the day of the Lord cometh, for it is nigh at hand; 2 A day
of darkness and gloominess, a day of clouds and of thick darkness, as the morning spread upon the mountains: a great people
and a strong; there hath not been ever the like, neither shall
be any more after it, even to the years of many generations.
3 A fire devoureth before them; and behind them a flame burneth;
the land is as the garden of Eden before them, and behind them
a desolate wilderness; yea, and nothing shall escape them. 4 The
appearance of them is as the appearance of horses; and as
horsemen so shall they run. 5 Like the noise of chariots on the
tops of mountains shall they leap, like the noise of a flame of
fire that devoureth the stubble, as a strong people set in battle
array. 6 Before their face the people shall be much pained: all
faces shall gather blackness. 7 They shall run like mighty men
of war; and they shall march every one on his ways, and they
shall not break their ranks: 8 Neither shall one thrust another;
they shall walk every one in his path: and when they fall upon
the sword, they shall not be wounded. 9 They shall run to and

fro in the city; they shall run upon the wall, they shall climb up upon the houses, they shall enter in at the windows like a thief. 10 The earth shall quake before them; the heavens shall tremble: the sun and the moon shall be dark, and the stars shall withdraw their shining: 11 And the Lord shall utter his voice before his army: for his camp is very great: for he is strong that executeth his word: for the day of the Lord is great and very terrible; and who can abide it?'' (Joel 2: 1-11).

SIXTH TRUMPET, SECOND "WOE," 9: 13-21.

''13 And the sixth angel sounded, and I heard a voice from the four horns of the golden altar which is before God, 14 Saying to the sixth angel which had the trumpet, Loose the four angels which are bound in the great river Euphrates. 15 And the four angels were loosed, which were prepared for an hour, and a day, and a month, and a year, for to slay the third part of men. 16 And the number of the army of the horsemen were two hundred thousand thousand: and I heard the number of them. 17 And thus I saw the horses in the vision, and them that sat on them, having breastplates of fire, and of jacinth, and brimstone: and the heads of the horses were as the heads of lions: and out of their mouths issued fire and smoke and brimstone. 18 By these three was the third part of men killed, by the fire, and by the smoke, and by the brimstone, which issued out of their mouths. 19 For their power is in their mouth, and in their tails: for their tails were like unto serpents, and had heads, and with them they do hurt. 20 And the rest of the men which were not killed by these plagues yet repented not of the works of their hands, that they should not worship devils, and idols of gold, and silver, and brass, and stone, and of wood; which neither can see, nor hear, nor walk: 21 Neither repented they of their murders, nor of their sorceries, nor of their fornication, nor of their thefts.''

The fateful proclamation announces the close of one ''woe'' and the imminence of two more. It is noteworthy that the command for the execution of this second ''woe'' was heard to proceed from ''the horns of the golden altar [the altar of incense] which is before God.'' This implies that this judgment results from the fearful power of imprecatory prayer. The voice of command ''from the *four horns* of the golden altar'' signifies the full authority and power of Christ Jesus responding to believing appeal for divine intervention through His name.

This voice of power commands the sixth trumpeter to "loose the four angels which are bound in the great river Euphrates." We take these to be powerful evil and satanic spirits. We need not hesitate to recognize such a thing as the localization of angels, good or bad. The Bible abundantly testifies to the definite appointment of good angels and to the localization of evil spirits, in relation to human or animal bodies, to districts of country, etc. These four angels were seen to be not only localized but held bound "in [or "at," 1911] the great river Euphrates." Moreover, their confinement was seen to be related to this service, and for an exact point of time—year, month, day, and very hour. The service will be "to slay the third part of men." It is not called for to consider this to be one-third of all mankind, but only of the people of the areas in the East which are to be the central theater of the apocalyptical judgments.

This destructive judgment is to be accomplished by means of an "army of......horsemen," two hundred million strong in exact number. Our imagination cannot harmonize the description with natural horses and human riders. The quotation taken from Joel not far back helps us to see under this remarkable description vast hordes of preternatural creatures more or less similar to the locusts of the first woe, and yet far more terrible and destructive. The expression, "these plagues" (v. 20), confirms the view that this vast cavalry force is to be classed with the locusts in kind rather than to be taken as literal horses and human riders. The characteristics of their deadly power can be still better comprehended if the idea be entertained that these are to be demonized creatures.

Just as in the case of the plagues of Egypt, the most important thing in this chapter to be noted is that "these plagues" of the first and second woes will be

designed to convict, soften and subdue wicked and rebellious men, but that, on the contrary, the actual effect
will be disappointing and futile, inasmuch as those
escaping death will go on defiantly and more obdurately
in devil-worship, idolatry and most heinous sins and
crimes.

In these last two scourges we seem to have a hitherto
unparalleled admixture of the natural, the preternatural,
or monstrous, and the supernatural, the supernatural
being, on the one hand, of God planning and employing
these agencies,—some holy and some devilish—and, on
the other hand, of Satan lending tormenting, death-deal-
ing virus even to animal creatures.

CHAPTER V.

THE SECOND CONTEMPORANEOUS INTERCALATION, CHAPTERS 10:1—11:14.

A CAREFUL reading of this whole section will justify its treatment as a passage not belonging to the regular course of the judgments upon the antichristian world, although dealing with most important matters contemporaneous therewith, which need to be brought to light before proceeding with the regular line of progress. That this long passage adds nothing to the progress of the sixth trumpet, or second woe judgments, is evident from 11:14, which notates the "second woe," described in 9:13-21, as finished, with "the third woe" to be immediately taken up.

As was seen in Chapter 7, so here again the sphere of revelation is shifted from that of judgment upon the godless to the contemporaneous course of things among the godly of that fearful coming time. Chapter 10, while belonging to this interjected section, yet is introductory and is anticipatory in outlook.

THE IMMINENT FINISH OF THE MYSTERY OF GOD ANNOUNCED, 10:1-7.

"1 And I saw another mighty angel come down from heaven, clothed with a cloud: and a rainbow was upon his head, and his face was as it were the sun, and his feet as pillars of fire: 2 And he had in his hand a little book open: and he set his right foot upon the sea, and his left foot on the earth, 3 And cried with a loud voice, as when a lion roareth: and when he had cried, seven thunders uttered their voices. 4 And when the seven thunders had uttered their voices, I was about to write: and I heard a voice from heaven saying unto me, Seal up those things which the seven thunders uttered, and write them not. 5 And the angel which I saw stand upon the sea and upon the earth lifted up his hand to heaven, 6 And sware by him that liveth

for ever and ever, who created heaven, and the things that
therein are, and the earth, and the things that therein are, and
the sea, and the things which are therein, that there should be
time no longer: 7 But in the days of the voice of the seventh
angel, when he shall begin to sound, the mystery of God should
be finished, as he hath declared to his servants the prophets.''

This is the second instance in which the Bible presents
a vivid angelic photograph which compels one to awe,—
almost to the homage which is due to the Deity alone.
Human conceptions are so puny, so trivial, so bemeaning,
so profane almost.   Angels, even God Himself, we commonly hold in such unworthy regard, that it is well to
have such actual vivid revelations of these beings on
record,—if such revelation never occurs in our personal
experience—to cause us to walk softly and reverently
before the unseen presences from the heavenly world.
God even, and angels too, are so humbly engaged in
ministry to us feeble mortals, that we are in danger of
behaving ourselves unseemly before them.   Did they but
disclose to us the hidings of their power, the beams of
their glory, the utterances of their intelligence and feeling, we would begin to know what worms we are before
God and to what vast a degree it is true that we are
''lower than the angels.''

In the vision of this mighty angel is combined entrancing beauty with glory too dazzling to behold stead-
fastly and with power that is paralysing to the senses.
The vesture of soft, cloudlike radiance and the rainbow
coronet invite one's confiding contemplation, although
the face almost forbids human gaze because of its dazzling, blinding radiance, and even the feet glow with the
fire of moral refinement almost too much for the most
sanctified man to behold in the flesh with composure.

Reference has been made to another angelic revelation
found in the Bible quite comparable with this one.   It is
recorded in Dan. 10: 5-10:

''5 Then I lifted up mine eyes and looked, and behold a
certain man clothed in linen, whose loins were girded with fine

gold of Uphaz: 6 His body was also like the beryl, and his face as the appearance of lightning, and his eyes as lamps of fire, and his arms and feet like the color of polished brass, and the voice of his words like the voice of a multitude. 7 And I Daniel alone saw the vision: for the men that were with me saw not the vision: but a great quaking fell upon them, so that they fled to hide themselves. 8 Therefore I was left alone, and saw this great vision, and there remained no strength in me: for my comeliness was turned in me into corruption, and I retained no strength. 9 Yet heard I the voice of his words: and when I heard the voice of his words, then was I in a deep sleep on my face, and my face toward the ground. 10 And, behold, a hand touched me, which set me upon my knees and upon the palms of my hands.''

THE ANGEL'S AUTHORITY, VS. 2-4.

This is a most imposing expression of unusual authority viewed from the earthly standpoint. The "little book open" implies the contrary of "sealed orders," of veiled or secret diplomacy; it implies the contrary of governmental purposes which were in danger of being frustrated through untimely discovery. This angel is seen to be on an errand of public moment calling for immediate universal attention.

As this is being written the French military has just "set his right foot upon" the "Ruhr Basin" in Germany. What demonstration of power and authority! But this demonstration of human authority, taking over in the name of a government some earthly territory, or any other demonstration of authority known in history, appears ridiculous in comparison with the demonstration here set before us. The angel—superb in person and appearance as he is—yet dramatically exercises an authority far above anything inherent in himself. He will, in the day not far distant, "take over" land and sea in the name of the glorified Son of man who, even before leaving the earth, said, "All power is given unto me in heaven and on earth."

And that "loud voice, as when a lion roareth"!

Has God made the king of beasts, and does He suffer him to hold sway in the wilds,—terrorizing beast or man that is so unfortunate as to cross his way—or to roar behind bars in the menagerie, just to give us an idea and to keep us in remembrance of the angelic voices, which are in "that day" to strike terror to the stoutest hearts on earth?

But what is the roar of a lion in comparison with rumbling, rolling, cracking thunder! Responding to the angel's lion-like voice were heard in the vision—shall be heard in reality full soon—the voices of seven angelic THUNDERERS. And the thunders will be intelligible, as they were in the vision. John heard intelligible communication through these voices of thunder, but he was arrested from writing it for us. We will hear them in "that day."

THE ANGEL'S PROCLAMATION, VS. 5-7.

That this mighty angel, who otherwise might easily be mistaken for our glorified Lord—more than once called in the Bible "the angel of the Lord"—is yet but a creature, is put beyond question by the language in which he was heard in the vision to authenticate his message. He sware by the Eternal, the Creator of skies, earth, sea, and all things in them. (Of course, "heaven" here is to be understood as that heaven—our skies—which is so often in the Bible directly associated with the earth and even with the sea also.)

The import of the proclamation is that "that day" has now arrived. The declaration, "that there should be time no longer," is to be taken in the light of what follows; namely, that the sounding of the trumpet of the seventh angel just imminent would open the final stage of divine accomplishment as revealed by God's servants the prophets. "Time no longer," then, does not mean that the end of all time is viewed as come, but only that delays are over, all preparatory stages fulfilled, and nothing conditional left that "the mystery of God should be finished."

Just what is meant by "the mystery of God" which is to be forthwith finished is to be gathered from the qualifying expression, "as he hath declared to his servants the prophets." The R. V. is very helpful here: "according to the *good tidings* which he declared to his servants the prophets." The C. V. runs a little more concisely and strikingly: "as he *evangelizes* to his own slaves and the prophets." All these translations agree in identifying the "mystery of God" as the *climax of the Gospel,* the finale of the glad tidings from God to His servants and His preachers. In brief, this is the familiar "gospel of the kingdom," the glad tidings of the visible reappearing of God's Son in the fulness of divine glory and power to reign in the earth, and of the coming of His saints with Him. This meaning is demanded by the whole objective of this Book of Revelation. It is true to the full Gospel as revealed by God to His servants from Adam down and as preached by all Spirit-moved prophets and preachers from Enoch to the present day. The point was here reached in the revelation given to John for the dramatic conclusion to be announced in the fulfillment of the mystery of God, which fulfillment had been begun by the first appearing of Jesus Christ. We have confirmation of this explanation of the mystery in Rom. 16: 25, 26, which at first reading seems to be somewhat involved and mystifying: "Now to him that is of power to stablish you according to my gospel, and the preaching of Jesus Christ, according to the revelation of the mystery, which was kept secret since the world began, but now is made manifest, and by the Scriptures of the prophets, according to the commandment of the everlasting God, made known to all nations for the obedience of faith."

The burden, then, of the mighty angel's proclamation was that the transactions to ensue directly upon the sounding of the seventh trumpet were to bring in without further delay the final revelation of God's Son on the earth, which has been the hidden purpose of God from before the foundation of the world, and which has been the crowning element of the Gospel throughout all human ages. That this juncture, in the progress of the revelation of the things to transpire rapidly in the last days, should be marked by so solemn and impressive an announcement, shows that the stage yet remaining is to be expected to constitute a distinctive epoch, unparallelled, in relation to which all else is anticipatory and preparatory.

THE LITTLE BOOK, VS. 8-11.

"8 And the voice which I heard from heaven spake unto me again, and said, Go and take the little book which is open in the hand of the angel which standeth upon the sea and upon the earth. 9 And I went unto the angel, and said unto him, Give me the little book. And he said unto me, Take it, and eat it up; and it shall make thy belly bitter, but it shall be in thy mouth sweet as honey. 10 And I took the little book out of the angel's hand, and ate it up; and it was in my mouth sweet as honey: and as soon as I had eaten it, my belly was bitter. 11 And he said unto me, Thou must prophesy again before many peoples, and nations, and tongues and kings."

It is evident that the little book has immediate reference to the closing epoch of the last days just mentioned above. And the book being seen "open" shows that the things contained therein have come due to be publicly accomplished. Of course this is the fact in the progress of the vision, not in the actual occurrences themselves.

The same voice—that of our Lord Jesus—which had abruptly forbidden John to record the utterances of the seven thunderers (v. 4), bade John to approach the mighty angel and to take from his hand the little book. Upon obeying this direction, the angel directs John to take the little book and to eat it up, adding that it would be bitter to John's stomach but sweet as honey in his mouth. This, as John took the book and ate it up, proved to be true,—it was as honey in his mouth, as gall in his stomach. It was then explained to him that the eating of this book meant that he had a new and distinctive body of prophecy to deliver "before ["over," R. V.] many peoples, and nations, and tongues, and kings." It also means that, while as God's word this communication should be like honey to his own taste, yet after the assimilation of it it should be like gall.

The calling and experience of Jeremiah lends to us here much that is helpful.

The young Jeremiah was informed by the Lord that even before his birth he had been "sanctified......and ordained...... a *prophet unto the nations.*" Although a prophet in Judah and mostly engaged directly in addressing apostatizing Judah, yet his prophetic office was preëminently of international, world-wide scope: "See I have this day set thee over the nations and over the kingdoms, to root out, and to pull down, and to destroy, and to throw down, to build, and to plant" (1:10). It was not Jeremiah's task to do those mighty things in a living, personal way, but as the one through whom Christ could lodge in the earth, in permanent public expression, His purpose with regard to the nations of that general segment of human history. We may see this most strikingly illustrated in the twenty-fifth chapter of Jeremiah.

And very sweet and very bitter both was Jeremiah's experience in becoming a prophet of Christ's word for those days. "Thy words were found," says he, in 15:16, "and I did eat them; and thy word was unto me the joy and rejoicing of mine heart: for I am called by thy name, O Lord of hosts." Yet this happy reminiscence is uttered in the same breath with the bitter complaint, "O Lord, thou knowest: remember me, and visit me, and revenge me of my persecutors; take me not away in thy longsuffering: know that for thy sake I have suffered rebuke" (v. 15). His persecutors brought him to where he cried, "I am in derision daily, every one mocketh me......because the word of the Lord was made a reproach unto me, and a derision daily." He even felt driven to renounce his commission: "Then I said, I will not make mention of him, nor speak any more in his name." However, he adds, "his word was in mine heart as a burning fire shut up in my bones, and I was weary with forbearing, and I could not stay" (20:7-9). How impressively have Jeremiah's international, worldwide prophecies been fulfilled!

Even more closely parallel and illuminating in some respects is the case of Ezekiel. He was called of Jesus Christ to a "rebellious nation......impudent children and stiff hearted." He was warned not to be "rebellious like that rebellious house." Then follows the symbolical manner of his endowment for his prophetic work:

"8 Open thy mouth, and eat that I give thee. 9 And when I looked, behold, a hand was sent unto me; and lo, a roll of a book was therein; 10 And he spread it before me; and it was written within and without: and there was written therein lamentations, and mourning, and woe. 1 Moreover he said unto me, Son of man, eat that thou findest; eat this roll, and go speak unto the house of Israel. 2 So I opened my mouth, and he caused me to eat the roll. 3 And he said unto me, Son of man, cause thy belly to eat, and fill thy bowels with this roll that I give thee. Then did I eat it, and it was in my mouth as honey for sweetness" (2:8—3:3).

To the servant who heeds his master's call to receive and deliver the word of God to his fellow-men, there is sweetness for him to taste, but there is bitterness also to come to his soul for the sake of that word, "when tribulation or persecution ariseth because of the word." Even the dreadful judgments of God's word, whether those of temporal character or that of eternal duration, are sweet to the taste of a heart in unison with God and to a loyal preacher. He will not fail to declare the whole counsel of God, even though he be made a savor "of death unto death," as well as "of life unto life." "How sweet are thy words unto my taste! yea, sweeter than honey to my mouth'' (Ps. 119: 103). This sweetness is not governed by the palatableness of the word to natural sentiment, but to the fact that it is God's word received by a mind and heart perfectly accordant with Him and His every word. The loyal follower of Jesus is not responsive to expurgated editions of God's word or to a "Shorter Bible."

In the case before us, John was in vision called in this dramatic way to add to the prophecies,—both beneficent and dire—which he has left on record up to the present point in the Book of Revelation, another body of bitter-sweet concerning the "many peoples, and nations, and tongues and kings" of the last days. From the manner of designation we are left to take the portion of the Book of Revelation embracing the period of the third woe, or of the seventh trumpet, as constituting a momentous, direful, epochal prophecy by itself.

THE TWO WITNESSES, 11: 1-14.

"1 And there was given me a reed like unto a rod: and the angel stood, saying, Rise, and measure the temple of God, and the altar, and them that worship therein. 2 But the court which is without the temple leave out, and measure it not; for it is given unto the Gentiles: and the holy city shall they tread under foot forty and two months. 3 And I will give power unto my two witnesses, and they shall prophesy a thousand two hundred and threescore days, clothed in sackcloth. 4 These are the two olive trees, and the two candlesticks standing before the God of the earth. 5 And if any man will hurt them, fire proceedeth out of their mouth, and devoureth their enemies: and if any man will hurt them, he must in this manner be killed. 6 These have power to shut heaven, that it rain not in the days of their prophecy: and have power over waters to turn them to blood, and to smite the earth with plagues, as often as they will. 7 And when they shall have finished their testimony, the beast that ascendeth out of the bottomless pit shall make war against them, and shall overcome them, and kill them. 8 And their dead bodies shall lie in the street of the great city, which spiritually is called Sodom, and Egypt, where also our Lord was crucified. 9 And they of the people and kindreds and tongues and nations shall see their dead bodies three days and a half, and shall not suffer their dead bodies to be put in graves. 10 And they that dwell upon the earth shall rejoice over them. and make merry, and shall send gifts one to another; because these two prophets tormented them that dwelt on the earth. 11 After three days and a half the spirit of life from God entered into them, and they stood upon their feet; and great fear fell upon them which saw them. 12 And they heard a great voice from heaven saying unto them, Come up hither. And they ascended up to heaven in a cloud; and their enemies beheld them. 13 And the same hour was there a great earthquake, and the tenth part of the city fell, and in the earthquake were slain of men seven thousand: and the remnant were affrighted, and gave glory to the God of heaven. 14 The second woe is past; and, behold, the third woe cometh quickly.''

This is a very important contribution to our knowledge of the course of things along the Jewish line during the first half of the last seven years—Daniel's seventieth week—before our Lord's return to the earth. As has been said, this passage brings the vision no further forward, but it does throw upon the screen a new and thrilling picture of international conditions revolving about Jerusalem, the Jewish capital, which will obtain during a period of three and one-half years. The time measurement of ''forty-two months,'' or ''a thousand two hundred and threescore days,'' delimits the period of time embraced, and the expression, ''the great city......where also our Lord was crucified,'' identifies the city of Jerusalem as the center of the events.

The angel's direction (v. 1), to ''measure the temple of God, and the altar, and them that worship therein,'' implies with one quick, graphic stroke great and important developments to take place in relation to Jerusalem and to the Jews in the closing epoch of this age. Jerusalem will again be the Jews' own capital, their national center. There will be again in full construction and use a temple of worship, an altar and the ceremonies of sacrifice. What was cut off in 70 A. D. will be once more in operation religiously speaking.

This is not a new disclosure altogether; Old and New Testament prophecies descant largely upon such developments. In 2 Thess. 2, it is clearly implied that a temple will be standing again, as "the temple of God," which "that man of sin," Anti-Christ, will sacrilegiously invade, "showing himself that he is God." Our Lord, in His great Olivet prophecy plainly implied all that has been stated above. See Matt. 24: 15-22. This last passage is based upon extensive representations to Daniel, especially 8: 10-14 and 9: 27. With all these passages Zechariah agrees in substance, while enlarging upon the picture with other particulars. See 12: 2-5; 14: 1-5, 6.

The direction given by the angel (v. 2) concerning the court which is without the temple proper—to "leave out, and measure it not"—indicates that the act of measuring signifies taking holy possession in dedication unto God. This is corroborated by the reason given for not measuring the outer court: "for it is given unto the Gentiles." The court will not be holy ground, but a profane place, and not just as a place of near approach for piously inclined Gentiles, but as a place from which hostile and impious Gentiles will not be debarred. This is the more evident from the manner of expression just following: "And the holy city shall they tread under foot forty and two months."

The situation of the Jews in their national capital, and even in their temple privileges, is to be galling and humiliating during all the three and one-half years, because of the jostling, threatening throngs of Gentiles who will be barred only from pressing into the very temple itself. It is to be recalled that Daniel (9: 27) prophesies that "the prince that shall come"—the Anti-Christ— "shall confirm the [a] covenant with many for one week," seven years. That is, the Anti-Christ will conclude a political compact with the mass of the Jews for the time embraced in Daniel's seventieth week. This treaty includes religious terms also; but our passage shows that even from the beginning these terms will in a galling way restrict the natural privileges and sanctities of the Jews. It will be like a sheepfold with wolves prowling and barking all about its very walls.

It is covering this period of one-half seven years— only expressed in days instead of months—that a remarkable ministry of prophecy, in word and in mighty deed, will be provided by our Lord. ''And I shall be endowing my two witnesses and they will be prophesying a thousand, two hundred and sixty days'' (C. V.). It is significantly added, ''clothed in sackcloth.'' What does this imply?

It is to be recognized that these representatives of Christ Jesus would by this penitential garb be expressing, not only their abhorrence of the Gentile profanation of the city and of the temple court, but also and chiefly their distress over the grievous spiritual state of their own people, on account of which this galling and perilous condition will exist. All Scriptures forecast a hardness, a blindness, an obduracy and an apostasy among the Jews of the last days so unparalleled that Jeremiah's heart-breaking situation will appear mild in comparison with that of these two witnesses. Yet in these very years of awful spiritual corruption—the final ripening for judgment—there will be given through these two witnesses an abundance of the Holy Spirit and of the light of the truth. For ''These are the two olive trees, and the two candlesticks standing before the God of the earth'' (v. 4).

Even as our Lord, in clear foresight and prevenient grace, had His timely witness for desperate days in Enoch, in Noah, in Moses, in Elijah, in Jeremiah, in John the Baptist,—as well as in others in more modern times —so likewise will our Lord not be without other timely witnesses in the last days of Israel's probation. It is to the glory of Christ Jesus that he never leaves Himself without witness, and that He is never at a loss for competent ministry at the right time in any emergency.

The defensive and the punitive powers of these two prophets, as described in vs. 5, 6, are extraordinary, even when compared with those of old-time prophets. They will sum up in themselves all the functions and signs of previous great prophets. Like Elijah, who called down fire to destroy the successive fifties sent by King Ahaziah to fetch him, these two prophets will by word of mouth smite to death with miraculous fire whoever shall attempt to harm them. Like Elijah, they will shut up heaven from raining, and like Moses they will turn earth's waters into blood and smite the earth with any calamity they may desire.

Up to this point we have been left to assume that the judgments of previous chapters will be inflicted otherwise than by human instrumentality. But the mighty punitive deeds here ascribed to these two witnesses are to be taken due account of in relation to these foregoing judgments. It comes to light that, during the progress of the six seals and of the first six trumpets of the seventh seal, Israel, although in treaty relations with the world-rule and under ostensible support from the same, yet is to stand under a hostile and treacherous menace from that rule, which will be held in measurable check only by these two men of faith and godly might. The likeness of their inflictions here depicted to the judgments upon the antichristian world previously described is very striking. And a clearer conception is now possible of the reason for the sealing of the twelve thousand from each tribe of Israel and of the part to be played by them during the era of the six trumpets, when outward stress from increasing Gentile rage and the greater strain from treacherous, apostatizing Jewish brethren will call for "servants of our God" intrepid in faith, unflinching in valor.

But again it will prove true, as one has said, that "God needs no great man." Enoch, Moses, Elijah

pass away, generally just when to man's view it seems
that they can least be spared; but it is not to God's loss
or cost, neither is He so exhausted in resources as to need
to send them back to earth's toil and conflict again. And
so these two witnesses are available just when God wants
them, and they will continue only until, as Jesus Christ
views it, "they shall have finished their testimony." A
revelation was at this point in the vision given to John
which is here first divulged in the Bible. It is here in-
cidentally disclosed that the ruler of the nations in the
days of these two witnesses—the Anti-Christ—is to be a
resurrected man, one that "ascendeth out of the bottomless pit." He is called "the beast" after the Scriptural
conception of the ravenous, devouring spirit of santanized
world-rulers.

The bottomless pit can be found nowhere else but in
the molten interior of this earthly globe. Thither Korah,
Dathan and Abiram with their company went down alive
bodily. Thither the legion of demons which possessed
the Gadarene begged not yet to be cast out. This pit is
described in Ezekiel (32:17-32) as "the nether parts of
the earth," whither the world-rulers of ancient times
are described as going down from their earthly glory.
The particular private individual or historic celebrity,
to be resurrected for final earthly dominion as the Anti-
Christ, will, of course, be the one of Christ's own choice,
even as He chose Judas Iscariot to fulfill, as "a familiar
friend," the dastardly task of betrayal before ordained
for him to fulfill.

The mysterious origin of the Anti-Christ easily accounts for the peculiar satanic witchery of his pretensions to antichristian world-rule. He will have good
ground for claiming following in preference to that
Christ which "liveth and was dead." It would not be
strange for supernatural powers to mark his person and
his operations. All the more apparent does it become
what a conflict the one hundred and forty-four thousand,

other heroes of faith, and especially the two witnesses, will have to meet, and how great will be their victories.

"Victories," Christian victories,—whether in the pre-christian dispensation (See Heb. 11) or in the Christian dispensation—have never been substantiated by the criterion of saving the body from destruction, but rather by keeping the faith at cost of bodily life for the sake of "a better resurrection." Hence we read concerning the two witnesses, "And when they shall have finished their testimony, the beast that cometh out of the bottomless pit shall make war against them." But that will soon prove to be a bad stroke of policy on the beast's part.

In a strange but very appropriate way will their bodies "lie in state" in the Sodomized, Egyptianized city "where also our Lord was crucified." In the very street of the great city shall the two corpses lie, exposed to the ribald gaze of the motley throngs crowding in holiday revelry the throughfares of Jerusalem. For "three days and an half"—exactly a day for each year of their irresistible prophetic repulse to the furious beast, their invincible *Ne passeront pas!* ("They shall not pass!")—their lifeless forms will be compulsorily kept from burial for a public show.

Those will be the days when international preparations for Israel's extinction will so far have matured, that Jerusalem will be the rendezvous of "the people and kindreds and tongues and nations." All nations will thus have eye-witnesses to the fact of the actual death of these two holy men. And the telegraph lines, the cables, the radios will be "hot" with the "great news" from Jerusalem, while over all the earth there will be a general merry-making, a time of mutual congratulation and of making gifts because of this event. Why? "Because these two prophets tormented them that dwelt on the earth." This reveals, at least largely, the secret of the human agency to be employed by the Lord in inflicting the judgments in the earth of the first half of the last seven years before Christ's appearing.

But heaven's turn to laugh comes. Nothing so spectacular will ever up to this time have occurred. Before the sightseers of all nations, in broad daylight, the two prophets suddenly spring alive to their feet under the resurrection touch of the Spirit of Christ. All faces become blanched with fear. Further awe and apprehension is inspired by the sound of a commanding voice from the sky: "Come up hither!" Other raptures presumably will have occurred without public sight thereof, but these two prophets will ascend in full public view. At the same time the earth will rock with terrific *temblors,* by which one-tenth of the city will fall in ruins and seven thousand lives perish. The remaining multitudes in a convulsion of terror will ascribe involuntary glory unto God instead of customary cursings. Thus will end, on different line of progress from that of Chapter 9, the period of the "second woe." But it is ominously stated that "the third woe cometh quickly" ("swiftly," 1911, "is coming swiftly," C. V.).

Before leaving behind this very significant passage we will seize the opportunity it furnishes for noting the most thrilling sign of the present hour relative to developments in the Jewish world.

While the passage shows that the spiritual state of the Jews during the first half of the last seven years will be such as to cause the "two witnesses" to be "clothed in sackcloth," yet, at the same time—as the passage proves—it will be a time of Christian faith and of spiritual power in Israel not surpassed at any period of her history. The angel's direction to "measure the temple of God, the altar, and them that worship therein," signifies that the Jewish nation will be reinstated not only politically, but also religiously and spiritually. It means that they "abide not still in unbelief," but that they are again "graffed in." In fact, it is reasonable to assume that the Gentile Church, after the rapture, will be left so weak and faltering as to be incompetent to meet the brunt of the antichristian opposition, and that Israel will then succeed to Christian leadership. The sealing of the hundred and forty-four thousand of the tribes of Israel, as well as features to appear later on in Revelation, confirm this assumption.

But this will involve a most vital change in the heart of Israel beforehand. Instead of Jewish conversion meaning ostracism, expulsion, death itself, in relations if not in fact,—as has been the case these centuries past —Christian faith will again take root within the pale of Israel, will grow up, become active and magnificently victorious. The "remnant" of the last days will be, like the Maccabees of old, the victors of faith left in, not cast out from, the Jewish Church.

Now, the most thrilling sign of the present hour is the indication that this spiritual change in Israel is already setting in.

In the first place, there is being an unprecedented spiritual awakening and eagerness among the Jews, especially of Central Europe. Not only is there an unwonted readiness to hear of Jesus from the missionary, but Gentile churches are frequented by Jews, and even synagogues are thrown open for Gospel meetings. Then, there is a consciousness seizing Hebrew Christians that they should proclaim the Gospel racially; that is, as Jewish believers to their fellow-Jews. And even Hebrew-Christian churches are being organized and are centers of great evangelistic zeal. Besides, there is fast growing among the Jews the practice of claiming Jesus of Nazareth as the great prophet of their own race. Furthermore, Jewish leaders are welcoming both Gentile and Hebrew believers in places of honor. At the dedication of the Hebrew University at Jerusalem, there were representatives of more than one hundred universities of the world, and the inaugural address was given by Earl Balfour. A devoted missionary of Tiberias, Palestine,—one of the world's greatest Hebrew scholars—

represented Glascow University and delivered an address in the revived Hebrew language. He writes of the high welcome and honor accorded to him as a Christian minister and missionary, as well as of the cordial invitation to a Hebrew Christian and his wife as practically Israelites. And he makes these significant declarations: "The Hebrew people are not far from acknowledging the Christian Jew as an integral part of the nation. When that is done formally, Israel will have reached the fulness of liberty. It will be the reviving of the race from its spiritual side."

CHAPTER VI.

SOUNDING OF THE SEVENTH TRUMPET, 11:15-19.

"15 And the seventh angel sounded; and there were great voices in heaven, saying, The kingdoms of this world are become the kingdoms of our Lord, and of his Christ; and he shall reign for ever and ever. 16 And the four and twenty elders, which sat before God on their seats, fell upon their faces, and worshipped God. 17 Saying, We give thee thanks, O Lord God Almighty, which art, and wast, and art to come; because thou hast taken to thee thy great power, and hast reigned. 18 And the nations were angry, and thy wrath is come, and the time of the dead, that they should be judged, and that thou shouldest give reward unto thy servants the prophets, and to the saints, and them that fear thy name, small and great; and shouldest destroy them which destroy the earth. 19 And the temple of God was opened in heaven, and there was seen in his temple the ark of his testament: and there were lightnings, and voices, and thunderings, and an earthquake, and great hail."

THIS annunciation is very comprehensive, embracing retrospect and prospect with reference to divine world-rule.

1. The Exalted Acclaim of High Angelic Powers.

Upon the sounding of the seventh trumpet the angelic realm (we may assume) resounds with the enthusiastic chorus that the world-kingdom—so long usurped, bedeviled and prostituted—is become the Lord's and His Christ's. Although the actual accomplishment of the results is not yet unfolded in the progress of the vision, yet it is evident that the stages of progress thus far accomplished, and the tone of the trumpet blast, will thrill the angelic spheres with the certainty of the end, as much as though the historical fulfillment thereof were actually beheld. It bears witness to the profound significance

187

of the question of world-empire, "The heavens do rule"
(Dan. 4 : 26). This rule—founded in creation, restored in
redemption—has long been disputed, apparently successfully. The interests at stake are beyond full compassing
by mortal minds,—they engage intensely the highest
angelic intelligence and emotion. Just as astute, discerning observers detect the point in a protracted conflict when the issue of complete ultimate victory sets in,
so in the case before us angelic prognosis is unhesitatingly
and exultantly heralded.

And the nature of the only true world-rule is
designated by the angelic concert. It is the personal rule
of Him who is the angel's Lord and of His Christ,—His
Anointed One, His Messiah, His Son. This acknowledgment of the direct and full association of the Father
and the Son in world-rule is very significant. It is in
accord with all Scriptural teaching and history, to the
effect that while the almighty Father is the supreme
sovereign of our heavens and earth—as well as of all
the universe—yet He commits all rule for direct active
administration into the hands of the Son. And it is in
accord with all the acknowledgments of the Lord Jesus
Christ that He does nothing of Himself independently
or for His own glory, but only from, in and for His
Father. Surely, then, if the angelic hosts honor the Son
as they honor the Father, it behooves natural man to do
the same, and nothing can palliate man's sin in failing
so to do.

Very striking now is the further utterance, "and he
shall reign for ever and ever." It reads not that they
shall thus reign; the number of the pronoun is singular,
—"he." And this pronoun must relate to the nearest
person mentioned before. This is Christ. Not that He
shall reign for ever any more independently than hitherto. It does, however, teach that the direct and active
world-rule is always to remain in Christ's hands. This
calls us again to a correct understanding of 1 Cor. 15:

27, 28. The words here—"Then shall the Son also himself be subject unto him that put all things under him,
that God may be all in all,"—are not to be taken to mean
that, after restoring to God's sovereignty all spheres now
in revolt, the Son will cease to be the Father's vice-
regent. This would be contrary to the teaching of Paul
in Eph. 1:10: "That in the dispensation of the fulness
of times he might gather together in one [better "rehead"] all things in Christ."   As all things were
"created by him [Christ] and for him" (Col. 1:16), so
that originally all creation was headed in Him—"the
first-born of all creation"—so by His redemption-work
all things will be "reheaded"—headed again—and that
for ever, in Him. What is meant by the language, "then
shall the Son also himself be subject unto him that put
all things under him, that God may be all in all," is that
the Son will remain the same filial servant of the Father
and not usurp to Himself that which He will have restored from the hands of the usurper, Satan.

The literal renderings of the duration of divine world-
rule present the idea wrapped up in the expression "for
ever and ever" very vividly and impressively. "And he
shall reign unto the ages of the ages." This expression
is not merely an effort to express indefinite duration by
an impressive figure. We are to see in this expression
something more than measureless time. In the chapter
on "The Cross of the Ages" the conception of an
organism, or of a structure of ages, will be brought out.
This idea meets us in the phrase, "the ages of the ages."
The ages are presented as confederated into one complete age, an empire of ages. There would be an articulat-
ing, inspiring, ruling principle thus organizing the
component ages. And the phrase, "the ages of the ages,"
reveals that there is growing up a plurality of such vast
time-empires corresponding to the empires of heavenly
spaces suggested by the expression, "the heavens of
heavens." How this enlarges and uplifts our conception
of the imperial sway "of our Lord and His Christ"!

2. *Acclaim of the Four and Twenty Elders.*

While, as has been noted, the interest of angelic intelligences in these coming events is evidently keen and discerning, yet here, as in 5:9-12, it is striking how much more practical and personal is the interest of human intelligence. *"We give thee thanks."* This is the emotion —that of the personal gratitude of intimate beneficiaries —which inspires this acclamation.

Again, the world rule of the Almighty is viewed and acknowledged in the language of historic fact. "Thou hast taken to thee thy great power, and hast reigned" ("Dost reign," C. V.). Such insight and foresight is not common among men while in the mortal state, excepting by prophetic endowment. Yet to an important degree the rule of the Almighty will at this stage have been established; namely, in the sky-regions.

This utterance of the elders contains clearly a forecast of the stupendous group of concluding events to be accomplished during the era opened by the sounding of the seventh and last trumpet. This group embraces three particulars of conclusive nature.

(1) The final premillennial Turbulence of the Nations of Earth.

"And the nations were angry, and thy wrath is come." This is a remarkable testimony to the outcome of postdiluvian history with respect to the relationship existing between the living nations and Almighty God with His Christ. Nations will prove to be sullen, rebellious, angered with the true God and the world's Saviour. This will not be due to divine injustice or harshness. It will be in spite of rich beneficence and wonderful long-suffering. Not that the righteous God never chastens sorely recalcitrant nations. Such measures are required at due times by every consideration of goodness as well as of righteousness. But the effect of all God's dealings through centuries and millenniums of goodness, for-

bearance, wisdom and faithfulness is a thoroughly
matured spirit of irritation, unruliness and angry re-
sentment. Further divine forbearance would not be a
virtue, further divine probation would be unjust to the
interests of humanity, further toleration would stultify
divine authority and holiness. "Thy wrath is come."
The premillennial age is an evil age,—"this present evil
world" (age). It is futile—it is fatal—to blink this un-
welcome but well-attested verdict of the Bible.   All
political, social, religious policies and elaborate endeavors
are as impotent to improve the age as a world-order—
even to tame the beast of unchristly imperialism, to
pacify the innate enmity, toward God and Jesus Christ
—as it is to get a friendly and safe grown-up lion out
of a kittenish cub by confiding, humanizing treatment.
The devil is "the prince of this world" (age), and he is
"the god of this world" (age). It is his to deceive the
nations until the millennium of his incarceration arrives.
Instead of the millennium being a product of this age,—
after the principle of "first the blade, then the ear, then
the full corn in the ear"—this age, in its essential, un-
convertible spirit and will must be overthrown by judgment, as was the antediluvian age. In fact, so inherent
and persistent will the antipathy to Christ of the
unregenerate world prove to be, that, even the millennial
rule of all nations outside Israel will have to be exercised
with a stern rod of iron, and after one thousand years
of personal, visible Messianic rule—with no dispute or
deception of Satan—the mass of humanity will again
enlist under Satan when "loosed out of his prison"
(Rev. 20:7) in a final determined, unprecedented effort
to overthrow wholly and forever the rule of heaven over
the earth.

(2). The Long Outstanding Judgment of Awards.

"And the time of the dead that they should be judged, and
that thou shouldest give reward unto thy servants the prophets,
and to the saints, and them that fear thy name, small and great."

It must be remembered that the consummations announced in our present passage, as forecast by the sounding of the seventh trumpet, constitute the outcome of the era left as "the last days" after the "forty and two months,"—the "thousand two hundred and threescore days" already covered in this chapter of The Revelation. The judgment of awards to all classes of believers, then, does not occur individually through the ages as the saints pass out of the body into the presence of the Lord; neither does it occur immediately upon the resurrection and the rapture of the saints, whether prior to or during the first three and one-half years of the tribulation. This judgment of awards, however, does constitute one of the conclusions reached by the last three and one-half years.

Further, this passage again proves, as has been found over and over throughout the Bible, that this judgment of awards includes the Lord's followers of all preceding times clear back to Adam and Eve. "That they without [apart from] us should not be made perfect" (Heb. 11: 40). That is, the promised consummation, to which "these all" of the pre-Christian times looked forward under the privileges of their dispensation, was not to be reached by them "apart from" our inclusion as we, under a dispensation of "some better" privileges, yet still look forward in faith. Thank God that the consummation common to believers of both dispensations was not fulfilled ere we of this age could be included!

The fact is very strongly emphasized that the range of the rewards as to ranks and classes is unlimited. While prophets are mentioned as though of first rank, yet they are classed as servants (slaves). One might feel hopeless of reward, even as least of "the saints"; but to be God-fearing only guarantees reward, even though one be but "small" in this class. It reminds one of Jesus' words: "Whosoever shall give to drink unto one of these little ones a cup of cold water in the name of a disciple, verily I say unto you, he shall in no wise lose his reward" (Mat. 10:42). The value of service is derived, not from its own magnitude or from the elevation of the immediate recipient of the service: the value of Christian service is derived from Him in whose name it is rendered. "Whosoever shall give you a cup of water to drink in my name, *because you belong to Christ,* verily I say unto you, he shall not lose his reward" (Mark 9:41). "The King shall answer and say unto them, Verily I say unto you, Inasmuch as ye have done it unto one of the least of these my brethren, *ye have done it unto me*" (Matt. 25:40).

In fact a still wider inclusion of merit in the Lord's judgment is guaranteed. Solomon (1 Kings 8:18) said, "And the Lord said unto David my father, Whereas it was *in thine heart* to build an house unto my name, *thou didst well that it was in thine heart.*" Which will receive the greater reward for the erection of Solomon's temple, Solomon himself or David his father? Certainly Christ took David nearer to His bosom in regard to the temple than He took Solomon. This principle entering into final rewards from the hands of Jesus is most encouraging, and it takes in a marvellous sweep of merit. In that day it will be revealed how the eye of Christ Jesus is ever scanning hearts—their promptings, their longings, their unaccomplished purposes—as well as their deeds, great and small.

Then, too, our Lord will judge and reward from a relative standpoint. "This poor widow hath cast more in than all they which have cast into the treasury; for all they did cast in of their abundance; but she of her want did cast in all that she had, even all her living" (Mark 12:43, 44).

All may be summed up in this, that reward will be according as one has proved in His sight to be in heart's affection and delight "rich toward God." "If there be first a willing mind, it is accepted according to that a man hath, and not according to that he hath not" (2 Cor. 8:12). "For God loveth a cheerful giver" (2 Cor. 9:7).

13

(3). The Destruction of Earth's Destroyers.

"And shouldest destroy them which destroy the earth." This word proves that the salvation of the earth from destruction depends upon our Lord's second coming, and that in destructive judgment. It is implied that the destructive forces in the world will not be extirpated or even abashed by civilizing, humanizing, modernizing or even Christianizing policies; on the contrary, it is implied that destructive tendencies—ever thus far betraying themselves, but as yet at least measurably restrained and baffled in purpose—will finally gain unrestrained dominance and would bring the earth to horrible ruin did not our Lord come forth upon the scene as "the Judge of the earth."

This word also faithfully and unblushingly confirms that Jesus Christ can at the proper time, and will, destroy men's lives in a swift, appalling way that will leave neither root nor branch. It implies that He is no Redeemer of mankind and that He is unfit to rule the earth, if He cannot be counted on to destroy earth's destroyers. He proved His judicial integrity in wiping out the antediluvian age, in destroying "the cities of the plains" of Jordan. Many another holocaust, if only rightly explained, would prove the same. As well suffer a mad beast to stalk unmolested through a village, tossing, stamping, goring every unprotected child, as to suffer maddened, bloodthirsty elements to seize defenseless society, to crush out all that is worth living for. But it is becoming ever more evident that destructive spirits are leaguing, organizing, training, plotting, assaying with ever increasing persistency and skill, for national, international, continental, world-wide overthrow of law, morality and religion. *"This know* also, that in the *last days......perilous times* shall come,.... Evil men and seducers shall wax *worse and worse,* deceiving and being deceived" (2 Tim. 3:1-13).

It is also becoming more and more evident that better

government is not improving, but is deteriorating. Unscrupulous politics, venality in office, commercial greed,
militaristic ruthlessness, imperialistic lust are bedevilling
elements which are not losing vitality in governmental
spheres. Satan is not out of his old business in earthly
affairs. He has not yet exhausted his wiles and devices
for deceiving the nations; his masterpiece of governmental deception is yet in reserve. Nothing but the destructive can be expected of him. To those who have
read the Bible up to this point intelligently it is good
tidings, that Jesus Christ is in due time to arise "to
shake terribly the earth." At the time when the present
point in John's vision is reached all the occupants of our
skies will exult over the imminent prospect, and all those
in the earth, who shall be taking "the sure word of
prophecy" as "a light in a dark place," will take new
heart,—even after those "two witnesses" fall in death
and ascend alive,—and they will gird up their loins for
supreme testing and for "a final and a glorious victory."

(4). The final verse of this introductory paragraph
presents a very comprehensive statement in two main
parts.

a. "And the temple of God was opened in heaven, and
there was seen in his temple the ark of his testament."
This describes the new point of procedure in the course
of judgments. This fact becomes the plainer when it is
noticed that this point of procedure is described a
second time in 15 : 5-8, when the recital of new judgments
is first really introduced following upon the extended inserted material lying between.

b. "And there were lightnings, and voices, and
thunderings, and an earthquake, and great hail." This
description of the effects of this new and final inaugura-
tion of the judgments of the seven-sealed scroll, embraces
results in the issues of the seventh vial judgment as described in 16 : 18-21.

This one verse, then, is an anticipatory epitome of the

whole judgment period of the third woe, a period embracing the latter three and one-half years of the reign of Anti-Christ. But further exposition of the items of this verse will be reserved for their later recurrence in the narrative of judgment itself.

CHAPTER VII.

THE THIRD CONTEMPORANEOUS INTERCALA-
TION, 12 : 1—15 : 4.

PART I, CHAPTER 12.

T HAT this long passage is intercalary; that is, a
passage parallel to, but not a part of the stages of
judgment, is evident from the very nature of its
contents and from the fact that, as has been noticed, the
anticipation of 11 : 19 is not straightway unfolded, but is
reintroduced in 15 : 5-8, after which the narration of
anticipated judgments immediately follows.

We are, therefore, to find in 12 : 1—15 : 4 a digression
following upon the forecast projected by 11 : 13-19. In
other words, 12 : 1—15 : 4 is an inserted passage which
is needed just at this point to supply information of
contemporaneous developments proceeding along the line,
not of the judgments upon the antichristian realm, but
of the victories of grace in the realm of heroic faith.

It will be both appropriate and convenient to treat
Chapter 12 first and separately. It calls for peculiarly
open-minded and close attention, bringing to it no pre-
conceived ideas or accepted theories of interpretation.
The chapter falls naturally into three paragraphs.

1. THE MAN CHILD, 12 : 1-6:

"1 And there appeared a great wonder in heaven; a woman
clothed with the sun, and the moon under her feet, and upon
her head a crown of twelve stars: 2 And she being with child
cried, travailing in birth, and pained to be delivered. 3 And
there appeared another wonder in heaven; and behold, a great
red dragon, having seven heads and ten horns, and seven crowns
upon his heads. 4 And his tail drew the third part of the stars
of heaven, and did cast them to the earth; and the dragon
stood before the woman which was ready to be delivered, for

to devour her child as soon as it was born. 5 And she brought
forth a man child, who was to rule all nations with a rod of iron:
and her child was caught up unto God, and to his throne. 6 And
the woman fled into the wilderness, where she hath a place
prepared of God, that they should feed her there a thousand two
hundred and threescore days.''

This paragraph pictures the birth and the triumphant
ascension of ''a man child'' who is ''to rule all nations
with a rod of iron.''

The passage gets well on the way to being clearly
understood, as soon as the place and the situation into
which the man child is to be translated is taken rightly
and in harmony with the descriptive terms of this Book
of Revelation. ''Caught up unto God and to his throne,''
or ''snatched away to God and to his throne,'' as the
C. V. reads. The very same place and situation has
been introduced already in 4:1-3: it is the celestial
region above the earth where God is to take possession
and dominion as the first stage of Christ's return. In
point of time this intercalary passage reaches back in
Chapter 12 to the very beginning of ''the things'' of 1:
1, 19, 4:1, which it is said ''must shortly come to pass,''
''which shall be hereafter,'' or ''which must be hereafter.''

The figure of the ''man child,'' then, would describe
the living earthly believers constituting in their part the
company first to be caught up to meet the Lord in the
air. They are to be identified in their part with
the throng of saints described in 5:9, 10 as singing the
''new song'': ''Thou art worthy to take the book, and to
open the seals thereof: for thou wast slain, and hast
redeemed us to God by thy blood out of every kindred,
and tongue, and people, and nation; and hast made us
unto our God kings and priests: and we shall reign on
the earth.'' In both passages the focal thought is the
earthly imperial rule immediately awaiting the translated ones. This is the true objective that is always
set before Christ's followers in this militant age. In

Rev. 2:26, 27 it was expressed in almost identical language: "And he that overcometh and keepeth my works unto the end, to him will I give power over the nations: And he shall rule them with a rod of iron; as the vessels of a potter shall they be broken to shivers: even as I received of my Father."

The Mother of the Man Child.

This portion of Chapter 12 describes how this class of the living saints of the first stages of the rapture are to be made ready. The process is described under the figure of parturition. The mother, is of course, the Church of the "latter days." As in the vision of 1:12-20, she is here again presented first in her mystical, heavenly ideal in Christ, "clothed with the sun, and the moon under her feet, and upon her head a crown of twelve stars." This is a most appropriate symbol of the Church even now in her victorious place in Christ—her Head. And the aspect of glorious, heavenly triumphs is appropriate in connection with the victorious ascension of the man child. The symbolism reminds one of Cant. 6:10: "Who is she that looketh forth as the morning, fair as the moon, clear as the sun, and terrible as an army with banners?" All these ranks of heavenly luminaries are employed in the symbolical description of this Queen,—the sun her garment, the moon the pavement under her feet, the ever-shining stars the chaplet on her brow.

But, just as in Chapters 2 and 3, "the things that are"—the "works" of the Church in earthly conditions and conflicts—presented her in painful contrast, so now this same woman is pictured as suffering the pains and struggles of mortal women in child-birth.

It is not difficult to discern the aptness of this symbolism. Up to child-birth mother and child share comparatively a common life, while the severance of the bond of vital union occasions the supreme agonies of mortal life. Following out the figure, there is an age-long enjoyment of community life in the Church in comparative comfort, but the preparation of this company out of the very womb of the Church for translation involves a process of spiritual parturition of acute suffering.

The real bridal spirit, which out of pure heart fervently cries out, ''Come, Lord Jesus,'' is pained by and is a pain to the spirit in the Church that would rather sleep on in earthly ease and apathy, a spirit which emasculates the ''blessed hope'' of all reality and vitality. On the one hand, the Church watches and waits in worldly separation for her Lord to appear: on the other hand, the Church prefers herself, and prefers in her own way and meaning to ''bring in the kingdom,'' with the Lord's visible return at the least indefinitely postponed. On the one hand, this age is an ''evil age'' to the Church, ripening for judgment at the Lord's appearing; on the other hand, this age is to the Church one to be exploited, converted and made meet for the Lord's return to express His pleasure and to pronounce all ''very good.''

One of the pronounced signs of the present day, indicative of the relative proximity of the Lord's return, is to be found in the sharp and painful contrast existing within the Church between a ''little flock'' of believers within the church and the general mass of professed Christians. To a few watchful saints it is thrillingly significant that within the last decade terrible scourges have occurred in the earth in a conjunction and on a scale not approached since the ascension of Christ Jesus. The compilation for this last decade is thus given:

1. *The worst war* the world has even seen, costing 10,-000,000 lives and over $200,000,000,000.

2. *The worst earthquake* in human history, the one in China during December, 1920, ''which literally shook the globe,'' and carried suddenly into eternity a quarter of a million lives. (Some authorities place the estimate far higher).

3. *The worst famine* "the world has hitherto known," that of Russia, in which millions perished miserably through starvation, and "added millions through starvation plus disease."

4. *The worst pestilence,* in some respects, known to man, world-wide in extent, and exacting toll of full 12,-000,000 lives. In the short space of twelve weeks nearly 6,000,000 persons died. In South Africa the mortality exceeded the combined mortality of three wars, and in India in a few months' time 5,000,000 deaths occurred.

Has this voice from God to humanity no significance to Christ's Church? Yet humanity is growing giddier and wickeder. As to the Church, one has said out of anguish of heart: "It is a mystery that the Church is not prostrate on its face before God, so acute is the crisis, and so awful and imminent the danger. It accentuates the tragedy that a section of the Church of Christ, of unknown magnitude, while these thunders are actually in its ear, begins to *tread the world's infidel way.*"

If the Lord Jesus Christ is actually to come soon and actually to find faith in the earth that suits Him,—faith in His coming, faith that cries "Come," faith that purifies one to "appear with Him in glory"—it is evident that already things are heading toward a *parturition of a child of the Church that is really a man in Christ Jesus, called and qualified to stand with Him in rule over the earth with the rod of iron.* It is to the honor of the Church that such a child can come out of her, while it is a tragedy that the child must leave his mother behind.

It is a remarkable sidelight that is thrown upon the transition of the earth from the present age to that of the rule of the man child by the words, "who was to rule all nations with a *rod of iron.*" The earth is not maturing for a rule with an olive wand or a golden scepter; this age will culminate in a condition demanding an iron rule,—stern, relentless, unsparing in compulsion. "With an *iron club*," reads the C. V. This administration is to be earth-wide, political, international,—"all nations."

One of the elements of anguish convulsing the Church in this child-birth must, then, be due to the dissent of the man-child element from the delusive hopes, theories, measures of international, millennial peace which are today more and more captivating the imagination, firing the ambition, absorbing the attention of Christians and heathendom alike. And why cast the pall of pessimistic prophecy over the fancied dawning of the fair day of self-operating international comity and accord? It is because the passage before us includes one more important personal factor to which the worldly wise are blind. This is the "god" and the "prince of this world" (age). "The rulers of the *darkness of this world*" (age), is the irremovable obstacle to the realization of the prevalent, comfortable hopes which are substituted for "the blessed hope." The man-child element in the Church wrestles "against the principalities, against the powers, against the world-rulers of this darkness, against the spiritual hosts of wickedness in the heavenly [aerial] places" (R. V.) ; the masses of the Church are not "able to stand against the wiles of the devil."

The Great Red Dragon.

It is under this symbol that the supreme head of the empire of "the darkness of this world" (age) is here portrayed. And it is a very fitting symbol. The literal dragon has never been known as an actual and particular creature,—as, for instance, some species of serpent, lizard, or other creature—but rather as the hideous imaginary embodiment of the frightful and repulsive characteristics of all such creatures; and as such it is employed as the emblem of the most malignant, passionate, poisonous and destructive principle warring against God, angels and mankind. Venom, savagery, terribleness, repulsiveness, treachery, deadliness, implacable passion, are all combined in this frightful symbol. As all such principle originates with and proceeds from Satan, it is a symbol perfectly applicable to him.

The heads and horns indicate superior power, and the crowns imply actual sovereignty. The numbers seven and ten intimate universal and unhindered sovereignty. It is to be noticed, however, that no crowns were seen upon the ten horns. The appearance of this "sign" in "heaven" shows that the seat of this power is in the skies. Yet the well-known Scriptural representation of the devil's interest and operations in earthly affairs are consistently carried out in the passage before us. This prospective child-birth will be of vital interest to him, and it will call for extraordinary action on his part. For is this not to be the birth of the human agent designed of God to "rule all nations with a rod of iron"? This clearly stands related to that mystic declaration of Gen. 3:15: "I will put enmity between thee and the woman, and between thy seed and her seed; it shall bruise thy head, and thou shalt bruise his heel."

When Adam was created and installed as the steward of God's Son in the earth, Satan's interest and action were called forth most markedly. So also when the Son of God was born into this world. Now again, Satan's sway over the earth is to be disputed, in fact overthrown, if timely action be not taken with respect to this man-child. Destruction is Satan's accustomed strategy; this child must be destroyed immediately upon its birth.

To this end, it is represented that Satan will draft one-third of his most brilliant regiments of wicked spirits in heavenly places, and hurl them into strategic position in earthly regions for the prompt destruction of the new-born child. This suffices to explain the travail in the bosom of the Church of the latter days already described as being created and directed by exceptional demoniacal presence, activity and power in the midst of Christendom.

And the plot will include apparently the bodily destruction of the saints constituting the man child; but this plot will be frustrated by the sudden rapture of those saints to "meet the Lord Jesus in the air." This will be not merely a fortunate escape; it will be crowning victory. It will prove afresh the truth of the promise of Jesus to the "little flock" that "the gates of hell shall not prevail." It will verify the word of Paul that "he who now letteth [hindereth, successfully obstructs] will let, until he be taken out of the way."

Consequently, the mother of the man child, the Church, henceforth devoid of a victorious element, can no longer "let" or successfully hinder Satan, so as to compel him to work his "wickedness" in "mystery,"—concealment. Flight will then be for her the better part of valor—her only resort, her only salvation (v. 6). But consideration of this important chapter in Church history will be best deferred until the next scene in this drama has been unfolded.

2. THE WAR IN HEAVEN, VS. 7-12.

"7 And there was war in heaven: Michael and his angels fought against the dragon; and the dragon fought and his angels, 8 And prevailed not; neither was their place found any more in heaven. 9 And the great dragon was cast out, that old serpent, called the Devil, and Satan, which deceiveth the whole world: he was cast out into the earth, and his angels were cast out with him. 10 And I heard a loud voice saying in heaven, Now is come salvation, and strength, and the kingdom of our God, and the power of his Christ: for the accuser of our brethren is cast down, which accused them before our God day and night. 11 And they overcame him by the blood of the Lamb, and by the word of their testimony; and they loved not their lives unto the death. 12 Therefore rejoice, ye heavens, and ye that dwell in them. Woe to the inhabiters of the earth and of the sea! for the devil is come down unto you, having great wrath, because he knoweth that he hath but a short time."

Singularly the past tense of this passage has often been taken as historical, instead of its being understood as merely being used by John in recording afterwards this part of his vision. It does not even mean that this battle will take place subsequently to the ascension of the man child. We have described to us here John's vision of one momentous factor essential to our understanding of a new situation, which is to exist in the skies and in the earth at the period of time when a prepared portion of the visible Church will be translated from her bosom unto God and to His throne in the skies, while the "Mother Church" will be left in singular plight in the earth.

Again, we would at once fall into serious misconception if we took "heaven"—the arena of this titanic conflict—as "heaven itself," instead of merely the skies from which Satan has always ruled this world.

Daniel left recorded in 7:9 this revelation: "I beheld [continued gazing upon the scenes of the vision] till the thrones were cast down, and the Ancient of days did sit" (take His throne there). The expression, "Thrones were cast down," briefly embraces what John in the passage before us more fully unfolds. The utter overturning of the satanic organism of government, based in the skies and swaying the earth, is here described as the issue of an unparalleled angelic combat between the spirits of light under the archangel Michael, and the spirits of darkness commanded by the dragon.

Imagination has a wide range of legitimate exercise over this coming crucial conflict, and the passage contributes much to assist one's understanding of many passages of Scripture which are too often taken in a vague, unreal, figurative sense.

The statement, "neither was their place found any more in heaven," means that thus is to terminate forever the presence and power of Satan and his hosts in the skies above us. This lends weight and vivid reality

to the passages—like Dan. 7:9, 10 and Rev. 4:2-11—
which describe the succession of Almighty God to throne
presence and power in the skies. Imagination is brought
to a still keener pitch by the further revelation that
Satan, the deceiver of the world for these ages, and his
angelic hosts are at this time to be cast down into the
narrow confines of the earth. Just what this will mean
to the skies above and to the earth is explained by a
"loud voice in heaven."

The expulsion of the dragon will signalize the arrival
in the skies of the salvation and imperial power of God
and the investiture of Christ with authority there in
place of Satan. This means, in other words, that the
"Advocate with the Father" has displaced "the accuser
of the brethren." Here again, great light is thrown upon
the need believers have for this Advocate, seeing that
the devil—which means slanderer—is ceaselessly engaged in plying before God damaging accusations of the
Lord Christ's brethren, as he did, for example, in the
case of Job. Concrete samples of Satan's accusations
may be found in the charges and insinuations he so
busily, though slyly, injects into the minds of Christians
against one another. The personal doubts, and fears, and
despairing moods which fall upon the hearts of believers
reflect this customary activity of Satan and his imps.
While the faithful Advocate quenches their fiery darts at
the throne of God, the believer has a way of victory for
his own peace of mind; and that is by ever resorting to
the blood of the Lamb of God, by maintaining bold and
open testimony, meanwhile practicing habitual self-
renunciation, till death itself, for Jesus' sake.

The "loud voice in heaven" calls upon the skies and
their sojourners to rejoice. It will be a glad consummation for all the faithful angels, who are ever sojourning
in these skies as foreign missionaries among implacable
enemies and amidst far worse than heathen darkness.
We cannot realize the keen and loyal interest, which

these faithful watchers and valiant warriors have maintained through the long ages, in the stupenduous drama of the recovery for God of the celestial regions, which were swept into spiritual darkness and under Christ-defying rule by the pre-Adamite revolution and disruption conceived and executed by the first traitor and rebel in God's universe. "Which things the angels desire to look into," says the Apostle Peter (1 Pet. 1:12), when speaking of the great themes of the prophets and evangelists. There is no lack of vigilant interest on the part of these sentinels of God in our skies regarding "the signs of the times." They are well acquainted with the program of the ages as divulged to God's people in the earth through the prophecies of the Old and the New Testaments. With alacrity, with fidelity and with efficiency have angelic messengers served in Bible times to communicate many of these prophecies to the human custodians of them. And these prophecies of this Book of Revelation were made known to the Apostle John through angelic mediumship (1:1). As a leading angel, encored by a multitude following him, sounded out to earthly listeners on Bethlehem's plains the anthem of the nativity, so will such a loud voice start a great angelic chorus in our skies, when the usurper with all his retinue is cast forever out of his aerial realm before the approach of God Almighty and of His Christ in salvation and dominion where darkness will have reigned so long.

But this momentous event of the complete and permanent overthrow of all satanic dominion in our heavens will mean a frightful situation for our earth. We may first, however, take a fresh view of the general situation.

This heaven and earth constitute one principality in God's universe. It was given by God into the charge of one of His highest, brightest and most powerful angelic creatures to rule under the supreme headship of Christ, the Son of God. The vice-regent, however, conceived hatred and rebellion against God and His Christ, re-

volted against their authority with a great following and
became "the adversary," the devil that he is, and Satan.
He has thus far been permitted to remain seated over his
magnificent province of skies and earth, and fatally to
affect their interests and welfare. After earth's restoration from the chaos entailed by Satan, and after man's
creation and investiture with the stewardship of the
earth under Christ the Lord, Satan brought about man's
disobedience and fall. From this juncture of temporal
history the Bible unfolds as the historical and prophetical
drama of the redemption of the aforesaid dual province
from Satan's sway, the center and seat of which has ever
been in the sky. Here, then, when Jesus Christ rises to
begin Satan's overthrow, He will begin His conquest.
This is true strategy. A masterly conqueror will always
make straight for his enemy's capital, and drive him
from his base and stronghold, and then hunt him down
to the outmost parts of his dominions. We have just re-
viewed the master-stroke by which Satan will lose further
place in our skies.

Whither but into the earth can the fugitive Satan flee?
There is nothing in all the Bible to indicate that, as the
sworn adversary of God's Christ, Satan ever has been or
will be permitted to cross the boundaries of this province
of earth and its skies into undefiled regions of the universe. While the azure dome above us presents to our
natural sight a beautiful symbol of heavenly purity and
peace, yet, could we penetrate the skies with spirit-sight,
most horrifying darkness, disorder, wickedness and moral
death—nowhere else in all the heavens of heavens to be
found—would meet our gaze. All likeness to this already
prevalent in the earth is but the manifested working of
"the prince of the power of the air, the spirit that now
worketh in the children of disobedience." Here will be
open to him still loyal territory of his own, not yet in-
vaded by the conquering Christ.

While Satan's expulsion from above implies the disruption of his long-standing system of antichristian government, yet there will be no extermination of the wicked spirits themselves and no change for the better, but, if anything, only for the worse, in their moral and spiritual nature, purposes and workings. Now for these hosts of satanic darkness to be hurled into and confined in this earth will manifestly create a situation inconceivably awful. Some inkling of a conception can be formed by those who are acquainted with actual demoniacal presences and influences, whose eyes are open to the satanic manifestations which ever expose themselves even upon the surface of human conditions and affairs. The very atmosphere will be thick and stifling with the congestion of demons. As to numbers, we have only to recall that enough could be spared for that one Gadarene to warrant his being called "Legion," or to take bodily possession of about two thousand hogs. Out of one woman, Mary Magdalene, went seven devils at Jesus' command. Countless multitudes of evil spirits are present in active and effective operations in the realms of mankind today. Yet the skies require hosts of them —especially the higher and mightier ranks and classes of them—to maintain Satan's battlelines against the angelic forces of God.

Then, as to morale, it will be the fighting mood of an infuriated, frenzied, cornered dragon. "Woe to the inhabiters of the earth! for the devil is come down unto you, having great wrath, because he knoweth that he hath but a short time." An unimaginable situation will exist in the earth, when Satan will have to make in the confined quarters of this globe his final stand and suffer his irreparable defeat before the conquering hosts of God's heavens. He will contend with the fury of a beast at bay, and with the recklessness of a foe whose hope is gone and who has nothing left but to do all the damage he can.

The thrilling story of John's vision does not, however,

14

digress from its main line of progress to engage our imagination in even the many momentous concerns involved for mankind in the new situation. One thing is to be inferred naturally and logically. That is, that the devil will exercise all his astuteness, as well as malignity, to conserve, if not repair, his fortunes and to strike his most telling blows against the interests of the Son of God in the earth. It is to be considered that the system of satanic operations, which has grown hoary in practice, and which has succeeded so wonderfully in apparent damage to the kingdom of God in earthly creation, will then have been smashed up beyond readjustment. The very base of operations will be terrestrial only, instead of celestial. New lines of defence will need to be established and new strategies of offence must be projected.

3. THE SATANIC PERSECUTION OF THE MOTHER CHURCH.

"13 And when the dragon saw that he was cast unto the earth, he persecuted the woman which brought forth the man child. 14 And to the woman were given two wings of a great eagle, that she might fly into the wilderness, into her place, where she is nourished for a time, and times, and half a time, from the face of the serpent. 15 And the serpent cast out of his mouth water as a flood after the woman, that he might cause her to be carried away of the flood. 16 And the earth helped the woman, and the earth opened her mouth, and swallowed up the flood which the dragon cast out of his mouth."

It is perfectly plain, that the devil's first line of operations will be to assail with vindictive anger the Christian system apparently accountable for the generation of the man child of royal destiny in the kingdom of Jesus Christ. However nominal the name Christian may be, whatever great division of the professed Christian Church,—Protestant, Roman or Greek Catholic, or Oriental—whatever minor denomination of any of these great ecclesiasticisms, may, under the all-pervasive searching and working of the Holy Spirit, have contributed any to the personnel of the first contingent of saints to be caught away without death to God and to His throne in the skies, whatever, in fine, shall retain the hated name Christian, will be by Satan held in measure responsible for his supreme disaster and will be by him held inimical to his remaining crown rights and interests. It is said that one may be known by the enemies he makes. Accordingly, the ''Mother Church,'' as we may fittingly call the ecclesiastical conglomeration to be left after the first rapture still professing on earth the name of Christian Church, demands of us a lingering veneration because of being counted still hateful and dangerous to the devil.

Right here verse six of this chapter, attention to which in direct order of the text was deferred, comes into full logical place and connection. This verse reads: ''And the woman fled into the wilderness, where she hath a place prepared of God, that they should feed her there a thousand two hundred and three score days.'' Verse thirteen shows that the reason for the woman's hegira will be this persecution instituted by the devil as his first effort after being expelled from the skies, whither the woman's child will have ascended to join the conquering Christ.

Verse fourteen described the woman's flight as swift and successful, as if on eagle's wings. Both verse six and verse fourteen represent that her flight is into ''the wilderness'' as ''her place,'' on the one hand, and as a place for her ''prepared of God,'' on the other hand. Note again the divine regard still continuing for the woman,—the poor, bereft, spiritless, helpless Christian Church. Not even yet will she be disowned and abandoned to the devil. What a lesson on present forbearance, reverence, spiritual helpfulness and hopefulness toward the Church general in her present degree of delinquency! Yea, verily! and all the more because she is yet to bring forth in complete parturition the child of the rapture.

But what is meant by her place prepared for her of

God in "the wilderness"? The conception is evidently drawn from Old Testament history and prophecy.

Israel, as the favored and witnessing body of God's people, was first led down into "the wilderness of the land of Egypt" (Ezk. 20:36). This was not Israel's appropriate place; but it was a place prepared for her of God for the time being, for the purpose of being nurtured and enabled in the period of weakness to prepare and multiply, as would have been impossible if left to contend for her promised place in the land of the still virile Canaanites.

Again, when Israel, through unbelief failed to follow her Lord into the promised land, He turned her back into the wilderness, through which He had led her so gloriously and speedily, there to find graves for that rebellious generation. But the Lord had her nevertheless in a prepared place of mercy and goodness. Of that very period of time Moses declared to them afterwards:

"The Lord thy God hath blessed thee in all the works of thy hand: he knoweth thy walking through this great wilderness: *these forty years* the Lord thy God hath been with thee; thou hast lacked nothing" (Deut. 2:7).

Also 8:2-4:

"And thou shalt remember all the way which the Lord thy God led thee these forty years in the wilderness, to humble thee, and to prove thee, to know what was in thine heart, whether thou wouldest keep his commandments, or not. And he humbled thee, and suffered thee to hunger, and fed thee with manna, which thou knewest not, neither did thy fathers know; that he might make thee know that man doth not live by bread only, but by every word that proceedeth out of the mouth of the Lord doth man live. Thy raiment waxed not old upon thee, neither did thy foot swell, these forty years."

And Neh. 9:19-21 is too beautiful to be left unnoticed:

"Yet thou in thy manifold mercies forsookest them not in the wilderness; the pillar of cloud departed not from them by day, to lead them in the way; neither the pillar of fire by night, to shew them light, and the way wherein they should go. Thou gavest also thy good spirit to instruct them, and withheldest not thy manna from their mouth, and gavest them water for their thirst. Yea, forty years didst thou sustain them in the wilderness, so that they lacked nothing; their clothes waxed not old, and their feet swelled not.''

Again, when Israel as a favored and witnessing kingdom, fell into decay,—spiritual and political—the Lord prophesied to her by Ezekiel His purpose in her captivity thus: ''I will bring you into the wilderness of the people [Gentiles], and there will I plead with you face to face'' (Ezk. 20: 35). By taking Israel out of the place of international notice, out of the place of witnessing responsibility in the earth, out of the place of certain extermination from her foes, her Lord could care for her still and accomplish spiritual ends with her.

Yet again, in the case of Israel as the favored and witnessing, ministering body of the Lord's people in the earth, Hosea prophesies of her long period ''in the wilderness'' now elapsing and of the Lord's gracious use of this time:

''Therefore, behold, I will allure her, and bring her into the wilderness, and speak comfortably unto her. And I will give her her vineyards from thence, and the Valley of Achor for a door of hope: and she shall sing there, as in the days of her youth, and as in the day she came up out of the land of Egypt. And it shall be at that day, saith the Lord, that thou shalt call me Ishi; and shalt call me no more Baali. For I will take away the names of Baalim out of her mouth, and they shall no more be remembered by their name. And in that day will I make a covenant for them with the beasts of the field, and with the fowls of heaven, and with the creeping things of the ground: for I will break the bow and the sword and the battle out of the earth, and will make them to lie down safely. And I will betroth thee unto me for ever; yea, I will betroth thee unto me in righteousness, and in judgment, and in lovingkindness, and in mercies. I will even betroth thee unto me in faithfulness: and thou shalt know the Lord. And it shall come to pass in that day, I will hear, saith the Lord, I will hear the heavens, and they shall hear the earth; And the earth shall hear the corn, and the wine and the oil; and they shall hear Jezreel. And I will sow her unto me in the earth; and I will have mercy upon her that had not obtained mercy; and I will say to them which were not my people, Thou art my people; and they shall say, Thou art my God'' (2: 14-23).

We may be reasonably certain that the case in hand is to be understood after the analogy of the cases just cited. The wilderness is a place of hiding rather than of public notice; a place of being nurtured as a child or as a sick person for the present incapable of performing virile task or of winning heroic victory; a foreign and inappropriate place, yet a desirable temporary resort; a place, indeed, of judgment, and yet a place of tender mercies from a compassionate Saviour. It is evident from the analogies cited that, after the first rapture, the visible Christian Church will be compelled to lose herself from public prominence, conspicuous offices, pronounced outward organic identity, and become dispersed and comparatively lost in the spheres of worldly society. The situation will be such that Satan cannot get at her effectually with his persecuting, exterminating purpose. In the case of Israel in dispersion, the more scattered, disorganized, unidentified she has been, the less exposed has she been to persecution and destruction. The survival of Israel for centuries has been due to decentralization, dispersion, public insignificance,—due, in fine, to her inability to help herself, and yet to the Lord's ability and willingness to keep and nurture her. So will it be with the "Mother Church." After the "little flock" has been taken aloft out of her bosom "the gates of hell" would easily prevail against her in frontal attack, mass against mass. She must become un-get-at-able. The non-Christian elements must so far absorb her as to be her screen, her camouflage. To reverse a familiar illustration, the wheat must be so strewn amidst the chaff that the devil cannot uproot the former without too much expense to the latter.

It is very interesting to note the two expressions employed in verses 6 and 14 regarding the time of the woman's seclusion in the wilderness. The two measurements must be co-equal. The thousand two hundred and threescore days equal three and one-half ("sacred") years; the "time, and times, and half a time" must, then, be a year, two years, and one-half a year, three and one-half years. This throws confirmatory light upon the same expression in Dan. 7:25 as meaning years. We, therefore, get the time designations of Daniel and of Revelation bound up harmoniously together into a strong and clear solution of the question of dates too often disputed over needlessly.

Now it is very important to notice the identify of this period of three and one-half years with the "forty and two months" and the "thousand two hundred and threescore days" of Chapter 11, verses 2 and 3. It is thus revealed that the time of the Church's seclusion from satanic reach is the time of Israel's return into the place of world-prominence as God's witnessing agency, taking the brunt, with miraculous powers of resistance, of Satan's open assaults.

Foiled in his efforts of persecution against the Church in retreat, the devil will try another, a more subtle measure.

In order to take the right path of interpretation here, it is first necessary to note that the whole paragraph of Scripture with which we are here dealing is clothed in figurative language. Therefore, the "water as a flood," which "the serpent" is represented as casting out "after the woman," is to be taken as a figure of speech. It is, however, not difficult to comprehend the plain sense of the figurative language. Water is one of the commonest symbols used in Scripture for the word of God as the agency of life proceeding out of the mouth of God. A flood of water, belching forth out of the mouth of the serpent—the devil and Satan—with destructive purpose, would signify one of those inundations of false and destructive doctrine—''doctrines of devils'' (1 Tim. 4:1)—which Satan has often broadcasted through ''seducing spirits.'' The present day is witnessing a veritable tidal wave of destructive doctrine, called scientific criticism, world-wide in its reach wherever the Church is to be found.

Almost strange to say, this artifice of the devil, it is represented, will fail. As has already been shown from Old Testament citations, Jesus Christ can sometimes safeguard His Church better in the wilderness than at Mount Zion. The Laodicean Church is so easily assailed and corrupted by demonizing teachings, whereas ''the Church in the wilderness''—debased from ''proud eminence''—is little inclined to listen to siren voices and more inclined to love her Bridegroom's voice. It is represented that the flood of lying doctrine to be cast forth by the serpent will be so greedily swallowed by the worldly, antichristian public, that the woman is indirectly helped thereby in being kept out of the destructive reach of the damnable heresy.

Indeed, so far from being crowned with success in this effort, the serpent will only be the more angered with the woman because of another result contrary to his expectations. This is revealed by the last verse of Chapter 12.

4. WAR INSTITUTED BY SATAN AGAINST THE REMNANT OF THE WOMAN'S SEED, 12:17:

''And the dragon was wroth with the woman, and went to make war with the remnant of her seed, which keep the commandments of God, and have the testimony of Jesus Christ.''

Different translations, while not at all disagreeing, yet lend interest and force to this passage by their variations: ''And the dragon was angered at the woman, and came away to do battle with the rest of her seed, who are keeping the precepts of God, and who have the testimony of Jesus'' (C. V.). ''And the dragon waxed wroth with the woman, and went away to make war with the rest of her seed, which keep the commandments of God, and hold the testimony of Jesus'' (R. V.). Another private translation reads: ''And the dragon was enraged at the woman, and went away to make war with the remnant of her seed, which keep the commandments of God, and have the testimony of Jesus.''

Several factors come to clear light from this verse.

(1). The ill-success of Satan, in his measures of malignant endeavor against the Church of Jesus Christ left in the earth—owing to her being screened as an outstanding, organized body, because decentralized, disorganized, dissolved into the general worldly body—will exasperate him all the more, and it will excite him to whatever diabolical enterprise circumstances may seem to afford him opportunity for and hope of success.

(2). The expression, ''the remnant of her seed,'' stands in antithesis to the woman's child mentioned in the early verses of this chapter. It follows that the parturition and the rapture of that part of the Church called the ''man child'' will not leave the Mother Church absolutely dead and infertile spiritually. This is as interesting as it is conclusive with regard to the question, whether all the Spirit-born will be at once raptured and that preceding the last seven years before Christ's descent to the earth. The expression, ''the rest,'' or ''the remnant of her seed,'' identifies this part of the Church membership with the raptured part as of like spiritual kind, but left behind because of not being embraced in the parturition of the raptured part. This point is all the more conclusive because this remnant of the woman's seed is distinguished from the woman herself. Satan is represented as being unable to effect his purpose against the woman and as turning his attention from her to seed from her; but that seed is represented as being ''the rest,'' or ''the remnant''; that is, all that will be left of that spiritual kind. Here then is what may be called a second parturition, a new and complete separation of the spiritual part of the Church from the nominal, that which is not Spirit-born, that which does not have the seed of God in it.

(3). That which characterizes this remnant of the woman's seed is strikingly, though so simply, expressed. We are again to project our imagination under the light of the vision of John into those coming days.

The rapture of 1 Thess. 4:15-17 will have occurred, including the "man child" of our present chapter. The satanic hordes will have scurried in an utter demoralized rout from the skies into the earthly sphere. The Church of Jesus Christ will have been left as weak as a woman after childbirth, with no militant spirit or strength. To be practically lost from sight and access as an institution will be her only salvation from the dragon's designs, while it will also be her favorable condition for compassionate, effective ministries from the Spirit of her Lord. For three and one-half years Jerusalem, the capital of politically revived Israel, will again be the sole religious center of world-wide attention, the base of mighty public demonstrations of the Holy Ghost and of power, as "the two witnesses" of Chapter 11 will be hurling, as from "big Berthas," the judgments of God against the aggressions of antichristian powers.

Meantime there will be transpiring a very important spiritual development within "the Church in the wilderness." The Spirit and the Word of God will be reviving, strengthening, enlightening, emboldening, multiplying responsive elements. These elements will be coming together independently, and more and more openly, in affinity of spirit, in noticeable godliness of life and in distinctive testimony of Jesus. They will be putting on the whole armor of God and getting ready for "the evil day" of open, unscreened, frontal, ferocious attack from the devil in all his powers and resources.

The two distinctive marks of this new out-gathering—not from the world, but from the Church—are noteworthy. They *"keep the commandments of God."* This is the essence, as it is the expression, of the life hid with Christ in God. Thus was Adam created; right here he fell. Salvation is summed up in restoration to this original relation to God. It is the dominant note of the One Hundred and Nineteenth Psalm,—that divinely inspired eulogy on God's law. It is not legality, it is spirituality,—fulfilling the righteousness of the law through walking after the Spirit and not after the flesh. Then those composing this remnant of the woman's seed "have the testimony of Jesus Christ." The variant readings omit the name Christ, rightly so no doubt. These outstanding believers will be distinguished for having, or holding, *"the testimony of Jesus."* Not Christ but Jesus is the name of opprobrium, and not at the name of Christ or of Jesus Christ, but of Jesus, shall every knee ultimately bow and every tongue confess that He, Jesus of Mary and of Nazareth, is Lord to the glory of God. The name of Jesus, as true God and eternal life manifested in the flesh, is the stone of stumbling and rock of offence. Saul of Tarsus did not deny or persecute Christ avowedly; so he heard the voice out of the dazzling glory say, not "I am Christ," but "I am Jesus whom thou persecutest." "And straightway he preached ......in the synagogues," not Christ, as reads the A. V., but "Jesus......that he is the Son of God" (Acts 9:20, R. V.). It was not because the man of Nazareth taught the truth about God and about Christ that He was crucified, but because He taught that He, the Nazarene, was Christ, the Son of God. Satan has always from his fall opposed Christ, but it is God's "holy child Jesus" that sets him beside himself. "Who is a liar but he that denieth that Jesus is the Christ" (1 John 2:22).

Chapter Twelve, thrilling, profound as it is, nevertheless is but an approach to the main theme of the great

inserted passage, 12:1—15:4. It is the dragon's war on
the remnant of the woman's seed during the second three
and one-half years that is the real theme. We have now
been brought to that point, on the line of who the object
of his warfare will come to be. The revelation must now
go back and start afresh to unfold how the dragon will
get the suitable implement of his warfare.

CHAPTER VIII.

THE THIRD CONTEMPORANEOUS INTERCALATION, 12:1-15:4.

PART II, CHAPTER 13.

This chapter also falls into three paragraphs.

1. THE BEAST, 13:1-5:

"1 And I stood upon the sand of the sea, and saw a beast rise up out of the sea, having seven heads and ten horns, and upon his horns ten crowns, and upon his heads the name of blasphemy. 2 And the beast which I saw was like unto a leopard, and his feet were as the feet of a bear, and his mouth as the mouth of a lion: and the dragon gave him his power, and his seat, and great authority. 3 And I saw one of his heads as it were wounded to death; and his deadly wound was healed: and all the world wondered after the beast. 4 And they worshipped the dragon which gave power unto the beast, saying; Who is like unto the beast? who is able to make war with him. 5 And there was given unto him a mouth speaking great things and blasphemies; and power was given unto him to continue forty and two months."

THE objective of this passage, taken in its place in the progress of the vision, is to be found in the last words, although their sense is probably somewhat obscured by the translation before us: "and power was given unto him to continue forty and two months." This beast has already been introduced in 11:7 in connection with the course of events in Jerusalem during the first "forty and two months." The word "continue" would, then, signify that the beast will be given power to go on for the last half of the last seven years before the arrival in the earth of Jesus Christ. But this is a rather tame statement. The R. V. makes it very little stronger: "and there was given to him authority to continue ('*to do* his works *during*,' Marg.) forty and two months."

The C. V. is stronger and clearer: "And to it was given authority to do what it wills forty-two months."

This last rendering links the passage to the description of the same power given in Dan. 11:36: "And the king shall do according to his will; and he shall exalt himself, and magnify himself above every god, and shall speak marvellous things against the God of gods, and shall prosper till the indignation be accomplished: for that that is determined shall be done." Here the license given to this last world-ruler, the Anti-Christ, is represented in its relation to the accomplishment of God's "indignation" against Daniel's people, the Jews. And this is the point on the Jewish line in the last days to which we have been brought by Rev. 11:1-14.

But we are at present being led along the line culminating in the dragon's war on the remnant of the Church's true spiritual seed. The vision has covered, in the story of the woman's hiding in the wilderness, the same forty-two months, and has brought us to the point when the spiritual remnant of the Church is viewed as prepared to suffer this onslaught of the dragon. We are now being shown that, just as in the case of the tribulation of the Jews subsequently to the first forty-two months, so also, in the case of the spiritual remnant of the Church, all barriers will be out of Satan's way and the instrument of his full authority and power will be at hand to conduct that campaign of the subsequent forty-two months—three and one-half years—against the remnant of the woman's seed which 12:17 brought us up to.

Hence the marginal reading of the A. V. would be very apt: "and power [authority] was given unto him to *make war* [i. e. to conduct against the remnant of the woman's seed that aforementioned war] forty and two months." Or perhaps better still is the reading of the other one of the three variant versions: "And authority was given unto him to *prevail* [just as in the case of Israel] forty-two months."

The passage we have just been considering is the culmination of a wonderful account (vss. 1-5) of the preparation of this implement of the dragon's warfare upon the remnant of the woman's seed.

Translations generally agree in correcting the serious mistranslation of the A. V. at the opening of 13:1. The R. V. reads: "And he [the dragon] stood upon the sand of the sea."

We are to remember that we are dealing through the vision with literal political and international developments of the last days. It would not be fanciful to understand by the expression here, "upon the sand of the sea," a literal, well-known geographical position. Did it read "the great sea," we would take it to mean, after the example of Dan. 7:2, the Mediterranean Sea. We hold a closer determination, therefore, in reserve for a little. We are the more impelled to consider that a literal geographical and international position is intended, by the statement that John saw this beast—the Anti-Christ—"rise out of the sea" (A. V.), "coming up out of the sea" (R. V.), "ascending out of the sea" (C. V.).

John saw this beast "having seven heads and ten horns," even as the dragon in 12:3. But there is this notable difference, that, whereas the dragon had crowns upon the seven heads but not upon the ten horns, this beast has crowns upon the ten horns, but none upon the seven heads. From this, much light is to be deduced. A remarkable conjunction of rulership between the dragon and the beast,—that is, between Satan and the Anti-Christ—is indicated. Each represents full rulership in a reign comprehended in one under the diversity of seven heads and of ten horns, but the actual rulership of the two is not throughout the complete reign and is not simultaneous. It is perfectly evident that the reign under the aspect of the ten horns is chronologically subsequent to that under the aspect of the seven heads.

Satan is represented as the actual ruler throughout the entire reign excepting a final aspect represented by the ten horns, under which aspect or period the Anti-Christ will be the actual ruler. And yet that this latter aspect is still the original satanic rule, only through a vice-regent, is evident from the fact that the beast has the same seven heads as the dragon, though uncrowned, and that his ten horns had already belonged to the dragon, although the dragon personally will fail to wear the crowns thereof. It is evidently a case of abdication by the dragon to the beast with respect to that closing aspect of the entire reign which is represented by the ten horns.

And it is just such abdication, or transfer of actual rule, that is described in the closing words of vs. 2: "and the dragon gave him his power, and his seat [throne], and great authority." This describes complete and absolute investiture of the Anti-Christ by the devil with all satanic power, with Satan's imperial seat and with full satanic authority. It is at this point to be recalled that this transaction will post-date the expulsion of Satan from the skies unto the earth. Hence, it appears that this is the system of rule under which the devil will reorganize his kingdom in the earth after the debacle he is to suffer in the skies.

Let the order of great events be recalled: the fall of Satan from the skies and the rapture of the man child into the skies—practically simultaneous; the investiture of the Anti-Christ as Satan's perfect visible, human crowned representative—subsequently, not prior, to the rapture of the man child.

This is the very order outlined in 2 Thess. 2:6-9:

"And now ye know what withholdeth [hindereth or restraineth] that he [the 'man of sin,' the Anti-Christ] might be revealed in his time. For the mystery of iniquity doth already work [that is; satanic working of iniquity is as yet in mystery, concealment, not open, visible and public]: only he who now letteth [preventeth] will let, until he [the final man child] be taken [raptured] out of the way. And then shall that wicked

[Anti-Christ, the incarnation of iniquity] be revealed, whom the Lord shall consume with the spirit of his mouth, and shall destroy with the brightness of his coming: even him [that Wicked], whose coming is after the working [energy] of Satan with all [his] power, and signs and lying wonders.''

Just as God the Father and Jesus Christ are one, the Son being the express image of the Father, to whom also the Father hath committed all power and authority and rule, so also Satan and Anti-Christ will be one, the latter the express image in public sight of the other, and the one to whom the other will commit all his power and authority. Then iniquity will not work in secret, in disguise and concealment, but in full public view through acknowledged and visible human agency. Until the "little flock," the man child, shall be taken out of the way, the gates of hell cannot prevail in unconcealed, public operations; but afterwards Satan's warfare can be carried out in broad daylight.

The earlier parts of vs. 2 must not be passed by. "The beast which I saw was like unto a leopard." This calls us straight back to Daniel 7:6, where the third of the "four great beasts" of Daniel's vision of the "four kings [empires] which," it was explained to him, "shall arise out of the earth" (vs. 17), is introduced as "a leopard." This beast was the symbol of the Grecian Empire. And it is a striking coincidence that now in our study in Revelation the Anti-Christ should be introduced under the symbol of the leopard. We recall that we learned from Dan. 8:9-12, 23, 25 that the Anti-Christ should spring from some quarter of the restored four quarters of the old Grecian Empire, and from Dan. 11:40 that it should be from the western, the Grecian, or Thracian quarter of the territory of the old Grecian Empire that he should arise. It will also be recalled that in Zech. 9:13 the final victory for Israel is represented as a victory for "thy sons, O Zion, against thy sons, O Greece."

This allocation of the beast through the symbol of the leopard with these Old Testament predictions of the rise of the Anti-Christ from the territory of the Thracian quarter of the old Grecian Empire, leads very directly to the conclusion, that the sea, on the shore of which the dragon stood in the vision while out of the sea the beast arose, is to be understood as the Ægean Sea.

But, while the beast was seen as a leopard in the main, yet he had attributes resembling the two ancient Empires prior to the Grecian; his feet—emblem of brute force— were like the feet of a bear (the symbol of the Medo-Persian Empire), and his mouth—emblem of intelligence—like the mouth of a lion (the symbol of the Babylonian Empire). We thus learn from John's vision that the ruler of the ten-crowned horns will be directly Grecian, but with striking Persian characteristic with respect to sheer force, and Babylonian with respect to brilliant intelligence. And, seeing that the ten horns are certainly to be indentified with the ten toes of Nebuchadnezzar's image and with the ten horns of Dan. 7: 7, 8, 20, and, therefore, are to be understood as the final manifestation of the imperial government of the world to be dominated by Anti-Christ, as Daniel's "little horn," we would find in the seven heads, crowned on the dragon, uncrowned on the Anti-Christ, symbols of the great ancient world-empires. It is to be perceived, then, that the Anti-Christ is to be the final successor to the rule of Satan over the past empires of earth, and to be himself endowed with all satanic power and authority to rule the final governmental situation in the earth.

It is mentioned as a most notable feature of this beast, the Anti-Christ, that one of his heads—emblem of an ancient world-empire—appeared "as it were wounded to death ("slain to death," C. V.); and his deadly wound was healed" ("death stroke was cured"). This clearly indicates the revival of a defunct empire amounting to a miracle of political, imperial resurrection.

This astonishing phenomenon carries the idea that there is chronological distinction between the heads, and that the seven heads may constitute in the vision a sevenfold succession of the world-empires of history, each subject in its day to the suzerainty of the dragon, the last one of which, after having been violently swept into oblivion with the others, yet experiences in the last days an amazing resurrection, to be imperially ruled under a tenfold division by the final great satanized earthly lord, the Anti-Christ. This is in accord with, although adding important revelation to, the disclosures of the image of Nebuchadnezzar and the vision of the four beasts given to Daniel, as recorded by him in Chapter 7.

It is represented by John that, because of this political marvel, the whole world "wondered after the beast." It will be remembered that the Anti-Christ himself is described in 11:7 as one who "ascendeth out of the bottomless pit." The resurrected empire will have, then, a resurrected monarch. As a resurrected man his reappearance out of the bottomless pit must occur somewhere geographically. John says that he saw him "ascending out of the sea," the Aegean as we have found. And his resurrection, it is evident, will be a well-attested fact, verified by witnesses and ample proofs. These will to the deceived world be ample parallels and offsets to the claims of the true Christ, coming as a resurrected One to rule a long-deceased, but newly resurrected Kingdom of Israel and empire of the world. Shall worship be held in reserve for the latter, or shall the masterpiece of Satan be acclaimed as the Chosen, the Anointed? John witnessed in vision the fateful decision which the impenitent world is to make. Even with "the sign of the Son of man in heaven," already hanging out in sight in the skies, and after the first stage of rapture shall have astounded the world, the consensus of mind and action will be expressed, "We will not have this man to rule over us," and, giving worship to the dragon-chief and to his super-man, the world will plight undying allegiance to the latter, saying, "Who is like unto the beast? who is able to make war with him?" It means not only who in his own strength can withstand the Anti-Christ, but also, who can withstand him by reliance upon Christ Himself? It will be a deliberate and final committal of fortunes to the Anti-Christ against the Christ such as to leave those who "keep the commandments of God, and have the testimony of Jesus" to be like victims thrown to the lions in the amphitheater.

This "Wicked" is to be endowed satanically with unparalleled ability to blaspheme outrageously everything sacred; and upon such a basis of blasphemous challenge will he especially wage the war upon the saints during the second forty-two months, v. 5. We remember to what unwonted sacrilegious daring Nebuchadnezzar was carried after he had destroyed Zion, the city of the great King Jehovah, as was exhibited on the occasion of dedicating the golden statue on the plain of Dura (Dan. 3). And we have seen in Rev. 11: 1-10 that it will be just at the end of the first forty-two months, that the two prophetic witnesses will be delivered to the will of the beast, and that all further divine restraint to his will is to be suspended. He will, therefore, be facing an open track for his own free and hellish will against the remnant of Hebrew believers and of Gentile believers alike.

2. THE BEAST'S WAR ON THE SAINTS, vs. 6-10.

"6 And he opened his mouth in blasphemy against God, to blaspheme his name, and his tabernacle, and them that dwell in heaven. 7 And it was given unto him to make war with the saints, and to overcome them: and power was given him over all kindreds, and tongues and nations. 8 And all that dwell upon the earth shall worship him, whose names are not written in the book of life of the Lamb slain from the foundation of the world. 9 If any man have an ear, let him hear. 10 He that leadeth into captivity shall go into captivity: he that killeth with the sword must be killed with the sword. Here is the patience and the faith of the saints."

With foregoing preparation, this brief, but pregnant and momentous passage reads to us so plainly as scarcely to need comment. Yet it deserves solemn and protracted meditation, lest its weight should not be felt.

First, the blasphemy of the Anti-Christ is exposed in horrifying details. This character of the Anti-Christ has always before been specially noted by Scripture. Daniel repeatedly points to it. "In this horn were eyes like the eyes of man, and a mouth speaking great things.......And a mouth that spake very great things......And he shall speak great words against the most High" (7:8, 20, 25). In the eighth chapter of Daniel is predicted how the "little horn" shall magnify himself against even Christ, the Prince of the house of Israel, take away the daily offerings and trample the sanctuary under his unholy feet. These sacrilegious outrages are predicted again in 9:27. And in 11:36-39 a yet fuller prediction of how the wilful king's unbounded contempt will be exhibited for everything sacred. In 2 Thess. 2:4 yet stronger and more graphic description is given of this blasphemer's doings: "Who opposeth and exalteth himself above all that is called God, or that is worshipped; so that he as God sitteth in the temple of God, shewing himself that he is God."

The beast's blasphemies will be explicable only by supernatural satanic endowment; "and there was *given* unto him a mouth speaking great things and blasphemies." Verse 6 specifies the objects of his blasphemous spleen: First, God Himself. "The wicked hath said in his heart, There is no God." "There is no God in all his thoughts," or better, "All his thoughts are —'No God.'" To the Anti-Christ God will be nothing, he will treat Him as nothing, he will burn Him in effigy amidst the howls of his frenzied devotees. Secondly, whatever belongs to God, to-wit: His name, His tabernacle, and "them that dwell in heaven." This no doubt refers to the things of God in the skies particularly related to the situation in the earth in that day. It will be the time of Jesus Christ's bodily and glorious presence in the skies, with all these regions acclaiming and adoring Him, where for so long abject obeisance had been exacted by the prince of darkness. It will, however, be the time of Jesus' glorified presence there hidden in His tabernacle or tarrying place. And those with him will be not only the happy and faithful angels, but also the raptured, glorified saints. All this magnificent setting in the skies, all this beatific and holy condition of the celestial classes and things, will be nothing to the beast but objects of execration, ribald jest and blatant defiance. It would seem that, not only thrilling events will have made known what a heavenly condition has supplanted in the skies the satanic conditions prevailing for ages before, but also visible signs—''the sign of the Son of man in heaven'' —will be in earthly sight. But this super-man will but toss his head and wag his blasphemous tongue against it all.

The next sententious statement expresses the course of the Anti-Christ toward the holy ones on earth. ''And it was given unto him to make war with the saints, and to overcome them,'' ''to battle with the saints, and to conquer them'' (C. V.). In the first three and one-half years his design against the saints—in this case Jewish saints—will be met by the stern repulses of the two witnesses. The achievements of faith will illustrate anew what is recorded in Heb. 11: 33-35: ''Who through faith subdued kingdoms, wrought righteousness, obtained promises, stopped the mouths of lions, quenched the violence of fire, escaped the edge of the sword, out of weakness were made strong, waxed valiant in fight, *turned to flight the armies of the aliens.* Women received their dead raised to life again.'' But now, during this period of the second forty-two months, it will be illustrative of the further and antithetical record in Heb. 11: 35-38:

"35 And others were tortured, not accepting deliverance; that they might obtain a better resurrection: 36 And others had trial of cruel mockings and scourgings, yea, moreover of bonds and imprisonment: 37 They were stoned, they were sawn asunder, were tempted, were slain with the sword: they wandered about in sheepskins and goatskins; being destitute, afflicted, tormented; 38 (Of whom the world was not worthy:) they wandered in deserts, and in mountains, and in dens and caves of the earth."

So long as Jesus' "hour was not yet" his enemies could not take Him; but later He said, "This is your hour, and the power of darkness." He was then "as a lamb led to the slaughter." So will it be with the faithful witnesses of Jesus in the days and years now under consideration. And this very Scripture will be light and strength and victory to them. They will know by this Scripture that it is by divine permission that the Anti-Christ can prevail over them. While doubtless faith will do many exploits, yet the great exploit will be that *"in all these things* we are *more* than conquerors through him that loved us."

The universal authority of the Anti-Christ is next foretold by our passage. The C. V. renders the passage with great force: "And authority was given to it [the beast] over every tribe and people and language and nation." Sometimes, even often, it seems to be warrantable to presume that statements of conditions to exist on earth in the last days apply only to the old imperial world of Bible history. But the language here is so explicit, emphatic and detailed as almost to require the application to be made on the world-wide scale. And this is logical. If the Anti-Christ is to rule in all the extent and strength of Satan's sway, it must certainly be world-wide in reach. This offers a very solemn and startling commentary upon hopes and theories and enterprises inspired by the expectation of "bringing in the kingdom over all the earth"—or any part of it—excepting through an unparalleled catastrophe ever drawing nearer, and through a "restitution of all things, which

God hath spoken by the mouth of all his holy prophets since the world began.''

And it is shown that this universal sway is to be spiritual as well as political: ''And all that dwell upon the earth shall worship him, whose names are not written in the book of life of the Lamb slain from the foundation of the world,'' v. 8. This shows how sharply the religious lines will be drawn. Every man on earth will then be a worshipper, and it will be a question of certain life or death whom every person worships, whether the Anti-Christ or Jesus, the Christ. To the former, there will be immunity from death for religious cause; to the latter, no immunity. Every believer will be ''always delivered unto death for Jesus' sake.''

''Whose names are not written in the book of life of the Lamb.'' This is not a criterion which is to hold only in that day as the evidence of salvation. It is the criterion as well now. Salvation is not commanded by profession, by religious works, or by ecclesiastical absolution and benediction. Salvation consists in being a partaker of the life of Jesus crucified and living again. And the Lord knoweth them that are His, and ''a *book* of remembrance was written before him for them that feared the Lord, and that thought upon his name.'' This book is not the ''Church-roll'' kept on earth by human hands. Many names engrossed in the latter will not be found in the former, and vice versa. The recorder above will make no mistake in including or in omitting. The Lord Himself knows when the virtue of life goes out from Him and whom it enters. His own consciousness is a self-recording book.

The expression, ''the Lamb slain from the foundation of the world'' is very suggestive. It has been fully discussed in the chapter on ''The Cross of the Ages.'' The truth that it embodies is that the dying of Jesus for the sin of the world is an event so related to all ages as to be the same in effect all before Calvary as since Calvary.

This is due to the fact that all ages constitute an organic whole, such that the cross stands in exactly the right place historically to pulsate with saving power throughout the entire body of the ages.

The C. V. reads "disruption of the world" instead of "foundation of the world." The difference arises simply from the sense in which the figure in the Greek word of *throwing down* is taken, whether as in laying a foundation or as in demolishing an existing structure. There is special appropriateness in representing the Lamb as slain from the throwing down violently, from the disruption of the world, for His death is the all-inclusive basis of restoration. We would then have the truth before us that from the time of world-ruin the cross of Jesus has been potent for world-salvation, for world-restoration. This teaching is especially germain to this Book of Revelation, which, as will be brought to light later, unfolds as no other part of the Bible does the final re-creation of the disrupted world of earth and skies.

The paragraph of the text now under study appends to the main material of revelation a peculiar message. It is a "word in season for him that is weary" in those awful days. Although so plainly and openly written, yet its voice is not for all ears. "If any man have an ear, let him hear." First, one must have an ear,—the ear. This is a spiritual function. But it is not even enough to have the function of spiritual perception; "let him hear." Attention, inquiry, searching and listening is necessary.

But what is the message for the spiritual listener? It is to the effect that the captor shall be taken captive, the slayer shall be slain. This, on the one hand, will deter the saints from retaliation in kind against their enemies, and, on the other hand, will assure them of a certain and speedy turning of the tables against those taking the saints captive or slaying them with the sword.

Although three and one-half years will seem long with their agonies and tragedies, yet how short a time really for this coming reign of unexampled terror! This message will ground and preserve the patient and believing endurance of the saints. This very verse 10 will be the sheet-anchor to hold attentive saints from fainting or flinching in that trying time.

3. ANOTHER BEAST, VS. 11-18.

"11 And I beheld another beast coming up out of the earth; and he had two horns like a lamb, and he spake as a dragon. 12 And he exerciseth all the power of the first beast before him, and causeth the earth and them which dwell therein to worship the first beast, whose deadly wound was healed. 13 And he doeth great wonders, so that he maketh fire come down from heaven on the earth in the sight of men, 14 And deceiveth them that dwell on the earth by the means of those miracles which he had power to do in the sight of the beast; saying to them that dwell on the earth, that they should make an image to the beast, which had the wound by a sword, and did live. 15 And he had power to give life unto the image of the beast, that the image of the beast should both speak, and cause that as many as would not worship the image of the beast should be killed. 16 And he causeth all, both small and great, rich and poor, free and bond, to receive a mark in their right hand, or in their foreheads: 17 And that no man might buy or sell, save he that had the mark, or the name of the beast, or the number of his name. 18 Here is wisdom. Let him that hath understanding count the number of the beast: for it is the number of a man; and his number is six hundred three score and six.''

The figure of a beast here implies another political personage. This seems to be the only passage in the Bible where this celebrity is mentioned. His symbolical representation is quite unique. Two incipient horns of a little lamb represent his inconsiderable power, while the frightful maw of a dragon represents the effectiveness of his utterances. His ascension to public notice "out of the earth" stands in apparently intended contrast with that of the first beast, "out of the sea." In either case the expression employed may imply literal human resurrection. This is the more warrantable conception because of the prominence which, as the accounts show, satanic signs and wonders will in that time assume.

The office of this unique personality will be that of prime minister to the Anti-Christ. He will be his plenipotentiary, proclaiming his liege lord with all authority, and causing the entire imperial world and all its peoples to bow down to him as their god and king. There will seem to be no bounds to the miraculous agencies at his disposal for effecting the bondage of all unregenerate men, soul and body, to the great vice-gerent of the devil. He will parallel the works of Elijah, he will outdo the works of the two witnesses, in bringing down fire out of the skies in public sight. Thus it is here shown that the "lying wonders," attributed by Paul in 2 Thess. 2:9 to "that Wicked," will be executed by this Grand Vizier of Anti-Christ. Thus will the Judge of all unregenerate men "send them strong delusion, that they should believe a lie: that they might all be damned who believed not the truth, but had pleasure in unrighteousness."

The supreme Pasha of the antichristian empire will require an image of his master to be made; likely some golden colossus after the prototype of the image which Nebuchadnezzar had set up in the plain of Dura. For the third time reference is in this connection made in v. 14 to the marvel of the healing of the deadly wound which one head of the beast had suffered. As has been shown, this signifies the return to full life of an earlier supreme political power which had passed apparently into hopeless oblivion. This political miracle, along with the fact of the Anti-Christ's personal resurrection from the dead, will influence the world's imagination to such a pitch as to render it ready to accord all admiration and homage to the beast. This captivation of the unregenerate public will reach its climax, when the great prophet of the Anti-Christ will actually endow his image with living breath and audible speech, and will require an all too-willing worship on the part of the unbelieving masses, under penalty of death, however, for all who refuse so to do.

In like manner this false prophet and executive of Anti-Christ will dominate the commercial and industrial spheres, to the extent of requiring, under penalty of utter economic disability, every person, low or high, rich or poor, free or bond, to exhibit constantly in a conspicuous way, on right hand or forehead, some emblem, the name or number denoting his serfdom under the terrible beast.

The object of this picture is, however, to bring to light how, again through such a specific prophetic method of testing, the elect of that day may avoid being deceived even if they shall not be able to escape boycott and death. Wisdom and understanding is ever promised to God's saints in every perplexity, entanglement and danger. With all this complicated, crafty, consummate contrivance of deception and intimidation, sorely besetting the servants of God Almighty and of His Christ, there will yet be a simple way of answering aright the question of the hour, "What think ye of Anti-Christ?" The answer which the spirit of wisdom and of discernment will promptly give the steady, devoted, trustful believer is, "Superman although he be, yet man, and only man, is he."

The simple-minded believer will take the accurate measurement and weight of dragon, beast number one and beast number two. As a trinity, rivalling the divine in pretence, they will be seen to fall fatally short of the divine; they cannot rise above the finite class, their number successively is only six, six and six. All the distance between the finite and the infinite,—which can never even be lessened; all the distance between creature and creator,—never a matter even of degrees; all the distance between the very God and His subjects,—where there is left no distinction of persons—remains. After the example of Shadrach, Meshach, and Abednego, the intrepid, unfaltering heroes of Christian faith in those coming days of testing will put themselves on record thus: O Anti-Christ, we are not careful to answer thee in this matter. If it be so, our God whom we serve is able to deliver us from boycott and from death, and He will deliver us out of thine hand, O King. But if not, be it known unto thee, O King, that we will not serve thy god (Satan), nor worship the golden image which thou hast set up.

CHAPTER IX.

THE THIRD CONTEMPORANEOUS INTERCALATION, 12:1—15:4.

PART III.   CELESTIAL SCENES, 14:1—15:4.

A T THIS point the vision is shifted again to the skies and a series of revelations from that standpoint is unfolded.

1. THE ONE HUNDRED AND FORTY-FOUR THOUSAND VIRGINS, 14:1-5:

"1 And I looked, and lo, a Lamb stood on the mount Sion, and with him an hundred and forty and four thousand, having his Father's name written in their foreheads. 2 And I heard a voice from heaven, as the voice of many waters, and as the voice of a great thunder: and I heard the voice of harpers harping with their harps: 3 And they sung as it were a new song before the throne, and before the four beasts, and the elders: and no man could learn that song but the hundred and forty and four thousand, which were redeeemed from the earth. 4 These are they which were not defiled with women; for they are virgins. These are they which follow the Lamb whithersoever he goeth. These were redeemed from among men, being the first-fruits unto God and to the Lamb. 5 And in their mouth was found no guile: for they are without fault before the throne of God."

The first thing to be perceived here is that "the mount Sion" is not earthly, but celestial. In the vision John heard the sonorous anthem of this unique choir as "a voice from heaven"; that is, out of the skies. Moreover they were seen singing "before the throne, and before the four beasts, and the elders." Thus the question is placed beyond debate. And it is not exceptional to find in the Bible that the earthly Jerusalem and Zion are types of celestial counterparts called Jerusalem and Zion. In Heb. 12:22 "mount Zion" is used as the sacred center of "the city of the living God, the *heavenly Jerusalem.*" This, however, is not to be understood as a matter of material celestial location and construction, but of spiritual reality. This subject will be fully unfolded later. Suffice it here to note, that it is seen that to this company the privilege of face to face worship and praise before the Lamb and before the four beasts and before the elders—that is, the privilege of the innermost circle of that combined concourse in our skies introduced in vision in Chapters 4 and 5—is to be accorded. Of such privilege it would be an earthly type for a special chosen company to occupy the most central place of worship and praise at Jerusalem and on mount Zion, on the occasion of Christ's coming glorified manifestation there, in the midst of the attending angels of God and of all the attending glorified saints.

These favored ones bear a mark standing in striking contrast to that which has just been spoken of in 13: 16, 17. These are stamped with the name, that is, the very being, of the Lamb and of His Father. They are thus stamped on their foreheads, the seal of both spiritual intelligence and of spiritual manifestation to all beholders.

Their singing is like to the distant roar of Niagara and to the reverberations through the ether of loud thunder. Their song is a new song, and one which no one outside themselves will be able to learn. What can and does this mean? The best songs are born of the experiences of the composers. Those only can truly learn and render those songs who themselves know the experiences which gave them birth. Go through the Psalms of David and note the many which are the offspring of well-known experiences of David. Their greatest service is as vehicles of emotion and expression to others down the centuries who have like experiences. We have already seen, in Chapter 7, a numberless throng of tribulation saints singing in common the song of their salvation out of a like general experience. But now, here is a company who have a hitherto unknown, unsung song, and one which no others will ever be able to learn to sing in a true sense. The reason must be that this company are in the last days to pass through altogether unique testing and triumphant experiences.

It seems both natural and reasonable to find in this company of one hundred and forty-four thousand—now come off more than conquerors and standing, translated and glorified, in highest possible privilege on the occasion of our Lord's tarrying presence in our skies—the company of the same number introduced in Chapter 7, a selected company from all the tribes of Israel, sealed in their foreheads with the "seal of the living God" and as His "servants." It was as special standard-bearers of the faith beginning with the era of the seventh seal that these Israelites were seen to be commissioned. Now, in the fourthteenth chapter, this company, it would seem, is presented again in the enjoyment of the rewards and commendations which will be theirs after their course has been finished. It is noteworthy that not one of the number is seen to have failed.

They are described as a company who, first, will have been "redeemed from the earth." This means much, in view of the state of the earth in their times. But it shows that the praise belongs to the Redeemer, and that by grace these shall be what they will prove to be. In the next place, they will be found and confessed to have kept themselves unspotted unto the Lord as chaste virgins. We may little dream of the spiritual temptresses which will practice their seductions upon these outstanding soldiers of the cross; but they will prove wholly sanctified and meet for the Master's use, following Him wherever He shall go before them. It next appears, that they will be the ensamples, the finest advance specimens, of the great company of true believers who shall weather the storms of the last days, "being the *first-fruits* unto

God and to the Lamb.'' Finally, as a simple, yet profound, mark of genuine sanctity there will be found in their mouth no guile, no compromise with the antichristian demands of their day, but they will come up before the throne of God in the skies fleckless, flawless, faultless.

2. THREE MOMENTOUS ANGELIC PROCLAMATIONS, 14: 6-13.

"6 And I saw another angel fly in the midst of heaven, having the everlasting gospel to preach unto them that dwell on the earth, and to every nation, and kindred, and tongue and people. 7 Saying with a loud voice, Fear God, and give glory to him; for the hour of his judgment is come: and worship him that made heaven, and earth, and the sea, and the fountains of waters. 8 And there followed another angel, saying, Babylon is fallen, is fallen, that great city, because she made all nations to drink of the wine of the wrath of her fornications. 9 And the third angel followed them, saying with a loud voice, If any man worship the beast and his image, and receive his mark in his forehead, or in his hand, 10 The same shall drink of the wine of the wrath of God, which is poured out without mixture into the cup of his indignation; and he shall be tormented with fire and brimstone in the presence of the holy angels, and in the presence of the Lamb: 11 And the smoke of their torment ascendeth up for ever and ever: and they have no rest day nor night, who worship the beast and his image, and whosoever receiveth the mark of his name. 12 Here is the patience of the saints: here are they that keep the commandments of God, and keep the faith of Jesus. 13 And I heard a voice from heaven, saying unto me, Write, Blessed are the dead which die in the Lord from henceforth: Yea, saith the Spirit, that they may rest from their labors; and their works do follow them.''

These eight verses group themselves together quite consistently both in outward form and in sequence of thought. There are three definite divisions of the passage.

(1). The Angelic Gospel, vs. 6, 7.

Calling to mind afresh the direful epoch now under survey, it must be admitted that very important is the place it is here shown the Gospel will then occupy. It clearly appears that at no time in even the last days is the Gospel to cease to be proclaimed. If it be here presupposed that the preaching of the Gospel will have ceased on the earth,—a supposition not at all called for in the case—yet it only means that God will have it preached from the skies. Preaching of the Gospel from mid-air by angelic voice is not here a new idea or a new fact. Paul, in Gal. 1:8, implies the easy possibility of this: "Though we, or an angel from heaven, preach any other gospel unto you"; only Paul here shows that the preaching of an angel has no sacred claim to acceptance excepting as it agrees perfectly with the original apostolical Gospel. The very fact of angelic proclamation of the glad tidings to human ears was illustrated on the night of our Lord's nativity at Bethlehem. And it is most heartening to know that in that awful coming night of spiritual eclipse, Gospel preaching will not only not cease, but will be supernaturally reinforced by angelic voice in mid-air.

The more impressive is the coming event because such angelic preaching is going to be not some singular, local occurrence, but it is to be a world-wide, thorough evangelization. There will be left no "regions beyond"; if never before, the Gospel at that time, at least, will be preached among all nations and to every creature.

And the Gospel preached will be "the everlasting gospel." This expression is a corrective to all tendency, because of differing descriptive terms,—like "the gospel of grace," and "the gospel of the kingdom"—to catalogue a variety of Gospels as belonging to different dispensations and peoples. Certainly the expression, "the everlasting gospel," implies one only and an ever-complete and changeless Gospel. It dates from before the foundation of the world and will never go out of date. Variations in description, such as have been instanced, are not different Gospels, or the Gospel for different times or peoples, but merely the different aspects belonging essentially and always to the one and the same Gospel. "The everlasting gospel" is not a distinctive Gospel, determined by the fact of being proclaimed in mid-air, by an angel and at such a point in the last days of the tribulation. It is our Gospel, to be sounded out in mid-air, the world around, by thunderous angelic voice, in those fateful days when such extraordinary Gospel preaching will be timely and appropriate.

And yet there is a principle of special adaptation in preaching the Gospel. Every Spirit-moved preacher will preach the Gospel appropriately to his audience and to the occasion, because the Gospel is not a fixed formula for ceaseless and unvarying repetition. Consequently the burden of this angel's Gospel message is appropriate to his world-wide audience and to the conditions and emergencies of the hour. It will be a most solemn and crucial hour in all the earth. Every individual inhabitant, every nation, every kindred, every tongue, every people will be facing supreme, urgent, decisive responsibility. As never before the call of the hour will be "Choose you this day whom ye will serve." It will be in most gracious as well as alarming tone that the angel will sound his message forth on every ear, to every nation, kindred, tongue and people, "Saying with a loud voice, Fear God, and give glory to him; for *the hour of his judgment is come:* and worship him that made heaven, and the earth, and the sea, and the fountains of waters." The call, coming in thrilling thunder-tone from the ether, from an awe-inspiring angel flying majestically in mid-air, perhaps in plain sight to all, will be reaching every ear and heart without interception; and it will once again more impressively than ever demand universal attention and individual decision regarding final position as between Christ and Anti-Christ. Every conscience will testify that to God alone belong reverence and glory. And every conscience will understand and bow under the declaration of immediately impending judgment. And every conscience will admit that, however mighty be the Anti-Christ, yet it is another who made heaven, earth, sea and all water-sources.

The angel's summons will not call for inconsiderate action, for it will be a time for public council as well as for individual consideration. Hence the decisions of nations, kindreds, tongues and peoples will be hammered out through heated campaign and clash of parliaments, chancellories and international conferences.

(2). The Angelic Verdict, v. 8.

Another angel will in due time sail through the sky in world-wide circuit, throwing into the trembling balances a most important consideration, "Babylon is fallen, is fallen, that great city." It is safe to say that this is not a city in the natural sense, and that her fall is not like the sudden wreck of Tokio, or Yokohama on September 1, 1923. The language expresses a fact already accomplished, and yet the judgment upon Babylon is placed in this book as of later occurrence. The charge against Babylon expressed in the lines following explains the nature of Babylon and her fall. "She made all nations drink of the wine of the wrath of her fornications," rather, "of the furious wine of her prostitution" (C. V.). Babylon is not municipal, political, or commercial in nature, but spiritual, as the language implies. And her fall is of a spiritual character which is represented as having reached its utmost depths. The angel's urgent, impressive announcement will be a moral warning against choosing in that fateful hour citizenship in the city of the devil rather than in the city of God, the one ripened in hellish depravity, the other abiding in unfading holiness and glory.

(3). The Angelic Warning, vs. 9-12.

What an era of angelic interposition, palpable to the physical senses and manifest to the public universal-

ly! Still a third angel of God will sweep through the
skies megaphoning the most fearful warning ever yet
heard. The message is directly applicable to the circumstances and issues of the hour. Warning is faithfully
given of the consequences of doing just those things
which the Anti-Christ, as was shown in 13:12, 15, 16,
will be requiring; namely, to worship him and his image,
and to receive his mark in forehead or in hand. The
warning is that such as obey these requirements "shall
drink of the wine"—not of Babylon, but—"of the wrath
of God." And it will not be as ever before, a wrath
mixed with many moderations, but wrath "poured out
without mixture into the cup of his indignation."

But warning will reach far beyond this fearful immediate, earthly and temporal visitation of divine wrath.
"And he shall be tortured with fire and brimstone in
the presence"; that is, before the very eyes, "of the
holy angels, and in the presence of the Lamb." That this
is future punishment, not on earth but in hell, not
temporal but eternal, is made plain by the further
words: "And the smoke of their torment ascendeth up
for ever and ever." We are not to infer that this final
future and endless punishment is immediately to ensue
on the wake of the first and temporal infliction. Later
teachings of this book show us when full, final and everlasting punishment is to begin.

The remainder of verse 11 is very striking as regards
the cardinal feature of the endless torment of the
damned, especially of those who refuse "the angelic
gospel" and ignore "the angelic verdict" and refuse
"the angelic warning," and who deliberately espouse
the dominion of the Anti-Christ: "and they have *no rest
day nor night*, who worship the beast and his image,
and whosoever receiveth the mark of his name." There
runs through all the Bible the sweet promise to the
children of God of eternal rest after this life's muta-
tions, but the promise to the antichristian classes is that

of unrelieved, incessant restlessness. "There is no peace, saith my God, to the wicked." As to the nature and the place of their endless torment as indicated by the expression "with fire and brimstone," a definite discussion is reserved until the last testimonies of the Scriptures on this subject in 20:10 and 21:8 are reached.

The importance to believers which this angelic warning will serve in those days and under the conditions then prevailing, is intimated by verse 12. It illustrates, just as is intimated in 13:9, 10 and 18, how valuable and necessary prophetic Scripture always is as "a light in a dark place," for the enlightenment, guidance and support of those who "take heed" thereunto. "Here is the patience of the saints: here are they that keep the commandments of God, and the faith of Jesus." A better translation is that of the C. V.: "Here is the endurance of the saints, who are keeping the precepts of God and the faith of Jesus." The timely angelic warning serves to arm them against fainting, wavering, or even questioning under the strain upon obedience and faith. And here again, the expression, "the faith of Jesus"; that is, the true faith in Jesus, is strictly relevant. The contention of those days will not be so much concerning "the Christ" as concerning Christ in Jesus of Nazareth, crucified for the sin of the world, risen, glorified, then already returned to the skies overhead and about to descend as "this same Jesus." This is the substance of Christian life now and ever—practicing the precepts of God and the faith in Jesus; but in those days very special help—even that of angelic warning sounded in mighty voice from mid-air—will be most timely and effective for the tested saints.

Verse 13 seems to belong to our present passage, serving as an appendix, especially to the last angelic message. The very expression, "the endurance of the saints," implies a time of fierce persecution and of common martyrdom. This new "voice out of heaven" does not seem to be heard by John in vision as, like the three angelic voices preceding, belonging to the progress of events in the last days, but it was a direction to John as to something to be written in his book just at this point. The matter to be written, however, is not one of general application, but one of particular application to the saints of that coming day, and to their peculiar experiences. The voice said, "Write: 'Happy are the dead who are dying in the Lord henceforth!' 'Yea,' the spirit is saying, 'that they will be resting from their toil, for their acts are accompanying them'" (C. V.).

True it is that happy are the dead who are dying in the Lord at whatever time. But so general and familiar a declaration as that would be incongruous as an appendix to the verses immediately preceding. The declaration should be taken in the limited application to the saints of those coming days. Moreover, the word "henceforth," of the phrase "from henceforth" as reads the A. V., indicates that a peculiar and special blessedness will from a certain point of progress in the last days await the dying saints who shall endure in obedience to God and faith in Jesus unto death.

This peculiar blessing must be sought for in the explanatory words following. These words—"that they may rest from their labors; and their works do follow them"—are so familiar to us in general quite vague application to dying saints in all ages, that we have difficulty in discovering anything new and distinctive in them. The translation of the C. V. already given helps somewhat: "that they will be resting from their toil, and their acts are accompanying them." Here the statement, "for their acts are accompanying them," is added to the statement "that they will be resting from their toil," as explaining a thought embodied therein. Evidently the connection of thought is, that, while these dying ones will be entering into rest from toil, yet they will not be entering into an intermediate state of bodily inactivity,—''their works do follow them,'' ''their acts do accompany them.'' Without doubt all dying saints enjoy after death activities such as belong to a disembodied state. But here the peculiar point is that accustomed activities are to accompany these saints through death. And yet those activities are to be at the same time a ''resting from......toil.'' It seems, then, to be clear that the peculiar blessing promised to the saints dying after a certain point in the last days is reached is that their dead bodies shall be immediately changed and translated, so that in their case, though dying, yet they will not pass into an intermediate, disembodied, physically inactive state, but pass instantly into immortality and glory with all the toilless, restful activities belonging to that state.

3. THE GREAT INGATHERINGS, 14:14—15:4.

It seems to be most logical to include 15:1-4 with the remainder of Chapter 14. Instead, however, of presenting the entire text at once together, it will be presented in three successive scenes.

(1). The Harvest of the Earth, 14:14-16.

''14 And I looked, and behold, a white cloud, and upon the cloud one sat like unto the Son of man, having on his head a golden crown, and in his hand a sharp sickle. 15 And another angel came out of the temple, crying with a loud voice to him that sat on the cloud, Thrust in thy sickle, and reap; for the time is come for thee to reap; for the harvest of the earth is ripe. 16 And he that sat on the cloud thrust in his sickle on the earth; and the earth was reaped.''

It should be remembered that the long passage, 12:1—15:4 has to do with the period of the last three and one-half years of this age, the time of Anti-Christ's unhindered sway. (Of course, as has been shown, chapter 12 leads up to this period.) We are therefore to see now what the above portion of chapter 14 reveals as belong-

ing to the very last days, the days of the supreme tribulation.

The first feature of this new vision is clearly that of
the glorified Jesus enthroned in the skies upon a cloud
of glory, with victor's wreath crowning His head, and
a keen-edged sickle in His hand. We recall that, according to 11 : 19, the action of this part of the Revelation is seen as proceeding from the temple in the skies,
the very sanctuary of God. So it is "out of the temple"
that this angel was seen to come. Not as a command, but
more as a prayer, he bids Jesus thrust in His sickle and
reap, because the field is white already to the harvest.
Finite intelligence observes and declares the ripeness
of the harvest, the high time for the divine reaper to
gather it in.

What is meant by "the harvest of the earth?" Beyond dispute or doubt it means saved souls. In James
5 : 7, 8 we have a kindred passage. "Be patient, therefore, brethren, unto the coming of the Lord. Behold, the
husbandman waiteth for the precious fruit of the earth,
and hath long patience for it, until he receive the early
and the latter rain. Be ye patient also; stablish your
hearts: for the coming of the Lord draweth nigh."

Both these passages show that down to the very coming
of Christ back to the earth there is to be spiritual
fruitage in the earth. The passage in James has to do
with the production of this fruitage; our present passage in Revelation has to do with the gathering of this
spiritual fruitage out of the earth into the Lord's storehouse of saints in the skies. "Precious fruit" implies
choice products; "of the earth" implies world-wide
product. "Harvest of the earth" implies abundance and
that abundance gathered into storehouse and barn. We
learn, therefore, that the last three and one-half years
of the age, long after the pre-tribulation rapture, and out
of the very midst of the supreme sway of Anti-Christ
over the earth, a vast and priceless harvest of believers

will be produced, ripened and gathered up on high. This great rapture-body of the second half of the last seven years corresponds to the great rapture-body of the first half seen in Chapter 7. It is most enlightening to us, as well as most cheering, to learn how richly fruitful in souls, saved and made meet for glory, will be the times of the tribulation.

(2). The Vintage of the Earth, 14:17—15:1.

"17 And another angel came out of the temple which is in heaven, he also having a sharp sickle. 18 And another angel came out from the altar, which had power over fire; and cried with a loud cry to him that had the sharp sickle, saying, Thrust in thy sharp sickle, and gather the clusters of the vine of the earth; for her grapes are fully ripe. 19 And the angel thrust in his sickle into the earth, and gathered the vine of the earth, and cast it into the great wine-press of the wrath of God. 20 And the wine-press was trodden without the city, and blood came out of the wine-press, even unto the horse-bridles, by the space of a thousand and six hundred furlongs. 1 And I saw another sign in heaven, great and marvellous, seven angels having the seven last plagues; for in them is filled up the wrath of God."

A very little attention serves to perceive the striking contrasts between this vintage and the foregoing reaping. Even the sharp sickle in the two cases is not the same, the former being one for cutting grain, the other for clipping grape stems.

In the first place this vintage is unto judgment. The treading of the wine-press stands in Scripture as a figure of divine judgment upon the wicked. This is the sense of the figure in Isa. 63:1-6, although this latter passage is so commonly misapplied. The "dyed garments" is there explained after the analogy of a treader of the grapes. The question is asked, "Wherefore art thou red in thine apparel, and thy garments like him that treadeth in the winefat?" The answer is given, "I have trodden the winepress alone." But what follows shows that it has no reference to the judgment borne by Jesus on Calvary, the blood shed for our sins.

"And of the people there was none with me: for I will *tread them in mine anger, and trample them in my fury;* and *their blood* shall be sprinkled upon my garments, and I will stain all my raiment. *For the day of vengeance is in mine heart,* and the year of my redeemed is come." This passage, therefore, predicts the very same execution of vengeance which is described in the passage of Revelation before us. This vintage is to be "cast.... into the great winepress of the wrath of God."

Again, the expression, "the clusters of the vine of the earth," is evidently a strong contrast to the expression, "the harvest of the earth." There is a vine the vintage of which is not earthly in nature but heavenly, not for divine judgment, but for divine acceptance. That vine is Jesus Christ, of which God the Father is the husbandman and believers are the branches. See John 15:1-8. And that "the harvest of the earth" is holy in character is implied by the fact that the Lord will claim and reap it Himself as His own. It is in James 5:7 called "the precious fruit of the earth," for which the divine husbandman waits with long patience until He receives both the early and the latter (spiritual) rain. As the early effusion of the Holy Spirit produced a great harvest of souls, so a similar effusion of the Spirit, with similar result, is reserved for the last days, even the latter half of the tribulation era. Notwithstanding the extreme provocation to execute precipitate vengeance offered to God by the outrageous effrontery of "that Wicked," yet God will sit calmly reserving His outpouring of wrath until He shall have a fully whitened "harvest of the earth" to gather into His garner in the skies. But this vintage of the earth will not be precious to Him. It is not He that "picks the grapevine of the earth" (C. V.), but it is an angel coming out of the temple who is charged to do this by another angel, who was seen to come "out from the altar, which had power over fire," or "jurisdiction over fire" (C. V.); that is, the fire of the sacrificial altar. This last feature is very striking. The angel out of the temple represents the holiness of God, while the angel of the altar of sacrifice represents the atonement for sin, the saving mercy of God through His slain Lamb. But here it is the very angel of the altar, who has charge of keeping the fire perpetually burning, that commands the cutting off of the vintage and the treading of it in the winepress of the vengeful fury of God. It all indicates the arrival of the time for final, unmitigated judgment, judgment with no further mercy in reserve; judgment, indeed, demanded by mercy itself.

A further ominous feature is that the "winepress was trodden without the city." This is the place of divine rejection, of final consignment to perpetual burning. The expression, however, localizes geographically the place where the execution of God's wrath, which is represented under the figure of the winepress, is to take place. The city is, of course, Jerusalem. Thus this symbolic picture of coming judgment in the last days connects itself with all those Old Testament prophecies, already noticed in their place, which represent the final, decisive premillennial infliction of destruction upon the international antichristian hosts, which will be gathered in the Holy Land and deployed about Jerusalem to besiege and destroy. It is in the Valley of Jehoshaphat that this host is to meet its Waterloo. Besides such passage as Ezk. 38:16—39:5, Zech. 12:19 and 14:12-15, the following is worthy of quotation in this connection:

"1 For, behold, in those days, and in that time, when I shall bring again the captivity of Judah and Jerusalem, 2 I will also gather all nations, and will bring them down into the valley of Jehoshaphat, and will plead with them there for my people and for my heritage Israel, whom they have scattered among the nations, and parted my land. 9 Proclaim ye this among the Gentiles; Prepare war, wake up the mighty men, let all the men of war draw near; let them come up: 10 Beat your plowshares into swords, and your pruninghooks into spears: let the weak

say, I am strong. 11 Assemble yourselves, and come, all ye
heathen, and gather yourselves together round about: thither
cause thy mighty ones to come down, O Lord. 12 Let the heathen
be wakened, and come up to the valley of Jehoshaphat; for
there will I sit to judge all the heathen round about. 13 Put
ye in the sickle, for the harvest is ripe: come, get you down;
for the press is full, the fats overflow; for their wickedness is
great. 14 Multitudes, multitudes in the valley of decision: for
the day of the Lord is near in the valley of decision. 15 The
sun and the moon shall be darkened, and the stars shall withdraw
their shining. 16 The Lord shall roar out of Zion, and utter
his voice from Jerusalem; and the heavens and the earth shall
shake: but the Lord will be the hope of his people, and the
strength of the children of Israel. 17 So shall ye know that I
am the Lord your God dwelling in Zion, my holy mountain:
then shall Jerusalem be holy, and there shall be no strangers pass
through her any more'' (Joel 3: 1, 2, 9-17).

The symbol of the winepress very consistently
represents the floods of blood, shed in the coming destruction of the antichristian hosts in the valley of
Jehoshaphat, as the blood of grapes gushing so copiously
from the winetrough as to reach to the horses' bridles, or
''bits'' (C. V.), ''By the space of a thousand and six
hundred furlongs,'' or, ''from a thousand six hundred
stadia'' (C. V.). We need not conceive of a stream
so deep for all this length of 183.86 miles, but only of its
attaining this depth at its mouth. But what are we to
understand by the figure as it passes over into literal
expression of distance?

It is a striking fact that this measurement serves very
accurately for the length of the Holy Land. The
prophecies with which we have become familiar indicate
that the antichristian armies of the last days, while they
will have the valley of Jezreel as their mustering ground,
Armegiddo—Mount Megiddo—as ''great headquarters,''
and while the great battle of God against this host will
occur in the valley of Jehoshaphat, under the walls of
Jerusalem, yet the whole land will be overrun by these
alien, ravaging troops, assembled from all nations. To

return to the symbol, Palestine will be the vineyard, occupied from end to end with ''the vine of the earth,''
whose clusters are to be picked and cast into the winepress
of the valley of Jehoshaphat, there to be trampled to
pulp till the blood flows in the deep, sharp valley to a
depth sufficient for horses to swim.

It seems most logical to connect with this subject the
first verse of Chapter 15, in which the angelic executioners of the unmitigated visitation of divine wrath
just considered are introduced. ''And I perceive another
sign in heaven,'' John records, ''great and marvellous,
seven messengers having the seven calamities'' (C.
V.). This throws important light upon the subject we
have been considering, showing that there is to be a
succession of divine inflictions upon the antichristian
world, running through the era of the last three and
one-half years, which will reach an exhaustive culmination and which will all together constitute the final outpouring ''of the wrath of God.''

(3). The Victors on the Sea of Glass, 15: 2-4.

''2 And I saw as it were a sea of glass mingled with fire:
and them that had gotten the victory over the beast, and over
his image, and over his mark, and over the number of his name,
stand on the sea of glass, having the harps of God. 3 And they
sing the song of Moses the servant of God, and the song of the
Lamb, saying, Great and marvellous are thy works, Lord God
Almighty; just and true are thy ways, thou King of saints. 4
Who shall not fear thee, O Lord, and glorify thy name? for
thou only art holy: for all nations shall come and worship before thee; for thy judgments are made manifest.''

Here again, it would be hasty and incorrect assumption to apply this beautiful picture to the resurrected
and translated saints in general, still more mistaken to
apply it to a happy condition entered upon by dying
saints at present. This is a special class of glorified
saints, not to be identified with those of 7: 9, and apparently not including the one hundred and forty-four
thousand of 14: 1-3.

That which differentiates and identifies this throng is the description of them as "them that had gotten the victory over the beast, and over his image, and over his mark, and over the number of his name." This identifies them as belonging to the part of the tribulation during which the conditions described in 13:4-17 will prevail; that is, during the second and latter "forty and two months" of the seven last years. That will be the time of the beast's unrestrained self-assertion and tyranny, when he will command universal worship and subjection, when he will have "given unto him to make war with the saints, and to overcome them," and will have "power ......over all kindreds, and tongues, and nations." These victors will not put him down or save their own lives from his hands, but these saints will "in all these things" prove "more than conquerors," for they will have no complicity with him, his image, his mark or his number, keeping true under all conditions to the precepts of God and to the faith of Jesus.

The sea, "as it were," "of glass mingled with fire," has already been mentioned in 4:6 as the pavement before the throne of God in the skies. This same apparition is recorded in Ex. 24:10, where, on the occasion when Moses, and Aaron, Nadab, and Abihu, and seventy of the elders of Israel went up in mount Sinai, "and they saw the God of Israel: and there was under his feet as it were a paved work of a sapphire stone, and as it were the body of heaven in his clearness." In this instance the color is blue instead of red, both being, along with the perfect transparency, fitting symbols of attributes of Christ Jesus in which victorious saints have their foundation and standing before the throne of God now and evermore.

"Having the harps of God," or "the lyres of the Lord God" (C. V.). Like all the other features of this charming picture, this feature inspires the imagination with the joy and praise awaiting these victors over the Anti-Christ. Exposition is submerged in sentiment, keen but beyond analysis. Certain aspects of this choral scene are explained to us.

First is the striking copulation of Moses' triumphant song, found in Ex. 15, and that of Jesus. Moses is described as the servant of God, Jesus as the Lamb. Both indicate the triumph over proudest earthly and satanic power through submission of faith to God. Both victories, therefore, are those of supernatural divine power and interposition. This conjunction is another of those testimonies to the unity of the Mosaic and Christian dispensations, of the Exodus and the Crucifixion, of Sinai and Calvary. It is not antithesis but synthesis. Both songs unite in celebrating the glory of the Almighty in judgment upon His enemies and salvation to His people.

Moses sang:

"I will sing unto the Lord, for he hath triumphed gloriously: the horse and his rider hath he thrown into the sea. The Lord is my strength and song, and he is become my salvation: . . . Thy right hand, O Lord, is become glorious in power: thy right hand, O Lord, hath dashed in pieces the enemy. And in the greatness of thine excellency thou hast overthrown them that rose up against thee: thou sentest forth thy wrath, which consumed them as stubble . . . Thou in thy mercy hast led forth the people which thou hast redeemed: thou hast guided them in thy strength unto thy holy habitation."

This might equally well be applied to the judgment of the last days of this age. Too little, far too little is the thought practically entertained, that there is to be another exodus of triumphant (spiritual) Israelites from a darker Egypt, a mightier Pharaoh, a deeper Red Sea.

Of this ancient triumph Habakkuk sang:

"God came from Teman, and the Holy One from mount Paran. Selah. His glory covered the heavens, and the earth was full of his praise. And his brightness was as the light; he had horns coming out of his hand; and there was the hiding of his power. Before him went the pestilence, and burning coals went forth at his feet. Thou didst march through the land in indignation, thou didst thresh the heathen in anger. Thou wentest forth for the salvation of thy people, even for salvation with thine anointed; thou woundedst the head out of the house of the wicked, by discovering the foundation unto his neck. Selah. Thou didst walk through the sea with thine horses, through the heap of great waters'' (Hab. 3: 3-5, 12, 13, 15).

It is the same theme,—judgment and salvation puissant —freely rendered and applied to fit the even greater triumph of the pilgrims of faith in the last days, which will be sounded forth with voice and harp unto God by these conquerors standing upon the jasper sea: ''Great and marvellous are thy works, Lord God Almighty; just and true are thy ways, thou King of saints [rather, of the ages]. Who shall not fear thee, O Lord, and glorify thy name? for thou only art holy: for all nations shall come and worship before thee; for thy judgments are made manifest.'' It is the victory of the Lamb in behalf of His blood-washed soldiers.

Thus the long intercalation of 12:1—15:4 closes. That it is an intercalation is very evident from the fact that the next verse takes up the thread of the vision introduced but dropped for the time being at 11:19. This long passage has covered a vast and magnificent sweep of revelation embracing what may be called the entire period of the last days; that is, the days consummating in and embracing the seven years of tribulation, which will issue in the final exodus out of earthly suffering into celestial rapture of the saints of God of that time. Yet the real objective of the passage is not the entire period and its outstanding features. Chapter 12 serves as an introduction, covering pre-tribulation antecedents and the first half of the seven years, to the last half of the tribulation era, which, in a very important sense spans ''*The Great Tribulation.*'' This last is the real objective, for this is the period still left under the

seventh trumpet, both for the final salvation of heroes
of faith and for the final judgment of their enemies.
It is the procession of the seven stages of that judgment
of the antichristian world that immediately follows in
the vision.

CHAPTER X.

THE SEVEN LAST PLAGUES. 15:5—16:21.

Introductory Vision, 15:5-8.

"5 And after that I looked, and behold, the temple of the tabernacle of the testimony in heaven was opened; 6 And the seven angels came out of the temple, having the seven plagues, clothed in pure white linen, and having their breasts girded with golden girdles. 7 And one of the four beasts gave unto the seven angels seven golden vials full of the wrath of God, who liveth for ever and ever. 8 And the temple was filled with smoke from the glory of God, and from his power; and no man was able to enter into the temple, till the seven plagues of the seven angels were fulfilled."

OF COURSE the phrase, "after that," does not mean that what is now presented is to be fulfilled subsequently to what has been unfolded, either in the previous verses of this chapter, or in the long passage reaching back to the close of Chapter 11. It simply means that John's vision is now turned in a new direction. In this case, as has already been intimated, his vision is now directed afresh toward the progress of judgment introduced by the sounding of the seventh trumpet. This era of judgment is called, in 11:14, "the third woe," the last. We found in 11:2, 3 that up to this last woe the first "forty and two months," or "thousand and two hundred and sixty days,"—that is, three and one-half years—will be expired, leaving, as was found explicitly in 13:5, the last "forty and two months," or three and one-half years, to be covered by the third woe. This division we have found corroborated by Chapter 12, where, in vs. 6, 14, the era of the woman's concealment in the wilderness, is identified in point of time with that of Chapter 11:1-13. It is most interesting as well as important to keep these divisions and these relations of parts of the general revelation clearly before the mind. For otherwise we would not know just where to place the seven last plagues, and just how long a period of time they cover.

In 12:12 this period is called "a short time." So it will be relatively for the dragon. Yet, compared with the entire procession of judgments preceding, it is a long period. For, we found from Chap. 12, that the practically contemporaneous events of the ascent of the man child and the descent of Satan mark the beginning of the "things which must be hereafter" introduced at Chapter 4. Seeing, then, that the period of the seven last plagues covers an equal period of time with that filled up by the august procession of events revealed in Chaps. 4-12 inclusive, it not only impresses one with the relatively long span of time to be covered by these last plagues, but it impresses one with the supreme weight of this closing stage of the last days.

"Behold, the temple of the tabernacle of the testimony in heaven was opened." Other series of judgments have been represented as proceeding from the throne in the skies, and from the golden altar in the skies. As these expressions were seen in their place in this study not to signify natural objects but the heavenly realities of which material throne and altar were "the patterns," the symbolical emblems, the expression, "the temple of the tabernacle of the testimony," is so to be taken also.

Put in other form, this expression would read, "the heavenly temple where the testimony resides." Of course, "the testimony" means the law of God. The decalogue especially was called the testimony. It is most impressive that the testimony of God given to Israel was, in a very true sense, a replica of God's eternal heavenly law. The decalogue was no arbitrary and temporary code; it was a pattern, in a prohibitory form, of the code of the Supreme Court of heaven. Not that it consisted of ten maxims of legalistic external

conduct constituting a self-righteousness for man. The
Mosaic testimony declares the main lines of conduct
which are forbidden by the Christian law of love to God
and to man, and which are destructive to the life hid
with Christ in God. It is just this which the teachings of
Jesus and of the Apostles expound and emphasize.
Herein consists the perfect spiritual unity between the
Mosaic and the Christian dispensations, between the Old
and the New Testaments. This testimony was not given
to be a covenant "which gendereth to bondage" but to
be to regenerated, sanctified, Spirit-filled saints, of old
or of new dispensation, "the perfect law of liberty."

Now this temple of the tabernacle of the testimony in
heaven is the eternal court of last resort. It is from that
quarter that judgment through the seven last plagues
is to go forth. The executioners of these plagues are
to be angels "clothed in pure and white linen, and having their breasts girded with golden girdles." This
description is noteworthy in view of the nature of the
business of these angels. Too often is it the case that
police and penal business is associated with coarse character and rough practices, and that the offices of legal
punishment tend to brutalize the officers. Here, however,
angelic officers, fittingly arrayed in the habiliments indicative of extreme purity, refinement and exaltation of
character, are the ones to execute the fearful plagues
of God's wrath. It does not look as though this business
were dismal and repulsive, but noble, holy and attractive.
This conception is confirmed by the statement that these
angels received their material of punishment in "seven
golden vials [bowls] full [brimming with] the wrath
[fury] of God, who liveth for ever and ever."

Moreover, "the temple was filled with smoke from
the glory of God, and from his power." How forcibly
the lesson is conveyed and driven home, that wrath,
fury, vengeance is pure, holy, glorious in God. Man has
an entirely wrong sentiment, who holds wrath to be in-

consistent in and unworthy of God, who can find no holy satisfaction and pleasure in divine justice and judgment, who qualifies and emasculates the fearful threatenings of Scripture, who hushes up the declarations regarding future punishment. One greatly lacks in fellowship with God who takes pleasure only in His mercies, but tries to forget His vengeances. Let it be remembered that the smoke of God's wrath is not only, or first, "from his power," but "from the glory of God." A true sympathy with righteousness in God must include complacency in His vindication of righteousness by due and timely punishment of obdurate unrighteousness.

"And no man was able to enter into the temple, till the seven plagues of the seven angels were fulfilled." This can mean nothing less than that this will be the time of judgment without mercy. No priestly intercession will be possible. Remember that the mercy-seat rested upon the ark enclosing the testimony of God's law. So long as a priest could have access to the Holy of Holies it was access to the mercy-seat and because for the time mercy rejoiced against justice. But this pictures a time when there shall be no access to the mercy-seat, when the testimony within the ark and beneath the mercy-seat shall assert control and manifestation without mercy, indeed with the full sanction and concurrence of mercy.

PROGRESS OF THE SEVEN LAST PLAGUES, Chap. 16.

"And I heard a great voice out of the temple saying to the seven angels, Go your ways, and pour out the vials of the wrath of God upon the earth" (v. 1).

One of the four beasts had, in the vision, given to the seven angels the golden vials full of the wrath of God. There is special propriety in this, taking the four beasts as supreme beings of human kind. The upper world at any rate is represented as being of one mind and pleasure in regard to the execution of God's wrath. Angels will be the direct celestial ministers; glorified humanity

will serve to the seven angels the vials; and now the
great voice of immediate command will be taken as that
of Jesus Christ acting in the name of the Father Almighty. Thus will the electric button, to use the figure,
be pressed, that will set in motion the drama of supreme
judgment upon the antichristian world running through
the last half of the seven unique years closing this age.

Plagues One and Two, vs. 2, 3.

"2 And the first went and poured out his vial upon the earth;
and there fell a noisome and grievous sore upon the men which
had the mark of the beast, and upon them which worshipped his
image. 3 And the second angel poured out his vial upon the sea;
and it became as the blood of a dead man; and every living
soul died in the sea."

The reasons for a literal understanding of the inflictions unfolded in this chapter, which were presented in
chapter 4 in connection with the eighth and ninth
chapters of Revelation, apply equally here. Therefore
scarcely a word of comment is needed on these verses.
Such plagues are already familiar to us as predicted in
chapters 8 and 9, and as recorded in Exodus in the
narrative of the ten plagues of Egypt. The marked
difference, however,—making these inflictions the most
stupendous—is that these plagues are not to be limited
in locality or partial in prevalence. The C. V. translates two expressions thus: "an evil and malignant
ulcer," and "every living soul died which is on the sea."

Plague Three, vs. 4-7.

"4 And the third angel poured out his vial upon the rivers
and fountains of waters: and they became blood. 5 And I heard
the angel of the waters say, Thou art righteous, O Lord, which
art, and wast, and shalt be, because thou hast judged thus.
6 For they have shed the blood of saints and prophets, and thou
hast given them blood to drink; for they are worthy. 7 And I
heard another out of the altar say, Even so, Lord God Almighty,
true and righteous are thy judgments,"

With this manner of plague we are also familiar from the history of Egyptian plagues long ago, and from the predictions in Rev. 8 of the plagues to come under the first woe. Here again the local and the fractional extent of the plague's prevalence is exchanged for the unlimited extent.

This stage in the progress of the last plagues will evoke from the angel, having jurisdiction in executing this infliction upon the waters of earth, an expression of great admiration of the righteousness of God manifested in this act, and of supreme complacency over it, because of the appropriateness of this judgment upon those who had, as it were, made the wounds of their Christian victims the springs from which to slake their bloodthirstiness. "They deserve it" (C. V.). And another angel from the altar (of incense) has no intercession for divine clemency, but only acclamation for the truth and justness of these judgments of the Lord God Almighty. Far from fellowship with Christ and His angels is one who knows not when to cease supplication and to exult in divine retribution.

Plague Four, vs. 8, 9.

"8 And the fourth angel poured out his vial upon the sun; and power was given unto him to scorch men with fire. 9 And men were scorched with great heat, and blasphemed the name of God, which hath power over these plagues: and they repented not to give him glory."

Advancement in the terrors of the plagues becomes plainly marked at this stage. "There is nothing hid from the heat thereof"; that is, the sun (Psa. 19; 6). But when this heat becomes a torture—oppressive, merciless, blistering, inescapable—what a plague! Fit symbol of the withering, incinerating flame of divine scorn and indignation! Here first the misuse of divine judgment is mentioned in this list. The challenge of the ten Egyptian plagues was for Pharaoh to yield to Christ and His will

for His people. While from time to time Pharaoh is said
to have repented, yet it was so insincerely that he soon
repented of repentance and became the more defiant. In
Rev. 9 it is foreshown how under these woes unregenerate
antichristian classes will refuse to repent. So here, instead of repentance toward Him ''who has the jurisdiction over these calamities'' (C. V.), there will be only
hellish blasphemy of His name and the more obdurate
refusal to give Him glory.

Plague Five, vs. 10, 11.

''10 And the fifth angel poured out his vial upon the seat of
the beast; and his kingdom was full of darkness; and they
gnawed their tongues for pain, 11 And blasphemed the God of
heaven, because of their pains and their sores, and repented not
of their deeds.''

The seat of the beast means his throne and capital.
From highest to lowest, from center to circumference
of Anti-Christ's kingdom, a darkness—not natural, not
merely a lack of light, but a plague of darkness, a darkness racking all with pain and aggravating their ulcers
—will universally prevail. But impenitency and blasphemy will wax still worse with these miserable sufferers,
who will ultimately gnaw their tongues for pain and
with them lash the name of the God of heaven with
satanic blasphemies.

Plague Six, vs. 12-16.

''12 And the sixth angel poured out his vial upon the great
river Euphrates; and the water thereof was dried up, that the
way of the kings of the east might be prepared. 13 And I saw
three unclean spirits like frogs come out of the mouth of the
dragon, and out of the mouth of the beast, and out of the
mouth of the false prophet. 14 For they are the spirits of devils,
working miracles, which go forth unto the kings of the earth
and of the whole world, to gather them to the battle of that great
day of God Almighty. 15 Behold, I come as a thief. Blessed
is he that watcheth, and keepeth his garments, lest he walk
naked, and they see his shame. 16 And he gathered them together
into a place called in the Hebrew tongue Armageddon.''

There is a marked change in the progress of the plagues. Divine dealing with men in the way of personal calamity and torment will reach its exhaustive degree in point of hardening effect. The first five plagues will be swift, decisive blows of brief duration and of relatively quick succession, like the plagues of Egypt. The sixth stage of progress will be preparatory to a final and conclusive calamity. Apparently, however, this stage will be one of great world-wide stir and enthusiasm, a great international militaristic epoch. The plague of it will consist in its being under satanic, demoniacal instigation, leading proud and impenitent mankind on to an unparalleled debacle.

The first part of the divine act will be a physical wonder, to which on a smaller scale the drying of the Red Sea and of the Jordan are to be likened. It will be the drying up of the waters of the Euphrates. The purpose will be to efface this barrier to the free and expeditious westward movement of the armies of the kings of the far East. This phenomenon is not here first mentioned in the Bible, although this purpose of it is here only mentioned. In Isa. 11:15, 16 we read: "And the Lord shall utterly destroy the tongue of the Egyptian sea; and with his mighty wind shall he shake his hand *over the river, and shall smite it in the seven streams, and make men go over dryshod*. And *there* shall be an highway for the remnant of his people, which shall be left, *from Assyria; like as it was* to Israel in the day that he came up out of the land of Egypt." No doubt this is the explanation, too, of that "highway" in Isa. 35:8; "And an highway shall be there, and a way, and it shall be called The way of holiness; the unclean shall not pass over it; but it shall be for those: the wayfaring men, though fools, shall not err therein."

More important than the foregoing physical and geographical preparation, will be the demoniacally wrought military preparation next described. By common agreement the evil trinity of dragon, beast and false prophet will issue a firman to all kings of the earth to mobilize their military forces. Unclean spirits will like frogs leap forward through this decree to deceive and instigate universal response. This militaristic movement will be supernaturally prosecuted by means of devilish signs, those mentioned in Chapter 13, vs. 13, 14. This is that general international mobilizing of armies, long and frequently predicted in Old Testament prophecy, for the battle of the great day of God Almighty. Some of these great outstanding prophecies were cited on pages 252-3 in connection with "the vintage of the earth." The special feature of our present passage in Revelation is the use made of satanic and demoniacal agencies through the Anti-Christ in awakening and organizing the nations for this vast military enterprise.

Once more in this blessed Book of Revelation is a timely word inserted parenthetically to serve the watchful but imperilled saints of that day, v. 15: "Behold, I come as a thief." Jesus will be speaking through this little verse, which clearly constitutes a parenthesis, an aside, a whispered message to His own. "Blessed is he that watcheth, and keepeth his garments, lest he walk naked, and they see his shame." To us this reveals that down to this late stage of the vial judgments, the Lord Jesus will be having His little flock still in the midst of the wolves, over which flock He will keep faithful watch-care.

Verse 16 is unique in the Bible in revealing just where the great headquarters of the international host will be established in the Holy Land. Armageddon is the Greek of the compound Hebrew Har-Megiddo, Mount Megiddo. This is the eminence overlooking the Plain of Esdraelon, or Valley of Jezreel, where the highway from Egypt to Mesopotamia passes out of the plain of Sharon over into that of Esdraelon. This latter plain is the theater of the many mighty conflicts of history waged for supremacy

over the Holy Land. Still it is a misnomer to speak of
"the Battle of Armageddon," for there the great battle
of God is not to occur; it is the center only of international mobilization on the fields of Palestine, from
which center the plans of conquest will proceed, but
where they will not be fought out. The actual theater of
the final battle will be, as we have seen, the Valley of
Jehoshaphat, under the walls of Jerusalem.

Plague Seven, vs. 17-21.

"17 And the seventh angel poured out his vial into the air; and
there came a great voice out of the temple of heaven, from the
throne, saying, It is done. 18 And there were voices and thunders,
and lightnings; and there was a great earthquake, such as was
not since men were upon the earth, so mighty an earthquake, and
so great. 19 And the great city was divided into three parts,
and the cities of the nations fell: and great Babylon came in
remembrance before God, to give unto her the cup of the wine
of the fierceness of his wrath. 20 And every island fled away,
and the mountains were not found. 21 And there fell upon men
a great hail out of heaven, every stone about the weight of a
talent: and men blasphemed God because of the plague of the
hail; for the plague thereof was exceeding great."

In these verses the final blow of divine fury upon the
antichristian world is briefly summarized. "It is
finished." The agencies of havoc to be employed are
shown to be the atmospheric,—"Lightnings," "voices,"
"thunders." These unparalleled electrical explosions
will be accompanied with a prodigious earthquake, with
which even the recent earthquake in Japan will stand
little comparison. Ezekiel prophesied of all this (38:19-
23). By this earthquake Jerusalem, "the great city"
shall be cleft tripartite. Zechariah definitely foretells this
cleaving of Jerusalem and her environs (14:4, 5). Special mention is made of "great Babylon's" coming into
remembrance before God, as if the very brunt of the
judgment of God's fierce wrath is to fall upon her.
Neighboring islands will disappear as if in flight and
mountains will subside from sight. And emphasized
mention is made of a fall of hail such as will have never

been known, the several stones being large as a talent. This awful pelting from the skies will bring anti-christian blasphemy to its highest pitch.

This description is very condensed and it will help the imagination to recall the more detailed description of some parts of these scenes given by Ezekiel (38:18-23):

"18 And it shall come to pass at the same time when Gog shall come against the land of Israel, saith the Lord God, that my fury shall come up in my face. 19 For in my jealousy and in the fire of my wrath have I spoken, Surely in that day there shall be a great shaking in the land of Israel; 20 So that the fishes of the sea, and the fowls of the heaven, and the beasts of the field, and all creeping things that creep upon the earth, and all the men that are upon the face of the earth, shall shake at my presence, and the mountains shall be thrown down, and the steep places shall fall, and every wall shall fall to the ground. 21 And I will call for a sword against him throughout all my mountains, saith the Lord God: every man's sword shall be against his brother. 22 And I will plead against him with pestilence and with blood; and I will rain upon him, and upon his bands, and upon the many people that are with him, an over-flowing rain, and great hailstones, fire and brimstone. 23 Thus will I magnify myself, and sanctify myself; and I will be known in the eyes of many nations, and they shall know that I am the Lord."

The predictions of this chapter are given in a very real and matter-of-fact way and as actual, intelligible revelation. Not that the facts are not beyond present comprehension, because they so far exceed human experience thus far. But to fail to let the Revelation tell its own story, or to put private construction or idealistic interpretation upon the statements given, would be to refuse the word as a revelation and treat it as a cryptic, intentionally mystifying piece of Scripture. This would throw us back upon affected human wisdom, which would be only vain speculation, certainly false, because treating the revelation as being nothing more than human wisdom and reason could know and declare without miraculous divine disclosure.

CHAPTER XI.

DIVINE RETRIBUTION UPON MYSTICAL BABYLON, 17 : 1—19 : 10.

IN THE midst of the concise summary of the momentous features of the final judgment of the seventh vial—comprehended in 16 : 17-21—lies this statement (v. 19) : "And great Babylon came in remembrance before God, to give unto her the cup of the wine of the fierceness of his wrath."

For the purposes of the revelation of this book this retributive judgment upon Babylon is viewed as of such importance as to call for the amplified description contained in this long passage. The passage falls into three divisions.

1. THE IDENTIFICATION OF MYSTICAL BABYLON, CHAPTER 17.

Introductory—The Angel's Proposal, 17 : 1, 2.

"1 And there came one of the seven angels which had the seven vials, and talked with me, saying unto me, Come hither; I will shew unto thee the judgment of the great whore that sitteth upon many waters: 2 With whom the kings of the earth have committed fornication, and the inhabitants of the earth have been made drunk with the wine of her fornication."

The action of this particular angel runs clear through and is complete in this chapter. Hence we should take the chapter as a whole. There is evident propriety in its being one of the vial angels to serve in this case. For the purpose in view is to "shew [unto John] the judgment." That it is the judgment of "Great Babylon" (16 : 19) is evident from the context of the chapter although not so designated in these introductory verses. Here it is called the "judgment of the great whore."

This is the first time that this expression occurs in definite and exclusive form. Its significance lies at hand for us, however, owing to the familiar use of the expressions, "go a whoring from the Lord," "play the whore," etc., which are found in the Bible. It always has spiritual meaning and describes the bestowment of spiritual devotion upon objects contrary to Jesus Christ. He calls all souls to spiritual union with and devotion to Himself; all other religious fellowship and devotion is spiritual whoredom according to the familiar language of Scripture. And as all who prove true and faithful to Him constitute *"the bride"* *"the Lamb's wife,"* so *"the great whore"* consists of all who are faithless to Him in spiritual fellowship, and who transfer their spiritual affections to the world, the flesh and the devil. We have now reached that late stage of the revelation of this book, where these two completed spiritual bodies, in process of growth through the ages, are to be delineated in sharp antithesis as two women holding opposite relations to the Lord Christ, the one fit for "the judgment of the great whore," the other "made ready" for her marriage as the wife of the Lamb.

The vial angel attributes three striking features to the great whore. First, it is she "that sitteth upon many waters." We would not expect this to be a geographical expression, but an expression suited to the symbol of the great whore. The phrase "sitteth upon" would imply domination, spiritual rule. And it is not uncommon for Scripture to describe multitudes of souls as waters. But no argument needs to be made, for the fifteenth verse of this chapter of Revelation expressly explains: "And he saith unto me, The waters which thou sawest, where the woman sitteth, are peoples, and multitudes, and nations, and tongues." Hence, the first feature attributed to the great whore is that of world-wide governing spiritual presence, not peculiar to any one people, mass, nation or tongue of the human race.

The next striking feature ascribed to the great whore is expressed in the words, "with whom the kings of the earth have committed fornication." The C. V. reads "commit prostitution," the present tense of regular habit. As all kings derive their authority and power from God, as Jesus declared even to Pilate (John 19:11), even so they owe all worship, honor and service to the blessed and only Potentate, the Son of God, as Nebuchadnezzar was finally brought to do (Dan. 4:34-37). To do contrariwise—as is the general practice of kings, even under the cloak of a Christian profession—is to practice fornication with the great whore. A very vivid and extended picture and illustration of this politico-spiritual whoredom is delineated in Ezekiel 23.

Finally, a striking feature attributed to the great whore is described in the words, "and the inhabitants of the earth have been made drunk with the wine of her fornication." How poisoned, perverted and stupefied the moral and spiritual sensibilities of the populaces of the earth become under the stimulation of a repulsive prostitution of Christless religion with Christless politics!

1. Mystical Babylon in Symbol. Character Sketch of the Woman Herself, 17:3-6.

"3 So he carried me away in the spirit into the wilderness: and I saw a woman sit upon a scarlet colored beast, full of names of blasphemy, having seven heads and ten horns. 4 And the woman was arrayed in purple and scarlet colour, and decked with gold and precious stones and pearls, having a golden cup in her hand full of abominations and filthiness of her fornication: 5 And upon her forehead was a name written, MYSTERY, BABYLON THE GREAT, THE MOTHER OF HARLOTS AND ABOMINATIONS OF THE EARTH. 6 And I saw the woman drunken with the blood of the saints, and with the blood of the martyrs of Jesus: and when I saw her, I wondered with great admiration."

"Come hither," the angel had first said to John, "Come along, and I will show you the judgment of the great whore."

So the angel conducted John, in spirit, into the sphere of conditions such as those just described. Truly such sphere is "the wilderness." It is where God's children are pilgrims and strangers and have "no continuing city." This will be the character of them of this world preëminently in the last days, as we have already had it presented to us in Rev. 12: 6, 14. It is there that John beheld in spirit this woman in the very act of prostitution with imperial government; namely, that of the Anti-Christ, already made familiar to us in Rev. 13: 1. The relation of the woman to the empire is that of spiritual rule on her part over the empire and of political support on the empire's part to her. It is the picture of spiritual pretensions prostituted to the favor of an utterly antichristian State.

In verse 4 the vision reveals this woman as in stately, gorgeous and costly costume. Excessive worldly display is the very garb of degenerate and faithless religion. But it is evident here that closer attention is intended to be fixed upon the debauching influence of the woman as she offers from cup of gold the abominations and filthiness of her prostitute spiritual ministries.

The vision of this bewitching but horrifying woman increases in interest as her characterizing name is read upon her forehead: "Mystery, Babylon the Great, the Mother of Harlots and Abominations of the Earth."

The appearance of this name in the forehead of the woman is to be understood not as a mere inscription, but as the revelation to public recognition of the woman's essential characteristics as registered upon and expressed by the forehead. This term of symbolism, "forehead," strongly marks the Book of Revelation. In 3: 12 we read: "Him that overcometh will I make a pillar in the temple of my God, and he shall go no more out: and I will write upon him the name of my God, and the name of the city of my God, which is new Jerusalem, which cometh down out of heaven from my God: and I will

write upon him my new name." The opening of the
seventh seal was delayed by the angel who had "the
seal of the living God" (7:2, 3) "till we," as he said,
"have sealed the servants of our God in their foreheads."
Again, in 14:1 we read: "And I looked, and, lo, a Lamb
stood on the mount Sion, and with him an hundred and
forty and four thousand, having his Father's name
written in their foreheads." Once more, in 22:4 we
read: "And they [the servants of the Lamb] shall see
his face; and his name shall be in their foreheads."

Per contra, the locusts from the bottomless pit were
commanded to attack "only those men which have not
the seal of God in their foreheads" (9:4). Also the second beast is to give to all followers and worshippers of
the first beast the mark of the beast in their right hand,
or in their foreheads (13:16, 17; 14:9, 11). But this situation will give opportunity for faithful worshippers of
the Lamb to gain the special victory of immunity from
"the mark of the beast" (15:2, 20:4).

Especially pertinent in this connection is Christ's
charge against Judah through Jeremiah (3:3), "thou
hadst a whore's forehead, thou refusedst to be ashamed."
Ezekiel charges "all the house of Israel" as "stiff of
forehead, and hard of heart" (3:7). But the Lord told
Ezekiel that He had made his "forehead strong against
their foreheads," yea, "as an adamant harder than flint
have I made thy forehead" (vs. 7, 8).

The name upon the woman's forehead is, then, to be
understood as a character name; to-wit, the character
name or stamp, suited to her character as described in
the words following, "Mother of harlots and abominations of the earth." It is not a geographical name, or
a political name, or any literal name at all, but a
"Mystery" name, designating a Mystical Babylon, a
spiritual Babylon, a whorish Babylon antithetical to the
Lamb's bride, "that [other] great city, the holy Jerusalem" (Rev. 21:9, 10), "the holy city, new Jerusalem,

coming down from God out of heaven, prepared as a bride adorned for her husband'' (v. 2).

''Babylon the great,'' therefore, is not to be taken as literal, easily ''known and read of all men,'' but as mystical, discerned in meaning only by revelation of God. It is an emblematic name; but it is also generic, covering many forms of offspring of like character, and describing the fountain-head of the spiritual abominations of all the earth in all the ages. The name is, then, not conventional, given or assumed by human choice, but characteristic, essential, inevitable. Neither is this name exclusive, particular, denominational, but comprehensive, all-inclusive, universal. Finally, this name is supremely, consummately awful, mothering to itself as its own legitimate brood all the spiritual harlotry and filthiness of all the earth in all the ages,—''having a golden goblet in her hand, *brimming* with the abominations and uncleanness of the prostitution of her and the earth'' (C. V.).

But it is in v. 6 that, for the purposes of the Book of Revelation, the real climax is reached; namely, in describing this woman's insatiable thirst for the blood of the saints and of the witnesses of Jesus. The apparent distinction between ''the saints'' and ''the martyrs of Jesus'' doubtless covers Christ's saints of pre-advent times and the martyrs for the name of Jesus of Nazareth since His human nativity, although this is not to detract from the shocking, persecuting and distinctive activity the vision is intended to show the woman to be engaged in in that final climactic period immediately under observation.

This paragraph of the chapter concludes with John's confession of the extreme, doubtless painful, degree of wonderment in which the vision of this marvellous symbolical apparition left him. The word ''admiration'' now poorly expresses his state of mind. Other closer translations read, ''I wondered with a great wonder,''

"I was astonished with great astonishment," "I marvel at the great marvel." While we have thus far been able with John to comprehend somewhat of this apparition, owing to light before thrown upon it, yet the mind of John was left in such a degree of perplexed, inquiring amazement as to call for clear exposition of the mystery of the woman.

2. Mystical Babylon in History. 17: 7-18.

"7 And the angel said unto me, wherefore didst thou marvel? I will tell thee the mystery of the woman, and of the beast that carrieth her, which hath the seven heads and ten horns. 8 The beast that thou sawest was, and is not; and shall ascend out of the bottomless pit, and go into perdition: and they that dwell on the earth shall wonder, whose names were not written in the book of life from the foundation of the world, when they behold the beast that was, and is not, and yet is. 9 And here is the mind which hath wisdom. The seven heads are seven mountains, on which the woman sitteth. 10 And there are seven kings: five are fallen. and one is, and the other is not yet come; and when he cometh he must continue a short space. 11 And the beast that was, and is not, even he is the eighth, and is of the seven, and goeth into perdition. 12 And the ten horns which thou sawest are ten kings, which have received no kingdom as yet; but receive power as kings one hour with the beast. 13 These have one mind, and shall give their power and strength unto the beast. 14 These shall make war with the Lamb, and the Lamb shall overcome them: for he is Lord of lords, and King of kings: and they that are with him are called, and chosen, and faithful."

That the apparition of "Babylon the great," under the figure of the resplendent harlot, is to be understood as purely symbolical, is proved by the declaration of the vial angel that he will immediately proceed to "tell [unto John] the mystery ["secret," C. V.] of the woman." Up to this point, then, John was himself in ignorance as to the identity of Babylon, the great whore, excepting that something more definite than he yet could comprehend corresponded to this mystical portraiture. We likewise, then, have up to this stage of the revelation no further light upon this point. But as the angel promised John to open to him the mystery, to tell him the secret of this symbolism, so we are assured that the verses before us constitute an intelligible and unmistakable explanation of the great whore called Babylon the great.

The symbol, however, is composite, consisting of two members,—the woman and the scarlet-colored beast—so the angel proposed to tell John the secret of both the woman and the beast, even the beast that had "the seven heads and the ten horns." The reason for this is that Babylon, the great whore, can be understood only from the standpoint of her relationship to the beast.

(1). History of the Beast.

In v. 8 the angel explains that the beast is characterized by the unique feature of having had an earthly existence prior to John's day,—the day of receiving the vision—of not being in earthly existence at that time, but of coming, at the future time in view in the vision, into a second earthly existence by virtue of "ascending out of the bottomless pit," only, however, to go into "perdition." (This already recalls to our mind Paul's designation, in 2 Thess. 2:3, of the Anti-Christ as "that man of sin ......the son of perdition.") This phenomenon of the beast will hold all the people of the world spellbound with wonder, whose names were not [will not have been] written in the book of life from the foundation of the world"; i. e., all the unregenerate people of the coming day.

We pause a little here to note that in this passage we should translate *"disruption"* instead of "foundation." This translation is correct as well as appropriate. The thought is that, from the great disruption between God and man caused by Satan in the Garden of Eden, there has been a book of life open to fallen man, and that a registration of names therein has been in progress from Adam and from Eve ("the mother of all living") consisting of "them that believe on his [Christ, the Lamb of

God's] name: which were born, not of blood, nor of the will of the flesh, nor of the will of man, but of God" (John 1:12, 13). But our passage implies that a class of humanity all the way down from Cain has refused enrollment on that register, and our passage shows that such shall be the marvel of the resurrected Anti-Christ, that those of his day, who will not be found enrolled in this book of life by new creation in Christ Jesus, will be deceived into worshipping the beast of the seven heads and ten horns.

It is not strange, however, that the natural mind, especially under such blinding influences as will then obtain,—the mind which does not even give attention to Scriptural and spiritual revelation—will perish in ignorance. But the angel proceeds to tell John the mystery of the woman and the beast, which can and will be apprehended and kept by "the mind which hath wisdom," especially by those of this class who will in that day most urgently need to know the truth.

"The seven heads are seven mountains, on which the woman sitteth. And these are seven kings," etc. The punctuation and the translation of the A. V. leaves confusion here which is cleared away by other versions. For instance, the R. V. presents the statement thus: "The seven heads are seven mountains, on which the woman sitteth: and *they are seven kings.*" The word "mountains" is first used figuratively for "heads," which in turn belong to the beast, which is itself a political and imperial symbol. The mountains are in almost the same breath explained to mean "kings." This is no new and novel use of figures of speech in the Bible, especially in the Old Testament. It is there customary, however, to identify the monarch with the realm, the king with the empire. King Louis of France said, "Le Roi, c'est l'Etat," the king is the State. "Thou, O King," said Daniel to Nebuchadnezzar, "art that head of gold,"—which stood for the empire of

Babylon, and that not only in Nebuchadnezzar's days, but throughout its entire history. Any familiarity with Biblical symbolism, therefore, enables us at once to recognize the propriety of designating political empires as mountains. "Behold, I am against thee, O destroying mountain, saith the Lord, which destroyed all the earth: and I will stretch out mine hand upon thee, and roll thee down from the rocks, and will make thee a burnt mountain," said Christ through Jeremiah concerning the later Babylonian Empire (Jer. 51:25).

"Five [of these empires] are fallen, and one is, and the other is not yet come; and when he cometh he must continue a short space." The angel's explanation, then, of the mystery of the seven-headed, scarlet-colored beast was that it was the symbol of seven chronologically successive supreme political powers,—world-empires— five of which in John's day had passed away, one of which was then having dominion, while the seventh was yet to come, but to be of very short duration.

It is perfectly easy to identify these empires and that with certainty. The empire having world-dominion in John's day was the Roman. The five which had preceded the Roman were—reckoning backward—the Grecian, the Medo-Persian, the later Babylonian, the Assyrian and the early Babylonian. A rise of imperial government again over the old world of Biblical times is here shown to be due in the closing days before our Lord's return.

In one sense this is not new to the discerning student of the prophetical Scriptures prior to the Book of Revelation. It has been repeatedly foreshown that imperialism will prevail in the last days, albeit an imperialism which, according to Daniel's interpretation of Nebuchadnezzar's dream, is to be modified by democratic counterpoise. But the disclosure before us is new in listing a seventh empire in the historical succession. The panoramas of the Book of Daniel seem to imply a continuance of the fourth (sixth) empire right through to the end, only that it is to be characterized by a tenfold federation.

We are helped at this point, however, by Rev. 13:3, 12, 14, where a special feature is brought out that is lacking in prior prophecy. It is there shown that the final "head" (empire) will be the marvel of the world, because of being a head "wounded to death; and his deadly wound was healed." This enables us to see that the seventh empire is really the sixth one revived from a long suspended career, from apparent final extinction. This tallies with historical progress thus far. Where is the Roman Empire today? Yet when will the witching dream, the bold claim of its revival and the international plotting for its revival, down for good? It never will down till it is accomplished for "a short space." Hence, Mussolini supplies a notable sign of present times.

"And the beast that was, and is not, even he is the eighth, and is of the seven, and goeth into perdition" (v. 11). Thus the angel continues his explanation of the beast to John which he began in v. 7. Here again the State and the ruler are identified as one, and the Anti-Christ is declared to be the head of an empire, which will not only be the sixth one revived as though resurrected from oblivion, but which will also be sufficiently distinctive to be classed as the eighth, while yet being none the less the consistent, essential child and successor of the seven. In this unique ruler and his peculiar empire, the whole series is to fall into perdition.

In verse 12 the unique composition of the Anti-Christ's empire as finally to be developed is described. "And the ten horns which thou sawest are ten kings, which have received no kingdom as yet; but receive power as kings one hour with the beast." Distinction appears to be made here between the ten governments operating in severalty and the same operating in imperial combination. In the vision of the four beasts of the seventh chapter of Daniel the climax of the vision is reached in the rise of an insignificant power ("horn") in the midst of the ten governmental divisions ("horns") of the imperial ter-

ritory. This upstart power was first to bring under him
three of these divisions by ruthless conquest. This conquest by "the little horn" is further revealed in Dan.
8 : 9 as occurring among the territorial divisions of the
old Grecian Empire, while in Dan. 11: 40 it comes to
light that the feeble beginning of this pretender will be
as head of Greece, from which base he will make conquest
of the other three divisions of the territory of the former
Grecian Empire.

Now, our present passage indicates that the ten existing kingdom-divisions of the old Roman Empire (embracing, but exceeding, the territory of the old Grecian
Empire) will all become federated voluntarily in imperial
organization under the Anti-Christ. "These have one
mind, and shall give their power and strength unto the
beast" (v. 13). We may well remember that there will
be a pronounced democratic side to these ten kingdoms.
"As the toes of the feet were part of iron, and part of
clay......They [these kings] shall mingle themselves
with the seed of men" (Dan. 2: 42, 43). This warrants
the assumption that, in forming this voluntary federation under the Anti-Christ as emperor, there will be not
merely the unanimous decision of the ten monarchs but
also, as the result of a popular plebiscite, an overwhelming vote in favor of it throughout the populace of each
kingdom. From the contributions of prior passages of
Revelation and of Daniel, touching the complete ascend-
ancy and ruthless doings of the Anti-Christ for a final
period of three and one-half years, it seems only consistent to identify the expressions, "he must continue a
short space," and "the ten horns......receive power as
kings *one hour* with the beast," with this final period of
three and one-half years.

This interpretation is corroborated by the concluding
statement of v. 14: "These shall make war with the
Lamb, and the Lamb shall overcome them: for he is
Lord of lords and King of kings: and they that are with

him are called, and chosen, and faithful.'' In Chapters
11, 12 and 13 it came clearly to light that, after the
forty-two months of the restraining ministry of the two
witnesses (Chapter 11), and (covering the same period)
after the ''thousand two hundred and threescore days''
(or ''a time, and times, and half a time'') of the devil's
ineffectual endeavor to swallow up in ''the wilderness''
the fugitive mother of the ''man child'' (Chapter 12),
in fine, after all restraining barriers shall be removed and
the devil shall have his proxy, the Anti-Christ, in full
position to exercise all satanic power and place (Chapter
13), the Anti-Christ shall ''continue forty and two
months'' (13:5). Our translators vary here, embracing
the following renderings: ''to make war,'' ''to prevail,''
''to do what it wills.'' All agree, however, in the idea
of utterly unrestrained, undaunted operations. And the
character of his operations is implied by the question,
''Who is able to make war with him?'' And the direction
of his operations is indicated by the saying: ''He opened
his mouth in blasphemy against God, to blaspheme his
name, and his tabernacle, and them that dwell in heaven''
(the skies), v. 6. And further, John says that during
these last forty-two months (three and one-half years)
''it was given unto him to make war with the saints, and
to overcome them: and power [authority] was given
him over all kindreds, and tongues, and nations. And
all that dwell upon the earth shall worship him, whose
names are not written in the book of life of the Lamb
slain from the foundation [disruption] of the world''
(13:7, 8). The challenge offered Him, according to the
last references, the Lamb will accept, and He will act
in judgment and in deliverance as the only true and
rightful sovereign over the earth. It is remarkable—and
most satisfying to us—how all prophetical Scriptures
consistently agree in confronting the reader over and
over with that concluding half-week of years and its
astounding denouement as ''that day,'' ''that notable

day of the Lord.'' It is the hinge on which swings the
door closing all premillennial ages and opening the
millennial age of the ever-anticipated reign of "the only
Potentate'' over the earth.

And it is no wonder that the pious reader's attention
is so steadily focussed upon that hour; for the Lamb is
not to come into this earthly victory and reign alone.
"And they that are *with him* are called, and chosen, and
faithful.'' Every child of God is "called''—to be co-
heir with the conquering Christ: those who suffer with
Him "shall be chosen'' to co-reign with Him, and the
"faithful'' shall be wealthy and distinguished inheritors
because of never having swerved from the objective of
keeping divorced from "man's day'' and devoted to
"the day of the Lord.'' The R. V. renders the last of
v. 14 very satisfyingly: "and they *also shall overcome*
that are with him, called, and chosen, and faithful.''
The thought, then, is that of a joint victory of Christ and
of His attendants at His coming.

(2). History of the Woman.

At this point we will return to the woman and to
John's promised revelation of this part of the mystery.
The fact is, that all through this chapter it is this woman
that occupies the center of the stage. It is for our right
understanding of her that all this historical panorama
of the beast is unfolded. The real objective is to bring
out the identity of the woman in world-history in order
to make the panorama of her judgment duly intelligible
and impressive.

Be it noticed, then, in the first place that this woman
is contemporaneous in career with this succession of
world-empires from early Babylon to the revived Roman
Empire, and to that beast who is to be of the seven and
yet himself the head of an eighth successive world-
dominion. This is placed beyond question by the statement that the seven heads of the beast are "seven

mountains, *on which the woman sitteth,*" these seven
mountains being then explained to be the seven world-
empires, from the early Babylonian to the Neo-Roman
inclusive. Furthermore, the statement that the woman
"sitteth" on these successive empires indicates a vital
dual relationship of the woman to them. On the one
hand, she is dependent for support upon them. The
distinction between the political power and the woman
is sharp and fixed. She is not political, but spiritual.
She does not seek to dominate politically, but religiously.
She is not the State, but the State Church. She rules
the State spiritually, while she depends upon the political
power of the State for maintenance and outward power.

We have, then, this historic situation pictured before
us. There has been a mystical, spiritual power contemporaneous with and vitally wedded to world-empire
throughout postdiluvian history. It is immediately
evident why this spiritual paramour of the political
power is called "Mystery—Babylon the Great." World-
empire political was founded by Nimrod as the first
"mighty one in the earth." "And the beginning of his
kingdom was Babel" (Babylon—Gen 10:10). This gave
to the first world-empire the name of Babylonian Empire
—the Early Babylonian Empire. This was the visible,
God-defying, Christ-denying political Babylon, which
set the type for all succeeding world-empires. Cohabit-
ing with the same was an intangible, idolatrous, Christ-
denying, forbidden spiritual spouse. The former was
Satan's counterfeit of the political kingdom of God—not
coming down from above, but assuming to reach unto
heaven in human pride and power; the other was
Satan's counterfeit of the bride of Christ waiting for
her earthly inheritance until her Lord should appear as
really the only "mighty One in the earth," "the only
Potentate, the King of kings and Lord of lords."

The particular form, or organized denomination, of
false religion existing in unholy wedlock with the empire

has not been the same throughout the full succession of empires, or even in any two members of the succession; but that mystical, satanic, spiritual thing has been the same unchangeably from Babel down. Satan has been her god, as he has been the prince of the world-empire and of the world; the human monarch has been her husband, her lord, her ''mighty one in the earth''; the ''spirit of this world'' has been her holy spirit. This spiritual whore has ever found satiety only in gorging herself ''with the blood of the saints, and with the martyrs of Jesus,'' and she has depended upon ''the sword of State'' as the instrument of her murderous business. The follower of Jesus Christ has never yet been given any calling in the earth but as a witness to the invisible but coming Lord, and the very word ''witness'' is *marturos,*—martyr. The only true self-dedication of the Christian thus far has been that of hating life itself for His sake and the Gospel's.

We are now able to draw certain important delineations and delimitations regarding the great whore.

a. She is called the great whore because she is of spiritual character and guilty of spiritual infidelity and prostitution. This abominable spiritual conduct consists in copartnership with the godless, self-determined political powers of this ungodly, Satan-ruled world, whereas true and faithful spirituality is known by acknowledgment of the Son of God alone as Lord and coming ruler of all.

b. She is called Babylon the Great because her career is to be properly dated from, as also to be denominated by, the founding of the first godless, self-existing, tyrannous world-empire at Babylon as the capital-seat. It was at Babylon that the human race determined to reverse God's order and—instead of dispersing throughout the earth, to cultivate, to replenish, to enjoy, and to live in fraternal equality and accord—to centralize, to organize, to dominate, yea, to deify man himself in respect to earthly power, privilege and achievement. While God frustrated this plan at the first by the infliction of the confusion of tongues, yet, later, Nimrod —a Hamite, belonging by dispersion in Africa—conceived from Satan this idea of world-empire in defiance of the confusion of tongues, and he aptly chose old Babel, located in territory allotted to the Shemites, for the object of his conquest and for the seat of his imperial organization.

Satan, however, has never founded a State without religion. To supply unregenerate man with false political government without supplying him at the same time with false religion, would spell failure from the outset. See, for illustration of the necessity for supplying the spiritual co-respondent of the self-determined political government, the case of Jeroboam in making calf-worship the religious bolster to his kingdom of the Ten Tribes. See 1 Kings 12: 25-33. *Per Contra,* for illustration of God's demand that all earthly government should acknowledge and exemplify the fact that "the heavens do rule," that "the most High ruleth in the kingdom of man," and that the earthly monarch should hold his office only to "praise and extol and honor the King of heaven" and to "show the signs and wonders that the high God hath wrought toward" him,—see Nebuchadnezzar's world-wide proclamation of his experiences with God to this end, as we have it all from his own hand in the fourth chapter of Daniel. Now this satanized religion of a satanized body politic is "the great whore," "Babylon the Great," not the political Babylon, standing out in publicity, but the spiritual Babylon, operating in "Mystery."

c. "Mystery, Babylon the Great," is, then, the substitute for, the antithesis to, true religion, and that not of some late historic times only, but of all the times of the world-empires. Neither is it some particular religious manifestation or organization. The religious paramour of the Christless State has not borne the same name, worn the same apparel, set up the same idols for worship at all times and in all places. This would not be "Mystery Babylon the Great." No one can put his finger on a mystery, or denominate a mystery, and say, "This is the mystery." As soon as this becomes possible there is no longer mystery. Mystery is indeed evident, but not apparent. The outward medium of evidence is not the mystery itself. Satan's strategy always has been to keep the spiritual whore of world-power mystical, indefinable, chameleon-like, so far as externals are concerned.

It has already been implied that there are signs by which this whorish spirituality can be detected. These signs may be classified as governing evil lusts.

(a) Lust for popular sway, "The great whore that sitteth upon many waters" (vs. 1); "and he saith unto me, The waters which thou sawest, where the whore sitteth, are peoples, and multitudes, and nations, and tongues" (v. 15). Religious propaganda and ambition for popular dominance is always an outstanding feature of whorish religion.

(b) Lust for political advantage. While political functions do not belong to the mystical Babylon, yet unscrupulous political alliance and influence is especially sought after and persistently practiced by the whore-religion.

(c) Lust for dazzling display. Access to financial wellsprings of luxury and imposing display—bartering essential spiritual privileges for sordid pelf—such are tokens of mystical Babylon, whether under the garb of the most civilized, cultured, artistic expression, or under the most barbarous, debased, grotesque expression of African savagery.

(d) Lust for the blood of dissenting saints. Religious bigotry and hatred, murder in spirit and practice, indelibly stamp, stain and betray this satanic counterfeit of spirituality.

These very ear-marks show that "Mystery Babylon" is not any one exclusive religious body, of a peculiar denomination, geographical center or historical period; for these ear-marks have been more or less prominent from Babel to this day, under various denominations and radiating from different centers, even simultaneously. Even movements originally evangelical may later decline spiritually, and become ambitious, worldly, unscrupulous, intolerant, murderous. It is this indefinable variety of forms, phases and expressions marking the ages from Babel to the end of this dispensation—all betraying the same evil spiritual genius—that gives occasion for "Mystery Babylon the Great" to be called "the mother of harlots and abominations of the earth." It is reasonable to suppose that in the days of the Anti-Christ—days of unparalleled political, commercial, industrial and social centralization and despotism—false ecclesiasticism may become more completely, inclusively organized and stereotyped than ever before, when the ear-marks of mystical Babylon will guide the eye more definitely, conclusively and amazingly to one certain monopolizing organization than has ever yet been the case. But even a final consummate manifestation of the great whore will be only illustratively and not comprehensively what is in Revelation called "Mystery Babylon the Great."

Just as imperialism is the spirit of which any given empire is but the body; just as militarism was not exiled with Napoleon; just as Moscow might be razed to the ground without halting the sway of Bolshevism; just as any ism may survive the medium of its public manifestation; so this "Mystery Babylon the Great" is set before us as the secret evil spiritual power of the imperial ages—changeless in principle, although ever changing and varying in external manifestations—which mere material, local, temporal measures cannot control.

3. More Especial Explanation of the Mystery from the Woman's Side, vs. 15-18.

"15 And he saith unto me, The waters which thou sawest, where the whore sitteth, are peoples, and multitudes, and nations, and tongues. 16 And the ten horns which thou sawest upon the beast, these shall hate the whore, and shall make her desolate and naked, and shall eat her flesh, and burn her with fire. 17 For God hath put in their hearts to fulfill his will, and to agree, and give their kingdom unto the beast, until the words of God shall be fulfilled. 18 And the woman which thou sawest is that great city, which reigneth over the kings of the earth.''

The context itself marks these verses off from the foregoing as a further explanatory paragraph.

It is first explained that the waters, upon which, according to v. 1, John had first seen the great whore sitting, were "peoples, and multitudes, and nations, and tongues." This exposes the widespread and profound popular control held by the faithless woman,—the defiling, inebriating spiritual system of the ages.

Evidently the territory of this baneful popular sway of the woman will be co-extensive with and especially that of the imperial federation of the ten kingdoms; for vs. 16, 17, go on to designate these powers as the agents of the Woman's destruction. The R. V. translates vs. 16, 17, in the perfect tense: "And the ten horns which thou sawest upon the beast, these shall hate the whore, and shall make her desolate and naked, and shall eat her flesh, and burn her with fire. For God did put in their hearts to do his mind, and to come to one mind, and to give their kingdom unto the beast, until the words of God should be accomplished." The C. V. translates these verses in the imperfect tense: "And the ten horns which you perceived, and the wild beast, these will be hating the prostitute, and they will be making her desolate and naked, and they will be consuming her flesh, and they will be burning her up with fire, for God imparts to their hearts to form his opinion, and to be

19

one in their opinion, even to give their kingdom to the wild beast, until God's words will be accomplished.''

It is concluded from the translations taken together, that the consumption of the Babylon religion is a process sufficiently gradual to cover largely the period—the ''one hour''—of the ten kingdom federation under the Anti-Christ; that is, that by a protracted destructive persecution shall this historic persecutor of the saints of ages come to her deserved end.

It was revealed in 13: 3-8, 12 that the beast, the Anti-Christ, should at last demand the worship of himself. With this other prophecies accord. This ordinance of worship will, of course, conflict with and involve the extinction of all previous religious order, not only the true order, but also the counterfeit order obtaining, as we have seen, throughout all previous ages and times. It is here revealed that God's will for the final consumption of this whorish religious system will become the unanimous verdict and effective policy of the final governmental organization. Such decision is peculiarly appropriate so far as the great whore is concerned because of her political relationship. The imperial power, which in all ages, from old Babel down, has been her secure support, will at last prove to be her ruin; instead of her enjoying longer fond and flattering dalliance with the kings of the world, they will become her mockers and bloodthirsty destroyers. So was it predicted for Aholah and Aholibah—faithless Israel and Judah of old, Ezekiel 23. Indeed, God's law for the recompense of adultery—whether physical or spiritual—is to have such prostitution bring results as though one took fire into one's bosom.

The essential distinction of the final form of false religion will be, not that of an adulterous alliance with the State, but that of an atheistical assumption of deity by the political head himself. It will no longer be a coalition of interests, political and religious, but a solidarity of political and spiritual world-power combined. All the false gods of history will go into the discard, and all false worship will become dragon-worship expressed in homage to the Anti-Christ.

The closing of this paragraph—more properly of the whole chapter, devoted as it is mainly to the identification of the great whore—seems at first irrelevant and confusing. Yet it is really most logical and timely. We should remember that in v. 7 it is recorded that the vial-angel told John that he would "tell—the *mystery* of the woman." The mystery of the woman consisted in what entitled her to the name "Babylon," that of the final mistress-city of the world and of historic ages. Her title, "Babylon"—Confusion—is very properly the same as that of the political capital, not only because of her adulterous coalition with the political throne there, but because she is in God's sight and in comparison with true religion the same in religion that Nimrod's throne was in government,—confusion. But her name Babylon is "Mystery"; that is, symbolical, not literal; religious, not political; ideal, not real; spiritual, not material.

Having given identification to the woman as the contemporary and the spiritual mistress of historic world-empires, the interpreter sums up the explanation of the two figures of the woman and mystical Babylon by saying, "And the *woman* which thou sawest is that *great city*, which reigneth ["*hath a kingdom*"—spiritual— C. V.] over the kings of the earth" (v. 18). That this rule is not political, but spiritual, is evident from the fact that it does not displace political imperialism and literal kingdoms. So this new explanation is not a diversion of our minds to a new object, or to some literal, latter-day city not already brought forward and explained. It is but the résumé of what had gone before; as though the interpreting angel had said, "That which you saw as a woman in your vision of the last days— the days of the Anti-Christ—and which you saw denominated in her forehead as 'Mystery Babylon the Great,' is that great spiritual organism, which, like an imperial capital—a veritable Babylon-mistress—has been having her malign spiritual rule over the kingdoms of this world all the way from Nimrod down, and which will so continue until, in the days of the last political organization of world-empire, her spiritual reign shall be destroyed to give way to another, the undivided satanic politico-religious sway of Anti-Christ.''

This change of metaphor has obvious relation to Chapter 18 and should prepare us for a right understanding of the symbolical nature of the city there dealt with. It is, indeed, a fair question whether this last verse of Chapter 17 should not be made the first verse of Chapter 18.

CHAPTER XII.

DIVINE RETRIBUTION UPON MYSTICAL BABYLON, 17:1—19:10.

(Continued.)

II. MYSTICAL BABYLON BROUGHT TO FINAL JUDGMENT, CHAPTER 18.

Introductory.

THE connection between Chapters 17 and 18 is most intimate, immediate and important. In 17:1, the angel says to John, "Come hither; I will shew thee the *judgment* of the great whore"; but in v. 7 he defers this disclosure in order to reveal to John first "the *mystery* of the woman, and of the beast that carrieth her." We have traced through the remainder of Chapter 17 this latter disclosure. John, therefore, having had revealed and identified to him the mystical woman and the mystical beast severally and in relationship to each other, now in Chapter 18 proceeds to transmit the promised revelation of the judgment upon the woman.

It is evident, then, that Chapter 18 is to be understood in the light of Chapter 17, especially in the light of 17: 5-18. We have there been shown a mysterious spiritual system, running contemporaneously and coitionally with political world-rule from Nimrod down to Anti-Christ, and religiously dominating the same, ever and anon commandeering the sword of the State to spill abundantly "the blood of the saints and—the blood of the martyrs of Jesus."

We have found this debauching spiritual system called by the name of the first imperial capital city of post-

diluvian history—Babylon; and it has been designated—
not apparently as any modern or coming literal city—
"that great city, which has a kingdom over the kings of
the earth." That is, this is "that great city" in "Mystery," which has been, still is and yet will be for some
time, the invisible mistress of all postdiluvian world-
capitals and realms of worldly mankind.

An unspeakably unholy, ambitious, soul-debauching,
implacably intolerant, murderous spiritual working has
been described to us in Chapter 17 and denominated a
whorish woman and an imperious city. In Chapter 18
the same descriptive terms are used, and they are with
grammatical precision applied to identically the same
object. Now, so long as the descriptive terms applying
to the same object are retained in Chapter 18, where the
judgment of this object is revealed, so long must we take
the language describing the judgment as corresponding
in form to the language of Chapter 17 which describes
the object itself. Seeing, then, that the descriptive terms
of Chapter 17, identifying this object, are mystical, not
natural; symbolical, not literal,—requiring careful explanation of what otherwise is confessedly unapparent
and unintelligible—so must we interpret correspondingly
the language describing the judgment of this object;
namely, as mystical, not natural; as symbolical, not literal. Consequently, we are to take the eighteenth chapter as the symbolical description of the execution of
divine wrath upon that which has already in the seven-
teenth chapter been identified through symbolical description. While no angelic interpretation of the
symbolism of Chapter 18 is given, yet the key to the
same is given in Chapter 17 by the angel's interpretation
of the identifying symbols there employed.

It is all-important that we follow this guiding and
controlling principle of interpretation, lest we be betrayed into humanly conceived, instead of divinely

authorized, meaning and application of the judgment of God upon mystical Babylon as described in the eighteenth chapter. To find here a literal city, consumed by material means and process, would be out of harmony with the identification of Babylon made in the previous chapter. It is enough for us to remember that "the woman" and "Babylon" are but two figurative designations of one and the same object; therefore, just as the woman was shown to be the spiritual mistress of world-empire from Babel to Anti-Christ, so "Babylon" the "great city" of 17:18 and of Chapter 18, designates not something material, confined to a given geographical locality and to one given past, present or yet coming period of time, still less to something political or commercial. Such a conception would fall immeasurably below what is demanded by the revelation of Chapter 17. This woman is ubiquitous both in the times and in the territories of the world-empires of post-diluvian history. Her several visible capitals, the centers of her adulterous spiritual co-regency with world-emperors, have successively fallen, but this spiritual mistress of world-emperors has no more ceased from the earth than political imperialism itself. Every shred of external medium of expression of this false woman opposed to "the mother of us all" (children born from above), of this "great city" of Satan opposed to the "city of God," might be demolished,—even as might the successive political expressions of world-empire—yet "Mystery Babylon the great" would remain intact in mystical organization and power. However much the judgment of mystical Babylon may involve external and material demolition, yet this would not constitute or accomplish the effectual judgment.

Moreover, chapter 17 furnishes us with another controlling factor in the interpretation of chapter 18.

Chapter 17 shows that the mystical Babylon is a system of spiritual power and rule which is counterfeit to evangelical religion and is its bloodthirsty persecutor, and that it pursues this persecution as the paramour of the emperor, by means of his political power, not, however, in his name, but in the name of heavenly divinity. And chapter 17 shows that the judgment of the great whore consists in the extermination of the religious principle and system of this kind, hoary with the ages of post-diluvian world-empire. We are also shown in this book of Revelation wherefore this revolt of imperialism against its long accustomed associate ecclesiasticism and wherefore this titantic, world-wide, mystical religious overthrow.

Chapter 13 reveals that the time is to come in the midst of the last days when the world-emperor—Anti-Christ—is to be satanically constituted as himself god, the only god of this world. He is to be the object of worship world-wide (13:4, 8), and this worship is to be compulsory (13:12, 15-17), under penalty of death or of exclusion from all means of earthly livelihood. This principle of "State Religion" is new; an appalling religious persecution and extermination is involved in the change, and it is not to be a persecution of "the saints, and—the martyrs of Jesus," but of their implacable persecutor through the ages of world-empire.

This new principle of religious faith and worship—the deification of the emperor, the union of political and spiritual tyranny in one personal authority, supplanting all celestial divinity as well as kingship—is forecast in earlier prophecies of the Bible. It is plainly involved in 2 Thess. 2:3, 4: "That man of sin —, the son of perdition; who *opposeth and exalteth himself above all that is called God, or that is worshipped;* so that he *as God* sitteth [taketh his seat] in the *temple of God,* shewing himself that *he is God.*" Likewise, in Daniel

11:36, 37: "He shall exalt himself, and magnify himself above every god, and shall speak marvellous things against the God of gods,—neither shall he regard the God of his fathers, nor the desire of women, nor regard any god: for he shall magnify himself above all" (i. e. all other gods). And we may probably be warranted in finding the same implied in John 5:43. "I am come *in my father's name,* and ye receive me not: if another shall come *in his own name,* him will ye receive."

There is involved in the change in the basis of world-religion already described a marked feature of control, as brought out in 2 Thess. 2:3, 6-9: "And that man of sin be *revealed,*....And now ye know what withholdeth [hinders] *that he might be revealed in his time.* For the *mystery of iniquity doth already work:* only he who [that which] now letteth [hinders] will let [hinder], until he [that which hinders; namely, the overcoming body of believers] be taken out of the way. And then shall that Wicked [One] be *revealed* . . . whose coming is after the working of Satan, with all power and signs and lying wonders." Here is the contrast between the working of antichristian iniquity in "mystery" and the same "revealed" in the person of "that man of sin." Now, it is the historic method of iniquity's working in "mystery" that is to be demolished to give place to the open, public, miraculous working of inquity by the personal Anti-Christ as Satan's full and undisguised medium of manifestation.

Although both principles and forms of false religion—that which consists of a mystical adulterous alliance between the beast and the woman, and that which unites visibly professed deity and emperorship in one personal head—are of Satan, yet none the less the change from the former to the latter involves an inconceivably terrible religious revolution and calamity, as it will also be the adequate execution of divine wrath upon that

which has through all postdiluvian ages fiendishly delighted in hounding the true followers of the Son of
God to the death. That this overthrow will amount to a
veritable world-wide and world-rocking cataclysm may
easily be imagined, from the fact that this religious power
has held its dominance for these thousands of years in
spite of the fluctuations and convulsions of world-
history. This has been due to Satan's great power, and it
will be due to nothing less than Satan's power ordained
by God that the revolution will be accomplished. See
17:13, 16, 17.

The Indictment, 18:1-3.

"1 And after these things I saw another angel come down
from heaven, having great power: and the earth was lightened
with his glory. 2 And he cried mightily with a strong voice,
saying, Babylon the great is fallen, is fallen, and is become the
habitation of devils, and the hold of every foul spirit, and a cage
of every unclean and hateful bird. 3 For all nations have drunk
of the wine of the wrath of her fornication, and the kings of the
earth have committed fornication with her, and the merchants
of the earth are waxed rich through the abundance of her
delicacies."

The sense of the word "power" in v. 1 is *authority*.
"Heaven" is to be understood in the prevailing sense of
the Book of Revelation; namely, as our earthly heaven,
and in that of Gen. 1:1. The vision is, therefore, of
the last stage of the angel's journey from the throne of
God in the skies. Hence the glory of his power, clothed
with such excellence and authority, illumines the earth
widely, as the glory of the angel of annunciation dazzled
the vision of the shepherds of Bethlehem. With sonorous,
awe-inspiring voice John hears the momentous pronouncement from the angel's holy lips:

"Babylon the great is fallen, is fallen."

It is all-important to mark the identity of this Babylon
with that of 17:5 as expounded later in chapter 17.
It is the historic, mystical, spiritual Babylon. This is

fully confirmed by the further words: "And is become the habitation of devils [demons], and the hold ['prison,' 'dungeon' or 'cage'] of every foul ['unclean'] spirit, and a cage ['den'] of every unclean and hateful bird."

This is descriptive of the most corrupt and repulsive moral, spiritual, and social state. Hence the term "fallen" is not descriptive of an external, material catastrophe, but of the extreme of spiritual declension. The C. V. more clearly than our other translations confirms this fact in the further words given in one and the same sentence with the two above quotations:

"Seeing that all nations have fallen [of course, morally and religiously] as a result of the furious wine of her fornication." The R. V. translates the same: "For by the wine of the wrath of her fornication all the nations of the earth are fallen."

The sense, then, in which mystical Babylon's fall is here pronounced is that of her utterly rotten internal moral and spiritual condition and influence, which cries out for God's judgment upon the great whore. The further statement, as translated by the C. V., is significant and weighty, standing as a new sentence: "And the kings of the earth commit prostitution with her and the merchants of the earth are rich as a result of her ability to indulge."

The present tense denotes the long-standing course of things. This is Babylon in no literal sense, confined to a distinct time, locality and limited religious establishment.

It is very important to note the emphasis given here to Babylon's attractions and value to the princely and commercial classes of the world. It has always been recognized that the Babylonish religion is of high political advantage to royalty in its unhallowed designs and policies; and it has also been recognized that the display and the extravagance of such religion is of immense profit to "big business." We need not be surprised to find these realms of mankind greatly stirred and affected when all this political and commercial benefit is demoralized because of the judgment befalling this medium thereof.

The Verdict, vs. 4-8.

"4 And I heard another voice from heaven, saying. Come out of her, my people, that ye be not partakers of her sins, and that ye receive not of her plagues. 5 For her sins have reached unto heaven, and God hath remembered her iniquities. 6 Reward her even as she rewarded you, and double unto her double according to her works: in the cup which she hath filled, fill to her double. 7 How much she hath glorified herself, and lived deliciously, so much torment and sorrow give her: for she saith in her heart, I sit a queen, and am no widow, and shall see no sorrow. 8 Therefore shall her plagues come in one day, death, and mourning, and famine; and she shall be utterly burned with fire: for strong is the Lord God who judgeth her."

Verses 4 and 5 show that even at so late a day there will be occasion for breaking the yoke of unequal, inconsistent spiritual fellowship. Whatever of mere external dissociation may be involved, the call is not primarily to the outward, but to the inward, the spiritual entanglement. It proves that there may be stages of religious apostasy at which separation from fellowship may not be absolutely, perhaps not advisedly, imperative on the part of the truly spiritual. There was a time in Ezekiel's days when true Israelites could still safely cling to the temple and its worship; but when "the glory of the Lord" lifted from its place in the Holy of Holies and, after tarrying a little at the temple threshold, and then "at the door of the east gate of the Lord's house, took its departure "from the midst of the city and stood [apart] upon the mountain which is on the east side of the city," it was time for the truly godly to break fellowship with all the forms and functions of professed religion connected with the doomed sanctuary. So here, further participation in this "State religion," whether to be so-called from the side of actual form, or of merely inward principle, will mean participation in "sins," because there will be then no further operations of divine mercy and grace; and such participation will involve inevitable sharing in judgment, because there will be recognized no exceptions, and discrimination between precious and vile will no longer be exercised.

By the way, it is very interesting, and a valuable contribution to our information and right understanding, to note that way down at this late hour in "the last days" Christ will have still His people on earth; His own to respond to the eleventh hour summons to "Come out," let it cost what it will. These are the very last gleanings from tribulation times, to be added to the Church still awaiting the marriage of the Lamb.

Verse 5 is in the category of various Scriptural records, when, as in the case of God's final investigation of the builders of the tower of Babel, God takes a critical personal estimate of moral conditions with a view to necessary and deserved judgment. There seems to be a probable reminiscence of old Babel in expressing the course of this mystical Babylon in building through the ages her tower of defiant sins up to the very battlements of heaven.

The word "double" in v. 6, is to be understood, not as twice as much, but as an exact equivalent, as it is an old legal expression denoting perfect duplicate, or exact equivalent.

Although it has been shown in chapter 17 that the immediate earthly executioners of the divine judgment upon the whore are to be the ten confederated kingdoms of Anti-Christ's empire, yet the most interested parties are those who shall have suffered through postdiluvian ages at her hands. The peoples of the earth, bewitched and debauched through her evil reign, will surely be changed into a rabble crying "Crucify her, crucify her." But the persecuted, tempted, martyred saints of all the centuries—whether those remaining still on earth or those above in the skies,—will give their eager consent to the judgment. And the faithful angels, who have watched and contended, who have gathered up lovingly the tear-drops and the blood-drops of distressed saints and witnesses, will gladly lend their hand in contributing effectively to the ends of divine wrath.

Verse 7 continues to ordain an exact equation of just judgment for the whore's criminality as a spiritual power in the earth. The language here employed in describing her perfidy makes all the clearer and stronger the fact that still the subject yet being treated is mystical and religious; and the language helps us to a more definite and tangible comprehension of this accursed woman. For the description reveals her as the antithesis to another figurative, mystical woman very prominent in the Bible; namely, the one not coquetting with earthly potentates, not courting present earthly regnancy, not abandoning herself to fleshly indulgence and promoting the same universally, the one not seeking her glory now and from the world lying in the evil one, the one not proud and self-exalting as a queen over superstitious subjects high and low,—No, not the pseudo-Christian Church, but the "virtuous woman," the "chaste virgin," the "little flock," the one loyally and faithfully waiting for her "Lord to appear," even the Lamb of God whose Bride and wife she is to become. These two women represent two classes of souls that have been since Cain and Abel undergoing spiritual incorporation and organization in permanent bodies under spiritual headship, the one under the devil's headship, the other under Christ's. The one head offers earthly inheritance but no promise for the future; the other calls to separation at present from all earthly inheritance unto an inheritance of heaven and earth with Christ in the ages to come. See Hosea 3:3.

The whore says in her very heart, "I sit a queen." She assumes the throne and reigns in power already with her earthly consort, from Nimrod down to Anti-Christ. Even though she calls herself "Christian," yet the appellation is a travesty upon the name and character of Jesus Christ. She muses in her heart, "I am not waiting, or going to wait, for an absent, a distantly coming lord, one who does not receive his kingdom from this world! I am no widow, husbandless in the world, forlorn and sorrowing. My garments are not the weeds of widowhood, but the robes of splendor and royalty." Her whole spirit, demeanor, state and profession is the diametrical contradiction of all that belongs to that other woman. To change the figure, she is "that great city," "Mystery Babylon," while the other is that "city of God," the "heavenly Jerusalem," "which is above—which is the mother of us [Spirit-born ones] all."

This distinctiveness of the Babylonish church shows how far this mother of harlots reaches in identity beyond the confines of any past or present known religions, organizations or bodies; for her manifestations and her members are to be found in outward contact and membership with the true followers of Jesus Christ quite universally. The tares and the wheat are growing side by side. And it will never be possible to destroy this universally pervasive spiritual organism by merely destroying something external, a visible solidarity—like an œcumenical ecclesiasticism or some particular city, like Rome or a Babylon *redivivus*. The judgment upon this false spiritual "queen" must exterminate that religious principle and spirit, wherever found, which has maintained itself by corrupt and corrupting spiritual alliance and partnership with the political and other powers of this present unregenerate world. It must expire, in order to give way to an undivided headship of civil and religious power in the person of the Anti-Christ. Of course, in the accomplishment of this extermination, institutions, organizations, municipalities,—interest temporal of all sorts—will be involved and affected, because this evil spiritual principle has from Babel down had its clutch upon the intricate mechanism of all things earthly and temporal. The consequence is that the graphic, practical, external aspects of this judgment could not be described otherwise than in such manner as is found in the rest of chapter 18, while the mystical character of the judgment and of the object judged remains unchanged.

Let us once more, before reading the graphic and astounding description of Babylon's destruction, summarize what has been found to be the real data controlling our understanding of the description.

A mysterious spiritual system, obtaining and governing from Babel down the souls of men in the earth outside the members of Jesus Christ, is to be destroyed by God in vengeance on account of the injustice and cruelty suffered from this system by His children and servants throughout these ages. Mere outward institutions do not constitute this mysterious system, so that their destruction would not destroy the system. Hence, from the standpoint of divine vengeance, it would miss the mark to interpret the object of this judgment— called "Mystery Babylon the great"—as merely or primarily external, local and material in sense. The end to be reached is to destroy this *spiritual* Babylonianism out of the very system of humanity in all the earth.

On the other hand, Satan, operating through the federation of the ten last kingdoms under the headship of the Anti-Christ, is to coöperate with God's purpose by an absolute repudiation of this spiritual Babylonianism, although it is his own creature, by which he has bewitched and corrupted the Christless world these ages. His determination will be to exterminate this secretive spiritual system,—the principle of which has ever been that of

coition with worldly political power—in order to replace
it with an unconcealed spiritual propaganda, the principle of which will be that of united spiritual and political headship in his incarnate manifestation, the Anti-
Christ. To effect this end the greatest war of the ages
must obtain. Yet not a "war," but a shock of ages, a
crash of systems, a death-grapple of worlds. Prussianism
needed to be destroyed by the great world war of 1914-
1918. Was that effected by the burning of Berlin?
But Prussianism meant militarism; i. e., military world-
rule, in the hands of Deutschland, more particularly of
Prussia, still more particularly of the house of Hohen-
zollern. Would militarism have been exterminated by
the defeat of German armies and the burning of Berlin?
No! Not if militarism runs like a fever through the
veins of modern Europe. Would Bolshevism be effectually judged, blotted out of the world forever, by the
burning of Moscow? Nay! Is not Bolshevism a poison
that has gotten to running through the veins of humanity
to such a degree that, however much its extinction might
involve frightful destruction in outward spheres, yet
the true conception of effectual judgment upon this
noxious ism would recognize, that all that outward
aspect of the case was but symptomatic instead of
systemic. The end to be reached is that the Anti-Christ—
the very incarnate revelation of Satan—shall stand in
the earth unrivaled and undisputed, in absolute personal
solidarity, as God alone to be worshipped as well as
king alone to be obeyed. In effecting this end, there will
be the wreck of a most hoary and powerful spiritual
constitution of unregenerate humanity, and the effect
upon all godless institutions and interests, especially
political and commercial, will be like an appalling earthquake, or the burning of a world-metropolis.

Lamentation Over Babylon's Judgment, vs. 8-24.

The description in the following paragraphs of Babylon's destruction is given but very meagerly as a direct spectacle and principally from the standpoint of its effect upon several prominent classes or spheres of intimate interest.

First, that of the governments of the world, vs. 9, 10:

"9 And the kings of the earth, who have committed fornication and lived deliciously with her, shall bewail her, and lament over her, when they shall see the smoke of her burning, 10 Standing afar off for the fear of her torment, saying Alas, alas, that great city Babylon, that mighty city! for in one hour is thy judgment come."

We remember that the ten kings federated under Anti-Christ will be executing this stupendous revolution. This makes it the more evident what momentous convulsions will shock the whole international political and governmental situation. Disentanglement from immemorial politico-religious affinities will necessarily be the general diplomacy of the time.

There is no discrepancy between the expression, "in one hour is thy judgment come" and the idea of a considerable period of time covering the process of exterminating this false spiritual system of the ages, seeing that the term "hour" is sometimes thus used in Scripture, especially in the Book of Revelation. The whole period of the confederacy of the ten kings under the Anti-Christ is designated as "one hour" (17:12), and the three and one-half years terminating this age are called (14:7) "the hour of his judgment."

Secondly, that of the commercial world, vs. 11-17a.

"11 And the merchants of the earth shall weep and mourn over her; for no man buyeth their merchandise any more: 12 The merchandise of gold, and silver, and precious stones, and of pearls, and fine linen, and purple, and silk, and scarlet, and all thyine wood, and all manner vessels of ivory, and all manner vessels of most precious wood, and of brass, and iron, and marble,

13 And cinnamon, and odours, and ointments, and frankincense, and wine, and oil, and fine flour, and wheat, and beasts, and sheep, and horses, and chariots, and slaves, and souls of men. 14 And the fruits that thy soul lusted after are departed from thee, and all things which were dainty and goodly are departed from thee, and thou shalt find them no more at all. 15 The merchants of these things, which were made rich by her, shall stand afar off for the fear of her torment, weeping and wailing, 16 And saying, Alas, alas, that great city, that was clothed in fine linen, and purple, and scarlet, and decked with gold, and precious stones, and pearls! 17 For in one hour so great riches is come to nought.''

An inconceivable extent of commercial disjointing is here clearly reflected. Imagine a crusade of extermination against present-day Roman Catholicism, or even of Protestantism. Would it not involve an unparelleled panic throughout the commercial world? Verse 14 expresses why such disastrous effects will befall commerce in that day. Lamentation is uttered over Babylon for the destruction of that "ability to indulge," which was attributed to her in v. 3 of this chapter and by which, as vs. 15, 16 show, brought immense profit to the world's merchants.

Thirdly, that of the maritime world, vs. 17b-19.

"17b And every shipmaster, and all the company in ships, and sailors, and as many as trade by sea, stood afar off, 18 And cried when they saw the smoke of her burning, saying, What city is like unto this great city! 19 And they cast dust on their heads, and cried, weeping and wailing, saying, Alas, alas, that great city, wherein were made rich all that had ships in the sea by reason of her costliness! for in one hour she is made desolate.''

Not only the commercial fabric of inland trade, but of marine traffic as well, will inevitably be imperilled and paralyzed as never before, and for the same reason as above. For the merchantmen of all waters, to an extent not before realized, will be found to owe their great profits to the balance of world-commerce, on land and on sea, embracing the enormous trade and influence

of this imperious, luxurious and ubiquitous system of
prostituting religion.

Fourthly, that of the heavenly world, v. 20.

"Rejoice over her, thou heaven, and ye holy apostles and
prophets; for God hath avenged you on her."

All our translations agree in two changes from the
A. V. above. Instead of "holy apostles" two classes are
specified; namely, "Ye saints and ye apostles," thus
making the threefold classification of saints, apostles and
prophets, besides the other classes in "heaven." We are
to recall the scene presented in this book, of the com-
mingled throngs in the earthly skies of angelic hosts and
of raptured saints of the ages, all clustering about the
Lord God Almighty enthroned and the Lamb.   The
most prominent leaders of the saints—apostles of the new
dispensation and prophets of the old—are specially
mentioned here.

Then, instead of reading "God hath avenged you on
her," the other translations practically agree in reading
"God hath judged your judgment on her."   That is,
"God hath executed your sentence of judgment upon her."
This carries in it the avenging; but it more explicitly
implies that the heavenly hosts—of angels, of saints,
apostles and prophets, those most intimately concerned
over the just dealing of God with Mystical Babylon—
will constitute the jury at heaven's court, when Jesus
Christ as prosecuting attorney will present and prosecute
before God Almighty the charges against Babylon for
her unpardonable wrongs against His followers on earth
and against His angelic messengers through all the ages.
The judgment of utter destruction of the Babylonish
system of religion on earth here set before us is presented
as executed in obedience to the unanimous verdict of all
this heavenly throng, who themselves have suffered
throughout postdiluvian ages at the hands of this mother
of harlots.

This revelation carries our attention and our conception yet further beyond a judgment confined to the relatively puny dimensions of a chiefly local, municipal, physical and ecclesiastical catastrophe. Review the ecclesiasticisms of the past, survey those of the present, forecast those of the future, in order to identify the great whore herself and to fasten this judgment upon her. While the earmarks of mystical Babylon will be found very pronounced in one ecclesiasticism and in another, yet in greater or lesser degree they will be found in all. They are, therefore, rather the harlot-daughters than the mother herself. But the mother is co-historic with Babylonian political imperialism. And none can put his finger upon this or that empire of yesterday or of today, and say, "This is Babylon imperial; destroy it and Babylonianism political will be no more." Symptoms are not the disease itself; destructive attack upon the symptoms will not kill the disease. Symptoms betray disease in the system, and it is the disease that needs to be attacked and cured.

So ecclesiasticisms betray more or less the hidden disease of spiritual Babylonianism. Destroy any one or more, or even all, yet the disease survives and will break out in new symptoms somewhere. Yet it is true that the cure of disease causes the symptoms to disappear and cease. This whole story of the extinction of harlot religion in the earth shows to what extent momentarily the outer world—of government, of commerce, of worldly society in every phase—will be affected. But these are effects only, symptoms again. But these effects do not constitute the judgment, or judgment will be found a failure. Neither do the outward objects thus affected constitute that "Mystery Babylon the great." *Harlotry in religion*—religious faithlessness to Jesus Christ and murderous religious envy toward His true followers—*is to be exterminated and no such religion is to remain in the earth even in principle, but a purely monarchistic religion is to sway the world in the scepter of Anti-Christ.*

Babylon's Doom of Oblivion, vs. 21-23.

This stupendous, world-rocking fall of this mystical harlot religion into utter and eternal extinction is described in these verses of Chapter 18:

"21 And a mighty angel took up a stone like a great millstone, and cast it into the sea, saying, Thus with violence shall that great city Babylon be thrown down, and shall be found no more at all. 22 And the voice of harpers, and musicians, and of pipers, and trumpeters, shall be heard no more at all in thee; and no craftsman, of whatsoever craft he be, shall be found any more in thee; and the sound of a millstone shall be heard no more at all in thee; 23 And the light of a candle shall shine no more at all in thee, and the voice of the bridegroom and of the bride shall be heard no more at all in thee: for thy merchants were the great men of the earth; for by thy sorceries were all nations deceived."

Thus by dramatic action and fateful words was pronounced in John's vision by this angel of great might and authority the verdict of Babylon's oblivion. The language of the pronouncement again reflects the elaborate contribution made by this harlot religion to the luxuries and excessive indulgences of temporal, earthly and fleshly living, to provide which the merchants of these things were made "the magnates of the earth."

Vindication of the Judgment, v. 24:

"And in her was found the blood of prophets, and of saints, and of all that were slain upon the earth."

This closing verse of chapter 18 is not taken as a part of the angel's message of doom. It is a suitable statement concluding the drama of Babylon's judgment, reiterating the governing reason for such a pitiless and extreme doom. And again this object of divine wrath is identified as that mystical bloody spiritual system, which has sated her madness against the Lord Christ by drinking from her golden bowl the blood of prophets and saints of olden and of present dispensations. What an epitaph to stand as God's ineffaceable indictment against a professed, world-wide, dominant religion hoary with the post-diluvian ages! Oh, the unpitied tears and groans and tortures and deaths of the trains of unfaltering martyrs—strong men, noble women, promising young men and women, tender youth and even little children! Every tear has gone into the Lord's bottle, every blood-drop into His chalice, every groan upon the record of His heart, every death-spasm upon the honor roll of the "faithful unto death." It will prove to be a fearful thing to fall into the hands of the living God when he avenges His elect.

Hallelujahs Over Babylon's Judgment, 19:1-2.

"1 And after these things I heard a great voice of much people in heaven, saying, Alleluia; Salvation, and glory, and honour, and power, unto the Lord our God: 2 For true and righteous are his judgments; for he hath judged the great whore, which did corrupt the earth with her fornications, and hath avenged the blood of his servants at her hand."

"Heaven" here is, of course, the skies where the raptured saints and the angels will be gathered about the newly erected throne of the Almighty and about the Lamb, the Lion of the Tribe of Judah. Those stupendous scenes of judgment in the earth will be perfectly clear to view and to understanding to all the vast throngs then assembled in the earthly skies. And these scenes will have even profounder significance to and effect upon those throngs than upon terrestrial classes of beholders as described in the previous chapter. And what contrasted emotions on the part of the terrestrial and of the celestial witnesses! On the part of the former only worldly lamentation! No recognition of God and His judgment, to lead to fear and repentance! No ascription of honor and approval for such just recompence! No

abhorrence of Babylon's abominations, no reprobation
for her corrupting sway over mankind! No pitying remembrance of her red-handed murders of the saints of
the ages! But on the part of the latter, what exultations
toward the "Lord," Jesus Christ, "our God." He will
have borne long with His elect who cried day and night
unto Him. It is necessary for Him to "suffer......thus
far," that none may be deprived of winning their crown.
What moral indignation will be satisfied in the hearts
above because of the corruptions of the "menstruous
whore," and what sympathies toward innocent martyrs
will be made glad!

The refrain of verse 1 would seem to be from the
throngs of raptured saints. For the first note of their
"Hallelujah" is "Salvation." They are partners in the
salvation in the interest of which this judgment will be
executed. Then, like true servants of Jesus Christ, they
see "glory" due to none but Him, and to Him they also
will ascribe the power which is almighty as exemplified
in this marvellous judgment. And, when their anthem of
praise has completed its noble recitation, they burst forth
afresh with a mighty "Hallelujah!"

As if closing the account John records through far-
reaching prospective vision: "And her smoke rose up
for ever and ever," (or, "is ascending for the eons of
eons," C. V.). Certainly the subject of this judgment, and the nature of the same, is something more
than, and primarily quite other than, a physical, visible,
municipal object and a material judgment. While, of
course, the physical, material, social, economic realms are
to be stupendously affected, yet the real object upon
which a consistent attention is held riveted is that
"Mystery Babylon the great," that "great whore" of all
postdiluvian ages. She has a mystical identity spanning
those ages, persecuting the saints throughout those ages,
combatted by the guardian angels and yet suffered to
test the valiant soldiers of King Emmanuel unto the

death. As she will have been known in mystery to earthly saints and heavenly angels through those ages, so also will there be a distinctive, recognizable, ceaseless ascending of the smoke for the eons of eons to follow.

"And the four and twenty elders and the four beasts fell down and worshipped God that sat on the throne, saying, Amen, Alleluia!" v. 4.

Thus the circle of celebrants takes in the great leaders of the raptured saints with whom we have been made so familiar in that capacity from the fourth and fifth chapters of Revelation. Probably their act of prostration in worship of the great divine Judge will be the sign for the vast human and glorified throng to follow suit. With one accord they proclaim their heartfelt approval —"Amen," so let it be—of God's judgment of the great prostitute.

Again the contrast between the effect of the judgment of mystical Babylon upon worldlings and upon heavenly beings is striking. God is not in all their thoughts, the thoughts of worldlings. That were not modernistic. But there is a view of God's fearful judgments which compels adoration and accordant hallelujahs. Eternal punishment will never give offence or grief to the fully sanctified and glorified saint.

"And a voice came out of the throne, saying, Praise our God, all ye his servants, and ye that fear him, small and great," v. 5.

This is a new act in this majestic drama in the skies celebrating God's finished judgment of the great whore of the ages. It is a call from the highest source of heavenly authority for all servants of God, small and great, in reverential fear to swell to utmost fulness the oratorio of praise unto God.

"And I heard as it were the voice of a great multitude, and as the voice of many waters, and as the voice of mighty thunderings, saying, Alleluia: for the Lord God omnipotent reigneth," v. 6

In the vision John hears as one voice—but that of a countless throng of immortal beings in glory, voluminous as measureless waters, resonant as thunderings at full swell—reiterating in climactic fulness and force the thrilling ''Alleluia.'' The cause for this outburst of full-voiced, unanimous triumphant praise is thus explained by the numberless host—''For the Lord our God, the Almighty, reigneth.'' It is thus attested that this judgment of God in the earth is to be a most momentous signal of unparalleled demonstration of His omnipotent sovereignty, far beyond what would be comprehended in the demolition of one more, even the greatest, of world-capitals of the ages.

''Let us be glad and rejoice, and give honour to him: for the marriage of the Lamb is come, and his wife hath made herself ready,'' v. 7.

This continuation of the united paean of praise unto God Almighty for this manifestation of His omnipotence —this self-summons of all God's throng of servants, angelic and redeemed, to highest gladness and rejoicing of heart and glorification of Him—takes a sudden and surprising turn, not anticipated by us, but perfectly natural to them. This act of divine, omnipotent sovereignty, which the innumerable throng celebrates, because of its bringing to endless obloquy the proud and bloody queen of the ages of Christian persecution, is exultantly recognized also as the signal for that consummation of the ages unto which tested believers have looked forward in faith unfaltering even though called to suffer unto death. *THE MARRIAGE OF THE LAMB IS COME.*

There is recognition here that two related consummations are anticipated throughout all these ages, and that these two consummations stand related vitally as well as synchronously through two women symbolically so called. The one woman—''Mystery Babylon the Great,'' or ''the

great whore,'' or ''that great city, which reigneth over
the kings of the earth''—we have just been viewing in
her coming fearful, final judgment. This woman has
been branded as the murderess of true saints through the
ages, especially from Babel to the Anti-Christ. She has
refused the Lord from heaven, and appropriate waiting
for Him, for queenship with the lords of this corrupt
world lying in the evil one. Her jealousy and hatred of
the true Church of the ages knows no bounds, no declension, but only increasing malignity. The other, contemporaneous woman is the pure virgin Church, espoused to
the Lamb of God, seeking no inheritance, fame, power or
indulgence at present, meekly, like a lamb—after the
example and in the spirit of her espoused Bridegroom—
submitting to all injustice, shame and cruelty, sustained
in faith and patience by the prospect of being in due time
wedded to the King of heaven and of all ages. She is the
''chaste virgin,'' the Lamb's intended wife, the city
called ''New Jerusalem,'' ''the holy city......descend-
ing out of heaven from God, having the glory of God.''
Over against the symbolism of the description of the
judgment of the former woman—''the great whore''—
will we meet in due point of progress in this study with
the symbolism of the description of the fadeless glory
of ''the great city, the holy Jerusalem.''

And what is the clear meaning in this connection
of the words, ''and his wife hath *made herself ready''?*

As has just been explained, the false mystical woman
and the true one have synchronous careers down to the
point of the false woman's judgment unto shameful
oblivion. At this point the true woman is shown as
reaching marriage to the Lamb as her magnetic attrac-
tion through all the ages.

But another thing is clear. Both these women are
throughout their preparatory careers being under probation and moving on to the completion thereof. The
false woman is continually ripening in perfidy and

spiritual corruption. Furthermore, she is the instrument
in large part of the probationary testing of the true
woman. So long as the false woman is allowed to continue unjudged there are believers yet to be tested
through her wiles and her cruelties. The marriage of
the Lamb, therefore, still is delayed until the last of these
saints have been tried out. In this sense, of including the
last of the Lamb's followers to be tried out in separation
from the great whore at any cost, will the Lamb's wife
not have become ready for the final ceremony of marriage. This corroborates the teaching, which has appeared consistently all the way along, that the Church
as the coming wife of the Lamb of God has been forming
for the ages past, that she is not to be blessedly married
to her Lord at the initial rapture, that her increase will
be going on through "the last days" thereafter until the
great harlot is judged, which is dated as occurring as
a prominent part of the judgments of the seventh, the
last, vial of God's wrath.

"And to her was granted that she should be arrayed in fine
linen, clean and white: for the fine linen is the righteousness of
saints," v. 8.

The translation here, "the righteousness of saints," is
ambiguous, as is implied by the translation "righteous
acts" in the R. V., "righteousness" in the 1911, or the
translation "righteous effects," or "rewards," in the
C. V. Scripture, however, has already made the meaning
clear. It is explainable by 2 Cor. 5:10: "For we must
all appear before the judgment seat of Christ; that every
one may receive the things *done in his body,* according to
that he hath done, whether it be good or bad." Inasmuch
as the words "done" and "his" are not found in the
original, as the italics show, this statement should read,
"that every one may receive the things in body [im-
mortal] according to that he hath done [in mortal body],
whether it be good or bad." Other prominent passages

should be noted, like Mat. 25:19, John 5:28, 29, 1 Cor. 3:8, 12-14, Rom. 2:6, Mat. 16:27, 1 Pet. 1:17, Rev. 22:12.

Our passages, then, suggest to us that, after all the membership of the Lamb's wife is made up—of those who, through the long ages shall have passed their probation in keeping undefiled by the strange woman—a judgment is to be held on their works past at the Lamb's judgment-seat in the heavens, as a result of which their suitable rewards shall be vested in glorified body. And it seems to be further implied, that this assignment of awards is here viewed not in personal severalty, but in the totality of the entire body of Christ's servants, then to be clad as a whole for the holy and higher functions of the age to come.

This all leads us on to a reliable conception of what is meant by the wedding of the bride to the Lamb. Earthly marriage *in the flesh* is distinctively a bodily union for the sake of combining in one physically two persons already united in heart. So the Lamb will wed the Church to Himself in glorified likeness and unity, for the purpose of together executing in glorified body the functions of the new age before Him, that of His millennial reign.

"9 And he saith unto me, Write, Blessed are they which are called unto the marriage supper of the Lamb."

The question arises here, whether these "which are called [invited] unto the marriage supper of the Lamb" constitute the Lamb's wife or some other company as guests merely. To interpret the figures according to ordinary analogy would favor, if not require, the latter conception. It would be an easy step, then, to the conclusion that, for the want of other beings, the angels would be the guests. And surely they will be happy over the whole event and deeply interested observers and ministers. If there is rejoicing in heaven among the angels over one sinner that repenteth, surely the angels will rejoice to see all penitent, sanctified and glorified saints united at last fully with their great Head, Jesus Christ.

But, in the light of Mat. 22:2-14 (Luke 14:15-24) it seems warrantable and preferable to identify the invited ones with the whole body of believers constituting the Lamb's wife. Just as in Dan. 12:12 some special occasion of superlative felicity is predicted as awaiting believers at a little time after what would naturally be taken as the final consummation, so here there is predicted for us a blissful repast with our Lord right after the full and final marital union with Him shall have been accomplished. Speculation and imagination may be warranted in picturing what joys and felicities will overwhelm us when we first sit down to "eat bread in the kingdom of God"; yet revelation gives not disclosure of what this special blessing will consist of, unless it be that of the Lord Jesus Christ Himself "as the bread from heaven." This wedding banquet may be found in prospect in Rev. 3:20; "Behold, I stand at the door, and knock: if any man hear my voice, and open the door, I will come in to him, and will sup with him, and he with me."

Any suggestion that there will be at the Lamb's wedding banquet two classes of redeemed saints—the one constituting the Lamb's wife, the other constituting a less favored class, of guests only,—is not warranted by the Scriptures, however easily worked out in human theory.

"And he saith unto me, These are the true sayings of God," v. 9.

Thus the messenger of Revelation assures John that these marvels are not new and strange disclosures, but really only a reiteration of what God has revealed all through His Word. Just as Jesus, opening at last the understanding of His disciples to what He had often sought to make them learn and believe, said, "O fools, and slow of heart to believe all that the prophets have spoken:......These are the words which I spake unto you, while I was yet with you, that all things must be fulfilled, which were written in the law of Moses and in the prophets, and in the Psalms, concerning me'' (Luke 24: 25, 44). How professed believers of today need to be vitally impressed with and governed by these and other ''sayings of God'' as practical realities!

''10 And I fell at his feet to worship him. And he said unto me, See thou do it not: I am thy fellow servant, and of thy brethren that have the testimony of Jesus: worship God: for the testimony of Jesus is the spirit of prophecy.''

The divine character and origin of the things revealed from Jesus by the angel were so manifest and overpowering that John fell for worship at the feet of the messenger himself, as if he were identified with the message in character, and as if he were the source of it. But the angel forbids such mistaken regard for him, explaining that he was but a fellow-servant of John and John's brethren with respect to having custody of the testimony regarding Jesus. One may be a High Commissioner relative to another, yet they are fellow commissioners. One American may be the United States Ambassador at the Court of St. James and another American but a private citizen touring Great Britain; yet there is a common classification embracing the two as subjects of the United States and representatives thereof. So the angel directs John to worship God alone. And he adds the reason: ''For the testimony of Jesus is the spirit of prophecy.'' Scripture teaches that prophecy is the exclusive prerogative of God Himself. See Isa. 41: 21-26, 42: 5-9, 45: 20, 21, 46: 9-11. He can communicate His will in prophecy to an angel, a man, or even an ass. ''No prophecy ever came by the [original] will of man: but men spake from God, being moved by the Holy Ghost,'' (R. V.); or, as another has put it, ''men moved by the Holy Ghost spake from God.'' The angel had already declared to John regarding the revelations given, "These are the true sayings of God." We can now see that the emphasis was placed on the word "God."

Our minds earnestly inquire for the peculiar turn of thought and shade of meaning to be found in the sentence, "for the testimony of Jesus is the spirit of prophecy." In the first place the word "for" shows that a logical reason is to be found here for the angel's word immediately preceding. What is the process of reasoning?

The matter circles about the angel's disclaiming John's worship of him, instead of God only, as the ground of angels and believing men having common standing as servants in the testimony of Jesus. But the angel adds that the testimony of Jesus is the spirit of prophecy,— they are one and the same in source and character, the latter inclusive in the other; so that the believer, John for instance, is eligible to the spirit of prophecy, albeit as a second-hand receiver and then transmitter, the same as the angel as a first-hand receiver and transmitter.

The important truth, then, is that all believers may have prophecy open to them as hearers and readers as really as if they were the first custodians thereof. As men of old moved by the Holy Ghost spake prophetically from God, so believers, to whom these prophecies descend in writing, by taking heed to them in their hearts will find them a shining light in a place otherwise dark, until the day dawn and the day star arise. But Peter emphasizes that "no prophecy of the scripture is of any private interpretation" any more than it is of the will of man originally.

This advantage of all believers, in having Biblical prophecy open to them in shining light, is not only a privilege, but it belongs to our "testimony of Jesus." This rebukes all idea that Biblical prophecy is relatively unessential, or that it is wrapped in obscurity, or that it needs preferential "interpreters" with their exclusive "keys of interpretation." The church needs today clear prophetical understanding, in such unanimity of vision as to preclude scisms and to secure in one voice and message a testimony on earth of the things to come to pass in Jesus. Thank God for the wide-spread restoration during the last few decades of the message of Jesus' return; but there is great need for such first-hand, self-evident reading of all prophecy, with attentive heart and simple mind, that the truth in all branches and details may be rescued from whims and fancies, conceits and false lights of men.

The Church Millennial

The Church Militant

CHAPTER I

MILLENNIAL ANTECEDENTS

A CAREFUL perusal of this section of the Book of Revelation readily detects that, like preceding divisions of this book, we have our attention focussed upon a special aspect of the Church, so that it constitutes a further member of a series of revelations from Jesus Christ concerning His Church. The revelation of this division clearly relates to her millennial position. The whole context proceeds step by step logically to its culmination in the undisputed co-rulership of the Church with Christ, her now wedded Lord, for the age of one thousand years.

See how beautiful is the order of revelation thus far given us in this book by Jesus Christ concerning His Church: 1. The Church purely spiritual, ideal and mystical in His priestly care and graces. 2. The Church in practical, probationary, militant character under the existing course of this age. 3. The Church, by resurrection and rapture in immortal bodies, being assembled in the earthly heaven about her returning Lord, from and out of the brief extraordinary epoch of tribulation lying between the present order of things and that of the millennium, that she in entirety might be wedded to the Lamb as a chaste virgin not defiled by the abominations of the great whore of the ages. 4. The Church brought into the joy of joint-heirship with her Spouse in the long-promised millennial kingdom of heaven on earth.

To sustain satisfactorily the position that this division of Revelation carries forward the Church as thus far before us, there is occasion to tarry at this point to examine the section which forms the climax, namely, 20:4-6.

There can be no question that the co-regents with Christ in the millennial reign are here under attention. But the question might be raised, Are these not limited to those so specifically described as the martyrs of the last great tribulation? And, again, does not the statement, "The rest of the dead lived not again until the thousand years were finished," imply that the final resurrection is a divisional resurrection among the saints and, therefore, that the co-regents with Christ will not embrace the Church as a whole? The following answers will clear up these questions:

1. Prior teachings as to who are included in the first resurrection saints must be borne in mind. Back in Dan. 12:2 the division of resurrection companies among Daniel's own people—the Jews—is only twofold, and that solely on the basis of the righteous and the wicked. In John 5:28, 29, the resurrection of "all that are in the graves" is divided into two resurrection events, the first, that ("all") of the righteous, the second, that of the wicked,—the former being "the resurrection of life," the other "the resurrection of damnation." Again Paul, in 1 Thess. 4:13-18, leaves no room for a discrimination between believers as touching resurrection at Christ's coming. The same is implied in 1 Cor. 15:23.

2. The explicit mention of the martyrs of the last days, and their extended identification as such, is not to be taken exclusively; and the further statement, "But the rest of the dead [whether believers or not] lived not again [were not resurrected] until the thousand years were finished," is not to be taken as emphasizing the exclusiveness of the martyrs of the last days as constituting Christ's millennial co-regents. The intention is explicitly and emphatically to include this martyr-class among the resurrected ones who shall reign with Christ. That this is so is proved by the preceding statement, with which verse 6 begins,—"And I saw thrones, and *they* sat upon them, and judgment [rulership] was given to

them." These demonstrative pronouns cannot refer forward, to the martyrs of the last days, but they must refer back to people already under discussion, and those ‚we find in 19:7-9, the whole company of the Lamb's wife. But, after declaring the enthronement and rulership of the Church as a whole, it is emphasized that those left even unto martyrdom in the last days—considerably later than the earlier rapture companies—shall live and reign with Christ as well as the rest. This point is made still stronger and clearer by the translation of the C. V., "they *also* live and reign with Christ a thousand years." The reason for the special mention regarding the martyr-class was doubtless to assure and sustain them in those coming days of extreme testing.

It requires but a cursory reading of the context before us, to see that it consists of various visions falling under three chronological subdivisions: 1. Millennial antecedents, 19:11—20:3. 2. The Millennial Age, 20:4-6. 3. Sequel to the Millennium, 20:7-15.

1. MILLENNIAL ANTECEDENTS.

(1). Descent of the Lord Jesus Christ to Earth, 19: 11-16:

"11 And I saw heaven opened, and behold a white horse; and he that sat upon him was called Faithful and True, and in righteousness he doth judge and make war. 12 His eyes were as a flame of fire, and on his head were many crowns; and he had a name written, that no man knew, but he himself. 13 And he was clothed with a vesture dipped in blood: and his name is called The Word of God. 14 And the armies which were in heaven followed him upon white horses, clothed in fine linen, white and clean. 15 And out of his mouth goeth a sharp sword, that with it he should smite the nations; and he shall rule them with a rod of iron: and he treadeth the winepress of the fierceness and wrath of Almighty God. 16 And he hath on his vesture and on his thigh a name written, KING OF KINGS, AND LORD OF LORDS."

Of course "heaven" in this passage is to be understood, as it generally means in the Bible from Gen. 1:1, and especially in the Book of Revelation, as the earthly heaven, the nearest heavens, *our* heavens or skies. Within their veil our ascending Lord was "received......out of their [the disciples'] sight." The two angels standing by told them, "this same Jesus, which is taken up from you into heaven, shall so come in like manner as ye have seen him go into heaven" (Acts 1:11). John in this vision saw the parting of the veil for the reappearing to earthly view of the returning Lord Jesus.

To Nathanael Jesus said (John 1:51), "Verily, verily, I say unto you, Hereafter ye shall see heaven open, and the angels of God ascending and descending [in attendance] upon the Son of man." And to the Sanhedrin, when adjuring Him to tell them whether He were the Christ, the Son of God, He declared, "Thou hast said." ("Let it stand as you have expressed it"). "Nevertheless I say unto you [in my own word], Hereafter shall ye see the Son of man sitting on the right hand of power, and coming in the clouds of heaven" (Matt. 26:63, 64).

The fulfillment of the above predictions and descriptions is found in the verse before us, only this new vision surpasses all that the others photograph upon human imagination.

In the Spring of 1878, the writer witnessed Emperor William the First's spring review of his troops garrisoned at Potsdam, Germany. Attention was drawn admiringly in various directions until William rode upon the field upon a magnificent black charger. His Majesty —majestic in form indeed, every inch a king—rode so easily upon his steed, the prancing charger bore his royal rider so proudly, that both seemed like one being, a perfect picture of royalty.

But how paltry this splendid earthly and human example in comparison with the appearing of Jesus

Christ upon the ethereal field coming earthward! The description, however, presents Him in military aspect. The white horse means this. And v. 11 closes with the statement that He will be decending to "judge and make war." This language is not to be qualified. Jehovah is a "God of battles," literal, bloody, destructive, victorious battles. He has shown Himself as such in history. He has confessed it in the Scriptures, both in general statement and in particular instances in Old Testament record. There is good reason to believe that He has continued to have His hand controllingly in the warfares of this dispensation. The question whether a disciple of Jesus Christ should engage in warfare under any circumstances and for any cause is answered by the fact that his Lord is "at the front," that He has His "Great Headquarters" in every war. And the question of whether it is not time to put an end to wars is not merely a question of sentimentality or of morality even. While the Scripture plainly teaches that Jesus Christ is controlling toward the end of making wars to cease and will eventually enforce that end, yet, sad to say, that happy time is not yet; when He comes (may it be soon!) He will have to deal with armed earthly hosts as a military enemy and destroyer of them. And the most fearful aspect of the matter is that in so doing He will display Himself as the "Faithful and True," acting "in righteousness" and establishing the same on earth. Of course, wars should now cease; they never should have been. The same can be said of all sins and of all evil. And Jesus Christ alone, interposing from above, and not by agencies now available in His church on earth or in present human society, can cause either to cease. Until then He is permitting sin and war-breeding conditions to continue on earth, which appeal for Him to unfurl His battle-flag over every battle-field for every Christian soldier to fight under, the ensign of "righteousness," the

standards of the "Faithful and True." While now the
provoking of war is always contrary to righteousness in
Him, yet the answer to such provocation for the Christian
is given us in the language of young David: "I come to
thee in the name of the Lord of hosts, the God of the
armies of......, whom thou hast defied." The question
of the hour is not so much whether we shall command
undisturbed peace, as whether we shall fight only, but
fight willingly and valiantly, "in the name of the Lord
of hosts" and "in righteousness......make war."

Further features here given of the military character
in which Jesus is to be seen descending, are found in the
"many crowns"; that is, conqueror's garlands, and in
the "vesture dipped in blood." This is not atoning
blood, His own blood spilt on Calvary; it is the blood
which He has before drawn from His enemies still crim-
soning His white uniform. When Jesus appears, conquering and to conquer on actual battlefields, there will
be upon His white uniform the blood-memorials of His
victory on every battlefield of history where righteousness has been at stake. And His garments will at His
second coming again be crimsoned, metaphorically speaking, with the blood of His antichristian enemies. See
Isa. 63: 1-6. And those "eyes—as a flame of fire"! It
is said of a certain Christian general that the enemy
feared his prayers more than his army. A noted American preacher and evangelist had sometimes to divert his
eyes from casually looking at people, lest the conviction
of the Holy Spirit should fall too poignantly upon
them. "A guilty conscience makes cowards of us all,"
while a conscience "void of offence" emboldens the mien
and fires the eye of one inspired by a righteous cause to
the dismay of wicked men and devils. The eyes of the
descending King of Righteousness will scrutinize all before Him with such soulful, consuming zeal of righteousness as to wither under His glance the wicked and

unbelieving. "He looketh on the earth, and it trembleth."

Our Lord is said by John to have "a name written, which no man knew, but he himself." And yet that name is given, "The Word of God." The "name" of a person, as the term is here used, connotes that person's very being. It is significant that the beloved apostle had Jesus revealed to him in His coming by that name, under which he had introduced and fully comprehended Him in that profound biographical description in his Gospel, 1: 1-14. Yet, while John saw Jesus Christ in both preincarnate and incarnate form as "the express image of the Father,"—the perfect utterance in personal, living expression of all the thought, will, feeling and being of the Father—yet John knew that he, or any other man, did not know that name as Christ Himself knew it. No human being can ever know what His name, "the Word," means to Jesus Christ Himself. But we may see and comprehend enough to read this name in Him and intelligently to call Him by it. Never before probably has the distinction between His own and those not His own been more decisively drawn than now under this same apostle's call for our unequivocal "Amen" to his fervent testimony: "We know that the *Son of God* is come, and hath given us an *understanding,* that we *may know* him that is true, and *we are in* Him that is true, even in *his Son Jesus Christ.* This is the *true God,* and *eternal life*" (John 5: 20).

There are still further features of the military character of our Lord's descent from above. The angelic hosts, which the Bible repeatedly asserts attend Him in action and powerful service, are here (v. 14) represented in military formations and activities, splendid with white uniform, and on white mounts. This is the appearance of the angels always given them in the Bible when representing them as opposing earthly military forces.

Again, verse 15, the metaphor of the "sharp sword"

issuing from the Lord's mouth carries out the military aspect of His descent; for He will have the destruction of literal military forces on earth to accomplish, albeit He will accomplish this with no material sword, but with the word from His mouth, "sharper than any two-edged sword."

We need to pause here a little to weigh the facts represented in verse 15 as to the relation of Christ's second coming to the nations of the earth.

"The nations" are the Gentile nations, exclusive of Israel. This phraseology is according to all Biblical usage. We see, therefore, that at our Lord's coming the Gentile nations will not be found in peace with heaven, with Jesus Christ, however much the international propaganda of "perpetual peace" or the ecclesiastical propaganda of "Christianizing" the nations of the earth may be advocated and pressed. Not that one iota of possible effort for peace and righteousness among nations should be neglected; but prophecy, rather than human sentiment or prognostication, is the "light in a dark place," by which we are to save ourselves from chasing after any "will o' the wisp." Such effort is a faithful witness, it is of real temporary and partial value, and it will no doubt in instances secure from our returning Lord less severity of judgment than would otherwise be the case. But the tenure of these premillennial compacts, leagues, and contrivances of this age, while Satan will still be deceiving the nations, is too weak and brittle to hold effectually.

The expression in verse 15, "that with it he should smite the nations," carries in it the sense of continuance. It seems to imply that our Lord will throughout His millennial administration be having rigorously to smite the nations with His sword of authority and corresponding penalties. And the translation of the C. V. still more clearly indicates the same, reading, "in order that with it he should be smiting the nations." The next sentence confirms the conception that these particulars not only characterize the manner of seizing the world-empire, but also of our Lord's rule of the same during the next ages, —"and he shall rule them with a rod of iron." "And he will be shepherding them with an iron club" (C. V.). Even in the coming age, under our Lord's visible em-perorship, the Gentile nations will continue to be unre-generate and rebelliously inclined, so that He, while a divine shepherd to them, will be obliged to treat them as obstinate goats, butting rams and fractious wethers. The glowing prophecies of such a thing as a nation "all righteous" applies only to regenerate and sanctified Israel. Finally, that this part of the context is portray-ing the character of the earthly rule of the Gentile world by Jesus Christ, is confirmed conclusively by the name seen to be written "on his vesture and on his thigh," "King of kings, and Lord of lords"; i. e., the universal earthly Emperor. This passage is having nothing to do with our coming King in relation to the Church or to Israel, but only to the Gentile nations.

It is of interest, and no doubt intended to be of im-portance, that this title of universal Emperor over the extra-Israelitish world should be seen written upon the vesture and upon the thigh of the descending Christ. The word "vesture" (A. V.) or "garment" (R. V.) needs to be more correctly and distinctly rendered "cloak" (C. V.). It designates the outer garment, loose but for the girdle, which served the purpose, on the one hand, of completing and dignifying the attire of the man while not engaged in labor, and, on the other hand, of furnishing a "slumber robe" by night. Of course, here the magnificent cloak of the military Com-mander-in-Chief,—in fact, in this case, of "the only Potentate"—is before us. The same is to be considered as gathered about the person with an appropriate girdle, with sword suspended down the thigh. Upon these two most prominent articles of His uniform Christ's imperial designation is seen written, the two articles of His attire which represent dignity and strength. Compare with this the equivocal title attached to the cross of the crucified dying One, "Jesus of Nazareth, the King of the Jews." This title was one both of shame and of verity. Of the Jews His coming means as direct King: of the Gentile nations His coming means as super-King, Emperor.

(2). *The Supper of the Great God, 19:17-21.*

"17 And I saw an angel standing in the sun; and he cried with a loud voice, saying to all the fowls that fly in the midst of heaven, Come and gather yourselves together unto the supper of the great God: 18 That ye may eat the flesh of kings, and the flesh of captains, and the flesh of mighty men, and the flesh of horses, and of them that sit on them, and the flesh of all men, both free and bond, both small and great. 19 And I saw the beast and the kings of the earth, and their armies, gathered together to make war against him that sat on the horse, and against his army. 20 And the beast was taken, and with him the false prophet that wrought miracles before him, with which he deceived them that had received the mark of the beast, and them that worshipped his image. These both were cast alive into a lake of fire burning with brimstone. 21 And the remnant were slain with the sword of him that sat upon the horse, which sword proceeded out of his mouth: and all the fowls were filled with their flesh."

This event unparalleled—of its kind—has been pointed to, as has been seen in pursuing our course of study through the Bible, many times, and as the great objective of Biblical prophecy on the line of divine judgment upon incorrigible mankind, preparing the way for the undisputed millennial reign of Jesus Christ; but it is also the accomplishment of that climax of the outpouring of the seven last vials of God's wrath, which was anticipated in the preparations described under the sixth vial (16:12-16) for what is there called "the battle of that great day of God Almighty" (v. 14). It is mistakenly quite commonly called today the "Battle of Armageddon.'' Armageddon is to be the mustering place in Palestine of the doomed hosts; their Waterloo is to be, like Sennacherib's, before the gates of Jerusalem.

Guests of the Banquet.

(1). *The Invited Guests, vs. 17, 18.*

"17 And I saw an angel standing in the sun; and he cried with a loud voice, saying to all the fowls that fly in the midst of heaven, Come and gather yourselves together unto the supper of the great God; 18 That ye may eat the flesh of kings, and the flesh of captains, and the flesh of mighty men, and the flesh of horses, and of them that sit on them, and the flesh of all *men, both* free and bond, both small and great.''

This coming holocaust of divine destruction is likened here to a great banquet spread by God as host. This manner of description is not new at this place. The passage seems almost like a quotation from Ezek. 39: 17-20 referring to the same event. Taking the two together it becomes unquestionable that the following description is to be taken literally, and also that we are to understand with certainty that the same manner of consuming the carcasses of the vast body of the troops of Anti-Christ is to be found in the literal interpretation of Matt. 24: 28: ''For wheresoever the carcass is, there will the eagles [vultures, scavenger birds] be gathered [preternaturally] together.'' If Jehovah could cause all kinds of dumb creation to assemble in pairs or in sevens to enter the ark with Noah, could command a raven to bring Elijah food and drink daily, could prepare ''a great fish to swallow up Jonah,'' and if Jesus could cause a fish to bring to Peter's hand a piece of silver for a tax payment, and if He could on two occasions cause schools of fishes to deliver themselves up to the nets of His disciples, He can preternaturally assemble these multitudes of fowls of the air—and also carnivorous animals—to devour the carcasses of Anti-Christ's hosts before their decomposition should cause a pestilence.

(2). *The Banquet Spread, vs. 19-21.*

"19 And I saw the beast, and the kings of the earth, and their armies, gathered together to make war against him that sat on the horse, and against his army. 20 And the beast was taken, and with him the false prophet that wrought miracles before him, with which he deceived them that had received the mark of the beast, and them that worshipped his image. These both were cast alive into a lake of fire burning with brimstone. 21 And the remnant were slain with the sword of him that sat upon the horse, which *sword* proceeded out of his mouth: and all the fowls were filled with their flesh."

This picture is for the most part readily intelligible to us from our foregoing study. It will at once be recognized as but a fresh and thrilling setting of the kaleidoscopic views of one and the same event—the overthrow of the Anti-Christ—so often reappearing through the Scriptural prophecies.

The vast international organization outlined in v. 19 was fully explained to us in chapter 17, especially vs. 11-13, and 17:14 states the object of this military combination—"and these shall make war with the Lamb"—in perfect accord with that objective as here stated in the words, "to make war against him that sat on the horse, and against his army." But to what a pitch of audacity this shows that the Anti-Christ will lead his followers, and to what a certain and awful catastrophe!

The beast and his false prophet—herald and advance agent—are to be first disposed of, being both arrested by angelic sheriffs and, without bodily punishment, being cast alive into "a lake of fire burning with brimstone," or "sulphur" (C. V.). This fate was partly implied in 14:9-11. The further explanation of this lake is reserved till we reach a more fitting place later in the book. Probably the fate of the beast here and thus described is to be taken as explaining what is stated in

17:8, 11, "shall—*go into perdition*" (8), "goeth into perdition," v. 11. It is to be remembered that the Anti-Christ will already before have died and been in the underworld, from which he will be resurrected. And most likely the expression in 13:11, concerning the false prophet as "another beast," "coming *up out* of the earth," signifies that the false prophet also is to be a resurrected person. These two, then, unlawfully resurrected, shall be sent back alive into the underworld, only this time it is to the place of final "perdition," for the Anti-Christ is "the son of perdition" (2 Thess. 2:3). It is an impressive and suggestive fact that Jesus called Judas "the son of perdition" (John 17:12), and that in Acts 1:25, it says of Judas, "Judas by transgression fell, that he might *go to his own place.*" Is there more than one "son of perdition"? Is Judas, forsooth, that coming Anti-Christ of whom it is written in Rev. 17:8: "The beast that thou sawest *was,* and *is not;* and *shall ascend* out of the *bottomless pit,* and *go into perdition*"? Does not "the son of perdition"—the invariable term,—identify the Anti-Christ with Judas? At this point Daniel 11:37 may be cited very appropriately, as a possible confirmation of the conception that Judas is to be the Anti-Christ, by paraphrasing it thus: "Neither shall he [the wilful king, the Anti-Christ] regard [acknowledge] the God [Almighty] of his [Hebrew] fathers, nor the desire [Messiah] of [Hebrew] women" (that is, the desire all Hebrew women, before Messiah appeared, had of being honored with giving Him birth).

Finally, verse 21 reads also very familiarly and intelligibly to all who are familiar with Biblical prophecy. The antichristian hosts are to experience a debacle altogether supernatural, although perfectly literal. The Lord's weapon of destructive offense is called a "sword," but it is added, "which sword proceedeth out of his mouth." This expression indicates clearly the exercise of the supernatural power of God Almighty through

Jesus Christ. "Speak the word only," said that believing centurion to Jesus. "He spake and it was done; he commanded, and it stood fast" (Psa. 33:9), is the explanation of all created existence. In 2 Thess. 2:8 the supernatural and divine nature of the Lord's sword, with which He will destroy His enemies, is attested, when it is asserted of "that Wicked" (Anti-Christ), "whom the Lord shall consume with *the spirit of his mouth.*" The "sword of the Lord" is the "sword of the Spirit."

It is true, nevertheless, that, as in the Lord's miracles usually, there is the material and "natural" side. In Ezekiel the Lord describes this same execution of His judgment upon the international hosts of the Anti-Christ:

"My fury shall come up in my face, 19 For in my jealousy and in the fire of my wrath have I spoken, Surely in that day there shall be a great shaking in the land of Israel; 20 So that the fishes of the sea, and the fowls of the heaven, and the beasts of the field, and all creeping things that creep upon the earth, and all the men that are upon the face of the earth, shall shake at my presence, and the mountains shall be thrown down, and the steep places shall fall, and every wall shall fall to the ground. 21 And I will call for a sword against him throughout all my mountains, saith the Lord God: every man's sword shall be against his brother. 22 And I will plead against him with pestilence and with blood; and I will rain upon him, and upon his bands, and upon the many people that are with him, an overflowing rain, and great hailstones, fire and brimstone. 23 Thus will I magnify myself, and sanctify myself; and I will be known in the eyes of many nations, and they shall know that I am the Lord" (Ezek. 38: 18-23).

Zechariah describes the same appalling event, partly in similar features, largely in different features:

"12 And this shall be the plague wherewith the Lord shall smite all the people that have fought against Jerusalem; Their flesh shall consume away while they stand upon their feet, and their eyes shall consume away in their holes, and their tongue shall consume away in their mouth. 13 And it shall come to pass in that day, that a great tumult from the Lord shall be among them; and they shall lay hold every one on the hand of his neighbor, and his hand shall rise up against the hand of his neighbor. 14 And Judah also shall fight at Jerusalem; and the wealth of all the heathen round about shall be gathered together, gold, and silver, and apparel, in great abundance. 15 And so shall be the plague of the horse, of the mule, of the camel, and of the ass, and of all the beasts that shall be in these tents, as this plague'' (14: 12-15).

Reference has already been made to the extended description given us in Ezek. 38: 1-22 of this destructive judgment of Jesus Christ upon His military enemies. It is there shown that he purposely entices this host into Palestine, there to entrap them and destroy them—all but one-sixth—and there to give their dead bodies ''unto the ravenous birds of every sort, and to the beasts of the field to be devoured''! The weapons of war are to supply firewood to Israel for seven years while the forests, orchards and vineyards will be recovering and flourishing again after the devastation wrought by the invaders. The skeletons left by the scavenger birds and animals, bestrewing the fields of destruction, will keep all the people of God employed exclusively for seven months in burying them, while thereafter especially appointed buriers are to continue in the work of cleaning up the land to the last offensive bone.

But through all this a higher end is to be reached than that merely of the destruction of Anti-Christ and his armies, or that of the rescue of the remnant of Israel from his intention to annihilate them as Christ's chosen people, so that He may not have a people to come to and take as His earthly kingdom. That purpose is expressed thus:

''21 And I will set my glory among the heathen, and all the heathen shall see my judgment that I have executed, and my hand that I have laid upon them. 22 So the house of Israel shall know that I am the Lord their God from that day and forward. 23 And the heathen shall know that the house of Israel went into captivity for their iniquity: because they trespassed against me, therefore hid I my face from them, and gave them into the hand of their enemies; so fell they all by the sword. 24 According to their uncleanness and according to their transgressions have I done unto them, and hid my face from them. 25 Therefore thus saith the Lord God; Now will I bring again the captivity of Jacob, and have mercy upon the whole house of Israel, and will be jealous for my holy name; 26 After that they have borne their shame, and all their trespasses whereby they have trespassed against me, when they dwelt safely in their land, and none made them afraid. 27 When I have brought them again from the people, and gathered them out of their enemies' lands, and am sanctified in them in the sight of many nations; 28 Then shall they know that I am the Lord their God, which caused them to be led into captivity among the heathen: but I have gathered them unto their own land, and have left none of them any more there. 29 Neither will I hide my face any more from them: for I have poured out my spirit upon the house of Israel, saith the Lord God'' (Ezek. 39: 21-29).

(3) *The Millennial Expulsion of Satan from Earth, 20: 1-3.*

''1 And I saw an angel come down from heaven, having the key of the bottomless pit and a great chain in his hand. 2 And he laid hold on the dragon, that old serpent, which is the Devil, and Satan, and bound him a thousand years. 3 And cast him into the bottomless pit, and shut him up, and set a seal upon him, that he should deceive the nations no more, till the thousand years should be fulfilled: and after that he must be loosed a little season.''

This passage is literal, while yet dressed in figures. The writer had a little girl friend of six, who had the Spirit of God upon her to take things Scriptural in reality and truth. She had a very vivid conception of the Devil. Before she could read herself, she heard this passage read one day. Forthwith she asked her ''Auntie'' (an earnest Christian woman to whom this motherless child had been committed) to turn the page down at this place. Many a time the child would be seen in her little rocking chair, with the Bible open in her lap at this place, rocking to and fro with delight depicted on her face, as she contemplated the time when Satan should be locked up in the bottomless pit and no one on earth should be troubled by him any more for a whole thousand years. Yes,—as a simple, real, impressive, happy prospect,—"O Father, Lord of heaven and earth," "I thank thee," said Jesus, "because thou hast hid these things from the wise and prudent, and hast revealed them unto babes."

It will be remembered, that in chapter 12 the vision is given (v. 9) of the expulsion of Satan from the skies into the earth, where he will operate in great rage because of knowing that even there but a short time will be allowed him to remain (v. 12). Our present paragraph reveals how he will be taken away in chains by an angelic sheriff, cast out into the bottomless pit and shut up there under seal for the millennial age. The reason for this exclusion from earthly relationship is given in most significant language "that he should *deceive the nations* no more."

It is the political and governmental question relative to the millennial age that stands at the front from 19:11 on. First, it is revealed that a great work of crushing general earthly revolt against the rule of righteousness and peace under the scepter of Jesus Christ will confront Him on His second coming from on high. This most formidable uprising against God and His Christ will betray the persistent rebelliousness of mankind toward God, which all measures ever before hopefully tried will have failed to conquer or to tame; and it will prove the necessity for just such an overwhelming, distinctive judgment as the returning Almighty and sovereign Word of God will inflict.

But it would be futile for Him to go no farther than to deal thus with the visible organized international antichristian forces, while failing to put out of the way effectually the all-commanding instigator of this human, world-wide animosity and rebelliousness toward God's Son as practical ruler of mankind. This original, implacable, super-human instigator and director of the

warfare of darkness against light, which has been on
since time immemorial, is Satan. And his efficient implement of success has been that of deception. He was
the deceiver of the first human pair; he has pursued
every human soul since, aiming to blind his eyes and to
keep him forever lost to God; he has successfully assayed
to deceive all nations and rulers of mankind. And
never will cease Satan's successes in deceiving individuals, collective bodies—social, commercial and ecclesiastical—and nations, small and great, whether petty
dynasties or the mightiest world-empires, until he himself is disposed of in the way described in our present
passage of study. The time for this is not yet; and no
program towards its accomplishment has yet been made
or can be made; it must be done by a sufficient intervention of power, super-human, and super-satanic;
namely, by archangelic power to be authorized and directed by Christ Jesus when He comes to earth again.

Perhaps no more subtle and fatal deception has been
devised by Satan than that reflected by the present-day
effort to create a secure and lasting peace on earth
through political conventions and ecclesiastical leadership. In none of these councils is Satan himself taken
into correct consideration—if consideration at all—and
in none of these measures and hopes is mention made of
our Lord's literal return as King of the Jews and world-
wide ruler. Praiseworthy as these combined, labored,
costly efforts may be, they are deluded and delusive pro-
grams, doomed to tragic disappointment and simply to
play the more aptly into the hands of the great deceiver.
He is snickering in his sleeve and chuckling in high
confidence. Yet the well-versed student of Scripture
sees in it all a striking sign of the nearing catastrophe
of this age. "For when *they* shall say, Peace and safety
[*a la* Locarno treaties] ; then sudden destruction cometh
upon them, as travail upon a woman with child; and
they shall not escape" (2 Thess. 5:3).

We are not meaning to imply that due measures should be neglected to expose, to hinder, to confound Satan, and to promote the peace, safety and true prosperity of all nations. But by what measures does Scripture show this can most effectively be done?

a. By the word of truth. Not by the spiritualizing interpretation of the plain and literal language of God's Word is the present to be guided and the future anticipated. As has been already expressed, this is where present-day propaganda of enduring peace is sinking in the quicksand. Daniel "understood by books." He took the Book of Jeremiah so literally as to understand that the Lord would "accomplish seventy years in the desolations of Jerusalem." He, therefore, knew that the existing desolations of Jerusalem were on the very eve of being finished, although there was no outward sign at all. So Peter says that "we have also a more sure word of prophecy; whereunto ye do well that ye take heed, as unto a *light that shineth in a dark place,* until the day dawn." And Paul says, "But ye, brethren, are not in darkness, that that day should overtake you as a thief."

b. By intercessory prayer. Because Daniel "understood by books," he betook himself to priestly travail in self-humiliation, in confession for himself personally and representatively, in an agony of supplications and intercessions, in powerful heart-appeal to the God of Israel. What for? For the accomplishment of God's *revealed plan and purpose,* as he, Daniel, learned it from the "books," the holy prophecies.

And the Jewish exiles in Babylon, so far from being bitter, hostile, disloyal, to the wicked power that held them in foreign bondage, were bidden by Christ through Jeremiah: "Seek the peace of the city whither I have caused you to be carried away captives, and pray unto the Lord for it: for in the peace thereof shall ye have peace" (Jer. 29:7). Paul enjoins upon all believers, "that—supplications, prayers, intercessions, and giving of thanks, be made—for kings, and for all that are in authority; that we may lead a quiet and peaceable life in all godliness and honesty" (1 Tim. 2: 1, 2). The Bible abounds with the teaching of the mighty power over earthly spheres and affairs which is lodged in the hands of God's children and ambassadors through the light of the truth and the coöperation with Jesus Christ above by prayer. This teaching is richly illustrated also in Biblical narrative. It is sadly true, however, that the Church of today thinks of such power only as belonging to distant times of the past; yet modern and present days furnish striking illustrations of the availability of this power.

It is most interesting and encouraging to the American Christian patriot, to know that the Constitution of the United States was given from heaven through the Continental Convention. After critically examining the constitutions of all ancient republics and of contemporaneous European States, and finding among them nothing suitable for the case in hand, the Assembly found itself "groping, as it were, in the dark to find political truth, and scarce able to distinguish it when presented." In this helpless, hopeless situation Benjamin Franklin questioned, "How has it happened, sir, that we have not hitherto once thought of humbly applying to the Father of Light to illuminate our understandings?

"I have lived, sir, a long time, and the longer I live the more convincing proofs I see of this truth, that God governs in the affairs of men. And if a sparrow cannot fall to the ground without His notice, is it probable that an empire can rise without His aid? We have been assured, sir, in the Sacred Writings that 'except the Lord build the house, they labor in vain that build it.' I firmly believe this, and I also believe that without His concurring aid we shall succeed in this political building no better than the builders of Babel; we shall be divided by our little, partial, local interests, our project will be confounded and we ourselves shall become a reproach and a byword down to future ages. And, what is worse, mankind may hereafter, from this unfortunate instance, despair of establishing government by human wisdom and leave it to chance, war, conquest.

"I therefore beg leave to move:

"That hereafter prayers, imploring the assistance of Heaven and its blessings on our deliberations, be held in this Assembly every morning before we proceed to business."

From the moment this resolution was passed, the Constitutional Convention began to make progress.

Again, a compelling and rapidly growing concern is gripping all classes of public-spirited men and women throughout the civilized world, over the menace to the foundations of moral, social, political, commercial and religious order which lawless, criminal, conscienceless, destructive and atheistical classes and organizations are secretly and openly propagating throughout all continents. This social upheaval is calling forth from statesmen, jurists, churchmen, and other keen-sighted watchmen, arousing notes of warning and dismal prognostications. Great political, social, legislative and ecclesiastical machinery is being invented and put into operation to cope with this diabolic octopus, but with little signs of success; and, to tell the candid truth, with less probability of success. The reason for this lies in the fact that human machinery is being pitted against moral, yea, devilish engines, and the odds are radically unequal. And it is not reprehensible, disheartening pessimism to declare this fact. Still, the effect of truthful warning would tend to fatal paralysis of human effort, if it be unaccompanied by the arousing, emboldening preachment that the belief of the word of truth and of the super-satanic power of prayer makes available ample victorious resources. This, too, is plainly taught by the

Holy Writings and exemplified by their historic records. Priests, kings, prophets of olden times—the times of Moses, Joshua, the Judges, the Kings and prophets of Israel—were ever and anon driven to the written oracles, to prayer and fasting, to secure omnipotent intervention under otherwise hopeless prospects. And such a course never proved insufficient.

When, in Samuel's days, "all the house of Israel lamented after the Lord," Samuel said, "If ye do return unto the Lord with all your hearts......prepare your hearts unto the Lord, and serve him only: and he will deliver you out of the hand of the Philistines." This Israel did, "and Samuel said, Gather all Israel to Mizpeh, and I will pray for you unto the Lord." The people gathered together, poured water out before the Lord, "fasted on that day, and said there, We have sinned against the Lord." This angered Satan's invisible hosts and brought his visible hosts, the Philistines, up against Israel to their great terror. They besought Samuel, "Cease not to cry unto the Lord our God for us, that he will save us out of the hand of the Philistines. And Samuel took a sucking lamb [Ah, the blood of God's Lambkin is the power of internal restoration and of external deliverance], and offered it for a burnt offering wholly unto the Lord: and Samuel cried unto the Lord for Israel; and the Lord heard him. And......the Lord thundered with a great thunder on that day upon the Philistines, and discomfited them; and they were smitten before Israel, and the men of Israel went out of Mizpeh, and pursued the Philistines, and smote them." Samuel then reared a memorial stone, calling it Eben-ezer, saying, "Hitherto hath the Lord helped us. So the Philistines were subdued, and they *came no more* into the coast of Israel: and the hand of the Lord was against the Philistines all the days of Samuel.......And there was peace between Israel and the Amorites." That is, other menacing neighbors became friendly.

c. By true, old-time Gospel revival work. When shameless degradation and red-handed lawlessness have taken the social reins out of the hands of the courts of justice, and when society is put to its wits' end for rescue by self-constituted or extreme emergency measures, the children of God are left in this world, neither to combine with society's self-efforts nor to stand by with folded hands. Through the word of truth and the power of prayer already mentioned, Christ's followers may march forth in the midst with the old-time Gospel of the supernatural conviction of and remedy for sin. Nothing else can cope successfully with the unseen, superhuman forces creating the emergency. Were it the province of civil government to employ Gospel agencies, it were better far to erect tents everywhere needed, and man them with real revivalists, than to declare martial law and seek to terrorize defiant culprits into submission.

For instance, a very recent object lesson was given to all the American nation, if not the world. At a certain mining center there occurred in 1922 a crime which shocked the world—"the brutal massacre of nineteen non-union and three union miners. Forty-four persons were indicted for murder, fifty-eight for rioting, and fifty-four for assault to murder; and yet at the close of two trials that followed, verdicts of 'not guilty' were brought in, and the special Assistant Attorney-General declared that 'intimidation, prejudice, or downright dishonesty actuated both juries, and that conviction was impossible.' From that time forward H......became the nation's outstanding example of lawlessness 'and barbarity. No power of man seemed able to cope successfully against the brutal instincts of the criminally inclined. Four times in two years the State Militia was called in to quell disturbances. Bloodshed had apparently become H......'s 'normal order.'........ 'Every human remedy had failed, but the divine remedy had not even been tried.' But God had a man ready to tell

H...... that 'there is no remedy for sin but from
above.' For seven weeks a young lay evangelist
'pounded the doctrine of the love of Christ into the
savage breasts of a people that apparently had stricken
love out of their vocabulary and utterly out of their
practice.' Night after night the people were asked to
read 'the great love chapter of the Bible, the thirteenth
of First Corinthians.' They did, and it worked. But the
evangelist at the same time, while thrumming the love
notes all the way through, 'was careful to condemn sin
without fear or favor.' Four hundred persons were converted, thousands of people came under the influence of
the meetings, a new era of brotherhood was developed,
'effacing very largely the cruel factions' which gave
H...... its notoriety. The well-known notorious
character of the community and the reported notable
character of the campaign so arrested public attention,
that a *committee from the State Legislature* was sent to
investigate whether the reported transformation had
really taken place; and among other things 'the legislature found men who could pray only in a foreign tongue,
standing shoulder to shoulder with the townsfolk who
once were armed against them.' 'They are convinced
that the city has returned to the ways of peace.' ''

And yet Satan, the tempter, left even Jesus but "for
a little." Mighty as is the subduing and transforming
agency of the Gospel preached with the power of the
Holy Ghost sent down from heaven, marvellous as has
been the Gospel's regenerative and transforming work
in lands of heathen degeneration and savagery, yet
Satan plies his wiles all too successfully in private lives,
social centers and in national organizations. He even
sows tares in the most promising wheat fields, he hides
leaven in the purest meal, he sends his foul birds to lodge
in the mustard trees. Refrain from holy vigilance and
practical diligence, and seven devils in place of one will
return and render the latter end worse than the first.

But our passage foretells the time and way when the deceiver shall, not by gradual advantage over him, but by sudden, superior, angelic intervention, be seized, bound, thrust violently down into the earth's bowels, and there locked up for a thousand years, beyond all further misguiding influence upon national or individual units in the earth. Yet "after that he must be loosed a little season."

2. THE MILLENNIAL REIGN OF THE SAINTS, 20:4-6.

"4 And I saw thrones, and they sat upon them, and judgment was given unto them: and I saw the souls of them that were beheaded for the witness of Jesus, and for the word of God, and which had not worshipped the beast, neither his image, neither had received his mark upon their foreheads, or in their hands; and they lived and reigned with Christ a thousand years. 5 But the rest of the dead lived not again until the thousand years were finished. This is the first resurrection. 6 Blessed and holy is he that hath part in the first resurrection: on such the second death hath no power, but they shall be priests of God and of Christ, and shall reign with him a thousand years."

It has already been explained at the beginning of this main division (19:11—20:6), that the revelation is intended to climax in a disclosure of the millennial exaltation of the Church with Jesus Christ over the earth. Consequently, our present paragraph of the text presupposes, by its opening with the mere pronoun "they," that those thereby referred to are well known and already uppermost in the mind. They are the Church of Christ, whom the whole Book of Revelation predominantly concerns, especially that United Church of all believers of all the ages now glorified in body, which stands before our view from 19:7 on. It has also been explained, that the lately beheaded witnesses specially described in 20:4 are not to be taken as exclusive, but only as inclusive; i. e., as included in those referred to by the pronoun "they" preceding.

The reading of the C. V. is discriminating and

luminous, leaving one's mind with a clear impression of this part of the vision: "And I perceived thrones, and they are seated on them, and judgment is granted them. And the souls of those who have been beheaded because of the testimony of Jesus and because of the word of God, and those who do not worship the wild beast or its image, and did not get the symbol on their forehead and on their hand—*they also* live and reign with Christ a thousand years. [The rest of the dead do not live until the thousand years may be finished.] This is the former resurrection."

This passage strongly corroborates the understanding of Scripture to the effect that, on the one hand, the Church of the millennial reign will include those who triumph over the exigencies—the extreme testings and the martyrdoms—of the tribulation era, even to its very end, while on the other hand "they," the more general body of believers, will come into millennial regency without experiencing the trials of the final tribulation.

It is interesting, instructive and thrilling, to note also how honorably believers of the tribulation era are described, especially for being true to the testimony of Jesus and to the word of God. How brilliantly these Christian, Spirit-filled luminaries of faith and valor will shine over against the prevailing darkness and ruthlessness of their brief day! Yes, "they also" are not to be overlooked "when the Lord shall make up his jewels." The passage emphasizes and illustrates the broad and gracious inclusiveness of the Lord's inheritance in His saints and of their co-regency with Him.

"I saw thrones, and they sat upon them, and judgment was given unto them." That which has all through the ages been promised to the children of God is here, in vision, "perceived" as a realization. The theme is worthy of an expanded treatment not possible here, even of a volume by itself. It is the point of convergence of all Biblical prophecy, it is the end unto which those whose "life is hid with Christ in God" were "predestinated according to the purpose of him who worketh all things after the counsel of his own will." The "thrones" imply more than citizenship in the millennial kingdom; they imply sharing in the conducting of the kingdom. The "judgment......given unto them" does not mean judgment—justice—rendered in their favor, but judgment committed into their hands, to be administered over some earthly sphere.

Let us put the matter somewhat into the definite, into the concrete, the practical aspect.

Our Lord is to take the direct kingship over Israel as the occupant of the throne of David. Not that He is to be limited to that throne in a purely earthly sense. A "prince," of human and earthly character, will doubtless be the acting ruler in the ordinary and apparent sense. Our Lord's ultimate supremacy will be exercised from the skies, with freedom of access and manifestation here below. His supreme season of earthly manifestation will be the occasion of the annual millennial Feast of Tabernacles. At this time His relationship to the Gentile nations also will be strikingly illustrated. For at that time all earthly nations will be representatively gathered before Him at Jerusalem to be taught all His will concerning them as nations and to receive judgment for their conduct for the twelve months preceding.

But, just as His rule is to proceed from a supreme seat in the skies, so will He have associated with Him in the skies the angelic hosts and His glorified saints, to administer under His direction a celestial oversight and rule over earthly persons and affairs in detail. While earthly order will be organized much as now, and while the glorified saints will not supplant earthly agencies in running the complex machinery of life on earth in all departments, yet these over-heads will have their spheres and functions of authority and activity touching all earthly administrations, which will bring to the natural human and earthly course of things the direct counsel, direction, check, encouragement and assistance in Jesus' name of these celestial representatives of His. There is not only reasonableness, but good evidence, that, in large degree, the high and effective offices to be filled by saints individually will correspond vitally to the apprentice- ships served by them in their mortal lives. We shall ap- pear at the judgment-seat of Christ (for awards) to re- ceive in (glorified) body the things done (while in the mortal body) whether good or bad. A life, for instance, has been given up in an apparently untimely, over- zealous and fruitless way, under the urge of the Spirit of Christ in behalf of others; but in glorified, deathless, painless, puissant body that soul is given charge to bring to pass, in that very locality and for that very people, what it ineffectually panted out its mortal life to achieve.

The six times that the phrase ''the [or a] thousand years,'' occurs in 20:1-6 constitute the exclusive authority for delimiting the next age to that period of time. The artificial argument that this age should con- stitute the seventh millennium of human history is con- fronted with the fact that, according to the better accredited Septuagint chronology, we are already several centuries on in the eighth millennium since Adam's crea- tion. But it would be very daring presumption even to question the literalness of this time measurement. And we are left well guarded against all delusive claims that the millennium has set in or will do so, before certain clearly revealed events and conditions transpire.

(1). In the first place, the expulsion of Satan and his entire personal entourage from his long-accustomed capitol and domain in our skies, and his confinement ex- clusively to the relatively puny quarters of this earth, must take place (according to Rev. 12:7-12). Also the reign of Anti-Christ—an entirely unique governmental regime, public and spectacular in character—must ensue for an epoch of time including, at the least, a period of seven closing years, years of Jewish political prominence and of unparalleled trouble in the earth. The Book of Revelation dilates upon these pre-millennial developments.

(2). The resurrection of Christ's departed saints must occur before the millennium begins, and they must reappear with the second visible and bodily reappearing here below of our Lord from the skies. This return is also attended by the most awful destruction of armed hosts—the international armies of Anti-Christ assembled in Palestine to annihilate the Jews regathered in their home-land. No such spectacle has yet occurred and such a debacle certainly cannot be hidden in a corner out of general sight.

(3). Further, there can be no millennium without the expulsion and effectual debarring of the devil from millennial relationship with the nations. But earthly government will be brought under the obvious sway of Jesus Christ and His prepared saints of all the ages. The glorified appearing of Moses and Elijah to the three disciples upon the Transfiguration Mount was an advance miniature of the frequent future appearings to earthly eyes in general—in glory aspect of body—of patriarchs, prophets, apostles and martyrs. Prophecy is given us to serve to the believing and watchful as a "light in a dark place," but only "until" the fulfillment thereof shall be dazzlingly realistic, even like the lightning that "lighteneth out of the one part under heaven," and "shineth unto the other part under heaven."

(4). There can be no millennial economy established without the manifest political organization of the Holy Land—from the Euphrates to the Red Sea and from the Mediterranean to the Indian Ocean—under Jesus Christ as King of the Jews and Emperor over all nations and under the associate regency of His glorified saints. The contrast between all previous international political order and that to be then inaugurated will be simply antipodal.

23

Ah, yes, in every conceivable way the new age will announce itself, even as it will be wholly superfluous and absurd when the Lord Himself reappears for any one to say to another, "Lo, here!" or "Lo, there!" "Every eye shall see."

(5). One of the most striking conditions attending the arrival of the millennium will be the new nation of the Jews. "Shall a nation be born at once?" Yes, what never had been seen or heard shall occur—a nation, all righteous and zealous for Jesus Christ their King, even the children after the flesh of those who cursed and crucified Him, shall suddenly "come up from the wilderness leaning upon her beloved." No longer shall a blind, unbelieving, stony-hearted Jew be found on the earth, but Isaiah's word concerning the entire remnant of Israel in the earth shall be fulfilled—"The ransomed of the Lord shall return, and come to Zion with songs and everlasting joy upon their heads: they shall obtain joy and gladness, and sorrow and sighing shall flee away" (35: 10).

"But the rest of the dead lived not again until the thousand years were finished. This is the first resurrection."

From this passage alone we would not know with certainty, whether all deceased saints will be included in the first resurrection. The question is settled, however, very positively by 1 Cor. 15:23, which classifies this resurrection as embracing all "they that are Christ's at his coming." About as conclusively is this fact made sure by 1 Thess. 4:16, where the members of this resurrection are described as "the dead in Christ." Going back to John 5:29 we can see clearly that the distinction between "the resurrection of life" and "the resurrection of damnation" corresponds to the first, or premillennial, resurrection, and the postmillennial resurrection. The same distinction consequently becomes clear in Dan. 12: 2. "Some [these] to everlasting life, and some [those] to shame and everlasting contempt."

"Blessed and holy is he that hath part in the first resurrection." This is not to be strained in an exclusive way beyond the expressions found in the other parallel passages, which clearly teach the inclusion of all "the dead in Christ" in the first resurrection.

"On such the second death hath no power" ("jurisdiction"—C. V.). Verse 14 explains the second death as "the lake of fire," of which comment will be made later.

"But they shall be priests of God and of Christ, and shall reign with him a ["the"—C. V.] thousand years." In harmony with other Scriptures this statement must not be strained to mean a uniformity of co-regency with Christ in the millennium, as though no distinction of awards is to be made among the saints of the first resurrection. It is a description of the glorified Church in solidarity.

This representation of the high offices and occupations of the Millennial Church is most interesting. We have been made very familiar before with the co-regency of Christ's glorified Church with Him, but not with her millennial priestly capacity. It is interesting to note the correspondence between the millennial offices of millennial Israel and the millennial Church. We have already learned from Isa. 61: 6 that millennial Israel shall fulfill her original calling as "a kingdom of priests" (Ex. 19: 6) : "Ye shall be named the Priests of the Lord: men shall call you the Ministers of our God." On the higher, celestial and glorified scale is the millennial Church to function in priesthood and in ruling ministry in behalf of earthly mankind. What an inviting calling, to be had now in view preparatory to the next age, as reward corresponding in measure to present life efficiency in prayer and in service for others!

3. SEQUEL TO THE MILLENNIUM, 20: 7-15.

"7 And when the thousand years are expired, Satan shall be loosed out of his prison, 8 And shall go out to deceive the nations

which are in the four quarters of the earth, Gog and Magog, to
gather them together to battle: the number of whom is as the
sand of the sea. 9 And they went up on the breadth of the
earth, and compassed the camp of the saints about, and the beloved
city: and fire came down from God out of heaven, and devoured
them. 10 And the devil that deceived them was cast into the
lake of fire and brimstone, where the beast and the false prophet
are, and shall be tormented day and night for ever and ever.
11 And I saw a great white throne, and him that sat on it, from
whose face the earth and the heaven fled away; and there was
found no place for them. 12 And I saw the dead, small and
great, stand before God; and the books were opened: and another
book was opened, which is the book of life: and the dead were
judged out of those things which were written in the books, according to their works. 13 And the sea gave up the dead which
were in it; and death and hell delivered up the dead which were
in them: and they were judged every man according to their
works. 14 And death and hell were cast into the lake of fire.
This is the second death. 15 And whosoever was not found written
in the book of life was cast into the lake of fire.''

This passage is clearly a sequel or needful appendix
to the millennial section proper. This is shown both
chronologically and logically. The chronological sequence
centers about the person of Satan, and the logical
sequence is demanded by the probationary nature of the
millennial age.

(1). Satan's Post-millennial Career on Earth, vs. 7-10.

''7 And when the thousand years are expired, Satan shall be
loosed out of his prison, 8 And shall go out to deceive the nations which are in the four quarters of the earth, Gog and Magog,
to gather them together to battle: the number of whom is as
the sand of the sea. 9 And they went up on the breadth of the
earth, and compassed the camp of the saints about, and the beloved city: and fire came down from God out of heaven, and
devoured them. 10 And the devil that deceived them was cast
into the lake of fire and brimstone, where the beast and the false
prophet are, and shall be tormented day and night for ever and
ever.''

In verses 2, 3 a return of Satan to earth for a brief season after the millennial age is anticipated. The millen-

nial story would be left unfinished without this further chapter in Satan's history.

The dethroned and exiled monarch of darkness is set free—it is not a self-procured escape—and he is allowed to return to the earthly sphere of his former realm, there to have liberty to exercise all possible devilish influence and strategy to regain and to retain forever his former control of impenitent mankind. Once again his diplomacy is that of beguiling the nations of earth politically. It is a shock to many superficial Bible readers to learn that the millennium does not begin and run through its ten centuries under world-wide ideal conditions, temporal and spiritual. But Scripture shows that outside the kingdom of Israel it is still an age of general impenitency, and that it, therefore, demands the rule of a "rod of iron." Still more surprising is it to learn that a thousand years of (enforced) peace and unparalleled prosperity will still leave the Gentile heart of humanity accessible and responsive to Satanic deception, and prone to revolt more decisively than ever against the kingdom of God. This exposes most vividly how delusive is the aim or faintest hope of the earth's "remotest nations submitting in this age to Messiah's reign," and how necessary is Messiah's personal coming again, to put under His foot the neck of an incorrigible and unregenerate humanity.

Apparently the most highly-organized and formidable military enterprise ever undertaken in history will result from Satan's post-millennial deceptive propaganda. The names "Gog and Magog"—familiar in connection with the pre-millennial antichristian invasion of the Holy Land, and here delimited as co-extensive with "the four quarters of the earth"—are now again thrust into "bad eminence," as surviving the millennial rule and ready, as of old, to respond to the devil's *jehad*, to his summons to a "Holy War" of extermination of all on earth who name the name of Christ.

The world-wide enlistment evidently will compel time-

ly flight of all believers to the only safe asylum of the
earth—the Holy Land. This territory—then fittingly
called "The Holy Land"—will present the appearance
of a vast camp, "the camp of the saints." Never before
such a "camp meeting"! Hosts of helpless fugitives
gathered like scared sheep "in the shelter of the fold"!
Onward the devil-driven, devil-inspired hosts will sweep
against the Holy Land from all sides, and close in nearer
and nearer to "the beloved city." We think that every
day and every hour Christian faith will be taking firmer
possession of every fugitive and of every Israelite's heart.
We think their earlier seasons of importunate prayer
will have turned to seasons of triumphant songs and
shouts. They will surely call to mind the drowning of
Pharaoh's army in the Red Sea, the destruction of
Sennacherib's host, the triumph of the Jews over their
enemies throughout the Persian Empire in spite of
Haman's decree, yea, the smiting of Anti-Christ and his
host by the sword out of the mouth of Jesus Christ. Yea,
more; after the wonders of Christ's millennial manifestations and demonstrations, Christian faith will be
equal to this final strain. The test will no doubt be
extreme. Perhaps Christ will be no longer visibly present.
Perhaps even that glory-sign of Isa. 4:5, 6 will be with-
drawn. Other speculations regarding both the testings
and the resources of faith at this crisis would not be un-
warranted, but they are unnecessary. Suffice it to say,
that on this the last and supreme occasion forever for the
earthly testing and victory of the people of God, the
stage will be set for the raising of the curtain to disclose
some divine intervention beyond all previous parallel.

And John was given to see in vision and to reveal to
us this timely intervention: "And fire came down from
God out of heaven, and devoured them." For the last
time will incorrigible humanity prove how deceptive is
Satan's promise of success in following his banners in
warfare against the Son of God. Heaven's resources of

judgment and destruction have been many times revealed in varied appropriate degrees, but never exhausted. A breath from the mouth of Christ Jesus, at the psychological moment in this supreme campaign of Satan's leadership on earth, will suffice to incinerate instantly this numberless host of the whole world's military force, just at the moment when all earthly saints seem doomed to fall a helpless prey to their ruthless hands.

But it is not the fate of the human hosts led on by Satan to this conclusive effort to annihilate God's people from the earth, that the revelation of this paragraph centers upon, but the final disposal of Satan himself. "And the devil that deceived them was cast into the lake of fire and brimstone, where the beast and the false prophet are, and shall be tormented by day and night for ever and ever" (v. 10). It is here freshly shown that the entire history of Satan's relation to and his prevailing influence over mankind is one of deception. This was the key to success for him in the garden of Eden; this was his strategy for the forty days of his temptation of Jesus Christ, before which man he first met defeat, and that utter defeat—defeat through which everyone believing in Jesus Christ has the power of victory.

We also learn from this statement of revelation what final disposition our Lord will make of the devil; he will be consigned to the lake of fire and brimstone as his abode, to ceaseless torment as his lot, to both the place and the condition everlastingly. These three points are here made as clear and certain as divinely inspired language could make them. To debate them adversely, or even questioningly, still more to expound the Scriptures contrarily, is a betrayal of simple confiding respect for the Bible as a divine revelation.

The expression, "by day and night," intends to teach us of the never intermitting torment of the devil. The author of all wicked torment shall not draw a breath without torment. Evidently, it is to be torment, not only incessant, but unalleviated.

The expression "for ever and ever" is literally "for the eons of the eons." Human conception and language could not more conclusively express the never-ending duration of this fate of the devil. It is true that an eon is a finite period of time. Hence even an eon of eons, —an organized series of eons—is still finite. And so are "eons of eons"—eons, or time-periods, comprising eons that hold in organization, not only one series of eons, but a series, even many series, of confederated eons—still only finite. But the expression is the utmost effort which the human mind can put forth to express interminable duration. Our mind is incapable of forming the concept of beginningless and endless time— which, in fact, is not "time." And an interminable prolonging of the existence of a creature will never constitute so much as a punctuation mark in what we mean by eternity.

But the expression, "the eons of eons," reveals to us, not only the utmost possible conception of interminable duration, but also that, in the progress of time subsequent to the consignment of the devil to his never changing abode, there will not be a mere flat continuance of time, but a marvellous, orderly, progressive march of history, having epochs, eons, an era of eons, many confederations of eons, and even empires of these confederations. And God's dealing with the devil—with him and his, with his and their "lake of fire and brimstone"— will no doubt constitute a striking and essential feature in the yet unrevealed program under the hands of God's Son for these ages upon ages.

WHERE IS HELL AND WHAT IS IT?

This seems to the writer to be the most suitable time and place in consecutive Bible teaching to discuss the location of hell, here called "the lake of fire and brimstone."

Can we ascertain from Scripture just where this

horrible abode will be? We affirm in reply that the Scriptures enable us definitely to locate hell and in a very realistic sense.

a. There is largely referred to in the Bible a place designated as one of fire, of burning, fuming brimstone, a "furnace of fire," and that "everlasting fire." This place is designated as "prepared for the devil and his angels." Clearly it is some literal and suitable place, definitely localized.

b. In 2 Pet. 2:4 and Jude 6 very important light is thrown upon the original occasion for a hell. The first passage reads: "For if God spared not the angels that sinned, but cast them down to hell, and delivered them into chains of darkness, to be reserved for judgment." The second passage reads: "And the angels which kept not their first estate, but left their own habitation, he hath reserved in everlasting chains under darkness unto the judgment of the great day." The apostate angels here mentioned most likely include the devil himself and "his angels." The passages imply that all the wicked spirits were originally created and appointed to a very different state and sphere from that now obtaining with them—even as different as light from darkness. Peter indicates that the cause of this reversion was their sinning, and Jude indicates that their sin consisted in political disloyalty and sedition, for which the Son of God as their appointed sovereign put them enchained into dungeons of darkness, to appear for final trial and disposal at a future occasion of momentous judgment.

c. As a result of this coming judgment the satanic order of beings is to be forever confined to the locality specified by various terms—Gehenna, Tartarus, Bottomless Pit, Deep, Abyss, Furnace of fire, Lake of fire and brimstone—all coördinating in different aspects with our most common term of "hell."

d. Where are we to find hell located? The satanic kingdom has its local sphere at present—the skies immediately above us—and it is certain that that kingdom must have some local confines somewhere hereafter. We have already found from the twelfth chapter of Revelation that Satan and his hosts will be cast out of that "heaven" into the earth no more thither to return. But their sojourn in the earth is to be only for "a little season," when, before our descending Lord, Satan is to be cast in chains into "the bottomless pit" (Rev. 21:1, 3) and there shut off for the millennial age from active influence on earth. The bottomless pit has already been mentioned in Rev. 9:1-3. There the opening of this pit results in the darkening of the atmosphere and the shrouding of the sun with "smoke out of the pit, as the smoke of a great furnace." Very clearly this pit is a literal subterranean interior,—without bottom because of constituting the interior globe of the earth within the solid encircling crust. It is inconceivable that the "hell prepared for the devil and his angels" should be outside the province of the universe which was wrested by Satan from allegiance to Jesus Christ. After being cast out of "heaven," and soon after taken in chains from the face of the earth, there remains only the regions "under the earth" for his incarceration. This is altogether fitting. Besides, all the descriptive details connected with hell correspond with the literal material facts.

e. The fiery molten bowels of the earth is the place of hell and of its fires which are reserved for the everlasting torment of the devil, his angels and all his human followers. They all will require some literal and suitable place together. Their place is distinctly described as under ground,—a "deep," a "bottomless pit," an "abyss," a place of fire and brimstone, a lake of fire. All this agrees with the material conditions obtaining in the interior of our earth. This is proved by the phenomena attending earthquakes, but more especially volcanic action. We need only to read the stories of

Vesuvius, Mauna Loa, Krakatoa, Pelee, and of almost numberless other volcanoes, to perceive that our earth consists within largely of fiery, molten gaseous and ashen material demanding channels of terrific explosion through the solid crust.

Vesuvius was not suspected of being volcanic in character until, suddenly, on August 24, A. D. 79 an eruption began with the appearance of a huge black cloud, which rose from the mountain. This was accompanied by an explosion that blew off the top and rained a mass of ashes, lapilli, and mud which buried Pompeii twenty feet under ashes and Herculaneum under a torrent of mud. Again, Mount Pelee, on the island of Martinique, was on April 25, 1902, burst open, and from it, on May 5, descended an avalanche of boiling black mud. On May 8 there issued a black cloud of explosive and exploded super-heated steam, charged with incandescent particles, which destroyed the city of St. Pierre with all its population of thirty thousand souls. The annihilating blow came with appalling swiftness, and there is reason to believe that for the great part of the victims death was well-nigh instantaneous, or at least brought about within two or three minutes. Only two of the inhabitants of the city proper appear to have survived their wounds. "The magnetic disturbance was transmitted to the antipodal region of the earth in about two minutes' time, while the noise of the eruption manifested itself forcibly at Maracaibo, Venezuela, and beyond, at a direct distance of eight hundred and fifty miles, or considerably more."

How forcibly the means and the manner of St. Pierre's destruction remind us of the sudden annihilation of Sodom and Gomorrah! At sunrise "the Lord rained upon Sodom and upon Gomorrah brimstone [sulphur] and fire from the Lord out of heaven." That is, an eruption shot the skies full of flaming, sulphurous substance, which descended in overwhelming, incinerating, encrusting torrents upon "those cities, and all the plain, and all the inhabitants of the cities, and that which grew upon the ground" (Gen. 19: 24, 25). The record, although so brief and simple, yet, taken together with many references to the event through the Bible, impresses us that this was one of the most stupendous volcanic eruptions from underground which has occurred in human history. And the most significant feature is the reference of the physical occurrence to God's appointment as executed through angelic agency.

Again, the judgment of God through Moses upon Korah, Dathan and Abiram, has spiritual relation to the underworld as the place in reserve for the wicked dead. "The ground clave asunder that was under them, and the earth opened her mouth, and swallowed them up, ...they, and all that appertained unto them went down alive [quick] into the pit, and the earth closed upon them." Then "there came out [from the fissure likely] a fire from the Lord, and consumed the two hundred and fifty men that offered incense" (Num. 16: 32, 33, 35).

Frequent seismic spasms and volcanic eruptions in our day prove that God's resources of pent-up subterranean combustibles and explosives are not exhausted, but only exhibited in samples, impatiently awaiting the touch of God's match to leap forth unquenchably to serve as His instrument of "the vengeance of eternal fire." "Upon the wicked he shall rain snares [quick burning coals], fire and brimstone, and an horrible [burning] tempest" (Psa. 11: 6).

f. To the Bible the thought of under-ground residence on the part of sentient beings, whether as a phenomenon of the past or a prospect of the future, is nothing novel. The places of intermediate abode, both of the righteous and of the wicked dead, are uniformly represented in Old Testament times as being under-ground, a comparatively inviting place there being assigned for the

former ("Today shalt thou be with me in paradise"),
but a repulsive one for the latter. It evidently means
more than mere bodily burial when Paul testifies that
Jesus "also descended first [before ascension from earth]
into the lower parts of the earth" (Eph. 4:9). There was
an under-world of beings for Jesus to visit, there was a
lower region of creature habitation for Him to penetrate,
that, in His return to glory, He might command the
"keys of hell and of death," that from glory above He
might "fill all things," and that the vision of John
might be rendered possible: "And every creature which
is in heaven [the skies], and on the earth, and *under the
earth,* and such as are in the sea, and all that are in them,
heard I say, Blessing, and honor, and glory, and power,
be unto him that sitteth upon the throne, and unto the
Lamb for ever and ever" (Rev. 5:13).

In view of even this incomplete summary of Scripture
testimony, how realistic and vivid do such statements as
the following become: "to go into hell, into the fire that
nevermore shall be quenched, where their worm dieth
not and their fire is not quenched" (given three times by
Jesus in Mark 9:43-48); "and he [that worships the
beast] shall be tormented with fire and brimstone in the
presence of the holy angels and in the presence of
the Lamb; and the smoke of their torment ascendeth up for
ever and ever" (Rev. 14:10, 11): "these both [the
beast and the false prophet] were cast alive into a lake
of fire burning with brimstone" (Rev. 19:10); "but
the fearful, and unbelieving, and the abominable, and
murderers, and whoremongers, and sorcerers, and
idolaters, and all liars, shall have their part in the lake
which burneth with fire and brimstone; which is the
second death" (Rev. 20:8); "and death and hell
[the grave] shall be cast into the lake of fire. This is the
second death. And whosoever was not found written in
the book of life was cast into the lake of fire" (Rev. 20:
14, 15).

No wonder is it that the devils possessing the two Gergesenes cried out in dire apprehension: "What have we to do with thee, Jesus, thou Son of God? Art thou come hither to *torment us before the time?*" (Mat. 8: 29).

The message of a real and literal hell, definitely localized and materialized, is the Spirit's implement in a fearless, faithful preacher's mouth, for bringing sinners out of carelessness and practical unbelief into a needed terrifying realization of the danger before them.

(2). The Final Judgment, vs. 11-15.

"11 And I saw a great white throne, and him that sat on it, from whose face the earth and the heavens fled away; and there was no place found for them. 12 And I saw the dead, small and great, stand before God; and the books were opened: and another book was opened, which is the book of life: and the dead were judged out of those things which were written in the books, according to their works. 13 And the sea gave up the dead which were in it; and death and hell delivered up the dead which were in them: and they were judged every man according to their works. 14 And death and hell were cast into the lake of fire. This is the second death. 15 And whosoever was not found written in the book of life was cast into the lake of fire."

We should approach this scene with awe. Briefly the essentials are stated of an event the most solemn probably of all human history. Man, in his pride, affects to express judgment upon issues here explained, as though either, without revelation, he may foresee the secret decision of the Almighty Judge, or he may assume to arbitrate his final destiny for himself. To humble faith it is a matter of wholesome impression and of deep satisfaction, that God has lifted the veil of secrecy, and that far in advance He has notified the moral universe of the final settlement of accounts with men and angels which He will carry out.

This passage falls into three parts:

a. The setting of the judgment scene, v. 11.

One is immediately impressed deeply by the simplicity

that makes it so august. Three features sum up the setting of the scene:

First, the majestic "white throne," "high and lifted up," throne of eternal glory, and seat of infinite authority and power.

Then, the person, the eternal, almighty, exclusive occupant of that throne, to whom every mortal creature owes his existence, his allegiance, his endless destiny.

Finally, the "face,"—the medium of self-expression. It is not through appurtenances, it is not through the general form, that one person really sees another,—with insight and acquaintance; it is only "face to face," eye to eye.

It was a fateful hour to Zedekiah, King of Judah, the covenant-breaking vassal of Nebuchadnezzar, when the words Jeremiah had given him were fulfilled, "thine eyes shall behold the eyes of the king of Babylon, and he shall speak with thee mouth to mouth." The result would be, "Thou shalt go to Babylon," sightless, as a captive, spirit and body.

The king of beasts shuns the face, the eye of man. The guilty soul recoils from the frank and innocent eye of a child. Gideon marvelled that he still lived after seeing "an angel of the Lord face to face." Manoah said to his wife, "we shall surely die, because we have seen God," although it was but God's angel. Daniel's "comeliness was turned......into corruption," and he "retained no strength," before the face of the prophetic angel. General Israel could not bear the reflection of divine glory upon Moses' face. And, although "the Lord spake unto Moses face to face, as a man speaketh unto his friend," yet God said to even Moses, "Thou canst not see my face; for there shall no man see me and live."

It remained true for Jesus to say, "No man hath seen God at any time; the only begotten Son which is in the bosom of the Father, he hath declared him." Yet how did guilty men quail before Him when He was here only as "a root out of dry ground." And when He said to the mob in the garden, "I am he, they went backward, and fell to the ground."

But now, in the vision before us, the time is brought forward, when God Almighty as supreme ruler will summon to judgment full and final before His very face. Before that face "the earth and the heaven fled away," says John; "and there was found no place for them." This phenomenon of earth and skies fugitive before the face of their Maker is beyond human conception, and it was probably beyond John's ability literally to describe it. It certainly does not mean annihilation; it certainly does not mean actual disappearance; it was in vision a flight, but a futile one, finding no place of hiding. But it reveals how poor fallen terrestrial creation—earth and skies—shrink in conscious shame and nakedness from that face. It reminds us of Bildad the Shuhite's confession: "How then can man be justified with God? or how can he be clean that is born of a woman? Behold even the moon, and it shineth not; yea, *the stars are not pure in his sight*. How much less man, that is a worm? and the son of man, which is a worm?" (Job 25: 4-6).

b. Subjects of the last judgment, vs. 12-13 a.

There are four weighty judgments associated with the millennium. The first of these judgments is that of the saints, upon their being gathered up before the Lord in the skies on His way back to earth. This judgment is briefly described in Rom. 14: 10 and 2 Cor. 5: 10. Discrimination will then be shown between the valueless and the durable works of believers, that the former may be consigned to ashes, the latter graciously and liberally rewarded. It appears that there will be a logical continuity between the good works contributed by believers while in the mortal body and the assignments of service as rewards, which will be liberally appointed to them in their immortal state. Warning is plainly held out of the danger of having to blush for shame in that day for the lack of any substantial contribution being found to one's credit.

The second judgment is that described especially in Mat. 25: 14-46. This is a twofold judgment, the one individual (vs. 14-30), the other collective (vs. 31-46), and both upon those living upon the earth at our Lord's arrival to assume earthly charge. Here again the Judge will pass judgment upon the merits of the earthly trustees of His interests while absent Himself on high. These trustees, taken individually, are likely more especially the Jewish custodians of Christ's cause in the last days. Such as shall be found faithful and profitable will be given high promotion under the millennial order of Christ's kingdom, especially that over Israel, while those found false to their trust will be deprived of any share in the kingdom.

The collective phase of our Lord's judgment upon arriving in the earth pertains to the Gentile nations and to their treatment of His ''brethren''—the Jews—in the last days, the days and conditions of their last great tribulation. The ''sheep''—the righteous nations, viewed from the standpoint of their dealings with needy and distressed Jewish believers—will be commended and rewarded with great honor under the millennial order, while the ''goats''—the contrary nations in relation to the Lord's brethren—will be consigned to the curse upon the devil and his angels.

The third great judgment of this series is that to be visited upon the world-wide post-millennial revolt which Satan will raise up and which has just been sufficiently treated of under vs. 7-10.

The fourth and last great judgment will be post-millennial, subsequent to the general resurrection, the one presented before us in vs. 11-15. It appears to be related especially to the final disposition of the wicked

24

dead. This seems to be the case, notwithstanding "the book of life" is in evidence in vs. 12 and 15. For in marked contrast to this book appear "the books," evidently the books containing the names and acts of the wicked, out of which judgment is drawn, while the book of life appears to be used for cross-reference, confirming judgment against the wicked because of the absence of their names from this book.

An awful picture is unfolded before our imagination. It is the arraignment of the unregenerate dead of all the race for their final judgment. In view of the "setting of the judgment-scene" (v. 11) the situation of the impenitent of all ages is unspeakably terrifying.

We know how bravery flees from a sinner's breast here and now when the sense of the divine presence in authority and power is for a little manifested. To face God in death is more fearful to the unforgiven, while the conditions and prospects of the intermediate state must be oppressively ominous.

But what will it be for him to meet the flaming eye of holy omniscience! The "books" of God's perfect remembrance will unfold the sinner's entire biography of impenitence, resistance and unbelief toward God his Maker and Jesus Christ his Redeemer. If the living impenitents will quail before the wrathful Lamb at His reappearing on earth and call upon the mountains and rocks, "Fall on us, and hide us from the face of him that sitteth upon the throne, and from the wrath of the Lamb: for the great day of his wrath is come; and who shall be able to stand?" "Thinkest thou this, O man......that thou shalt escape the judgment of God," thou who "after thy hardness and impenitent heart *treasurest up* unto thyself wrath against the day of wrath and revelation of the righteous judgment of God; who will render to every man according to his deeds: ......unto those that......do not obey the truth, but obey unrighteousness, indignation, and wrath, tribula-

tion and anguish, upon every soul that doeth evil?"
(Rom. 2:3, 5, 6, 8).

c. The Sentence of the great white Throne, vs. 13b-15.

The C. V. makes an important correction of the translation in v. 13. Instead of reading merely, "and they were judged every man according to their works," which would be but a repetition from v. 12, the correct translation should be, "and they were *condemned*, each in accord with his acts."

The great white throne judgment, then, is unto condemnation, convicting and sentencing the guilty. While it is implied that condemnation will differ in degree according to acts, yet all that fall short of the glory of God will be condemned and sentenced. The reference to the "book of life" implies the probability that the regenerate dead of the second resurrection—the believers dying during the millennium, or yet in the body at its close—will stand before the great white throne; yet the absence of any mention of a sentence upon them proves that they will not be there to come under trial, but to be demonstrably approved as being such as Jesus promised "shall never come into condemnation," or such as stand before the throne of the Almighty with the great Daysman to acknowledge them and present them perfect in Himself.

But, alas, for those who obtain no recognition from the Daysman on that fateful occasion! The day of mercy is past: no longer does that tender voice plead, "Come unto me!" But, as the Almighty God refers the verdict to His Son, the sentence goes forth, "I never knew you; depart from me, ye that work iniquity." And this sentence will be without partiality. Jesus says that many will try to justify themselves with the plea, "Lord, Lord, have we not prophesied in thy name? and in thy name have cast out devils? and in thy name done many wonderful works?" (Matt. 7:22). Yet all in vain, if their names are not found written in "the book of life." Jesus alone is the life, those who have not His Spirit are none of His, their names are not found recorded by the finger of the Spirit in Him. Unspeakably awful will be that hour for all there, high or low, religious or confessedly reprobate, who "shall be punished with everlasting destruction from the presence of the Lord, and from the glory of His power" (2 Thess. 1:9). Language cannot make more certain the punishment of never-ending conscious, hopeless banishment from all happy relationship to or favor from the only Mediator between God and man. Into hell—the lake of fire and brimstone within this earth's renewed crust—all that belongs to death, grave, shades of darkness and of woe, will be cast with its convicts of devils and unregenerate souls. These facts need to be plainly, faithfully and convincingly promulgated the world around, to every human being, that all may know their need of fleeing to the cross of Jesus and to the shelter of His fold.

The Church Glorified
Chapters 21:1—22:7

CHAPTER I.

THE DISRUPTION OF THE WORLD.

W HILE the Book of Revelation consists, in main bulk, of the disclosure of things coming to pass swiftly in their time—the things unfolded in 4: 1 —19: 10 and focussing on the avenging of the Church— yet, as we met with brief treatment of two prior aspects of the Church—the first in 1: 10-20, "The Church Mystical," the second in Chapters 2 and 3, The Church Militant—so we find two subsequent aspects of the Church briefly treated—the first, which we have just studied in 19: 11—20: 15, "The Church Millennial," and now the second, in 21: 1—22: 5, "The Church Glorified."

We should first note the temporal standpoint of this stage of the revelation. It is post-millennial, and subsequent to the completed history of the redemption of original terrestrial creation from its fall. The fall involved the human race and the entire creation directly related to mankind. The vision now set before us reveals the perfect restoration of believing mankind and its creature sphere. While ages upon ages will follow on, yet, so far as restitution is concerned, the drama of the Bible is finished, and the endless golden age, anticipated in original creation, but thrown into apparently hopeless chaos and perdition, is established.

Here may perhaps be most suitably introduced a word-study of great importance.

In the English versions of the New Testament the phrase, "from the foundation of the world," quite often occurs. Discrimination in translation should be made between two words in the Greek, which are commonly translated alike in the New Testament by the word "foundation." One of these words stands regularly for the idea of placing something as a substructure, the laying of a foundation, as of a building. The other word, however, and quite to the contrary, carries the idea of casting down, demolishing, disrupting the very foundations. The former word is *Themelios,* the latter *Katabole.*

We can see readily that the latter word expresses demolition, disruption, from its use in our science of physiology. The word is a compound, the second member of which—*bole*—forms our terminal "bolism." In physiology we use three words with this terminal in common. These three words are *"Ana*bolism," *"K(C)ata*bolism" and *"Meta*bolism," (We at once recognize the word Katabole in "K(C)atabolism," and whatever sense belongs to the prefix *Kata* in the Greek word must belong to it in the English word, especially as it is intended to distinguish sharply.)

Now, in physiology, Anabolism indicates the process of cell construction, K(C)atabolism denotes antithetically cell destruction, while Metabolism (*meta* means between) denotes the resulting maintenance of the bodily structure after contribution of suitable material, on the one hand, and elimination of unsuitable material, on the other hand, is accomplished.

Now the Greek word unexceptionally used in the phrase translated "the foundation of the world" is *Katabole,* our anglicized K(C)atabolism. It cannot mean "foundation" in our common conception of that term; it is not substruction, but disruption, not laying of the foundation, but the overthrow of the very foundation.

The word *"Themelios"* is used in the following and similar New Testament passages: Luke 6:48, 49, "laid the foundation on a rock," "that without a foundation built a house"; Eph. 2:20, "are built on the foundation of the prophets"; Heb. 1:10, "Thou, Lord, hast laid the foundation"; Rom. 15:20; 1 Cor. 3:10, 11, 12; 1 Tim. 6:19; 2 Tim. 2:19; Heb. 6:1. In all these and other like cases the sense is obvious and the same.

To use the same English word in the same sense in translating *"Katabole"*—in the expression "the foundation of the world"—would leave us with the thought of original creative substruction of the world according to Gen. 1:1. But while *Katabole* cannot describe an orderly, beautiful, purposeful and serviceable order of creation, it does apply in its true sense to the picture of Gen. 1:2, the appalling disruption of that original creation. And it is from disruption to recreation that the whole drama of the Bible is unfolded. The contention over "the days of creation," whether days of twenty-four hours or of vast periods, really finds no occasion from Genesis 1, for v. 1 alone has reference to original creation. That furnishes no part of the Bible revelation, saving to make known that the dual terrestrial sphere of skies and earth —the theater of the Biblical drama—was, to begin with, created by God. Geology, for instance, testifies not of the process of creation so much as of the catastrophe which befell the geological construction. So also astronomy, and other sciences. Their fields of research reveal the debris of a disrupted creation and the processes of cosmic restoration. The tale of creation itself is not told; the tragedy of the disruption of the original world—material and moral—is not told; but little of the cosmic renewal is told; very briefly is the tale of the first century—approximately speaking—of human existence on the earth told us; but the needful information, of how the newly created Adam fell under subjection, with his whole estate, to the already ruling fiend of the skies, is sufficiently recounted to give us the opening chapter of the marvellous all-Bible drama of the redemption, the finishing point of which is reached only when we read: "I saw a new heaven and a new earth."

So the great date, *from* which this drama proceeds, is not "the foundation of the world," but this disruption of the world. The frequent Biblical reference to that impresses upon our minds the awful significance of the event to the mind of God, and at the same time, it portrays against that background the more forcibly and luminously the glories of redemption.

Let us now ponder for a season over the passages which in our English should substitute the word "disruption," or some word of equivalent meaning, for "foundation."

Matthew 13:35: "I will open my mouth in parables; I will utter things which have been kept secret from the foundation [i. e., disruption] of the world." That is, the disruption occasioned concealments of truth and teaching on God's part from his human creatures such as were not necessary in man's unfallen and undarkened condition. Matt. 25:34: "Come, ye blessed of my Father, inherit the kingdom prepared for you since the foundation [disruption] of the world." That is, whereas Adam, who by his fall forfeited to himself and his seed that heirship on earth first given to him, has, by redemption from the effects of the fall, the kingdom-estate restored to him in right and in prospect through the Redeemer since the very fall itself. Luke 11:50: "That the blood of all the prophets, which was shed from the foundation [disruption] of the world, may be required of this generation." That is, from the earliest days of the disruption of the original created order, murderous antagonism leaped forth in mankind against God's truth-bearers; namely, from Cain down. John 17:24: "Thou [Father] lovedst me [Christ] before the foundation [disruption] of the world." Note that here it is not "from," or "since," but "before." What a revelation springs to light here! The Son of God Himself, as divine mediator of and head over the original created world, was affected by the disruption of the world, so that not until redemption's end is accomplished will His own original glory and honor from His loving Father be fully restored; but even that expression of the Father's love will Christ share with His disciples. Eph. 1:4: "He hath chosen us in him before the foundation [disruption] of the world." That is, the intervention of the disruption of the world has not forfeited, lowered or altered for us the place in His Son originally given us when God ordained the creation of man in His image —"Christ, who is his image" (2 Cor. 4: 4). Halleluia!

Heb. 4: 3: "Although the works were finished from the foundation [disruption] of the world." The Apostle is here discussing God's denial to disbelieving Israel of entrance into the promised possession of Canaan, as an illustration for the forfeiture always of Gospel inheritance through unbelief, in substituting human works for the finished work of God's grace. The teaching here is that, as in Israel's case, so always, the Gospel demands faith and faith only, without works of human ability and merit, because all such conditions for us have been wrought in Christ Himself since the time disruption of the world created the need for them. Heb. 9: 26: "For then must he often have suffered since the foundation [disruption] of the world." That is, if the sacrifice of Christ Jesus be only of *ex post facto* efficacy; i. e., efficacy only after the act, then it is also only of temporary and fractional efficacy, needing to be repeated constantly from the beginning of the breach between man and God, as in the case of the powerless symbols of the Jewish ritual, and as is the case of the symbol of the mass today of the Church of Rome. The rest of this verse reads, properly translated, "but now once, at the *focusing point of the ages,* hath He appeared to put away sin by the sacrifice of Himself." That is, the cross stands at just that juncture of the ages—past, present and future—which gives it equal efficacy for all times, even from the disruption itself of the world which called for atonement between God and man.

1 Pet. 1: 20: "Who verily was foreordained before the foundation [disruption] of the world." That is, this bleeding Lamb had been taken and reserved for sacrifice, even before the disruption itself, which called for the atoning sacrifice.

Rev. 13:8: "The book of life of the Lamb slain from the foundation [disruption] of the world." Note again, that in the last verse it read *"before* the foundation" [disruption], while here it is *"from,"* etc. That is, a book has been open since the disruption of the world for lost souls, who receive eternal life through "the Lamb slain for the sin of the world."

Rev. 17:9: "Whose names were not written in the book of life from the foundation [disruption] of the world." This certainly means this much, that that book for the registration of souls recreated in Christ Jesus has been open and receiving names ever since the disruption itself. Does it also mean, that the names of all the saved were already written in that book by the omniscient Spirit, even from the date of the disruption itself? The form of language will bear even this interpretation.

We have now come in our course straight down through the Bible to where the world enters upon its endless ages of restored, recreated condition and destiny.

CHAPTER II

THE NEW TERRESTRIAL CREATION, 21:1

"And I saw a new heaven and a new earth; for the first heaven and the first earth were passed away; and there was no more sea." "And I perceived a new heaven and a new earth, for the former heaven and the former earth pass away, and the sea is no more" (C. V.).

THIS translation is far preferable. The word "perceived" means more than mere eyesight; it indicates an arrested, impressed imagination. There was immensely more in the vision than a spectacle to the physical eye. It rivets, it enthralls the eye of the soul as well. The word "former" is true to fact. The *first* heaven and the *first* earth of Gen. 1:1 long, long ago passed away, as is shown by Gen. 1:2. That is, the earth and its skies were long, long ago—even before Biblical history began—dissolved, disrupted, subverted from original character, condition and purpose. Yet they did not "pass away" in the sense of extinction; they were reconstituted as described in the further account of the first chapter of Genesis.

Now again, the apocalyptic seer perceives in the vision this old, old "former" (not "first") heaven and earth—this "groaning creation"—perfectly renovated and reconstructed for the endless ages to come.

This is in accord with the sense in which the word "new" is frequently used in Scripture. This word does not necessarily, or principally, mean another something, but that something made over new. It will be well illustrated by the case of the "new commandment" of 1 John 2:7, 8. The apostle John is there writing about loving one's brother. He says, "I write no new commandment unto you, but an old commandment which

you had from the beginning." Here "new" means
another. After reiterating, "The old commandment is
the word which ye had from the beginning," he proceeds to say, "A new commandment I write unto you";
but he qualifies and explains it by adding, "which
thing is true in him and in you: because the darkness
is past, and the true light now shineth." Here "new"
means not another, but the *old made new;* namely, as
revealed afresh "in *Him*" and so also "*in you.*" As
Jesus put the same point in John 13 : 34 : "A new commandment I give unto you, That ye love one another;
as I have loved you, that ye also love one another."
"Darkness" had come to veil, almost eclipse, the original
commandment of brotherly love, so that in effect it was a
new commandment—the old commandment in "True
Light"—for Jesus to command His apostles to love one
another after the example of His love unto them.

Again, the "new heart," the "new creation," the
"new man," the "new covenant," the "new name," the
"new spirit," the "new song," the "new tongues"—all
these expressions imply not something substituted by
another, but something made all new again. Several
times in the Bible it is foretold that the Lord God
will create new heavens and new earth; but Peter explains their newness from the spiritual standpoint thus,
"wherein dwelleth righteousness."

And we have very clear explanation of the coming
newness of terrestrial creation in Rom. 8 : 21 : "Because
the creature [our creature sphere] itself shall be *delivered from the bondage of corruption into the glorious
liberty of the children of God";* i. e., into the freedom
of the glorified children of God. How superior is this
prospect, how much more to God's honor and glory, how
much more consistent as the ultimate triumph of His
original creative purpose—than to think of the annihilation of the present creation to be replaced by an absolutely different one! That which Paul chiefly empha-

sizes in the passage just quoted, is the transformation
of entire terrestrial creation from the corruptibility
imposed by the fall into the same deathless, fadeless,
puissant glory, in which the glorified saints shall appear
at the return of Jesus Christ.

We must remember that "the creature" was not created "subject to vanity" (perishability), but was afterwards—by the great "disruption"—so constituted,
"not willingly, but by reason of him who hath subjected the same"; viz., the devil. In this state of
"vanity" "the whole creation groaneth and travaileth
in pain together until now." But we are also to remember that the creation lies under this "bondage of corruption" *"in hope,"*—namely, the great hope of being
in due time "delivered" therefrom "into the glorious
liberty of the sons of God." Therefore, "the *earnest
expectation* of the creature waiteth for the manifestation
of the sons of God"; that is, the whole creature world
about us is waiting in tip-toe, expectant eagerness for the
appearing of us "sons of God" in glorified bodies as the
first-fruits and samples of the "new heavens and......
new earth," with all contained therein.

"And there was no more sea." If this does not mean
just what it says, neither can we trust the previous
statement to be literally true, nor can anyone tell us
what this new statement does mean, for it is not by God
explained otherwise than as it reads.

But we are invited to ponder this mighty statement of
five or six monosyllables.

As the "new heaven" and the "new earth" are presented in contrast with the heaven and the earth dating
from the great "disruption" pictured in Gen. 1:2, so
this vision of the creation with "no more sea" stands in
contrast with the order, not of original creation, but of
that succeeding the awful "disruption."

From Gen. 1:2 it is plain that the chaos, into which
terrestrial creation was plunged, was just one shapeless,

useless, murky watery mass—"the deep." The beginning of the creative Spirit's reviving work—commonly,
but mistakenly, considered as original creation—was in
"moving upon the face of the waters." The exclusive
aqueous state was, then, that of the creation in utter dissolution. *The earth reduced to one great sunless, star-
less, non-lucent fluid mass was the negation of creation.*

God's first achievement was to penetrate the otherwise impenetrable shroud of thick atmospheric darkness
with sufficient lucency to establish the day in alternation
with the night. He then took a new victory over "the
deep" by dividing its watery contents, by uplifting huge
quantities thereof into the skies in rarified condition,
with a "firmament" (Heb. "expansion") to "divide
the waters [above] from the waters [beneath]." This is
good tactics of conquest, to divide the enemy's forces.
God then proceeded to overcome further unlawful dominion of the waters by causing emergence of land areas,
and by imprisoning the lower waters into huge reservoirs
by themselves, thus constituting of the defiant chaotic
sea the many "seas" of the present earth. Doubtless
further great changes were wrought by omnipotence
through the convulsions in the aqueous spheres of the
Noachian Flood. While the seas as God has left them
in this present order of the terrestrial creation have
been made largely useful, yet they have, like the refrac-
tory horse and mule, to be "broken," to be "held in with
bit and bridle, lest they come nigh thee." "Who shut
up the sea with doors, when it brake forth, as if it had
issued out of the womb? When I made the cloud the
garment thereof, and thick darkness a swaddling band
for it, and marked out for it my bound, and set bars and
doors, and said, Hitherto shalt thou come but no further; and here shall thy proud waves be stayed?" (Job
38:8-11, R. V.)

Scripture thus attributes to the sea a proud, aggres-
sive, usurping, destructive, rebellious disposition which

God Almighty has had to smite, to subjugate, bind and bar, and merely to tolerate for the time being under forcible restraints, while He has some uses for it. It is these "proud waters" which serve as the figure of the ruthless hostilities of the wicked against the righteous, of reprobate Gentiles against Israel, of the hosts of Anti-Christ against the remnant of the last days: "If it had not been the Lord who was on our side, now may Israel say: If it had not been the Lord who was on our side when men rose up against us; then the waters had overwhelmed us, the stream had gone over our soul" (Psa. 124: 1-5). The sea would, if unrestrained, submerge the land, destroy its productions, devour its inhabitants, and reduce the earth to a tumultuous, howling, profitless waste. It really is a relief to read from the apocalyptic page, that in the new heaven and the new earth "the sea is no more."

CHAPTER III

GOD'S TABERNACLING AMONG MEN, Vs. 2-8

"2 And I John saw the holy city, new Jerusalem, coming down
from God out of heaven, prepared as a bride adorned for her
husband. 3 And I heard a great voice out of heaven saying,
Behold, the tabernacle of God is with men, and he will dwell
with them, and they shall be his people, and God himself shall
be with them, and be their God. 4 And God shall wipe away
all tears from their eyes; and there shall be no more death,
neither sorrow, nor crying, neither shall there be any more pain:
for the former things are passed away. 5 And he that sat upon
the throne said, Behold, I make all things new. And he said
unto me, Write: for these words are true and faithful. 6 And
he said unto me, It is done. I am Alpha and Omega, the beginning
and the end. I will give unto him that is athirst of the fountain
of the water of life freely. 7 He that overcometh shall inherit
all things; and I will be his God, and he shall be my son. 8 But
the fearful, and unbelieving, and the abominable, and murderers,
and whoremongers, and sorcerers, and idolaters, and all liars,
shall have their part in the lake which burneth with fire and
brimstone: which is the second death."

HERE again John's gaze is riveted, his attention
absorbed, by a fresh marvel of the renewed heaven
and earth. It is the descent of the Holy City
from "heaven itself" into the terrestrial sphere. The
nature of this city is intimated by the words "prepared
as a bride adorned for her husband." This at once
identifies this city with the glorious Church of Jesus
Christ. In 19: 7, 8 we have recorded the vision of the
wedding occasion which is implied by the present picture. "The marriage of the Lamb is come, and his wife
hath made herself ready. And to her was granted that
she should be arrayed in fine linen, clean and white:
for the fine linen is the righteousness of saints."

The revelation now made is that, while this final glorified and wedded state of the Church of Jesus Christ is

to be consummated in the Father's eternal heavenly home, yet the Lamb's wife is to have her new home back in the old familiar, but perfectly renewed, terrestrial sphere. This withdraws our expectation from that of spending our immortal ages in some immeasurably distant, unaccustomed, imaginary sphere.

But we are not left to conjecture here. For John writes, ''I heard a great voice out of heaven [or, 'the throne'] saying.'' What follows is the Almighty's own explanation of this city and of the reason for its descent among mankind here below. ''Behold, the tabernacle of God.'' That explains the ''holy city.'' It is God's abode in His glorified saints of all the ages constituting His Son, the Lamb's wife. This ''habitation of God through the Spirit''—consisting of the saints redeemed and glorified out of the ages of the former heaven and earth—is not to be far aloof from the abodes of the human race in the ages of the new heaven and earth.

For, as the passage clearly implies, the new earth is to be peopled by continuing human beings and generations. God, in the descended Church of Jesus Christ as His holy city of habitation, will dwell with the earthly peoples and be their God, ''and *they* shall be *His* people [too], and God himself shall be with *them* [too], and be *their* God.'' How fitting this is—a united humanity, with one God, occupying one sphere of the universe together, only the glorified part of humanity dwelling in ''the new heaven'' and the peoples in immortal, but not glorified, bodies dwelling in ''the new earth.''

One detail of this charming spectacle remains to be noticed. It is the name of the holy city—''New Jerusalem.'' Several times in foregoing Scriptures this celestial Jerusalem has been mentioned. These instances corroborate the explanation just given of the nature of the city. In Gal. 4:26 Paul describes it as ''Jerusalem which is *above*'' and ''which is the *mother* of us [believers] all.'' It is, therefore, the habitation of God in those who are born from above, of the Spirit of God.

In Heb. 12 : 22 it is called ''the city of God, the heavenly Jerusalem.'' Already, the writer declares, his believing readers had ''come unto'' that city; and doubtless this city is that which is defined in the next verse as ''the church of the firstborn.'' In Rev. 3 : 12 it is promised to the overcomer of the church in Philadelphia— ''I will write upon him the name of my God, and the name of the city of my God, which is new Jerusalem, which cometh down out of heaven from my God; and I will write upon him my new name.''

The conception of God's habitation through the Spirit in His redeemed and glorified people as a city is very appropriate. All down through the Bible runs the representation of God's one loving aim, to obtain peaceful, happy, full abode in man. Consequently the various figures of such indwelling are brought under requisition. Man is thus called God's ''abode,'' ''house,'' ''habitation,'' ''temple.'' And collectively the saints of Jesus Christ are called by these figurative names. Other figures, such as vine and branches, body, family, sheepfold, etc., are used; but the various terms for indwelling are favorites. Jesus said to the disciples, ''In my Father's house are many mansions.'' That is, in this habitation of God in His children through the Spirit— the very thing Jesus is speaking of throughout John 14 —are many mansions, more literally translated abodes, individual cubicles. ''I go to prepare that you shall be cubicles of His indwelling presence, as chambers of His great spiritual house.''

Now the term city is the highest conception of an habitation. Its structure is the most elaborate, its organization the most developed, its activities the most composite, its privileges the most favored. ''City of God'' is, then, the supreme conception and description of God's residence in the whole glorified Church. And it is most

appropriate for that city to be called Jerusalem, the
new, the heavenly Jerusalem.

It is not, however, this "holy city, new Jerusalem,"
that occupies the center of attention in this entrancing
vision. That is presented only as the medium of God's
new relationship to earthly humanity in the final and
everlasting restoration. Consequently v. 4 describes the
happy changes of condition to be wrought of God for
earthly humanity. Nevermore shall a tear fall from a
human eye; no more mortality; no further mourning,
discord or misery; for the former things will have
passed away.

The Almighty Sovereign emphasizes the complete re-
versal of conditions to be made for mankind in the
new earth, "Behold, I make all things new." In no
respect, comprehensive or detailed, will the new sphere,
lot and condition of terrestrial humanity resemble the
old, the present. And yet, we are to remember that it
does not involve annihilation and another creation. God
has created nothing for ultimate destruction in the sense
of annihilating one and substituting it with another
creation. It is not otherness, but newness, that is to
characterize human abode, conditions and relations in the
final and everlasting order. And the most striking thing
in this picture is God's personal, sympathetic and delighted achievement of these things. Little wonder that
John is specially instructed by the written affidavit:
"These words are true and faithful."

But even stronger certification is furnished, amounting to as good as the accomplished fact—"it is done";
namely, the personal relation to all of the One affirming
it. This is expressed in the words, "I am Alpha and
Omega, the beginning and the end," that is "the Origin
and the Finish."

Human and earthly creation is not merely a production of Christ's almighty hand. The gravity of the truth
concerning the origin, history and destiny of mundane

creation does not consist in a differentiation between
creation by divine fiat or by creaturely evolution; it
consists in the facts of the vital relationship of this
creation to the Son of God Himself as its Alpha and its
Omega, its origin, its redemption and its restored perfection. Many Scriptural passages emphasize these facts.
Col. 1: 15: "Who is the image of the invisible God, the
firstborn of every creature." This two-way personal
relationship of the Son of God is striking and marvellous. Godward He is the perfect personal revelation of
the otherwise invisible deity; creatureward He is personal head unto all and several. This latter is set forth
at length and most impressively: "For *by him* were
all things *created,* that are in heaven, and that are in
earth, visible and invisible, whether they be thrones, or
dominions, or principalities, or powers: all things were
created *by* him, and *for* him: and he is *before* all things,
and by him all things *consist*" (vs. 16, 17).

Here surely is a vital and personal relationship between Jesus Christ and the mundane creation, which
warrants, as it also elucidates, His own description of it,
"I am its Alpha and its Omega, its Origin and its Finish." And when creation fell, it was a personal matter
to Him, and creation's redemption lay with Him, yea,
in Him: "For it pleased the Father that—having made
peace through the blood of his cross, by him to *reconcile*
all things unto himself; *by him*—whether they be
things in earth, or things in heaven" (vs. 19, 20).

Finally, most logically belongs it with Jesus Christ
by vital personal relationship to bring the redeemed creation to perfect and perpetual restoration; "That in the
dispensation of the fulness of times he might gather together in one (better translated, *rehead) all things in
Christ,* both which are in heaven, and which are on earth;
even *in him*" (Eph. 1: 10).

Therefore, the mystery of creature-existence lies in the
fact that it belongs essentially to the Christ to reveal

God in handiwork, in redemption of that handiwork, and in its imperishable restored perfection.

Our paragraph concludes with plain exposition of the spiritual conditions governing the experience of these felicities. "I will give unto him that is athirst of the fountain of the water of life freely" (v. 6). To the thirsty of spirit Jesus, God's Lamb, proffers in pure, abundant grace a never-failing flow of eternal life from His own being. What invitation! Further, "he that overcometh shall inherit all [these] things; and I will be his God, and he shall be my son" (v. 7). What incentive! On the other hand, all those of contrary spirit and practice (v. 8) shall have their part "in the lake which burneth with fire and brimstone: which is the second death." What warning!

CHAPTER IV

HOLY JERUSALEM, 21:9—22:7

ATTENTION is now turned directly and extendedly —as the climax of the whole revelation—upon that "holy city," new Jerusalem, coming down from God out of heaven, prepared as a bride adorned for her husband," called also "the tabernacle of God," in which, as previous verses have described, He is to reside, in intimate communion and blessed ministry through the everlasting ages, with the populations of the renewed, perfected, imperishable earth.

"9 And there came unto me one of the seven angels which had the seven vials full of the seven last plagues, and talked with me, saying, Come hither, I will shew thee the bride. the Lamb's wife. 10 And he carried me away in the spirit to a great and high mountain, and shewed me that great city, the holy Jerusalem, descending out of heaven from God, 11a Having the glory of God:"

The angel of v. 9 may be the same as the one of 22:6 and, therefore, the angel by whom, according to 1:1, the whole revelation was ministered to John. His authority and qualification for the matter in hand cannot be questioned.

The matter taken up by him with John is so definitely explained and is so intelligible to us, that we have no reasonable question left as to the understanding of the vision.

The angel calls John in rapture away with him to a suitable position for showing him "the bride, the Lamb's wife"; that is, the glorified Church.

Therefore, to John—"in the spirit," from "a great and high mountain"—the angel showed the consort of the Lamb in the character and capacity, yea, in the symbolism of a "great city, holy Jerusalem, descending out of heaven from God, having the glory of God."

The language here restricts us, and also accurately guides us, in our understanding of this description. The "great city" is identical with "the bride," and cannot, therefore, be a city in a natural sense, but only a symbolical sense, and the name "holy Jerusalem" is identical with "the Lamb's wife,"—*is her name*.

This is, therefore, a purely spiritual representation of the bride, the Church. It is not a new manner of definition, as we have seen in previous pages. It especially reminds us of Rev. 2:12, where the promise is given to the Philadelphian overcomer: "I will write upon him the name of my God, and the name of the city of my God, which is new Jerusalem, which cometh down out of heaven from my God: and I will write upon him my new name." Here is a blending of different aspects of one and the same spiritual conception. And the rather leading aspect is that to this overcomer God will give acknowledgment of finding in him an abiding place in His glory. We are reminded again of Jesus' words to the apostles, "In my Father's house are many mansions"—abodes, or chambers, of His indwelling. Jesus "was come from God" to reveal Him and what it is to have His indwelling; and He "went to God" to prepare for His followers places of God's like abode in them and through the Spirit.

And now John is shown in symbolical vision what is to be consummated, in the way of the entire glorified Church becoming the spiritual city, the residence of God, descending in His glory out of heaven to earth as a marvellous medium of His presence, residence and ministration in relation to the terrestrial residents of humanity in the everlasting ages of the restored world.

The conception "passeth understanding" and is, with good reason, portrayed symbolically, picturing allegorically—not to confuse us, or mislead us, but to assist the

poverty of our imaginations. It were presumptuous for
one to treat the description following with dogmatic
interpretation. The summation of all is given in advance
in the words, "having the glory of God." All that
follows is an exposition of the glories of God to be manifest by the perfected Church of Jesus Christ. But how
could those glories be described to us? Certainly not in
literal terms, for they surpass our present powers of
comprehension and far outreach the limits of human
language to express.

We are somewhat helped here by the case of the old
"worldly sanctuary" of the Jews. The whole structure,
and its rituals of service, was but "a *figure* for the time
then present," "the *patterns* of things in the heavens,"
"the *figures* of the true." In other words, all was symbolical, the pictorial, not the real. The "things in the
heavens," the realities of "the true," antedated the
symbolism so precisely prescribed, were the reality behind the symbolism with which faith had to do, and they
subsisted unaffected when the symbolical structure was
reduced to ashes. The summation of it all consisted in
"the riches of grace in Christ Jesus." Until He came,
displaying those riches in person, the symbolism was
helpful to faith. So, until the Lamb's wife is revealed,
"having the glory of God," as Jesus promised (John
17:22), it is helpful to faith and understanding to have
this symbolical vision of her glories.

"11 . . . Having the glory of God: and her light *was* like
unto a stone most precious, even like a jasper stone, clear as
crystal; 12 And had a wall great and high, *and* had twelve gates,
and at the gates twelve angels, and names written thereon, which
are *the names* of the twelve tribes of the children of Israel: 13
On the east three gates; on the north three gates; on the south
three gates; and on the west three gates. 14 And the wall of
the city had twelve foundations, and in them the names of the
twelve apostles of the Lamb. 15 And he that talked with me
had a golden reed to measure the city, and the gates thereof, and
the wall thereof. 16 And the city lieth foursquare, and the length
is as large as the breadth: and he measured the city with the

reed, twelve thousand furlongs. The length, and the breadth, and
the height of it are equal. 17 And he measured the wall thereof,
an hundred *and* forty *and* four cubits, *according to* the measure
of a man, that is, of the angel. 18 And the building of the wall
of it was *of* jasper; and the city *was* pure gold, like unto clear
glass.''

The seer is first impressed with the radiance of the
city, as of a most highly polished jasper stone (v. 11),
polished even to crystalline clearness. And it is ''a
glorious church,'' that the Lamb will have ''to present—
to himself,'' ''not having spot, or wrinkle, or any such
thing; but that it should be holy and without blemish.

With a golden reed the measurements of the city were
taken in John's sight; namely, ''foursquare,'' equilateral,
''twelve thousand furlongs'' (15,000 miles) to each side,
and, amazing to behold! the same in height, making a
perfect cube of such immense amplitude. This is form
comprehensive to the utmost, and it reminds us of the
crowning achievement of ''the riches of [God's] glory,''
namely, to be so strengthened unto Christ's indwelling
as to ''be able to *comprehend with all saints what is the
breadth, and length, and depth, and height;* and to
know the love of Christ, which passeth knowledge, that
ye might be *filled with all the fulness of God''* (Eph. 3:
16-19).

In verse 18 the city as a whole in its wonderful luster
is thus described: ''And the city was pure gold, like unto
clear glass.'' ''And had a wall great and high'' (v. 12).
Here is security and strength. It is a city with ample
defense. ''We have a strong city; salvation will God
appoint for walls and bulwarks'' (Isa. 26:1). Furthermore, the wall rests upon ''twelve foundations'' (v. 14)
engraved with ''the names of the twelve apostles of the
Lamb.'' This is not unfamiliar language. In Gal. 2:9
Paul speaks of James, Cephas and John, who ''seemed
to be *pillars.*'' In Eph. 2:20 Paul assures the Gentile
believers of their being ''built *upon the foundation of the
apostles and prophets,* Jesus Christ himself being the

chief cornerstone." And we may fearlessly quote the words of Jesus to Simon Barjona: "And I say also unto thee, That thou art Peter, and upon this *rock I will build my church;* and the gates of hell shall not prevail against it" (Mat. 16:18). And Paul says of himself with regard to the Corinthian Church as the temple of God, "I have laid the foundation" (1 Cor. 3:10); namely, that "foundation—which is Jesus Christ" (v. 11). "And he measured the wall thereof, one hundred and forty and four cubits" (v. 17); i. e., a wall 264 feet high, "and the building of the wall was of jasper" (v. 18). Surely the language of Isaiah (60:18) will be most applicable to the glorified Church—"Thou shalt call *thy walls salvation.*"

Yes, "and thy gates praise." For John remarked that this strongly walled city "had twelve gates, and at the gates twelve angels, and names written thereon [on the gates], which are the names of the twelve tribes of the children of Israel: on the east three gates; on the north three gates; on the south three gates; and on the west three gates" (vs. 12, 13).

We have had frequent occasion in traversing this unique book of the Bible, to note the large and harmonious commingling of Old Testament features with the latest developments of the New Testament economy. This is true to what we have found all along to be the unity of all Biblical revelations, dispensations and stratifications of saints, if we may so express it. So with the gates of this city of God. There are twelve and they are named after the twelve tribes of Israel.

Now, gates are the entrance-ways into a walled city. While they serve when shut to exclude, yet, their real object is to serve to "go in and out." So the twelve tribes of Israel were appointed avenues of entrance into the city of God. Israel is spoken of as "the church in the wilderness" (Acts 7:38). This is called Christ's "house" (Heb. 3:2-6) to which Moses belonged, in which he was "faithful......as a servant," which "house are we, if we hold fast the confidence and the rejoicing of the hope firm unto the end."

While in literal house-building foundations are laid before gates are set up, yet there is nothing spiritually incongruous in the gates of this city being named after the tribes of Israel, while "the names of the twelve apostles of the Lamb" were written in the foundations. It is expressly stated that "God is not ashamed to be called *their* God: for he hath prepared for *them a city*" (Heb. 11:16). And it is peculiarly appropriate that there were "at the gates *twelve angels*," for the covenant of the Mosaic law was "Ordained by angels in the hand of a mediator" (Gal. 3:19), and Israel "received the law by the disposition of angels" (Acts 7:53) and "the word spoken by angels was steadfast" (Heb. 2:2).

Further description of the city-wall, especially its foundations, and of the city-gates is given in vs. 19-21:

"19 And the foundations of the walls of the city were garnished with all manner of precious stones. The first foundation was jasper; the second, sapphire; the third, a chalcedony; the fourth, an emerald; 20 The fifth, sardonyx; the sixth, sardius; the seventh, chrysolyte; the eighth, beryl; the ninth, a topaz; the tenth, a chrysoprasus; the eleventh, a jacinth; the twelfth, an amethyst. 21 And the twelve gates were twelve pearls; every several gate was of one pearl: And the street of the city was pure gold, as it were transparent glass."

Here it is a matter of the beautiful garniture of the same. The mineral world—God's laboratory of exquisite and priceless gems—is drawn upon exhaustively for symbols of the spiritual colorings and iridescent beauties of salvation manifested in the Church, as she will stand glorified upon her foundations in Jesus Christ.

This spiritual symbolism of precious stones is not hitherto foreign to Scripture. Paul mentions symbolically "precious stones" as building material for the temple of the Church built upon the foundation of Jesus Christ (1 Cor. 3:12). Peter calls believers "lively stones'' of ''a spiritual house'' (1 Pet. 2:5). The most striking and pertinent parallel to our present passage is found in Isa. 54:11, 12, relating to the restoration and beautification awaiting earthly Israel from Christ her King: ''O thou afflicted, tossed with tempest and not comforted, behold, I will lay thy stones with fair colours, and lay thy foundations with sapphires. And I will make thy windows of agates, and thy gates of carbuncles, and all thy borders of pleasant stones.'' The immediate context, both preceding and following, shows that these expressions are symbols of spiritual characteristics. And those beautiful stones, placed in the Hebrew high priest's garments of beauty and glory, were largely the same as those named in our passage, and they were no doubt richly symbolical of spiritual things not easy to set forth excepting in symbolism.

What has been presented relating to the foundations applies to the city-gates of pearl and to the street of ''pure gold, as it were transparent glass'' (v. 21). While imagination might find room in this description to roam afar and wide, yet even the soberest conception discerns exquisite spiritual conditions as attending the daily public travel and traffic of this city.

Attention is next directed to the transcendent provision of this city for community worship, vs. 22, 23:

''22 And I saw no temple therein: for the Lord God Almighty and the Lamb are the temple of it. 23 And the city had no need of the sun, neither of the moon, to shine in it: for the glory of God did lighten it, and the Lamb is the light thereof.''

The purely spiritual and realistic nature of true worship, in exclusion and independence of everything artificial, is exemplified when ''the Lord God Almighty and the Lamb'' are not only the sole object of worship, but also themselves in ever omnipresence the sanctuary of worship itself. Abiding in Him is abiding, worshiping in the temple unintermittently. ''They rest not day and night, saying Holy, holy, holy, Lord God Almighty.''

As for the illumination of this city an abbreviated quotation is drawn from Isa. 60:19, 20: "The sun shall be no more thy light by day: neither for brightness shall the moon give light unto thee: but the Lord shall be unto thee an everlasting light, and thy God thy glory. Thy sun shall no more go down; neither shall thy moon withdraw itself: for the Lord shall be thine everlasting light, and the days of thy mourning shall be ended." This quotation throws light upon the spiritual signification of the symbolism here.

Verses 24-27:

"24 And the nations of them which are saved shall walk in the light of it: and the kings of the earth do bring their glory and honor into it. 25 And the gates of it shall not be shut at all by day: for there shall be no night there. 26 And they shall bring the glory and honor of all nations into it. 27 And there shall in no wise enter into it any thing that defileth, neither whatsoever worketh abomination, or maketh a lie: but they which are written in the Lamb's book of life."

In this paragraph closing Chapter Twenty-one the most important, pregnant light of all the Bible is given us regarding the holy and happy relationships which will, to the endless ages of the new heavens and earth, subsist between the terrestrial peoples and the glorified Church. This most engaging subject was introduced in vs. 2-4 of this chapter. The further treatment before us impresses us with the transcendent importance of the matter.

1. We need to recognize afresh that the location of the glorified Church; that is, the "Lamb's wife," "the holy city, new Jerusalem," "that great city, the holy Jerusalem, descending out of heaven from God, having the glory of God"—that her permanent future location is to be in the renovated earthly skies and in immediate relationship to the earth and its peoples. Our future and everlasting sphere of residence and action is not to be in some unknown, distant, imaginary heaven, unrelated by creation, history and redemption to this earthly sphere,

to which by origin and probationary experience we belong. But, even though temporarily—pending the final preparation of this dual mundane sphere of the universe —we may have more distant and foreign abode, yet in due time, as depicted in this chapter, we will come back home to earth for unending residence, only as citizens of the surrounding skies.

2. The renovated earth is to be the abode of the humanity surviving the purgatorial dealings of God and progressing in its posterity and history according to God's original purpose for male and female. This human race is to consist "of them which are saved" (v. 24); that is, saved from being destroyed out of the earth by God's renovating judgment. Moreover, all such survivors of the generations affected by that judgment will be only and all "they which are written in the Lamb's book of life." They will, therefore, be fellow-members of Jesus Christ with His glorified saints. The simple truth, then, is that the redeemed are eventually to consist of a fixed multitude of glorified saints, residing in aerial regions surrounding the globe, and of a multiplying earthly population, who will never taste of death, resurrection or after bodily change.

Moreover, the earthly populations will be constituted, not merely of surviving individuals, but of surviving national remnants, "the nations of them which are saved." These nationals will have their distinctive kings —"the kings of the earth." There will be finally realized the territorial distribution of the living earthly race as indicated in Deut. 32:8: "When the Most High divided to the nations their inheritance, when he separated the sons of Adam, he set the bounds of the people according to the number of the children of Israel."

3. The relationships between the two classes of redeemed humanity, and their spheres of residence and of activity, will be most intimate, happy, spiritual—reciprocally beneficial.

The light of the city—the Lamb's wife—that is, the Lamb Himself who "is the light thereof," will be the light in which "the nations of them which are saved shall walk," for they shall be "written in the Lamb's book of life."' Not in the millennial age even is such "obedience to the faith among all nations" to be realized, although an approximation to it will then be manifested, especially in outward form. This world-wide imperialism of the Lamb is due to Him, "the King of the ages" (15:3), and the word of Scripture and of God would fall utterly short did not the vision before us come to pass.

But not only are the nations of the endless ages to enjoy full privilege with the Bride in the Lamb, but the nations are to contribute to her spouse's glory and honor. "The kings of the earth do bring their glory and honor into it." In those ages it will be neither State vs. Church, nor State and Church separate, but it will be State and Church serving each other beyond all our present power to conceive.

This reciprocity is to be uninterrupted by any temporal alternations, as of day and night. "The gates of it [the city] shall not be shut at all by day." It is explained that this means not at all, "for there shall be no night there." And this reciprocity will never be betrayed or marred by sinister intrusion of anybody or anything, defiling, injurious or false. What a glorious monarchy!

It is very striking to note the approximation to this vision by the prophetic prospects of the condition awaiting Israel in the millennial age and the relations of Gentile nations to her. For instance: "Arise, shine; for thy light is come, and the glory of the Lord is risen upon thee,......The Lord shall arise upon thee and his glory shall be seen upon thee. And the Gentiles shall come to thy light, and kings to the brightness of thy rising......the abundance of the sea shall be converted unto thee, and the forces of the Gentiles shall come unto

thee.......Therefore thy gates shall be open continually;
they shall not be shut day nor night; that men may
bring unto thee the forces of the Gentiles, and that their
kings may be brought" (Isa. 60:1-3, 5, 11). "Awake,
awake; put on thy strength, O Zion; put on thy beautiful garments, O Jerusalem, the holy city: for henceforth
there shall no more come into thee the uncircumcised
and the unclean" (Isa. 52:1).

"1 And he shewed me a pure river of water of life, clear as
crystal, proceeding out of the throne of God and of the Lamb.
2 In the midst of the street of it, and on either side of the
river, was there the tree of life, which bare twelve manner of
fruits, and yielded her fruit every month: and the leaves of the
tree were for the healing of the nations. 3 And there shall be
no more curse: but the throne of God and of the Lamb shall
be in it; and his servants shall serve him: 4 And they shall
see his face; and his name shall be in their foreheads. 5 And
there shall be no night there; and they shall need no candle,
neither light of the sun; for the Lord God giveth them light:
and they shall reign for ever and ever. 6 And he said unto me,
These sayings are faithful and true: and the Lord God of the
holy prophets sent his angel to shew unto his servants the
things which must shortly be done. 7 Behold, I come quickly:
blessed is he that keepeth the sayings of the prophecy of this
book" (22:1-7).

With this passage the revelation proper is finished,
the rest of the chapter being in the nature of an epilogue
to the book. Symbolism here, so rich and significant, has
first to do with the provision of eternal life. Under the
figure of water life in Christ Jesus is very familiar in
Scripture. "A pure," or *the* pure, "river of water of
life," signifies the fulness of the living Spirit of God to
be ceaselessly supplied through the Lamb right out from
the very throne. This shows that the water of life in
everlasting fulness will be available by sovereign grace,
in which the righteousness and authority of God will be
eminently preserved and exemplified. "The tree of life"
represents our Lord as the fruit-producing Head of His
glorified people, and it calls us back to Edenic provision,

so foolishly lost by man, but now to be everlastingly regained. "The leaves of the tree" may well be taken to
signify the blessed, wholesome, life-giving words of the
Son of God. And here again we meet the fact that the
earthly peoples are to share appropriately in the life-
giving provisions of the city of God. While it seems
hardly appropriate to infer from the word "healing,"
that the nations of the restored earth will be subject to
sickness, yet the term does suggest, just as the word
"replenish" in Gen. 1: 28, that recovering of the nations
from the effects of previous ages will be going on in the
ages to come. The perfections of the regenesis will still
leave room for progress and betterment.

Verse 3 explains that all "curse" for sin and ill-desert
will be forever gone. The purpose of the cross in this
respect will be in full effect. This applies to all spheres of
the creation. All reflection of divine displeasure and
judgment will be effaced, and the sway of God and of
the Lamb will prevail. How impressive is the frequent
proviso, "and the Lamb"! It shows that to everlasting
ages, as emphatically as now, the blood of Jesus Christ
will maintain the favored conditions of both the glorified
Church and the terrestrial humanity.

Then, the picture is drawn of willing, loving, intelligent service of God on the part of humanity. The
prayer, "Thy kingdom come; thy will be done, on earth
as it is in heaven," will be fulfilled. Service will not be
slavish, but that of friends of God. Old, carnal Israel
shunned the face of God and could not even look upon
Moses' face so long as the glory shone there. But now the
servants of God will bask in the privilege of beholding
the divine face and their very foreheads will reveal the
knowledge and the glory of God.

The declaration of v. 5, that night will have passed
away and all dependence upon the celestial luminaries
for illumination, produces something of a shock, even
as did the statement of 21: 1, "and there was no more

sea." In our present state night is welcome as a time of
rest, its luminaries are beautiful to our sight, and the
return of the sun "to rule the day" is a diurnal rejoicing.

Yet some observations are in order. First, probably the
lighting of the holy city only is here in view. We remember the Shekinah, we remember "the pillar of fire
by night," we remember "the shining of a flaming fire
by night: for upon [above] all the *glory* shall be a defence" (covering) (Isa. 4:5). From these we learn of
higher modes of illumination than we are accustomed to
at present, whether in nature or in modern discovery and
invention. Then, it is our accustomed old effete state
—inadequate to that future—which demands present
modes of illumination. They belong to a state of in-
firmity, physical, mental, industrial and every other way.
They belong to a state of shifting change and alternation, of confessed imperfection. There is no indication
that darkness belonged at all to original physical creation, but rather that it came with "the disruption of the
world," and has since as yet been merely put under
limitations and to measures of temporary usefulness.
"The works of darkness" bear an ill repute. In the
eternity coming there will be no such works.

Moreover, the substitute for "natural" lights here
promised dispels all possible regret. "For the Lord God
giveth them light." That is, the creator of light and of
all light-bearers, will be Himself the illumination. "The
light dwelleth with Him." In Rev. 18:1 it is said of
even an angel—"the earth was lightened with his glory."
And Jesus said that His appearing should be "as the
lightning, that lighteneth out of the one part under
heaven, shineth unto the other part under heaven"
(Luke 17:24), even as the prophet Ezekiel, who was
given to see in vision the return of Jesus in glory to the
millennial Jerusalem and temple, said, "and the earth
shined with his glory" (43:2).

Finally, this affirmation evidently belongs to the

climactic representation of the endless future prepared
for us, "and they shall reign for ever and ever." The
subject of remark is the Lamb's wife, the holy Jerusalem. That consecrated devotion already noted, which
will characterize the Lamb's wife, will be rewarded with
full participation with Him, both in light and glory, and
in power. This is now inconceivable, yet so constraining
to a present consecration, which welcomes thousands of
coming ages for carrying out that consecration. A token
of one's destination for that day and estate is one's
impulse right here and now to enter into the dedicated
spirit of that day. Our passage reminds us of Prov.
10:30: "The righteous shall never be removed: but
the wicked shall not inherit the earth."

Again, in v. 6, the Lord Himself speaks with emphasis
of the certainty of these sayings as "faithful and true"
—to be believed and depended upon. "These sayings."
Beware how you deal with these sayings! Trifle not
with them by far-fetched interpretations, which bring
credit to the professed interpreter, but perversion to
"these sayings"! Again is declared the fact, that the
things this revelation foreshows are sent by angelic
medium from "the Lord God of the holy prophets" to
be made known to "His servants." The Revelation is of
vital consequence to those who belong to and are engaged
to serve Him. He returns to His opening affirmation of
His speedy coming and of the blessing attending the
cherishing of "the sayings of the prophecy of this book."

These are the last words of the revelation proper.
They impress us with the concern of Jesus Christ, that
we should be ever holding this book fresh in mind and
close to heart. It is implied that the simple, first-hand,
layman's reading of its connected, apocalyptic—not
cryptic—sayings will yield the blessing, whereas neglect
to read and to keep,—through distrust of the self-evident
intelligibility of the disclosures or through deference to
the mystifying, theoretical, misleading "keys of interpretation" of human invention—will leave one unblest.

CHAPTER V

THE EPILOGUE, 22 : 8-21.

Verses 8-21 are of the nature of an epilogue or "closing remarks."

JOHN AND THE ANGEL, VS. 8-9.

"8 And I John saw these things, and heard them. And when I had heard and seen, I fell down to worship before the feet of the angel which shewed me these things. 9 Then saith he unto me, See thou do it not: for I am thy fellow servant, and of thy brethren the prophets, and of them which keep the sayings of this book: worship God."

AGAIN John gives us his own personal voucher as eyewitness and direct auditor of these things. The impression of them upon him was such as to prompt him—the apostle John—to worship the Lord's messenger and revelator of these things. This impresses us with the real momentousness of the things themselves, and with the exalted character of one who could disclose them to a human seer. John's prostration before the angel gave the latter occasion to illustrate the humble disposition of such illustrious beings. He forbids the act of John on the ground that he is himself but a subordinate with John, with all the prophets and even with the humblest readers and keepers of the "sayings" contained in the book we have been perusing. "Worship God," is the angel's charge.

The writer has been deeply impressed with the angel's humility, as he has searched Revelation time and again to find the angel sent by Jesus to show all to John. But the passage before us is the only place where he is in certain evidence, whereas one would naturally expect his personal presence to be everywhere apparent. The author's most plausible surmise—very diffidently advanced—is that the angel of Chapter 10 is the angel of the Apocalypse.

THE TIME AT HAND, VS. 10, 11.

"10 And he saith unto me, Seal not the sayings of the prophecy of this book: for the time is at hand. 11 He that is unjust, let him be unjust still: and he which is filthy, let him be filthy still: and he that is righteous, let him be righteous still: and he that is holy, let him be holy still."

Here again is stressed the immediately impending time of these revealed events. Not that they were necessarily to occur right soon, as we measure time. But, relative to eras, the era of these things was next in order, and would transpire swiftly. Hence the revelation of them was to be held open—unsealed. This harmonizes with the urgent injunction to read and to keep the sayings of this book. Even though hundreds of years have already elapsed, yet "those things which are written therein" are "things which must shortly come to pass," and "the time is at hand." That is to say, there is no further probation for us than the present, whether in the body or out of the body. And such is the brevity of our individual portion of this dispensation—just preceding these "things which must shortly come to pass"—that we are quickly and finally fixing our character and our destiny for that future.

JESUS' LAST ADMONITION, VS. 12-15.

"12 And, behold, I come quickly; and my reward is with me, to give every man according as his work shall be. 13 I am Alpha and Omega, the beginning and the end, the first and the last. 14 Blessed are they that do his commandments, that they may have right to the tree of life, and may enter in through the gates into the city. 15 For without are dogs, and sorcerers, and whoremongers, and murderers, and idolaters, and whosoever loveth and maketh a lie."

Verse 12 takes up the thought of verse 11 as to the present predetermination of one's final moral alignment with the adjustments of that coming day. It is the day of the sudden appearing of Jesus Christ, when He shall reward every man according to his present record. The basis of decision will be that of "Jesus Only"—from A to Z, from beginning to end, from origin to consummation. It is a question of doing His commandments. Obedience unto Him now will be the passport then to the tree of life, to the freedom of that city. What are His commandments? They are the principles and particulars of the spiritual life, all the instructions of the Bible in the way everlasting, all the monitions, promptings, constraints of the Holy Spirit given to us to take of the things of Jesus, make them known to us and fulfill them in us. This is not a reward of merit, it is simply living as already in that day. "Let us walk honestly, *as in that day*" (Rom. 13:13). How greatly we need to "read," to "hear," to "keep" this saying of the book! What place will we find outside the gates of the city? Only the place peopled by characters catalogued in v. 15.

JESUS' LAST INVITATION, VS. 16-17.

"16 I Jesus have sent mine angel to testify unto you these things in the churches. I am the root and the offspring of David, and the bright and morning star. 17 And the Spirit and the bride say, Come. And let him that heareth say, Come. And let him that is athirst come. And whosoever will, let him take of the water of life freely."

The emphasis is upon "I Jesus." He it is who testifies these things to the churches by His angelic messenger. From Him as pre-existent and divine root sprang David, both in respect to his spiritual life and in respect to his royal dignity, and from David by miracle-birth came Jesus as to the flesh, to inherit the throne and to make effective the kingdom of God and of heaven upon the earth. He is the promised day-star that shall never go down, but only shine more and more unto the perfect day. For His coming, the Spirit cries of Himself and through the bride, the sanctified believers. This cry is not only in secret, but should be also upon the housetop, that others may hear and may join in crying, "Come." And what is there so heart-searching to the unsaved, as this cry while they are unprepared for His coming? To these thirsty ones Jesus sends out by us the gracious invitation "Come," "Let him who is wanting it take the living water gratuitously."

JESUS' LAST TESTIMONY, VS. 18-19.

"18 For I testify unto every man that heareth the words of the prophecy of this book, If any man shall add unto these things, God shall add unto him the plagues that are written in this book: 19 And if any man shall take away from the words of the book of this prophecy, God shall take away his part out of the book of life, and out of the holy city, and from the things which are written in this book."

Verse 18 should not begin with "For." There is no rhetorical connection. This new word is like a thunder bolt out of a clear sky. It pertains to our dealing with "the words of the book of this prophecy." They are not to be "handled deceitfully," whether by sensational "interpretation" or by time-serving dilution. This is a book of "prophecy." Back in Isaiah we hear the Lord claiming the exclusive ability and prerogative of prophecy. It were, then, a daring, dangerous sacrilege for any creature to qualify, in one way or other, the intended, self-evident communication of God in prophecy. This warning against trifling with prophecy, here especially the Book of Revelation, extends to the very "words." This is verbal inspiration, so far as the original is concerned. In this day of revived interest in prophecy and of voluminous teaching on the subject, is there not urgent call to us all to examine closely our principles, methods and findings—what we believe and what we teach, even to the very "words"—to the end of neither adding to nor taking from that which God only can disclose, from

that which He has intelligibly disclosed in prophecy?
"Revelation" must be intelligible, or it is not a revelation. Its disclosures must be apparent to every eye. It
is a non-sealed book (22:10). "Keys" are not needed
with which to open it, for it never was locked. It was
given expressly "to shew" (1:1), to show, not to mystics,
but "unto his servants." The spirit of implicit obedience
to Jesus, "the fear of the Lord," is the key of interpretation to the reader of The Revelation.

Verse 20 the Apostle John appends,

"He which testifieth these things saith, Surely I come quickly.
Amen. Even so, come, Lord Jesus."

"He which testifieth." It is Jesus, and it is present,
continuous tense. By "the words of the book of this
prophecy" Jesus is ceaselessly testifying to the "things
which must shortly come to pass." He is thereby constantly saying to His servants: "Yea, I am coming
quickly." His wide-awake servant is likewise constantly
saying in response "Amen! Be it so! Be coming, Lord
Jesus!"

APOSTOLIC BENEDICTION, V. 21.

"The grace of the Lord Jesus be with all the saints. Amen."

CHAPTER VI.

THE CROSS OF THE AGES.

T HROUGHOUT this study of the Scriptures it has been found that the immediate, personal and known presence of Jesus Christ, in the characters and offices familiar since His visible advent, was enjoyed in all the Old Testament times. Because of the importance of the subject, and for assistance to readers, an express chapter on "The Christ of the Ages" was presented. In like manner, abundant evidence has been found that the Church of Jesus Christ has been in the building all the way down from the fall of man; and for the same reason as above this subject has been treated in a special chapter on "The Church of the Ages." Once more, the power of the cross of Jesus Christ has been found in full effect from Adam to Christ, as well as since our Lord's death. The importance of this holy theme and the desire to help our readers call for a separate discussion of "The Cross of the Ages."

These three revelations stand interrelated as the three sides of one complete triangle of fundamental truth. The proof of any one of the three carries the certainty of the other two. If Christ be found throughout the Old Testament as Redeemer and Saviour, then the Church must be of Old Testament origin and, in due part, of Old Testament formation; and the power of the blood of Jesus Christ must be found operating in appropriate effects all through these ancient times. The like conclusion must be true whichever one of the three revelations is first perceived. The matter to be presented in this chapter is the prevalence throughout Old Testament times of the power and effects of the atoning work of Jesus Christ.

The subject of "The Cross of the Ages" will be treated under three heads: I. The Cross in Mystery. II. The Cross in Manifestation. III. The Cross amidst the Ages.

I. THE CROSS IN MYSTERY.

By mystery is not meant unreality. Neither is that which is in mystery beyond discernment. A divine mystery is something as real as a divine manifestation, and it is as plainly revealed to spiritual discernment as when it is disclosed to sensible view. "Faith is the evidence of things not seen." Jesus Christ was in mystery to Old Testament saints; but how real He was to them, how plainly revealed to spiritual apprehension, is indicated in Heb. 11:27 by the key there given to Moses' patient walk of faith with Christ: "*as seeing him* who is invisible." Likewise the Church as the spiritual body of Christ was in mystery to Old Testament believers; but it was a fundamental reality, discernible to the eye of faith while waiting for its public disclosure. "Even the mystery which hath been hid from ages and from generations, but now is made manifest to His saints," which mystery is "Christ in you, the hope of glory" (Col. 1:26, 27). So also the atoning work of Jesus Christ was in mystery of old, but most real, most deeply experienced through faith.

It is a modified way of admitting this truth to say that "*In the mind of God* His Lamb was viewed from the foundation of the world as slain, so that *in the mind of God believers* were viewed in the Old Testament as saved." This is not a mystery, however, it is an unreality. Such salvation is not as yet actual and experimental; it remains at best but a prospective, long-deferred salvation. And this still leaves the question, "When does the salvation of Old Testament believers really occur?" to a merely theoretical answer. The best solution that is offered is, that after Christ appeared and shed His blood atonement was first available, and that it was applied *retroactively*. But do we have revelation from God to this effect? Another question is, "Were Old Testament saints also viewed in God's mind as prospective members of the Church of Jesus Christ, to be taken in retroactively; or are they, in spite of the retroactive application of the atonement, to be forever excluded from the Church? This question also can be answered from this position only theoretically.

Another modified way of admitting the truth of the Old Testament salvation is to say that faith then looked forward through types to an atoning Saviour to come some time to remove sin by His blood. In this view atonement was in former times only external and typical, and salvation was only prospective, impossible actually before the death of Christ upon the cross. Accordingly He was left unknown as Redeemer and Saviour, and His Church waited for Pentecost for its origin.

These two theories have nothing really in common with the postulate of this chapter. It remains necessary to take account of data sufficient to show that real, full and unqualified effects of the cross of Jesus Christ were current in Old Testament times.

1. Mercy and salvation are the theme and the refrain of the Old Testament, not in any other tense or sense than in the New Testament. The word "salvation" occurs three times as often in the Old Testament as in the New. The difference is even greater in the occurrence of the words "mercy" and "mercies"; and they are not distant, but present, mercies, spiritual and not merely or commonly temporal. The set refrain of Israel's psalmody was, "The Lord is good, and His mercy endureth forever." "Restore unto me the joy of thy salvation," pleads David. He knew salvation and its joy, the loss of which joy brought an agony which led to broken-hearted confession and earnest prayer for its restoration. David also clearly testified to the inefficiency and worthlessness of mere works of atonement, and to an

efficacy of present atonement which was apart from
all ceremonial sacrifices: "Thou desirest not sacrifice;
else would I give it: Thou delightest not in burnt offering. The sacrifices of God are a broken and a contrite
spirit: a broken and a contrite heart, O God, Thou wilt
not despise" (Psa. 51 : 16, 17). "Even as David also de-
scribeth the blessedness of the man, unto whom God
imputeth righteousness without works, saying, Blessed
are they whose *iniquities are forgiven,* and whose *sins are
covered.* Blessed is the man, to whom the Lord *will not
impute sin*" (Rom. 4 : 6-8). If these passages do not mean
that forgiveness, justification, blessedness, etc., were then
of full power and value, then these passages have no real
power and value for us.

Another important fact is that very many times in the
Old Testament the word salvation is used in a personal
sense. As such the word means Jesus personally; for
the Hebrew word for salvation is Jesus. When the
dying Jacob said, "I have waited for thy salvation,"
he was testifying to a satisfying vision of the present
Jesus; so he worshipped Him, leaning on the top of his
staff in touching reminder of the night when Jacob
wrestled with Him and prevailed, although at the expense of lifelong lameness in the hip. When, also, the
aged Simeon "took Him [the visible infant Jesus] up in
his arms, and blessed God," he said, "Lord, now lettest
Thou thy servant depart in peace, according to thy
word: for mine eyes have seen thy salvation,"—Thy
Jesus—(Luke 2 : 28-30). This was no new salvation,
no new Saviour, no new Jesus. There was a needs be
in the direction "Thou shalt call His name Jesus"—
salvation; for that was His name before incarnation and
He could rightly be called by none other. "For He
[incarnate] shall save His people from their sins" (just
as He had been doing while preincarnate).

And we have to remember that, if the atonement was
not effective before the tragedy of Calvary, then the

words and deeds of grace, of forgiveness and salvation
ministered by Jesus on the way to the cross were inef-
fective, being merely prospective—in the thought of
God......not immediately yielding human experience,
but waiting so to do retroactively afterwards.   How
strangely the Gospels would read under such construction! While Jesus was faithfully and prominently holding forth His prospective death, yet He never hinted that
any one had to wait for his salvation until that event.
"Behold, the Lamb of God," cried John the Baptist,
"which taketh [not, is about to take] away the sin of the
world."

2. "By their fruits shall ye know them."   This
principle of perceiving cause by effect was declared by
Jesus Himself; and by this principle we can perceive
abundant workings of the cross of Jesus in lives before
Calvary, both in those contemporary with Him before
He died and in those running clear back to our first
parents.

Jesus reproved Nicodemus for failing as a ruler of
the Jews to be familiar, by doctrine and by experience,
with the truth of regeneration by the Holy Spirit. "Art
thou a ruler of the Jews and knowest not these things?"
......that a man must be born from above, of the Spirit
and of the Word of God, and that thereby any man of
any day might enter the eternal, spiritual kingdom of
God.   It is of Old Testament times, and not confined
either to the pale of Israel, that it is said of the saving
results of ante-Calvary times: "But as many as received
Him, to them gave He [Jesus Christ] power [the right]
to become the sons of God, even to them that believe on
His name [that is, on Him in personal presence to them]:
which were born [then as now], not of blood, nor of the
will of the flesh, nor of the will of man, but of God"
(John 1:12, 13).

When we look for characters, lives and deeds which are
worthy of our study and emulation spiritually, are they

not to be found chiefly in the Old Testament as the album
of such persons? In discussing the efficacy as well as the
sufficiency of faith for salvation, sanctification, victory
and prospective glory, where does Paul find examples,
but in Abraham and David? And where does the writer
of Hebrews find abundant illustrations of the nature,
actions and results of our Christian faith? He begins
with Abel, follows up with Enoch, Noah, Abraham,
Sarah, Isaac, Jacob, Moses, Rahab; he then confesses
that there is not time more than to cite the names of a
half dozen others individually; and then he bulks an un-
told number of prophets and heroes, ''of whom the world
was not worthy.'' The conclusion is then stated: ''These
all having obtained a good report through faith,'' our
Christian faith. Note the reading here of the Revision:
''These all, having had witness borne to them through
their faith.'' Whose witness? Certainly the witness of
the Spirit. That they ''received not the promise'' does
not mean that they did not have salvation further than
by promise. And that God had ''provided some better
thing for us'' does not imply that that better thing is
salvation, or a better salvation. ''That they without us
should not be made perfect'' signifies that, while we have
had somewhat of God's program in Christ fulfilled in
our dispensation beyond their privilege, yet we both are
waiting still to be together ''made perfect''; that is, to
be brought into the full consummation of the program
in Christ Jesus which was from the beginning before the
eye of faith.

3. The secret of Old Testament salvation was the same
as that of New Testament salvation so far as the instrumentality of the Word of God, especially the Scriptures, is concerned.

It was altogether of the Old Testament Scripture that
Paul spoke in 2 Tim. 3:15-17: ''From a child thou
hast known the holy scriptures, which are able to make
thee *wise unto salvation through faith which is in Jesus*

Christ. All [Old Testament] scripture is given by inspiration of God, and is profitable for doctrine, for
reproof, for correction, for instruction in righteousness:
that the man of God may be perfect, thoroughly furnished unto all good works.''

This shows that the Bible, from its first sentences,
fixes an attentive soul in saving faith upon Jesus Christ
as a present Saviour and builds up such a soul unto
perfection in all good works. ''Faith which is in Jesus
Christ'' was never primarily a believing forward-look
unto His first coming any more than it is such a look now
unto His second coming; saving faith is present reliance
upon a present Jesus Christ as an immediate, present,
living Saviour.

Now, where shall we go for the richest expressions of
appreciation of the saving, sanctifying, conquering power
of God's Word? Is it not to Psalm 119? Why did the
Spirit cause to be penned such an appreciation of the
saving, quickening, renovating, transforming ministries
of Scripture hundreds of years before Calvary, if the
atoning ground of such experiences was not in effective
operation? ''Thy word have I hid in my heart that I
might not sin against thee.'' ''Let thy mercies come also unto me, O Lord, even thy salvation, according to thy
word.'' ''I entreated thy favor with my whole heart: be
merciful unto me according to thy word.'' ''My soul
fainteth for thy salvation: but I hope in thy word.''
''O how love I thy law! it is my meditation all the day.''
''Thy word is a lamp unto my feet, and a light unto my
path.'' ''Mine eyes fail for thy salvation, and for the
word of thy righteousness.'' ''Deal with thy servant
according to thy word and teach me thy statutes.'' ''The
entrance of thy word giveth light: it giveth understanding unto the simple.'' ''I cried unto thee—Save me,
that I may keep thy testimonies.'' Salvation in order
to obedience! The whole Old Testament plan is not that
of works of law in order to a legal justification, but it is

that of salvation by grace in order to a life in God's law. Such love of God's law, such diligent and beneficent use of it as this Psalm expresses was no more needed than now and was then no more possible without gospel salvation than now. ''The law is the Gospel contained; the Gospel is the law maintained.''

4. As has been brought out in previous pages, the whole Levitical system testified primarily, not to a salvation to be available only at a future time, but to a then present salvation through a present Redeemer and Saviour.

All these significant details, ordained by God for approach to and communion with Him, were not first types of things to come in an incarnate Saviour, but they were symbols of things then available in a present preincarnate Saviour. And as symbols, they were not primarily means or works of righteousness. This was the error into which formalists then fell even as they do now—the error of thinking that outward, creaturely things can procure heavenly realities. Simon, the sorcerer, could just as well buy with gold the power to confer the Holy Ghost as Abraham could obtain a real atonement by a mere lamb or bullock. Any offering, presented without faith in the mystical Sacrifice as figured in the offering, was a dishonor to the Son of God and an offence to His Father. Abraham's circumcision was ''a seal [symbol] of the *righteousness of the faith* which he had yet being uncircumcised.'' David testifies that, without ''a broken spirit: a broken and a contrite heart,'' God had no desire for the symbolical sacrifice and took no pleasure in the symbolical burnt offering. Actual conviction of sin, contrition over it, whole-hearted confession of it, full conscious forgiveness of it through faith in a merciful Redeemer, actual purging of sin, victory over it in life, —all these spiritual effects coming from no possible source but that of the cross of Calvary, effects which have abundant illustration in Old Testament times among both

Jews and Gentiles — all these preceded the various offerings and alone rendered those offerings appropriate and pleasing to God. There is no cause in the universe to which to attribute these effects, but to Jesus Christ and Him crucified; therefore, His atoning work was then in effect and He was the Lamb of God then as well as now.

5. There is no other evidence of the power and the effect of the cross under the old dispensation so conclusive as the exposition given by Jesus of "the law and the prophets" as a whole.

"A lawyer [an expounder of the law of Moses] asked Him a question, tempting Him [putting Him to a theological test], and saying, Master, which is the great commandment in the law? Jesus said unto him, Thou shalt love the Lord thy God with all thy heart, and with all thy soul, and with all thy mind. This is the first and great commandment. And the second is like unto it, Thou shalt love thy neighbor as thyself. On these two commandments hang all the law and the prophets" (Mat. 22: 35-40).

This summary of law and prophets, by Him who gave the law by Moses and all applications of it by the prophets, is most weighty and important, and it is absolutely conclusive. The word "hang" is illuminating. In oriental houses long pins of tough wood were set into the masonry of the walls to take the places of closets and wardrobes. All kinds of things were hung upon these pins. Jesus uses the figure of the pin when He says, "On these two commandments *hang* all the law and the prophets." That is to say, upon love—supreme toward God, equal toward fellowman—depends every item of Old Testament law, every moral and spiritual precept of the prophets. In other words, the whole body of the law and the prophets is interpreted, directed and fulfilled by Christian love.

And the remarkable thing is, that Jesus was not declaring any new doctrine, issuing any new exposition, but was reminding the lawyer of what the Old Testament everywhere teaches. Indeed, Jesus' words are directly quoted from the books of Mosaic legislation (Deut. 6: 5, 10, 12, 30: 6 and Lev. 19: 18). We do not begin to find the Old Testament, to understand it and to make right application and exposition of it, until we feel the pulsation of Calvary all through it. The New Testament proposes no new law of spiritual life, when it teaches "that He died for all, that they which live should not henceforth live unto themselves, but unto Him which died for them, and rose again" (2 Cor. 5: 15), and "because He laid down His life for us......we ought to lay down our lives for the brethren," 1 John 3: 16. The Old and the New Testaments are absolutely one in the doctrine and in the fruit of spiritual life; and, as the cross is the exclusive ground in the latter case, so is it, so must it be, in the former also. It is only through faith in an atoning Saviour that fallen man can be restored to this perfect love. Jesus, to be sure, issued in His living, human example a bright, new edition of the old, original, eternal law of love; but it was not a new writing, or a revised edition. When He judges His people for their works, will He find that the Church of this dispensation has fulfilled "the law of Christ" better than did the chosen people of old? Certainly, there should be more fruit of love now than then, both because it then was so disappointing, and because of what will appear from the next line of discussion.

II. THE CROSS IN MANIFESTATION.

"There is nothing hid, which shall not be manifested, neither was anything kept secret, but that it should come abroad." Thus spoke Jesus Himself in Mark 4: 22. "Great is the mystery of godliness: God was manifest[ed] in the flesh" (1 Tim. 3: 16).

Nothing stands out more prominently in the Old Testament than the promise of the human bodily coming of

the Son of God, and that coming was to be for salvation.
It was fully revealed to the fallen Adam through the
words spoken by Christ to Satan: "I will put enmity
between thee and the woman, and between thy seed and
her seed; it shall bruise thy head, and thou shalt bruise
his heel" (Gen. 3:15). The Son of God as born of woman was to crush the power of "that old serpent, called the
Devil, and Satan." This connects right up with two
striking New Testament passages regarding the cross in
relation to Satan. Heb. 2:24: "For as much then as
the children are partakers of flesh and blood, He also
took part of the same; that *through death,* He might
destroy him that had the power of death, that is, the
devil." Col. 2:14, 15: "Nailing it to his cross; and
having spoiled principalities and powers [satanic], he
made a show of them openly, *triumphing over them in
it,*" or on it, the cross.

In Gen. 23:18 the promise is given to Abraham concerning the Son of God as his seed: "And in thy Seed
shall all the nations of the earth be blessed." Connect
this with Acts 3:25, 26: "Ye are the children of the
prophets, and of the covenant which God made with our
fathers, saying unto Abraham, And in thy seed shall all
the kindreds of the earth be blessed. Unto you [Israel]
first [of all nations] God, having raised up His Son
Jesus, sent Him to *bless you,* in turning away every one
of you from his iniquities."

In 1 Chron. 17:11, 12 the promise is given to David
concerning the Son of God as his Seed: "I will raise up
[i. e., resurrect] thy Seed after thee, which shall be *of
thy sons:* and I will *establish his kingdom.* He shall
build me an house, and I will stablish his throne for
ever." Connect this with Acts 2:30-33, 36: "Therefore
[David] being a prophet, and knowing that God had
sworn with an oath to him, that of the fruit of his loins,
according to the flesh, he would *raise up Christ* to sit
on his throne; he [David] seeing this before spake of

the *resurrection of Christ*......Therefore being by the right hand of God exalted......let all the house of Israel know assuredly, that God hath made that same Jesus, whom ye crucified, both Lord and Christ.''

Thus Old and New Testaments run parallel in Jesus Christ all the way through as promise and fulfillment, as mystery and manifestation. And it is very striking to note how prominent in the New Testament are certain words which indicate the presence of Jesus Christ, not as a new and before unknown person, nor as one in new character and offices, but only as one coming out from invisible presence into visible, out of spiritual presence into physical.

1. The word ''appear.'' ''Now once in the end of the world hath he *appeared* to put away sin by the sacrifice of himself'' (Heb. 9 : 26). This is the more striking when taken in connection with verse 24—''Now to *appear* in the presence of God for us,'' and with verse 28, ''shall he *appear* the second time [in the world] without sin unto salvation.'' Here are three visible, personal appearings, differing in time, place and purpose, but all relating to the same person. ''But after that the kindness and love of God our Saviour toward man *appeared*'' (Ti. 3 : 4). There is no intimation here that Jesus was unknown before as ''God our Saviour,'' or that His ''kindness and love'' were any new, before unknown, feeling; but the marvel consists in the human appearing, in kindness and love, of God our Saviour. Again, similarly, in Ti. 2 : 11, ''For the grace of God that bringeth salvation hath *appeared* to all men.''

2. The word ''manifest.'' ''Great is the mystery of godliness, God was *manifest*[ed] in the flesh'' (1 Tim. 3 : 16). The difference is not between unreality and reality, but between invisibility and visibility, between unincarnate and incarnate presence. ''That eternal life, which was with the Father, and was *manifested* unto us'' (1 John 1 : 2). John greatly emphasizes this physical

manifestation of Christ as the same eternal life of man
as He was when unincarnate. "That which *was from the
beginning,* [but] which [now] we have heard, which we
have seen with our eyes, which we have looked [gazed]
upon, and our hands have handled of the Word of life;
[for the life was *manifested,* and we have seen it]." "In
this was *manifested* the love of God toward us, because
that God sent His only begotten Son [in incarnate mani-
festation] into the world, that we might live through
Him" (1 John 4:9). "According to His own purpose
and grace, which was given us in Christ Jesus before the
world began, but is now *made manifest* by the appearing
of our Saviour Jesus Christ" (2 Tim. 1:9, 10). How
clearly this shows that salvation and holy calling were
prepared for man in divine purpose and grace in God's
Son as Saviour even before there was a fallen man to
need the same, and that the same was given public,
visible manifestation by the human appearing of Jesus
Christ! "Christ, as......a lamb......verily was foreordained before the foundation of the world, but was
manifest in these last times for you" (1 Pet. 1:19, 20).

3. The word "came." "But before [Christ the object
of] faith *came,* we were kept [in safeguard] under [the
restraints of] the law, shut up [closeted] unto [Christ
the object of] faith, which [who] should afterwards be
revealed" (Gal. 3:23). "This is a faithful saying, and
worthy of all acceptation, that Christ Jesus *came* into
the world to save sinners, of whom I am chief" (1 Tim.
1:15). It is farthest from the thought of this verse that
Jesus Christ had not before coming into the world in
body been saving sinners. "Every spirit that confesseth
that Jesus [is the] Christ......*come* in the flesh is of
God." 1 John 4:2 "I am the bread which *came down*
[in visible manifestation] from heaven" (John 8:41).
"Moses gave you not that bread from Heaven"; that is,
in the manna (v. 32); but, when in the Psalms it says,
"He gave them bread from heaven," it meant "the true

bread from heaven" (v. 32), "the bread of God......he which *cometh down* from heaven, and [in human presence] giveth life unto the world" (v. 33); "I am the bread of life" (v. 35). This plainly teaches that God's Son was being given as the bread of life to Israel in the wilderness, and unto the world from the beginning, but that now He had come down incarnate for the same purpose. "In him was life, and the life was the light of men......Light *is come* into the world......I am the light of the world" (John 1:3; 3:19; 8:12). "He was in the world......I *came forth* from the Father, and *am come* into the world: again, I leave the world, and go to the Father.......And now I am no more in the world." "Lo, I am with you alway." (John 1:10; 16:29; 17:11; Matt. 28:20.) Of course, these apparent contradictions are due to the contrast between spiritual presence and bodily presence.

This group of passages might be extended greatly, but it is not necessary. Enough has been presented to illustrate how much the New Testament emphasized the public unveiling in Jesus of Nazareth of the things of the Son of God which were just as real in the Old Testament, though veiled.

The discussion of this chapter as thus far conducted serves to force to the front the question, "Why, then, the literal cross at all? If the atonement was in full force before the literal cross was erected, was the literal cross really necessary? Or, was the literal necessary only for the sake of demonstration? Did the Lamb of God, slain from the foundation of the world, come in visible form and die merely that what had ever been true invisibly might be brought to light before the eyes of man?"

There is language in Rom. 3:24-26 which might be taken to favor the explanation of the service of Christ's physical death just mooted. "Being justified freely by his grace through the redemption that is in Christ

Jesus: whom God hath set forth to be a propitiation through faith in his blood, to declare his righteousness for the remission of sins that are past, through the forbearance of God; to declare, I say, at this time his righteousness: that he might be just, and the justifier of him which believeth in Jesus."

This passage plainly teaches that remission of sins was enjoyed in Old Testament times. But the passage also implies that, while justification was on terms of faith the same as now since Jesus came, yet in Chist's coming God "hath set forth," or openly manifested, Jesus Christ as "a propitiation," and this to the end of *declaring;* that is, of literally and manifestly showing, the justness of God's act in justifying a penitent and trusting sinner "freely by His grace." It is the same truth which has been presented at large already—that in all the past propitiation was in effect, as was proved by God's exercise of "forbearance" in "the remission of sins"; but that also the ground for and the righteousness of God's course have now been plainly declared in the appearing and atoning work of Christ Jesus.

And the expression in v. 24, "the redemption which is *in Christ Jesus" suggests* the idea that redemption is primarily in the person of Christ Jesus rather than in His visible work on the cross. It *suggests* that the mystery of redemption lies in the person and functions of the preincarnate Christ, yea, in the eternal Son of God. It is a fascinating suggestion, that the expression, "the Lamb slain from the foundation of the world," implies that a function of atoning sacrifice subsists and operates in the very nature and personality of the eternal Son of God; in other words, that one person of the adorable trinity is originally and eternally a slain Lamb in such a sense that Calvary serves only as a visible and human revelation of Him as such. Other passages of Scripture could be grouped together in support of this suggestive explanation of the service of Christ's death.

But, inasmuch as it is a mere suggestive solution of a confessed dilemma confronting us, nothing need be added to the above presentation. The gist of this explanation would be, that Christ's death on Calvary in atonement for the sins of the world is but the public, human revelation of a mystical sacrifice obtaining originally and subsisting ceaselessly in the person and official functions of the eternal Son of God.

III. THE CROSS AMIDST THE AGES.

Returning to the question—"If the atonement was in full force and effect before the literal cross was erected, was the literal cross really necessary?"—we answer, the Scripture itself puts an end to such question. In its light there can be no question of the necessity for the actual atoning death of the Son of God on Calvary. Jesus Himself declared to His immediate disciples: "Thus it is written, and thus it *behoved* Christ to suffer, and to rise from the dead the third day" (Luke 24: 46). All Old Testament Scripture foretold Christ's death and resurrection, not only as a coming event, but as a necessity. This is because, in the nature of the case, it *"behoved* Christ to suffer."* Only predetermined theory can read out of this expression the necessity for the actual bodily sufferings of Christ on the cross. Again, at Thessalonica, Paul was on three successive Sabbath days "opening and alleging, that Christ *must needs* have suffered, and have risen again from the dead" (Acts 17: 3). That this necessity means here only for the purpose of physical demonstration is repugnant to intelligence; and, in spite of the dilemma already confessed and which should be frankly faced, such construction is repugnant to the evangelical believer's spirit as well as to his intelligence.

Taking the apostolical preaching of the cross as a whole, no room is left to doubt that there was such need

for the actual death of Jesus Christ that, without it,—
the actual death of Jesus of Nazareth on Calvary's tree
—the sin of the world had never been taken away. These
very apostles were themselves experienced in the power
and effect of the "cross in mystery." Nevertheless Jesus
diligently pointed them to the cross on which He was so
soon to give up His life as an offering for sin. His words
fell on dull and listless ears. His actual death dismayed
and disheartened them. Even after the risen Christ had
shown Himself two or three times to the Apostles, Peter
knew nothing to be doing but to propose to the others,
"I go a fishing." And the other six in company with
him said, "We also go with thee." Yet, as a mere
spectacle, they had witnessed the Lamb dying and had
seen Him again in resurrected body.

But from the day of Pentecost—when the Spirit of
the glorified Lamb revealed to them "those things which
God before had shewed by the mouth of all His prophets,
that Christ should suffer" (Acts 3:18), these same men
began straightway to turn the world upside-down with
their preaching of the crucified and risen Jesus. Human
hearts rejoiced unspeakably for the peace with God
brought to them through one look of faith at the mercies
of God beaming from the cross. Ecclesiastical authorities
quailed and writhed and gnashed their teeth in abject,
cowardly rage before these simple fishermen. Kings,
potentates, imperial thrones vainly strove to arrest "this
way."

Without taking up the Apostles' teaching right
through,—which would mean a review of the whole body
of their preaching and teaching—it will suffice to make
use of just one apostolical testimony, to prove the
primary and imperative necessity for Christ's actual
death on the cross.

In 1 Cor. 15:3, 4, Paul summarizes the Gospel under
three essential, literal facts: "Christ *died for our sins*
according to the Scriptures;—He was *buried,* and—He

rose again the third day according to the Scriptures."
Now, in v. 17 Paul states, "If Christ *be not raised,* your
faith is vain; ye are *yet in your sins."* So when, for
example, we read in Rom. 4: 25, "Who was delivered
for our offences, and raised again for our justification,"
language could not make it plainer that, without the
actual death of Jesus, there would be no propitiation for
our sins, and that without the actual resurrection of
Jesus to appear as man's Advocate before the Father on
high, there would be no justification for man before God
and no peace for man with God.   The same conclusion
applies to the almost countless passages of the New Testament Scripture along this line. All would be summed up
in the pithy statement, "Without shedding of blood,
there is no remission" (Heb. 9: 22). This admits of no
less meaning than that without the shedding of the blood
of the man Christ Jesus, there is no remission of sins,
—past, present or future.

We seem, then, to be confronted with a dilemma inexplicable to the human mind. The dilemma is, how can
it be true that atonement for man's sins is confined pro-
visionally to the actual cross of Calvary, while yet the
power and the effects of the atonement are to be found
in full force all the way back to the first fallen man?
Human reason would here stoutly assert that one or the
other of these alleged facts must be rejected. And does
not reason commonly determine doctrine at this point?
Does not reason commonly close its eye to the plain
evidence of the prevalence of the power and effects of
the atonement all through the Old Testament? And does
not reason commonly dictate in consequence, that Christian salvation was not known experimentally of old;
that the Son of God was not a Redeemer and Saviour of
old excepting in prospect; that Old Testament saints
were still unforgiven and unregenerate sinners, at least
only justified by the law (notwithstanding Paul says in
Rom. 3: 20: "by the deeds of the law there shall no

flesh be justified''); or that only at Jesus' death did
redemption become available, and then only *retroactively* (where in all the Bible is such an idea suggested?); and that the spiritual family and house of
God, the spiritual body of Christ—the Church—did not
have birth and origin until the day of Pentecost and
will never include Old Testament members? It is evident that the subject of this chapter governs the true
understanding of several of the fundamentals—and most
important fundamentals—of all Biblical truth and revelation.

But why precipitately indulge in assertions of reason
on such profound, important and unsearchable themes,
instead of patiently waiting to search out the teachings
of revelation? Why close the eye to one revelation,
which at first, and only to untaught reason, seems to be
inconsistent with another equally clear revelation? Why
not wait, and pray, and search, until another revelation
yields up the secret which shall harmonize the other
two? Unrenewed reason is not promised satisfaction in
Biblical truth; but reason when exercised according to
faith in God and in His Word is promised true and
happy understanding; *"By faith we understand."* And
might we not expect to meet with revelations in the realm
of divine things, which devout reason can heartily and
believingly accept as facts and truths, although unable
for the present fully to comprehend and explain them?

In the case before us, the author has the testimony to
give, that for years both sides of this apparent contradiction grew upon him, so that he was brought into great
anxiety. He could not hesitate to recognize and proclaim
the prevalence of the power and effects of the cross in
all pre-Christian times; yet he feared so to recognize and
proclaim the same as even to appear to be implying that
there was not absolute necessity for the actual Calvary,
the same as if it meant that no one could be saved before
Jesus bowed His head in death upon the accursed tree.

For years there was increasing prayerful searching in the Word for a revelation, which would either eliminate one side of the apparent contradiction or harmonize the two facts which to natural reason were contradictory and mutually exclusive.

The solution of this problem which is found in Scripture places in our possession one more of the marvellous revelations from God, of which the mind of man could never conceive. A clear exposition of the mystery is to be found in Heb. 9: 24-26: "Christ is not entered into the holy places made with hands, which are figures of the true; but into heaven itself, now to appear in the presence of God for us; nor yet that he should offer himself often, as the high priest entereth into the holy place every year with blood of others; for then must he often have suffered since the foundation of the world: but now once in the end of the world hath he appeared to put away sin by the sacrifice of himself." The last verse especially gives us the revelation needed.

It is here admitted that sacrifice for sin was needed from the disruption of the world. And it is clearly implied that from the disruption of the world the sacrifice of Christ for sin was effective. It is virtually declared that, if such were not the case, this sacrifice must have been made actually way back there, or for all men living before Calvary never forgiveness could be found. There is no hint of a retroactive power of Jesus' blood, by which sin could have been forgiven after the event of Christ's death. Furthermore, it is clearly implied that, if Christ's sacrifice had needed to be made at the beginning in order to be effective, it must also have needed to be often repeated. This would mean that the sacrifice of Christ Jesus for sin was limited and temporary in power, like the symbolical sacrifices of the Levitical code. The passage clearly implies, on the contrary, that Christ's one sacrifice on Calvary, far down in the history of mankind, operated in as full saving power immediately for fallen Adam, as if it had been enacted on that fateful evening when the anxious Christ cried after the fugitive pair, "Where art thou?" It is, however, natural, even for sanctified reason—and it is perfectly legitimate—to inquire, "How could this be?"

This inquiry is clearly and beautifully answered in this very verse, although it is somewhat obscured by the common version. No doubt, many have been confused by the expression, "in the end of the world." One would say that that time has not even yet come. But the Revised Version correctly translates, instead of "world," "ages,"—"Once at the end of the ages." One's mind is, however, still confused; for the ages had not then, neither have they yet, reached their termination. But termination is not here at all the intended meaning of the word "end." The marginal rendering—a perfectly correct one—is "consummation": *"once at the consummation of the ages* hath He appeared to put away sin by the sacrifice of Himself." What a glorious light this passage now throws for us upon the death of Jesus! His cross marks the "end" of all the ages, in the sense of the objective, the goal, the conjunctive, the confluence, —yea, His cross marks the *"consummation"* of all the ages.

Our conception of the ages has been wrong entirely and needing correction. The ages are not mere successive periods of time, or stages of progress; they constitute a unity, an organism, a constructive whole. The ages are like a living, highly organized body. The dying Lamb of God is the heart in this complex organism, pulsating with equal saving energy throughout the whole body of the ages, whether in the freshly desecrated garden of Eden, or in the New Jerusalem, of which it is said, "the Lord God Almighty and *the Lamb* are the temple of it."

Our passage significantly represents that the Cross of Christ has this once-for-all efficacy because, not by the

"blood of others"—and those only dumb animals—
"but by the sacrifice of Himself," He "put away sin."
Said John the Baptist, "Behold the Lamb of God, which
taketh away the sin of the world." This was declared
by John before Calvary, and yet declared as ever present
fact, without limitations of time, degree or subjects.

With this as a key-passage, the whole Bible opens
anew. Most gloriously are harmonized profound and
fundamental facts which, if otherwise seized at all, are
held hestitatingly, at least with perplexed grasp. Not a
passage is found in all the Bible which does not blend
in perfect symphony with this one in its true meaning.

We learn once more how different the divine view
often is from the human. Poor human reason can of
itself conceive of efficacy from an act only as *ex post
facto,* subsequent to the event; effect must follow cause
in time as well as in power. But it is not so at all with
God, and it is not so with enlightened faith. "By faith
we understand," under the light of God's Word, that
Jesus is God's slain Lamb of all the ages conjointly, and
hence equally. The ages are so unified that His blood
would have been otherwise, it would have been but partial, *ex post facto* in efficacy—just as man commonly
thinks—if Jesus Christ had died at the beginning of the
ages as a mere succession of times, instead of at the
"consummation of the ages" as a composite whole.
Faith, illumined by revelation, sees all the ages, not as a
mere flow of time in successive measurements, but as a
single, corporate design.

What a new and inspiring revelation comes to us now
out of such a passage as Heb. 1:2, where it is said of
God and His Son, "through whom He made the ages."
The ages are a creation, created by Christ Jesus for His
Father according to the Father's sovereign design.
They all together form an incomparable mosaic, of which
the Lamb is the centralizing, organizing, harmonizing,
commanding objective. Place Him anywhere else than

at "the consummation," the confluence, and the pattern becomes untelligible and beautiless.

Again, in Heb. 11:3 we read: "By faith we understand that the ages were *framed* by the word [personal Word] of God." Marvellous revelation as it now opens to us! The ages constitute an imposing piece of divine architecture. The Architect and Builder is God the Son, "the Word of God," Jesus Christ. Unbelieving mortal, however great a self-styled philosopher or scientist, can see no wondrous temple of the ages, with the Lamb as the chief cornerstone, the Lamb as the capstone, the Lamb as the architectural "theme" of this design, the symphony of all the exquisite, intricate, delicate expression of this edifice; but "by faith we understand" this magnificent, boundless revelation.

How impressively does that word now come to us which is found in Rom. 5:6: "For when we were yet without strength, *in due time* [according to the time, Marg.] Christ died for the ungodly." What failure, what catastrophe, had been the result had the Lamb been slain at any other time, no man can tell; but we now shudder to contemplate the possible consequences. In God's view thousands of years of persistent, but futile, human effort to regain his lost moral and spiritual strength were needed by man to render the only possible provision of recovery exactly and fully "due." And yet no contrite soul, needing and seeking one "strong to deliver," had needed to wait till this "due time" of Christ's death for his personal recovery of eternal life.

The subject, the discussion of which has engaged the present chapter, is a fitting climax to *"Revelation the Crown-Jewel of Biblical Prophecy."* In this last book of the Bible, in which all the lines of Biblical revelation and prophecy are consistently carried forward into concluding revelation, even of the "ages of the ages,"—the endless times of the new heaven and the new earth—the greatly predominating form in which

Jesus Christ is presented is that of "the Lamb." It seems that the further the ages wheel into place historically, the more all realms of beings will be impressed with Him—the central personality of all ages—as

THE LAMB OF THE AGES.